brainwashing

brain washing

The Fictions of Mind Control

A Study of Novels and Films

Since World War II

David Seed

The Kent State University Press

Kent and London

Library of Congress Catalog Card Number 2004010977
ISBN 0-87338-813-5
Manufactured in the United States of America

08 07 06 05 04   5 4 3 2 1

LIBRARY OF CONGRESS CATALOGING-IN-PUBLICATION DATA

Seed, David.
Brainwashing : the fictions of mind control :
a study of novels and films since World War II / David Seed.
      p.   cm.
Includes bibliographical references and index.
ISBN 0-87338-813-5 (alk. paper)
1. English fiction—20th century—History and criticism.
2. Brainwashing in literature.
3. American fiction—20th century—History and criticism.
4. Literature and science—English-speaking countries.
5. World War, 1939–1945—Literature and the war.
6. World War, 1939–1945—Influence.
7. Brainwashing in motion pictures.
8. Alien abduction in literature.
9. Conspiracies in literature.
I. Title.
PR888.B72S44 2004
823'.91409353—dc22
2004010977

British Library Cataloging-in-Publication data are available.

To Joanna with love

contents

Acknowledgments

■ I would like to record thanks to the following who gave assistance to this project: Elliot Atkins, Mark Bould, Pat Cadigan, Susan Carruthers, John Clute, Robert Crossley, Thomas M. Disch, Martin Durham, Alan C. Elms, Pat Gehrke, Bennett Huffman, David Karp, Ken Kesey, Alastair Spark, Brian Stableford, Wil Verhoeven, Jenny Wolmark; to Liverpool University for a semester's leave to complete this study; and to my wife, Joanna, for her support throughout and for her help in producing the final manuscript.

Introduction

Brainwashing:
A method for systematically changing attitudes or altering beliefs, originated in totalitarian countries, especially through the use of torture,
drugs, or psychological-stress techniques.
— Random House Dictionary

The systematic and often forcible elimination from a person's mind of
all established ideas, esp. political ones, so that another set of ideas
may take their place.
— Oxford English Dictionary

■ There has been no critical account published of representations of brainwashing in prose fiction and film. This continues to be a visible absence,
particularly in view of the reassessment of Cold War culture that has produced a number of important studies of nuclear war fiction, one analysis of
Korean War fiction by Arne Axellson, and monographs on containment (Alan
Nadel) and surveillance (Timothy Melley and Patrick O'Donnell).[1] Brainwashing as a subject cuts across genres as varied as dystopias, war fiction, and
invasion fantasies, even extending into contemporary dramatizations of the
interface between mind and machines. Its postwar cultural representations
bring the concept of the singular discrete self under increasing pressure.

Since its assimilation into discussions of the Cold War in the 1950s and 1960s, the term "brainwashing" and its associated images have tended to suffer critical neglect from their very familiarity although they express the deep-seated fear that the mind—the traditional seat of individual selfhood—can be reshaped by technical means. The word cannot help but trigger the image of Laurence Harvey's wooden stare as he acts out the role of the trained assassin in *The Manchurian Candidate.* And yet it is a word with a complex, if brief, history, first denoting the workings of an alien system of mind control beyond the United States and then becoming relocated within American culture to suggest similar processes that seemed even more unnerving by being so near home. It will be the basic argument of this study that the notion of brainwashing triggered and sustained an extended crisis of cultural self-examination throughout the early Cold War period and has continued to inform narratives that examine the relation of technology to consciousness long after its initial political meaning had lapsed. The historian Walter Bowart has described brainwashing as a domestic issue, "largely a campaign waged in the United States home press. It served as a sharp-edged propaganda weapon and was aimed at the American people to add to the already considerable fear of the Communists."[2] For Bowart, the U.S. government had a vested interest in promoting the fear of brainwashing because it diverted public attention from embarrassing defections and helped to justify covert experiments that it sponsored during the period of the Korean War and beyond.

The roots of the notion of brainwashing lie in the experiments carried out between the two world wars by Russian physiologist Ivan Pavlov and his American equivalent John B. Watson. Both researchers were hostile to introspection as a mode of investigation, and both were determined to establish a scientific study of the mind based on measurable physical phenomena. Both exploited the stimulus-and-response pattern in their experiments, and Watson made no bones about applying his discoveries to social planning. He conducted notorious experiments at inducing fear responses by introducing a rat into the crib of an infant named Albert, experiments that were subsequently alluded to in *Brave New World, Nineteen Eighty-Four,* and later novels. Watson was one of the earliest to make the argument that induced conditioning was simply repeating in a more structured and directed way the process of socialization undergone by every individual. Then in his 1924 monograph *Behaviorism* Watson made his notorious claim that, if he was given twelve healthy infants and his own "specified world" to bring them up in, he could train them to fulfill any role, regardless of the children's talents.

Watson later admitted that he had gone beyond the facts in making this claim, but it only exaggerates his stance as a social technician. His writings were full of terms like *implanting, building in*, and *unlearning*, which collectively suggest that, in suitably skilled hands, the behavior of any individual can be shaped at will. And, although Watson concentrates on externals, his writings further suggest that the individual's mind can be altered too.

While there are early signs in pre-1945 fiction of practices that resembled brainwashing, the concept and the term were Cold War phenomena, both promoting the grand narrative of Communist conspiracy. When Allen Dulles, the director of the CIA, admitted that brainwashing was of "great psychological interest to the West" but was "never practised" there, he was making at once an understatement and a disingenuous claim that it belonged exclusively within the Communist bloc.[3] The shocks to the administration of the trial of Cardinal Mindszenty and of reports that American POWs in Korea were being manipulated into turning against their own country triggered a massive covert wave of psychological experimentation funded by the CIA and other agencies throughout the 1950s. These programs, the most notorious of which was the CIA's MK-ULTRA project, included pharmacological trials of LSD and other substances, the use of hypnosis, sensory deprivation, electroshocks, the application of radioactive elements, and even ESP. In short, every conceivable means of mind control was investigated during the 1950s and 1960s. In his survey *The Making of the Cold War Enemy*, Ron Robin has shown that this government-sponsored research usually applied behavioristic methods heavily colored by domestic ideological assumptions in order to construct models of "alien" practice. Most of these projects have been well documented in such pioneering studies as Peter Watson's *War on the Mind*, Walter Bowart's *Operation Mind Control*, and many other studies that will be cited in later chapters.

The analysis of brainwashing or mind control self-evidently involves an examination of how power relations are represented, and I have repeatedly drawn on Michel Foucault's argument in *Discipline and Punish* that the subjects of surveillance internalize the official gaze. In "Panopticism" Foucault describes the way in which Jeremy Bentham's circular model prison dissociates seeing from the seen, so that the inmates cannot see their observers but are sure that they themselves can be observed at any time. Thus the inmate "inscribes in himself the power relation in which he simultaneously plays both roles."[4] Independently, R. D. Laing arrived at a similar position when he stated in his introduction to the 1965 edition of *The Divided Self* that "psychiatry can so easily be a technique of brainwashing, of inducing behaviour that is adjusted, by (preferably) non-injurious torture. In the best places, where straitjackets are abolished, doors unlocked, leucotomies largely forgone, these can be replaced by more subtle lobotomies and tranquillizers that place the bars of Bedlam and the locked doors *inside* the patient."[5] Whether the context is political, psychiatric, or social, we shall see this internalization of processes of monitoring and surveillance occurring again and again in fictional texts from *Nineteen Eighty-Four* onward.

Two recent monographs on cultural paranoia have helped to focus the analysis of narrative structures in this study, both published in 2000. Timothy Melley's *Empire of Conspiracy* pursues the notion of what he calls "agency panic" to extrapolate a theme of crisis over selfhood that he finds running through postwar American writing. Melley helpfully links fiction to contemporary social commentary by David Riesman, Vance Packard, and others to demonstrate the repeated difficulties authors have in imagining a coherent causality for actions. He shows how ideological power in works like *Invisible Man, The Manchurian Candidate*, and *One Flew Over the Cuckoo's Nest* is represented as a "female force that invades, empties, and reconstructs the male subject."[6] Patrick O'Donnell's *Latent Destinies* undertakes a broader conceptualization of paranoia, which he breaks down into a series of five main aspects: paranoia is the "last refuge of individuality"; it reflects a "commodification and virtualization of temporality itself"; it evokes pleasure from the "totalized world of available objects"; it suggests a desire to escape the "totality of late capitalism" by trying to control the latter; and paranoia might well constitute the "final form of human knowledge before knowledge passes away into information."[7] Where Melley keeps a tight focus on narrative discourse and structure, O'Donnell considers broader kinds of narrative work that constantly resituate the subject in his or her culture. For both critics, paranoia is a cultural symptom, not a sign of individual pathology.

This study does not set out to produce new historical data about covert experiments on mind control. Its concern is with fiction and film, in other words with the imagining of such experiments and their consequences. It also constantly draws on the historical analyses of secret programs of research funded by the CIA and similar agencies. Two works deserve special acknowledgement here. Alan Scheflin and Edward M. Opton's *The Mind Manipulators* remains an indispensable mine of information and documents many of the points of contact between authors and such programs. They criticize the term "brainwashing" as an "emotional scare word," but do not dismiss the subject as a result. Instead, they draw the following discrimination: "Brainwashing is not an exotic, irresistible procedure which cleanses the mind so that others may remold it. It is a process of extreme physical deprivation, akin to torture, which depletes a person's capacity to stand firm against interrogation and indoctrination."[8] *The Mind Manipulators* covers many areas of psychological research, whereas John Marks's *The Search for the "Manchurian Candidate"* examines thousands of declassified documents specifically to ask whether the kind of programmed assassin described by Richard Condon was possible. Partly because the CIA had destroyed many relevant records, Marks could not come up with a definitive answer, but his study kept the possibility open and documented experimentation in a number of important areas, such as hypnosis and drugs.

Researchers like Marks have performed an invaluable general service to the reader of mind control fiction. We dismiss at our peril even the most extreme conspiracy, experiment, or means of control. Our presumptions about the nature of day-to-day reality become next to useless in this context since mind control narratives question our cherished beliefs in autonomy and agency. These narratives approach the hypotheses of the experimenters being thought experiments themselves. Both narratives and experimental undertakings performed acts of speculation, the former being particularly alert to possible consequences for the human subjects involved.

Again and again in the discussion that follows we shall be encountering evidence of how the "battle for men's minds" conflated psychology and warfare so thoroughly that the very concept of illness became politicized, as recent researchers have shown.[9] Introducing their survey of Soviet political hospitals, Sidney Bloch and Peter Reddaway make a point that applies equally well to Western psychiatric practice. They argue that the traditional concept of "adjustment to society" was turned by critics into a confirmation of the "political stance, either covert or overt, taken by the psychiatrist when he makes those who behave in ways unacceptable to society modify their behaviour so that they can re-find their place in the community."[10] Such a revision of the notion of psychiatry takes place within Robert Heinlein's tautly paranoid 1941 story "They," which begins with a dialogue between the protagonist, known officially as a "case," and his doctor. As "They" progresses, the reader develops a strong suspicion that the protagonist has been suffering from a persecution complex that makes him analyze every event for possible discrepancies and hidden purposes. At the end of the story, Heinlein breaks the fiction when the man's companion is revealed as a "creature" and the hospital into a place of psychological manipulation where false memories can be "grafted" on to his consciousness. For Harold Berger this story powerfully articulates the fear that "our social and even physical environment (that is, what we call reality) is a hoax and that each of us is alone sharing his life with a race of deceivers."[11]

A new model of the self without any clear boundaries emerges from experiments of the 1950s. The psychologist Donald Hebb asked whether the mature adult exists independently of place and circumstances. Brainwashing, he insisted, demonstrated that the answer was no: "the adult is still a function of his sensory environment." More complexly, José Delgado argued that there was necessary continuity between environment, senses, and mind: "cerebral activity is essentially dependent on sensory inputs from the environment not only at birth but also throughout life." If selfhood is a constantly shifting "composite of materials borrowed from the environment," then it follows that *the individual mind is not self-sufficient* (his emphasis).[12] If self-sufficiency is phrased as "independence," it gives a political dimension to the processes of brainwashing that can be figured as an Orwellian violation of the self's space, hence the popularity of invasion narratives, either on the national level of the body politic or on the level of the single body.

The term "brainwashing" suggests both a metaphor and a narrative. For Thomas Szasz this metaphor connotes "one of the most universal human experiences and events, namely . . . one person influencing another," but with a heavily adverse judgment built into it. Szasz was trying to play down the connotations of the term in order to drain some of the sensationalism out of cases like that of Patty Hearst, which in the mid-1970s was seen as one of cult brainwashing.[13] Since it is virtually a paradox (we wash clothes but how can we wash an internal organ of the body?), the term's circulation throve on mystery, according to Albert D. Biderman. Although its use was promoted by journalists and victims, since it was defined as a mystery, the meaning of the word could only be explained by experts; and the term accrued a further dimension of meaning by being shaped by the "diabolical view of Communism," which the U.S. government was then encouraging.[14]

The metaphor of washing, traditionally applied in religious contexts to signify the individual's purging of sin, entails a human agent and also suggests purging or cleansing; in other words a process. The standard pattern emerged as a sequence of phases. First, the subject was brought under total control, then debilitated by prolonged isolation and sleep deprivation; then personal humiliation was exploited as the immediate preliminary to the subject's admission of guilt. This could be one goal—the admission of crimes against the state; or alternatively the subject might be coerced into becoming an advocate of the regime's ideology.[15] In the narratives discussed in this study, the emphasis varies between process and goal, but in every case the vulnerability of the individual subject is foregrounded. Brainwashing can thus be considered as a particular instance of what Louis Althusser describes as the functioning of "ideological state apparatuses." He argues that every ideology interpellates individuals as subjects through a complex set of practices and brainwashing is an unusually direct confirmation of this process of ideological consolidation.[16] If a repressive regime arrests a subject (one of the prime meanings of the French verb *interpeller*), it then enacts a symbolic confirmation of its own authority by reducing the subject to a passive agent for its own purposes, whether to suppress dissidence or produce an assassin. The key drama in brainwashing narratives plays itself out as an encounter between subject and ideology and between an individual and different kinds of authoritarian structures.

Accordingly, most of the narratives considered here revolve around conspiracies against the state or self. This is a motivated paranoia, however, in that it responds to early signs—subsequently confirmed in graphic detail—of covert processes at work within America. In early naive accounts the threat is demonized and external, but conspiracy rapidly becomes internalized as a perception of the subject's loss of autonomy. Tony Tanner has expressed this perception as an "abiding dread" in postwar American fiction "that someone else is patterning your life, that there are all sorts of invisible plots afoot to rob you of your autonomy of thought and action, that conditioning is ubiquitous."[17]

Such a perception produces a narrative tension between resistance and enquiry where the self is simultaneously being subjected to processes beyond its control and attempting to understand those processes. Whether the narrative draws on the genre of science fiction or psychological realism, the self is being coerced into ideologically prescribed patterns of behavior or, worse still, being used as an unwitting guinea pig in an experiment. In the most extreme cases the subject is caught in the catch-22 of attempting to understand a situation where the very means of understanding and verification are themselves liable to manipulation. Such narratives spiral into a sequence of images and representations that can never authenticate themselves, by which point the reader or viewer begins to feel as entrapped as the protagonists.

Mind control or brainwashing was initially conceived in the postwar period as a politically motivated process, but by the late 1950s it had become extended to the media and advertising in the social criticism of Vance Packard and others. In effect a double displacement of the original meaning of brain-washing occurs here. First, it is transposed on to the home scene, thereby apparently losing its original demonized sense of an alien process. Second, it takes place through the most familiar day-to-day social activities. In *The Hidden Persuaders* Packard attacked the use of motivational research in advertising by drawing on the trope of invasion that lies at the center of many 1950s narratives of mind control: "The most serious offense many of the depth manipulators commit . . . is that they try to invade the privacy of our minds."[18]

It was only a matter of time, therefore, until writers further extended the concept into society as a whole. From 1959 onward, Allen Ginsberg repeatedly attacked what he described as a "huge sadistic police bureaucracy" that, particularly through the agencies of the FBI and CIA, was infiltrating the media, producing "identity brainwash accelerated now to mass neurosis."[19] Ginsberg's perception was shared, albeit in less conspiratorial terms, by Malcolm X, whose 1963 autobiography criticized the routine indoctrination of racist ideology in American culture as a form of brainwashing. That same year, in her study *The Feminine Mystique*, Betty Friedan drew on the analogy with returning POWs from Korea to explain a passivity in American women that had been gradually induced through the 1950s so severe as to produce virtual zombies. The similarity between the two groups was proposed as evidence of deterioration in the American character.[20] By this point the initially alien concept of brainwashing had become thoroughly internalized into critiques of American society.

This application was made repeatedly in the writings of Robert Anton Wilson, coauthor of the *Illuminatus!* trilogy (1975). Wilson had studied the psychology of perception in the 1950s and then broadened his interests to include Wilhelm Reich (whose persecution he saw as a result of repressive American laws), psychedelic drugs, and Korzybski's General Semantics. In the second volume of *Illuminatus!* the use of electronically controlled brain implants (discussed in chapter 6) is despecified as a parable of an authoritarian society. The cultural equivalent of such implants is named as the "logogram" or set of conditioned verbal habits that can be exploited as follows: "All authority is based on conditioning men and women to act from the logogram."[21] Wilson's *Prometheus Rising* (1983) similarly attacks stereotyping of thought: "Human society as a whole," he declared, "is a vast brainwashing machine whose semantic rules and sex roles create a social robot."[22] Alert to the metaphor in "brainwashing," Wilson in turn deploys a series of different tropes to indicate unconscious formations of the self that can be altered. In the 1999 collection *Everything Is Under Control*, Wilson followed other psychologists in identifying three phases to the brainwashing process: isolation, humiliation, and relearning.[23] Whether using the metaphors of bonds, imprints, or brain "wiring," Wilson implies that the individual can correct the blinkering effects of what Mark Twain calls "training," i.e. the instilling of cultural habits.[24] Wilson cites the major religions as institutions that constantly reinforce consensus reality and argues that the army practices an institutional brainwashing in its treatment of new recruits.

Wilson's diagnosis of widespread social manipulation echoes similar positions adopted by Ken Kesey, William Burroughs, Allen Ginsberg, and other writers who, during the 1960s particularly, voiced their protests against a perceived lack of social awareness around them. The protagonist of John Kennedy Toole's *A Confederacy of Dunces* (written in the 1960s but not published until 1980) harangues his mother in terms that would be congenial to the writers just mentioned when he insists: "Don't you understand? Psychiatry is worse than communism. I refuse to be brainwashed. I won't be a robot."[25] Toole ironically substitutes one totem-word for another to satirize a way of thinking in which his character refuses to participate.

■ Although brainwashing makes up a major narrative concern of Cold War politics, the origins of mind control as a subject for fiction lie ultimately in Gothic fiction, where the proud unscrupulous villain with his flashing eyes exerts power over his entranced subjects. By the late nineteenth century hypnosis had become a staple of novels like *Dracula* where swirling lights are induced by the vampire, or *Trilby* where Svengali "plays" his pupil like an instrument. In John Buchan's 1924 novel *The Three Hostages*, the nature of such demonic figures has undergone a significant change. In that novel an insidiously attractive businessman named Medina reduces Richard Hannay to helpless passivity. Although it is the other's eyes that initiate the process, Hannay succumbs to a "dreadful overmastering aura." He repeats words automatically and finds his consciousness split in two, as if he were witnessing a performance by a version of himself: "I felt abominably helpless, my voice was not my own. . . . I seemed to be repeating a lesson at someone's dictation."[26] Hannay finds himself transformed into a puppet, a repeated trope of manipulation in postwar narratives. Furthermore, Medina, like Fu-Manchu, has a large organization behind him.

While *The Three Hostages* is a transitional work that combines both individual and group manipulation, Joseph O'Neill's *Land Under England* (1935) anticipates postwar narratives of brainwashing and applied behaviorism.[27] The novel describes the descent of Anthony Julian through a trapdoor under Hadrian's Wall into an underground world modeled on the dictatorships of the 1930s, where individualism has become superseded by a centralized state-directed consciousness. When the narrator first sees these figures, he is startled by their fixed stare. Their eyes are at once "vacuous" and "penetrative" in that they attempt to invade the other's consciousness and "absorb" him into the new collective. When he visits the schools, the narrator witnesses a process similar to that described by Aldous Huxley in *Brave New World* and one that anticipates later behavioristic manipulation whereby the children are "taught" through hypnotic suggestion: "I could see that their knowledge of tendencies, psychic reflexes, and the various automatic reactions of the mind, made it possible for them to turn into account the different forms of suggestion which produced an automatic functioning of this or that tendency."[28] O'Neill's account clearly anticipates later descriptions of mental conditioning (his term "mind-murder" looks forward to discussions of "menticide" in the 1950s), particularly of mental processes being repeatable and therefore open to manipulation; and his narrator experiences a series of vertiginous crises where he feels his self-control slipping out of his grasp. The underground people communicate through a form of telepathic projection that gives an eerie silence to their city and reinforces the narrator's perception that the citizens have become virtual robots within a "monstrous machine." The monstrous aspect of their regime does not emerge through any specific offensive act so much as from the collective assault on the narrator's subjectivity.

The resistance by O'Neill's narrator to "absorption" is construed by his assailants as a sign of mental illness, and after the Second World War brainwashing was repeatedly depicted as a politically directed form of psychiatry. One of the earliest instances of this concept occurs in H. G. Wells's *Men Like Gods* (1923) where a group of Englishmen travel through a time warp to a future utopia. There they learn that the regime requires no "concentration of authority." One of Wells's characters asks what would happen if someone refuses to conform to the rules of the regime. The answer: "We should make an inquiry into his mental and moral health." At this point the visitor senses a covert process of ideological enforcement where "the mind doctor takes the place of the policeman."[29] Although the point is not developed, Wells's character points to a dystopian identification of social non-compliance with illness, which in Zamyatin's *We* (1924) can be "cured" by surgery, or in Huxley's *Brave New World* obviated by intensive Pavlovian conditioning. Similarly, in Wells's "A Short Story of the Days to Come," as a group, hypnotists effect social planning by "effacing unpleasant ideas, controlling and overcoming instinctive but undesirable impulses."[30] This function is hardly shown in the narrative proper, merely described with a presumption of normality challenging to the reader.

Huxley's novel anticipates a number of processes subsequently described in the fiction of brainwashing. By conflating the Taylorian factory method of production with Pavlovian conditioning, Huxley creates a regime that approximates to the perception outlined in his 1946 foreword to that novel: "A really efficient totalitarian state would be one in which the all-powerful executive of political bosses and their army of managers control a population of slaves who do not have to be coerced, because they love their servitude."[31] The ideology of efficiency promoted by Huxley's regime had already been anticipated in Hugo Gernsback's *Ralph 124C41+* (1925) where the eponymous "great American inventor" devises a "hypnobioscope" virtually identical to the hypnopaedia machines in *Brave New World*. Gernsback's mechanism transmits words direct to the sleeping brain and is premised on a principle of efficiency and a crudely automatic model of learning: "while in a passive state, the mind absorbed the impressions quite readily and mechanically."[32] Conditioning in Huxley's novel is described in similarly mechanistic terms and occurs before and after birth in the first case, "decanting" individuals whose destiny has already been shaped through a form of biological determinism. The siren and electrified floor (an anticipation of Ralph Ellison's *Invisible Man*) extend an induced aversion to books, thereby blocking off one avenue of independent thought and potential subversion. Correspondingly the Solidarity service described in chapter 5 enacts a secular ritual of coding where the loving cup, circular movement, and other symbolic details, like the ceremony of the Church of State in David Karp's *One*, reinforce the participants' conformity to induced norms. So, although the slogans in *Brave New World* somewhat resemble Orwellian Newspeak, as Krishan Kumar points out, there is no need for Big Brother or an elaborate system of surveillance since the whole population has become infantilised.[33] Conformity has been internalized as a set of unexamined norms, which can only be subjected to ironic disruption by a misfit who has somehow slipped through the system.

Despite the internalized regulation of Huxley's utopia there is paradoxically a police force whose very existence implies at least the possibility of dissidence or resistance. However, their appearance is minimal, confined to a near riot in a hospital when the daily *soma* ration is hurled through a window. The police in this case function as an extension of the ruling elite of technicians when they activate a soothing electronic voice that does service for the drug and simply varies the political narcosis that prolongs the regime's existence.

Huxley sets the tone for the few treatments of technological brain control that we find in 1930s science fiction. John Wyndham's 1933 novel, *Exiles on Asperus* describes a Wellsian situation on a planetoid where a small group of Earthmen is surrounded by thousands of "Batrachs," a subterranean race conditioned to hate the surface world by a system of applied behaviorism. Any approach to fire or light triggers revulsion, which has become internalized as a deep-level inhibition. Significantly, it is a doctor who defends the practice: "Every thought of yours is based on somebody's teaching, or a scrap of information picked up from somebody else. One might even say that there is no 'you'—you are no more than a conglomeration of bits of other people."[34] Wyndham creates a parable of political apathy out of this technology since the masses refuse to react against their conditioning. There is no indication of how this conditioning was put into effect here, or in Frank K. Kelley's 1934 short story "Famine on Mars," where an Earthman learns from a Martian that, after that planet declared independence, a repressive regime came into operation. Thus a Martian explains: "I . . . had been flexed and shaped by the insistent pounding of the Combine; my brain had been conditioned to believe what it was desired that I should believe, nothing beyond that."[35] This instance figures the enforcement of ideology as a mechanistic process where the subject is "stamped" with the requisite beliefs, just as in Wyndham the equivalent metaphor is one of ideological "assembly" out of parts, a factory-line production of citizens.

Not all treatments of mind control are negative, however. In John W. Campbell's "The Brain Stealers of Mars" (1936) a note of admiration creeps in when an Earthling recounts his experiences at the hands of the Martians. He undergoes an accelerated form of the hypnopaedia described in *Brave New World*: "That old bird just opened up my skull and poured a new set of brains in. Hypnotic teaching—a complete university education in thirty seconds."[36] Although Campbell's title denotes theft, the crudely mechanistic account given here suggests a more ambiguous process of replacement. The speaker can be thrown into a silent trance at will by the Martians, but his words show that he has retained memory, and briefly he even comes to sound like a salesman for a new learning technique. What is not in doubt here is the exercise of power by the Martians that totally subdues their subjects.

The reversal of this process formed the subject of Ayn Rand's political parable *Anthem* (written in 1937 but not published until 1946), which mounts a sustained attack on collectivism by identifying it with slavery. In this work, listed in 1960 by the CIA-funded Society for the Investigation of Human Ecology as part of the fiction of brainwashing, the state ideology has already reduced citizens to ciphers by inducing a collective and inexplicable act of surrender. Rand shows the effect of brainwashing as a condition of discourse that can only be reversed with great difficulty. Rand's narrator uses the "we" pronoun virtually until the end of the novel, to conform to the World Council slogan, "We are one in all and all in one. There are no men but only the great WE, One, indivisible and forever." The very act of narrating transgresses this council's restrictions and takes the narrator on a rite of rediscovering the past and with it individuality (the original title was to be *Ego*). The visible sign of this change is a shift to the first person singular in the self-celebratory line "I AM. I THINK. I WILL."[37]

Electrical experiments on the brain are described as early as 1926 in Charlotte Haldane's *Man's World*, where volunteers for scientific research are exhibited, after their skulls have been opened, experiencing electronic stimuli to different parts of the brain to identify their various functions.[38] The consciousness of a technology of collective mind control was heightened during the Second World War in two narratives published in 1942, the first of which concerns a Nazi method of dealing with an occupied country. Storm Jameson's *Then We Shall Hear Singing* describes an autocratic regime's plan to subjugate an invaded people to the docility of trained animals. In the novel, Dr. Hesse, a Nazi doctor, has perfected a method of "destroying the higher functions of the brain" so effective that it can reduce captive populations to the status of drones. He explains: "The mind is, you may say, gone. . . . A trifling injury to the fore-brain . . . an electrical disturbance a thousandth of a thousandth of a visit too powerful. . . . The body is left living and fit to work. You'll be able to drop all pretence at educating them, they'll need training, that's all. You can imagine yourself directing a Zoo."[39] The plan is never put into practice. Rather, the novel concerns itself with revealing the scientist's latent hatred of humanity, which leads him to design a process of dehumanization. Nor is the technology ever specified. Rather, Jameson uses the project as a focus of moral debate over its application—in other words over the ethical limits to government-directed practices.

Jameson's novel contrasts markedly with Olaf Stapledon's *Darkness and the Light* in which, as Robert Crossley explains, two sequences of imagined postwar history are combined. The dark vision derives from Huxley, among other writers, and describes the triumph of a fascistic regime.[40] A Chinese world empire implements an enormous apparatus of repression where miniature brain implants (a very early anticipation of José Delgado's experiments) can be used for political monitoring: "Advances in the technique of radio made it easy to transmit this record [of brain changes] over great distances, and to decode it automatically in such a way that the thoughts and impulses of the observed person could be accurately 'read' by observers in far-away government offices." The implanted device is both transmitter and receiver with the result that anyone suspected of "dangerous thoughts" could be subjected to a form of hypnopaedia: "while he was going to sleep he might be invaded by music and incantations calculated to mould his mind into the temper approved by the government." Stapledon's concept is more sophisticated than Jameson's notion of a kind of electronic lobotomy, since he briefly outlines just the elaborate system of surveillance that was to take political center stage in *Nineteen Eighty-Four*. Furthermore, Stapledon gives an ironic twist to the system in that its controllers are themselves enslaved by it: "the technicians were hypnotised in their [the leaders'] service, hypnotised, not through the cunning and resolution of the rules themselves, but through the vast momentum of traditional culture."[41] Intended as a system of control, the system itself *becomes* the control, and Stapledon briefly evokes a technology of transmitted hypnotic impulses that was to be elaborated in 1950s narratives of remotely triggered assassins.

Not even the huge time-span of Stapledon's novel conveys a sustained narrative of mind alteration. His perspective suggests a self-mystifying system within which technology can be deployed to serve the ideological aims of a regime. Most early narratives that refer to conditioning or mind alteration do not even go this far, identifying instead the processes that might take place without embodying them in a narrative. A possible exception might be William Faulkner's *Sanctuary* (1931), which, Kevin A. Boon argues, anticipates the paradigm of brainwashing. Temple Drake, the novel's sexually victimized subject, undergoes isolation, deprivation of social and intellectual stimulation, and other aspects of what came to be designated as brainwashing, succumbing ultimately to a male ideology "that allows them to objectify women's possessions."[42] In general, however, for the full political narrative of brainwashing we have to wait until the fiction of Arthur Koestler and Orwell fleshes out the state's "purging" of the dissident individual.

■ The chapters of this study trace the evolving conception of mind control, starting with four seminal novels that are constantly cited in this context: *We*, *Brave New World*, *Darkness At Noon*, and *Nineteen Eighty-Four*. All four explore ways in which the privacy of the self can be erased through an elaborate system of surveillance so that the individual is reinscribed as a subject of the state. In *Nineteen Eighty-Four* O'Brien seems to know so much about Winston Smith that it is as if he has the capacity to read his mind. In short, the system maximizes public perceptions of its power by constantly hinting at other monitoring processes beyond the subject's knowledge. Orwell was writing only shortly before the coinage of "brainwashing," which is discussed in chapter 2. In the hands of commentators like Edward Hunter and Aldous Huxley, the term emerges from one of the crises of the Cold War and is promoted within the "battle for men's minds" of the 1950s where two broad meanings emerge: the "soft" view that brainwashing merely entails a newly systematic form of interrogation, and the "hard" view that new technology has enabled new, more radical changes to be brought about in the human mind when the subject is isolated. Chapter 3 demonstrates how, simultaneously with this public debate, a series of novels dramatized processes of brainwashing in a whole range of contexts, political and social. Many focus on the institutionalized "invasion" of personal, local, or even national space; and many, as in the famous case of *Invasion of the Body Snatchers*, describe the transformation of humans into zombies.

Appropriately, since brainwashing emerged specifically from the political impasse of the Korean War, chapter 4 considers how Korean War fiction begins to apply psychiatric procedures to the situation of captivity so as to bring the self-images and cultural presumptions of American POWs under maximum pressure. The interrogations central to these narratives probe individuals' commitment to their nation and by so doing become enquiries into different aspects of American cultural values. This chapter supplies the immediate context for *The Manchurian Candidate*, the subject of chapter 5, which is a narrative conflating the alien Communist conspiracy and the familiar characteristics of the American political right. Freudian melodrama is deployed in making the family the site for political betrayal. The conditioning used to underpin the assassination plot forms a link with the fiction of William S. Burroughs (chapter 6); in turn, Burroughs assembles a veritable encyclopedia of different forms of mind control. Burroughs's heightened awareness of the ideological construction of the "reality studio" makes him represent governmental conspiracy as a virtual norm and encourages him to define selfhood in informational terms.

Chapter 7 will elaborate the analogy between brainwashing and psychiatry drawn by R. D. Laing and others through a discussion of Ken Kesey's *One Flew Over the Cuckoo's Nest*, Sylvia Plath's *The Bell Jar*, and related works where psychotherapy is depicted as a covert means of enforcing social conformity. Here a double analogy is brought into play between nonconformity and illness, and between therapy and punishment for the crime of noncompliance. Chapter 8 extends this theme into narratives dealing with the social problem of violence. Here the central works are *A Clockwork Orange* and *The Terminal Man*, where the novels are compared with their film adaptations. Already a number of chapters will have described instances of individuals unwittingly acting out the role of experimental guinea pigs. Chapter 9 will consider the experimental subject in such works as Thomas M. Disch's *Camp Concentration*, the BBC TV series *The Prisoner*, and Thomas Pynchon's *Gravity's Rainbow*, in order to foreground how experimentation deconstructs the selves in question. Finally, the concluding chapter examines ways in which cyberpunk fiction and other recent novels revise the notion of mind control, and considers whether brainwashing persists as a discrete subject within the new context of increasingly sophisticated interfacing between humans and computerized systems.

one

Precursors:
Nineteen Eighty-Four in Context

All commentators on brainwashing agree that the term denotes an exercise of power over a state's own citizens or members of an enemy regime. The very fact that the term caught on so quickly suggests that it designated a process already existing in representations of political action. The process may form part of the state's consolidation of its power or a strategy within an ongoing struggle between ideologies. In his analysis of ideology in relation to the state Louis Althusser attempts to distinguish between Repressive and Ideological State Apparatuses. Both categories include institutions that enact themselves through concrete social practices that are "governed by the *rituals* in which these practices are inscribed." For Althusser "*all ideology hails or interpellates concrete individuals as concrete subjects.*" Althusser's example is of a conversational opening such as "Hey, you there"; but the French verb *interpeller* occurs in situations more charged ideologically, particularly in the legal context to summon someone to answer. Here the challenge is to a subject's capacity to demonstrate his or her ideological allegiance.[1]

Brainwashing and other forms of mind control take this process to an extreme where means are found to circumvent the subject's consent. Yevgeny Zamyatin's *We* (1924), Huxley's *Brave New World* (1932), Arthur Koestler's *Darkness at Noon* (1940), and Orwell's *Nineteen Eighty-Four* (1949) all describe different kinds of brainwashing before the letter. All four focus on a quasi-religious "subjection to the Subject," where the Leader has assumed mythic dimensions as a personification of the state; and all three describe the working of the most powerful apparatus of the state—its security arm— as it redirects the desire of deviants to accept their subjection. Two of these novels, *Brave New World* and *Nineteen Eighty-Four*, will recur throughout this study as major reference points. In the 1950s and later, they virtually became paradigmatic representations of a mechanized society and of a totalitarian regime. Both works were constantly reprinted throughout the cold war. *Brave New World* was supplemented by a steady flow of articles and lectures by Huxley on the technology of mind control, the most important collection of these being *Brave New World Revisited*, first published in 1958. As we now know, the 1956 film adaptation of *Nineteen Eighty-Four* came about through initiatives from the CIA and consultations with the American Committee for Cultural Freedom.[2]

Zamyatin's *We* describes state harmony symbolically through the collective construction of a spaceship called the *Integration*. The members of the OneState become indistinguishable not only from each other but also from machines in their ideal realization of Taylorian productivity. On the Day of Unanimity the Benefactor is ritually reelected as premier. Under the impact of his relationship with I-330, a female operative, Zamyatin's narrator–protagonist D-503 is initiated into dangerously heterodox desires: for a new revolution, to move beyond the wall encircling the state city, even to question the Benefactor. The official ideology is to promote mechanism as an evolutionary ideal through rationalizations from history and the infallible "OneState Science." Within this logic, imagination is viewed as a disease (a "worm" or "fever") to be "cured" by an operation on the brain.

D-503, whose consciousness toward the end of the novel begins to resemble a "blank, white page" ready for official inscription, is first challenged by the Benefactor to disprove the proposition that "a true algebraic love of mankind will inevitably be inhuman, and the inevitable sign of the truth is its cruelty." After this appeal to reason, the narrator is arrested and undergoes the Great Operation (capitalized throughout as an initiation ritual) where a new self is born: "They extracted a kind of splinter from my head, and now my head is easy and empty. Or I should say, not empty, but there's nothing strange there that keeps me from smiling (a smile is the normal state of a normal person)."[3] This figure reifies heterodoxy as inert matter. The metaphor is not one of alteration or cleansing, but rather of obstruction removal. The total identification of the individual with the regime explains Zamyatin's pun in the latter's name. "OneState" combines political singularity with norms of behavior and feeling. The novel's coda expresses a postoperative euphoria that totally estranges the narrator from his earlier actions. Now the style itself demonstrates a lack of affect and other "distractions" from the facts. D-503's new confidence that "reason has to win" arises from the conquest of his self.

When he came to review *We* in 1946, Orwell compared it to *Brave New World*, arguing that both works "deal with the rebellion of the primitive human spirit against a rationalized, mechanical, painless world."[4] Orwell's humanistic interpretation has colored most subsequent readings of *We*, but Istvan Csicsery-Ronay has opened up a new perspective by suggesting that the novel presents a "micromyth about eternal ahistorical oppositions which have little, if anything, to do with human responsibility or choice."[5] According to this persuasive argument, the polarities of the novel (reason or imagination, collective or individual) form the ground of the action that D-503 is totally unable to affect.

The notion of rebellion within *Brave New World* is similarly problematic. When he had finished his novel Huxley explained to his father with pointed irony that *Brave New World* dealt with "such social reforms as Pavlovian conditioning of all children from birth and before birth."[6] Like *We*, the novel describes a regime ideally modeled on the machine, where negative and positive conditioning is used to ensure that the wheels of the state turn smoothly. The association between books and horrendous noises, and flowers and electric shocks, give two early examples of inducing aversion. Near the opening, the Director of Hatcheries and Conditioning explains to his student visitors: "It was decided to abolish the love of nature, at any rate among the lower classes. . . . We condition the masses to hate the country. . . . But simultaneously we condition them to love all country sports."[7] To pursue these sports they are further conditioned to use expensive equipment, so the citizens become unwitting consumers. In the Director's explanation, the decision process is anonymised into a natural or inevitable process where the administrative elite exercise power over the unthinking masses. Indeed, within Huxley's central machine metaphor these masses are dehumanized into the passive "machinery" waiting to be worked on by the operators or Directors.

The design society of *Brave New World* should make dissent impossible. The misfit Bernard Marx really only becomes a rebel as a result of an error in the management of his gestation. For the most part, the novel shows an endless sequence of actions that reinforce the state ideology of collectivism. Slogans and catch phrases continually reassure characters that their thinking is as uniform as their clothes.[8] The Solidarity Services show a similar group bonding as the participants dance around in a circle and the drug "soma" actualizes the narcosis of the masses by the state. As Richard A. Posner and others have argued, *Brave New World* is packed with instances of mind and body alteration, and "people are brainwashed to want ever more, ever newer consumer goods."[9] Where dystopias like *We* express anonymity through the numbers given to citizens, Huxley names his characters after behaviorists (Watson, Pavlova), industrialists, and politicians. Characters thus become the unconscious bearers of the names of those figures who helped form the World State, which in turn is modeled on the controlled order of a laboratory. Within this social laboratory any kind of dissent or even difference becomes encoded as illness.

Though written too early (1920–21) to depict Stalin's regime, *We* nevertheless anticipates the cult of the leader and above all the view of political dissidence as a disease that can be cured by a "scientific" operation. D-503's self is erased (washed away) by this process so efficiently that he eagerly participates in the betrayals of other deviants. This process was to be described in much greater detail by Arthur Koestler.

In *The Yogi and the Commissar* (1945) Koestler identifies what he designated the "Soviet myth" as a persistence of Western European millenarian hopes that insulated the true believer from criticizing any of the subsequent events in the Soviet Union. This will to believe makes objective discussion impossible: "arguments are not considered on their merit, but by whether they fit into the system, and if not, how they can be made to fit."[10] This is exactly the kind of intellectual enclosure Koestler dramatizes in *Darkness at Noon* (1940), which was based on the trials of figures like Bukharin. In his preface to Alex Weissberg's 1952 study of the Moscow trials, *Conspiracy of Silence*, Koestler identifies the following process that could stand as a retrospective summary of his novel: "To pick them, recondition them, transform their personalities, break them down and build them up for the selected part, was one of the functions of the G.P.U." Koestler originally planned to place the novel within a trilogy and call it *The Vicious Circle*, no doubt to foreground the Soviet regime's self-perpetuating ideology. It was to describe a group of characters who, charged by the state with one set of crimes, identify a different guilt in themselves of "having placed the interests of mankind above the interests of man, having sacrificed morality to expediency, the Means to the Ends."[11] In the event he focused the novel on a single member of the Communist old guard, Rubashov, who is arrested and under extended interrogation persuaded to sign a confession of counter-revolutionary activities. He is subsequently tried and shot.

Darkness at Noon describes a procedure designed to consolidate the regime by removing a dissident member of its administration, but the effect of the narrative is the very opposite: to expose the contradictions of the regime's practices. This becomes apparent from the novel's use of prison rooms as the main settings. Apart from the obviously claustrophobic effect of Rubashov's captivity, a late phase of his interrogation induces the impression that "time stood still." This is both caused and exemplified by his second interrogator Gletkin, a young apparachnik who keeps the curtains of his room closed and his lamp burning at all hours. Although Party ideology appeals to the absolute of History to justify its actions, Gletkin (himself a man with no past and therefore no history) manages to suspend time, trapping Rubashov in an extended present. The description of the latter's arrest has already blurred distinctions between the Party and Rubashov's earlier arrest in Germany by the Nazis. Koestler avoids the use of Party names, instead deploying identificatory signs (uniform, insignia, and so on) that simultaneously invite recognition from the reader and speculation about similarities between totalitarian regimes.

The aim of the Party is to produce a monologic official discourse that excludes difference and rival points of view. However, a crucial progression that takes place throughout the novel is a fracturing of Rubashov's discourse, to such an extent that the individual self, "to which the Party refuses to attribute any significance" gradually comes to be recognized by Rubashov even though that recognition does nothing to alter his fate. First he visualizes himself through the perspective of the authorities. An early thought sequence gradually shifts the grammatical person: "So I shall be shot, thought Rubashov. . . . 'So they are going to shoot you,' he told himself. . . . 'So you are going to be destroyed,' he said to himself half-aloud."[12] Perceptions of the self as subject and object separate out so that Rubashov finally anticipates an impersonal process where the agents of his death have been elided. The grammar of his discourse becomes a charged political issue, as his first interrogator Ivanov points out, because Rubashov implies an unacceptable separation of self from State and Party. The slippage of pronouns (I, you, we) throughout the novel reflects Rubashov's shifts of allegiance and shifts in self-perception.

The suppressed oppositional voice within Rubashov's discourse is thematised at one moment of Dostoevskyan insight: "He found out that those processes wrongly known as 'monologues' are really dialogues of a special kind; dialogues in which one partner remains silent while the other, against all grammatical rules, addresses him as 'I' instead of 'you,' in order to creep into his confidence and to fathom his intentions." This second voice exists within the interstices of Rubashov's discourse initially, as an inflection of pronouns, an incomplete subversive utterance censored before it can be spoken, and a disconcerting continuation of the supposedly logical sequence of his conscious thoughts. Rubashov designates this voice abstractly as a "grammatical fiction," but it takes on more and more substance as the novel proceeds, deriving in part from all the other disquieting reports he remembers hearing from party members. In one sense then the novel dramatizes an inner drama where Rubashov's interrogators play the role of catalysts. Ivanov's voice is internalized as an "echo" in Rubashov's head. Gletkin is more of an antagonist, but even here the power is articulated as mutual dependence: "we each hold the other by the throat." Koestler later described the interrogations as being "determined by the mental climate of the closed system; they were not invented but deduced by the quasi-mathematical proceedings of the unconscious from that rigid logical framework that held both the accused and the accuser, the victim and the executioner in its grip."[13] Starting from premises Rubashov has himself accepted and applied, like the proposition that "the Party can never be mistaken," the interrogations revolve around a functional notion of truth as either helping or hindering the unique historical experiment of the Soviet Union. No distinction is made between Rubashov's actual and potential behavior once he has admitted to heterodox opinions. If No.1 (Stalin) embodies the state and if Rubashov has subversive opinions against that state, then merely holding those opinions is tantamount to plotting against No. 1's life, his main alleged crime.

Two central metaphors are used in the novel to articulate the relation of the individual to the state: the corporate body and the theatre. During one of the recent show trials, party members, for Rubashov, resembled a "marionette-play with figures, moving on wires." Here the implication is of direction from elsewhere, while the theatre analogy in general suggests performance according to a script—officially the script of historical necessity, unofficially the pragmatic plotting of the Party leader. The second metaphor of the body makes a consistently ironic criticism of Party policy. Traditionally signifying the harmonious working of the state, the body politic in Koestler's novel fragments into a series of instances where every significant character is damaged in some way. Ivanov has lost a leg, Gletkin is scarred, Rubashov suffers from myopia and toothache. Disease is repeatedly foregrounded as a perception of the times, the Party (it has "gout and varicose veins in every limb"), or economic determinism (for Rubashov the "cancer which was eating into [humanity's] entrails").[14] The Party's euphemistic description of its acts as necessary surgery is rejected and revised by Rubashov as wanton brutality where the skin of the body politic is stripped away to reveal the innards.

Both metaphors critique a state policy that has to fulfill itself through the ideological state apparatus of ritual confession, trial, and execution. In ironically literal confirmation of Althusser's example of the individual participating in ideology as a subject, Rubashov is interpellated by being arrested. The first grim irony lies in his startling fall from a position of status to that of victim; the second in his acceptance that confession without martyrdom is the last service he can pay his party. Rubashov's trial has a performatory significance quite independent of any true guilt in the accused. Like the OneState "liturgy" in *We* and Hate Week in *Nineteen Eighty-Four*, such trials bond the masses together against their enemies, reinforcing the unique status of No.1, the Benefactor, and Big Brother. The functioning of the party is so ubiquitous in *Darkness at Noon* that it becomes impossible to imagine an "outside," and Rubashov is such an indoctrinated member that even when he is locked in a cell he assesses its orderliness as an official, not a victim, of the system. By the end of the novel Rubashov has at once recognized what Koestler was to call the "necessary lie" in state ideology and at the same time has acquiesced to the ritual of state reinforcement.[15]

The process that Rubashov undergoes anticipates the pattern later attributed to brainwashing. He is at one and the same time performing a script that will lead to his death, but also, he supposes, strengthen the state. Once the sequence is initiated by arrest there is no doubt about its outcome, only about the intervening phases. Rubashov's ordeal follows the paradigm of the Yeshov method of interrogation used by Stalin's Commissar for Internal Affairs in the 1930s and then applied by the Chinese Communists for their thought reform programs of the 1950s. The sequence consists broadly of an accusation phase, a confession phase, and a phase of "reconstructed confession," during which the prisoner develops a need to be guilty. In the novel the Party demonstrates its capacity to control Rubashov's entire environment, his sense of time, physical details like the temperature of the shower, and so on. This method has been explained as a method of brainwashing *avant la lettre* insofar as "once a person has emerged from the Yeshov treatment, he is totally ideological. He not only acts in an ideologically 'correct' way, he also reflects in the ideologically appropriate way before he acts, and he is given to reflecting upon and therefore criticizing himself on the basis of interiorized ideological standards. He is both consciously and *self*-consciously communist."[16]

Rubashov anticipates Winston Smith in recording the demise of the individual in a medium traditionally associated with personal privacy—the diary. Smith predicts his own execution, Rubashov admits the legitimacy of his own treatment: "We admitted no private sphere, not even inside a man's skull."[17] The diary records Rubashov's efforts to stifle his own selfhood and, by implication, to prepare himself for the ultimate sacrifice. In contrast to an individual's perception of death, death for the Party resembles more the "oceanic" feeling of merging with a larger unit and not an individual ending. Rubashov's ultimate suppression of his self comes when he realizes that his "last service" erases his individuality within the grand narrative of Party progress. As Koestler later explained of the group he originally intended to describe, "they re-value their lives and each one discovers that he is guilty, though not of the crimes for which he is going to die. The common denominator of their guilt is having . . . sacrificed morality to expediency, the Means to the Ends. Now they must die, because their death is expedient to the Cause."[18]

Rubashov himself experiences no physical torture but remembers his experiences at the hands of the Nazis and hears of torture elsewhere in the prison through the so-called "steambath." The reader never learns what this device involves; Rubashov tries to defuse its threat by visualization: "He imagined the situation in detail and tried to analyse the physical sensations to be expected, in order to rid them of their uncanniness." This attempt proves premature because all information reaching Rubashov might be stage-managed. He later hears of another prisoner being sentenced and screaming, in surreal contrast to the silence of the prison, and later still sees a former comrade being dragged by his cell door on the way to execution. The prison environment is exploited by Gletkin, the technician of interrogation, to disorient Rubashov as much as possible. Ironically, this process is pursuing the logical implications of a principle Rubashov himself has cherished: "we admitted no private sphere, not even inside a man's skull." The first interrogator's role is to persuade Rubashov of the logical necessity of his own death, but this can only go so far since Koestler had become convinced that Communism was a utopian faith inaccessible to rational persuasion. Once Gletkin takes over, a whole series of strategies come into play: sleep deprivation, limited rations, the physical discomfort of a bright light shining in his eyes, but never actual physical torture. Earlier reflecting on the mystery of No. 1's brain, Rubashov finds himself transformed into an experimental subject where the task of the "scientist" is to induce admissions culminating in a confession of motive. His loss of the sense of time corresponds to a loss of distinctions between real and potential acts, and prepares for his total acquiescence to the interrogator's prescription of necessity. Finally Rubashov becomes appropriated into the state discourse where at his trial he himself points out the moral to events sublimating himself to the higher cause of History: "My story will demonstrate to you how the slightest deflection from the line of the Party must inevitably end in counter-revolutionary banditry."[19]

Koestler's narrative limits itself for the most part to Rubashov's perceptual horizons and obviously halts at the point of his death. Koestler makes no attempt to explain the provenance of the narrative, only using it to challenge the then silence of Communist Party members on this subject and to preempt a Party promise that in the millennium "the material of the secret archives will be published." The novel attacks this deferral to dramatize the Party's consumption of itself, and juxtaposes Rubashov's continuing individuality with his assimilation into the Stalinist role of the "accused." Exemplifying what Berger and Luckmann designate "nihilation" (that is, a liquidation of everything outside the known universe), Rubashov acknowledges in his trial the "political death" of ideological life outside the true church of the state.[20]

After the war Koestler hardened his critique of Stalinism as a form of political neurosis, promoted particularly in *The God That Failed*, the 1949 collection of memoirs by former Communists. It may be a sign of his hardening political position that in 1951 he met Frank Wisner, the then chief of CIA covert operations, and we shall see that he had a connection with that agency's covert drug experimentations.[21]

■ The ideas of Zamyatin and Koestler intersect in the novel that was to become a major point of reference in the subsequent debate over brainwashing. Orwell reviewed *Darkness at Noon* somewhat critically, for he perceived a sympathy toward the Communist old guard and was horrified at the attempts of Western intellectuals to justify the Moscow trials. However, he felt that the novel would help to combat this attitude.[22] After 1945 the two writers became closer friends, both campaigning for the foundation of a League for the Defence of Democracy in 1946.[23] In that same year Orwell finally reviewed *We*, declaring it to be more relevant to the present than *Brave New World* and praising its dramatization of the hunger for power of the political elite. Assessing the manuscript of *Nineteen Eighty-Four* for publication, Fredric Warburg recognized that part 3 was influenced by Koestler though the treatment was "more brutal." When the first American reviews began to describe the novel as an attack on Socialism, Orwell dictated a press release that insisted that "the danger lies in the structure imposed on Socialists and on Liberal capitalist communities by the necessity to prepare for total war with the U.S.S.R.," the danger in other words of the "acceptance of a totalitarian outlook."[24]

Orwell's claim of a general attack on totalitarianism was, however, rendered rather disingenuous by the fact that fascism was virtually dead by 1949 and also because he was enlisted that year by the secret Information Research Department of the British Foreign Office set up in 1948 to combat Communist propaganda. In May, Orwell sent Celia Kirwan, Koestler's sister-in-law and member of that department, a list of thirty-five names of alleged Communists and fellow travelers. She reported that Orwell had "expressed his wholehearted and enthusiastic approval" of the department's aims. The existence of this list confirms other evidence that Orwell had a deep fear of the spread of Soviet influence in postwar Britain. This explains in turn why *Nineteen Eighty-Four* depicts a Stalinist regime transposed onto a British setting.[25] By the 1950s Orwell's beast parable and dystopia had become appropriated into the anti-Communist cause. The CIA funded the film version of *Animal Farm*, which, along with the 1956 movie adaptation of *Nineteen Eighty-Four*, was actively promoted by CIA-supported bodies.

The Moscow trials were written into Orwell's novel as purges taking place in the mid-1960s to establish a pattern prior to Winston Smith's experiences. Although the novel combines allusions to contemporary Britain and Nazi Germany, it is Stalin's consolidation of his power in the 1930s that—transposed—supplies the main history for *Nineteen Eighty-Four*. Winston Smith's final "confession" was originally planned to echo the Moscow trials. The following passage was eventually deleted from the novel: "Bit by bit the listing of a whole lifetime of active crime was dragged out of him: murder and conspiracy to murder, distribution of seditious pamphlets, intelligence with the enemy."[26] When glossing the gradual physical and emotional humiliation of Smith, O. John Rogge stressed its continuity with the Moscow trials, arguing that "martyrdom and confessions are basically the same thing: they are both efforts to gain love."[27] The novel's closing line partially confirms Rogge's case in so far as Smith recognizes love for Big Brother.

Orwell anticipates Althusser's notion of interpellation in his image of Big Brother, which combines visual echoes of the Kitchener poster from the First World War and the pictures of No. 1 in Koestler. Like the latter, the pictures of Big Brother are the signs of an absent principle of power accessible only through its representations. Big Brother is a far more aggressive image than Koestler's, however. Orwell creates the archetypal icon of surveillance since his poster is dynamic ("so contrived that the eyes follow you about when you move") and symbolic of centralized state power in that it "gazed down from every commanding corner." Althusser's notion of "hailing" has been predicted here as a visual warning to citizens. Big Brother's gaze sums up the activities of the Thought Police—a shadowy but ubiquitous agency—and the two-way telescreen, implying that no areas of public or private experience are exempt from its scrutiny. So, contemplating the frontispiece of a child's history book, Smith experiences a fantastic anticipation of his later interrogation: "The hypnotic eyes gazed into his own. It was as though some huge force was pressing down upon you—something that penetrated inside your skull, battering against your brain, frightening you out of your beliefs, persuading you, almost, to deny the evidence of your senses."[28] The Party's constant rewriting of the past is the immediate trigger to this sensation, but Smith figures the gaze through aggressive metaphors of invasion and attack. When his interrogation finally takes place, it demonstrates an ironic inadequacy to the qualifier "almost," since Smith is forced into a direct confrontation between Party authority and what he himself can see.

Smith hypothesizes different kinds of invitation in Big Brother's gaze. For example, when his image replaces the sheep-like features of Goldstein during the Hate Week rituals, it projects a public reassurance. Primarily, however, the poster anticipates the full significance of the phrase the "place with no darkness," which, unbeknown to Smith, could at once describe the state and his own mental space. Clinging to a vestige of individuality, Smith can only imagine this as a space within a space: "They could lay bare in the utmost detail everything you had done or said on thought; but the inner heart, whose workings were mysterious even to yourself, remained impregnable." The regime engages in an attempted total monitoring through the "telescreen with its never-sleeping ear," where the ideological situating of the subject involves a seemingly endless reconfirmation of his or her orthodoxy. The two-way telescreen has been described as "powerful metaphor for the loss of privacy in a totalitarian state," although we should remember that it only represents one means of control among many.[29] The state has an elaborate apparatus of propaganda and education to control thought. The telescreen disturbs because it reverses the direction of the medium (the viewer becomes the viewed) and thereby takes surveillance into domestic spaces.

The 1956 film adaptation of *Nineteen Eighty-Four* rightly exploits the imagery of observation. Smith's work place is shown as a kind of administrative panopticon, a huge open-plan hemispherical building whose workers can be observed at any moment. The recurring image throughout this film is that of an electronic eye, a chilling suggestion of observation being taken beyond known limits. And when Smith finally succumbs to his brainwashing, it is shown as a kind of technological entrapment. In these scenes we see Smith on a telescreen with electrodes fixed on either side of his skull; in other words, we see him as literally framed by the electronic apparatus of the state.

From *Darkness at Noon* Orwell extrapolated Thought Crime as an initially private deviance that must be monitored since it could lead directly to political action. Winston Smith naively assumes that the authorities have limited powers: "They could spy upon you night and day, but if you kept your head you could still outwit them. With all their cleverness they had never mastered the secret of finding out what another human being was thinking."[30] In 1956 William H. Whyte contrasted Orwell's world with developments in contemporary America: "In the 1984 of Big Brother one would at least know who the enemy was—a bunch of bad men who wanted power because they liked power. But in the other kind of 1984 one would be disarmed for not knowing who the enemy was." They might appear to be a "mild-looking group of therapists."[31] Whyte's anxiety over identifying enemies reflects a paranoid suspicion of psychotherapy being used for manipulative purposes, a suspicion that we shall see being developed in fiction from the 1950s onward, but his neat contrast presumes a clarity that does not match Winston Smith's experience. The foregrounding of the media in *Nineteen Eighty-Four* raises the possibility that Big Brother and the enemies of the state are political fictions devised to maintain the power of the regime. Smith assumes he can see a kinship of spirit in O'Brien, but this marks an error of vision so radical that it leads to his arrest. Indeed, the regime holds onto power by exploiting an uncertainty in the population about who the enemies are. This uncertainty creates a paranoia that is exploited to create a widespread surveillance by the citizens on each other.

Just as surveillance involves control by the eye, Newspeak leads to control of the voice. The psychologist Perry London has drawn a valuable comparison between the practices of Big Brother and classical Pavlovian conditioning. He writes: "The signals in classical conditioning are parts of a code; they have no intrinsic meaning of their own but represent whatever the code's inventor wishes." Thus, in dictatorships meanings are promoted by the state apparatus without any direct regard for their rationality. Terms like *Volk* (Hitler) or "deviationism" (Stalin) function as bonding or dividing cues within their regimes. London continues: "Orwell's Big Brother destroys denotative meanings totally with slogans like 'war is peace' and 'slavery is freedom.'"[32] His choice of identifying opposites is not only parodic, but makes the point that meaning has become such an imposed habit that opposites have collapsed together. Orwell's vulnerable argument in "Politics and the English Language" that there *is* an essential connection between words and actuality attempts to counter the strategies of the dictators, which are shown in miniature when O'Brien asks Smith to count his fingers when in custody. Like the slogans above, it is an exercise in breaking a commonsense continuity between sense-observation and words.

Countless signs in *Nineteen Eighty-Four* suggest that the arrest, interrogation, and indoctrination of Winston Smith are all absolutely inevitable, and Daniel Kies has noted how Orwell minimizes agency throughout the novel to present Smith as a passive victim of the system.[33] As soon as he prints "DOWN WITH BIG BROTHER" in his diary, he predicts is own guilt and doom: "It was always at night—the arrests invariably happened at night. The sudden jerk out of sleep, the rough hand shaking your shoulder, the lights glaring in your eyes."[34] In the 1984 film adaptation this point is made by synchronizing Smith's private admission of committing the "essential crime" with a televised confession from a deviant, i.e. with an embodiment of Smith's imminent future. Throughout the novel Smith is described in passive terms as if he were a template for ideological inscription. Here he has blanked out his own selfhood so that he is reduced to an anonymous instance of a process impossible to resist. "They"—the Thought Police—are equally anonymous, and here lies their unnerving power. Grammatically, their title could be internal (the imagined police) or external; hence from an early stage in the novel the distinction between thought and action collapses. In the apparent privacy of his thoughts Smith already plays out the drama of deviance being identified and corrected, thus confirming Krishan Kumar's view that "since there are no laws in Oceania, and since police surveillance and action must always be to some extent insufficient, the goal is to make all Party members police themselves. They must internalise the Thought Police."[35]

It follows then that Smith recapitulates the internal drama we already saw in *Darkness at Noon*, alternately vocalizing in his thoughts rival positions of disobedience and punishment. The difference in Orwell's novel is that Smith's ambivalence toward the state is represented as a condition of the novel's discourse. Noting how the narrative voice is limited to the horizon of Smith's thoughts and perceptions, Lynette Hunter argues that our difficulty in separating character from narrator parallels Smith's own difficulty of self-definition. In fact, from the very beginning Smith is positioned within the state so that he strikingly embodies what Michel Pêcheux describes as the discrepancy by which the individual is interpellated as a subject while still being "always—already a subject." His very name inscribes him historically (Winston) and culturally (Smith connoting anonymity). Correspondingly it is appropriate for the reader to be unable to locate where his thoughts shade into narrative comment since his words are already another's. Smith internalizes this narrative function in his capacity to visualize himself within the dominant narrative of Oceania: the ritual purging of deviance. This narrative is accepted so completely by Smith that it is virtually identified with his own lifespan, so his actions could be taken to demonstrate, if not a death wish, then at least an acceleration of his own mortality. "We are the dead" thus becomes an appropriate refrain. When Smith meets O'Brien the event heightens his sense of process as if he were the helpless agent in a sequence from thoughts through words to acts. "The end was contained in the beginning. . . . it was like a foretaste of death." The novel is packed with such proleptic anticipations that precede Smith's arrest and multiply after it. The reviewer Daniel Bell punned unconsciously on the term "end" when he described the novel as a "morality play which preaches the absolute truth that man is an end in himself"[36] and had to admit that the narrative showed a manipulative process so efficient that he could not begin to imagine ways of resisting it.

While the reader is left with no doubt about the outcome of *Nineteen Eighty-Four*, many details are overlooked by Smith in confirming the novel's deterministic foreshadowings. To take one example, the shop where Smith and Julia meet is naively imagined to lie outside the system because there is no telescreen in their room. It is, however, probably infected with vermin: Julia casually remarks that the bed is probably "full of bugs" and the picture on the wall is sure to have "bugs behind it." The postwar period saw "bug" used to mean a hidden microphone or monitoring device and of course this meaning is confirmed by their arrest. In one sense the idealized site of romantic union proves to be "infected" by a state surveillance system. In another Smith and Julia are themselves infected by the bug of deviance and the term suggests a subtextual metaphor of illness that is brought to the surface by O'Brien in part 3 when he claims the role of therapist. In short, the narrative trajectory of the novel is not from latent to overt dissidence, followed by arrest and interrogation. Rather, the earlier episodes could be read as confirmation of a guilt Smith has already recognized in himself. The diary entries thus appear to be gestures of deviance but can also be taken as anticipatory admissions that will be read by the Thought Police. Smith's compulsion to write is inseparable from his perception of guilt: "it had got to be written down, it had got to be confessed."[37]

Part 3 of *Nineteen Eighty Four*, therefore, represents the culmination of the novel in making explicit many of its earlier representations, and it anticipates the paradigm of brainwashing that was to emerge as a pattern of physical alternating with psychological duress resulting in a "confession" by the subject of ideological guilt. The political space of the state is now narrowed down to the confinement of different cells that can be totally monitored. Brutality is first imagined by Smith, then witnessed, and finally experienced. His anticipations of death are now realized symbolically as a destruction of his earlier self. Beatings break down his body consciousness to uncoordinated limbs (members) while he is questioned endlessly before a panel of Party members. Like Zamyatin's D-503, he can only undergo a reintegration into the body politic after his "illness" has been cured and electroshock performs the function of surgery: he feels "as though a piece had been taken out of his brain." Prior to this Smith has dreamed or hallucinated a self-negation through the image of gazing eyes where he "dived into the eyes and was swallowed up."[38] Again and again there are figures of Winston Smith's self being wiped out. Because the party controls all means of verifying an individual's existence, O'Brien can boast fantastically that the party can convert individuals into gas since they remove all evidence of their having existed. Here lies a crucial difference between Koestler and Orwell. Rubashov rationalizes his compliance as one last service to the Party, whereas Smith can only experience a total loss of self, as we shall see.

One of the few critics to discuss the issue of brainwashing in *Nineteen Eighty-Four* has argued that Winston Smith undergoes a "reverse of separation—individuation," a kind of "psychological death" as he is compelled to merge into the state collectivity and acknowledge what Czeslaw Milosz in *The Captive Mind* (1953) calls the "good of the whole as the sole norm of his behaviour."[39] Again, in echo of Zamyatin, this process is designated as "reintegration," a term suggesting holism and loss of division as well as mathematics.

Smith's interrogation and indoctrination are enacted through a dialogue with O'Brien whose stated aim is to confirm Smith's status as a subject. Althusser plays on different dimensions to the meaning of this term when he describes individuals' "subjection to the Subject." If the capitalized Subject is the deity, then the Benefactor, No.1, and Big Brother are clearly images of the deity's displacement, a point O'Brien makes clear when he declares: "we are the priests of power." O'Brien personifies the authority of the state, not only in the force of the arguments he puts to Smith but also in the diversity of functions he adopts: "He had the air of a doctor, a teacher, even a priest, anxious to explain and persuade rather than to punish." Typically, Smith infers O'Brien's presence before he sees him, transforming into a single person engrossing all the roles of the moment: "he was the tormentor, he was the protector, he was the inquisitor, he was the friend." Modeled on Dostoevsky's Grand Inquisitor, O'Brien's composite role is to challenge any presumptions about reality and history in order to prove the absolute position that "whatever the Party holds to be truth, *is* truth." Of course the means of persuasion are not verbal and Orwell demonstrates throughout part 3 that sleep deprivation, disorientation, physical beating, and other practices can radically undermine the subject's self-perception. Smith's very "power of arguing and reasoning" comes under attack with the result that he confesses to anything in order to appease his interrogators. O'Brien even insists that Big Brother exists but that Smith does not, and as if in confirmation places him in front of a mirror where Smith recoils in horror from recognizing the "bowed, grey-coloured, skeleton-like thing" he sees in it. The terms applied to Smith suggest humiliation, loss of distinctive appearance, and above all that he is the walking dead. The ultimate crisis with the rat cage triggers a hallucinatory image where his self traverses a boundless space under erasure: "he was blind, helpless, mindless."[40] Orwell originally planned to call his novel *The Last Man in Europe*, which was wisely dropped as it suggests an apocalyptic ultimacy to Smith's fate whereas the novel demonstrates that he is an anonymous instance, one case within a repeating process.

Smith's interrogation resembles processes of measurement and a distorted kind of psychotherapy (another analogy developed in the 1950s) where his inquisitor asks factual questions as tests of his subject's attitude. One deleted passage from the manuscript captures the officials' pretence of concern: "There were men in white coats who stroked his forehead & looked deep into his eyes while metronomes ticked somewhere near at hand."[41] The metronome links the interrogation to Pavlov's experiments and briefly casts Smith in the role of guinea pig. The famous case of how many fingers O'Brien is holding up makes the point clearly that no commonsense notion of the real can substitute for Smith's required "act of submission." The mathematical question further infantilizes Smith and makes it even clearer than in *Darkness at Noon* that the interrogation is a ritual, a series of cues for ideological recognition, not appeals to any body of fact. This is a form of unlearning that Smith has to endure, whose goal is uncertainty. So, paradoxically, he can only "truly" see once his eyes are closed. Then and only then can he admit to sincere ignorance and be rewarded with a pain-killing drug, the whole exemplifying what came to be known as the alternation between "hard" and "soft" treatment.

The assault on Smith constitutes an attempt by O'Brien to naturalize the state ideology. Not only is the regime of Big Brother rendered as timeless, without origin or limit; but also each shift of state policy has to erase former ones so as to promote the impression that things had always been thus. Smith himself works in one of the most manipulative ideological state apparatuses in retrospectively reinventing the small details of recent history. O'Brien thus redirects against Smith the very procedures Smith had been exploiting for public consumption and attempts to introduce a relational concept of the self to replace that of individuality. He refuses to allow Smith to imagine himself other than as part of a larger whole, a "cell" within a body. And, since power is collective, "the individual only has power in so far as he ceases to be an individual."[42] So, by his logic, the Party maintains itself by a perpetual erasure of past events and of potentially deviant individuals.

O'Brien requires an "act of self-destruction" preparatory to Smith's reeducation. He reduces Smith to a state of automatism ("a mouth that uttered, a hand that signed"), but only as a prelude to "conversion." For this reason he has been described as a "re-creator surrounded by religious connotations of confession and rebirth." The analogy with a church of true believers, which O'Brien confirms, anticipates the terms of reference used to discuss brainwashing and Communism in general through the 1950s, and was to be made explicit as the Church of State in David Karp's *One* (1953). Not only does O'Brien direct events; he provides a running commentary on them, which once again anticipates subsequent accounts of brainwashing. Consider, for example, his following statements: "we convert him [the heretic], we capture his inner mind, we reshape him; we bring him over to our side, not in appearance, but genuinely, heart and soul"; "everyone is washed clean" and deviants after their "treatment" are "only the shells of men." The central metaphor of cleansing contains a crucial ambiguity of reference. Traditionally the figure is of purifying the individual body. Here, however, the metaphor of the collective body politic takes precedence over any tropes of the individual self, so that cleansing comes to signify erasure: "you will be lifted clean out of the stream of history," Smith is told. Instead of *carrying* blemish his consciousness *is* a blemish: "You are a stain that must be wiped out."[43]

O'Brien is a skilled manipulator of metaphors of transforming the self—by occupation, purging, and cleansing. He rejects all earlier forms of martyrdom as inefficient because the victims had not been converted. Accordingly he predicts to Smith that his inner space will be removed: "you will be hollow," the emptiness connoting his accessibility to ideological reconfirmation. If consciousness is figured as a vessel, this explains why Smith's electric shock treatment creates a "large patch of emptiness, as though a piece had been taken out of his brain." This echo of the operation in Zamyatin (a prelude to Smith's "reintegration") can be read as an individual reenactment of the erasure brought about by other state processes. Thus Chad Walsh has argued that "Newspeak is the Orwellian equivalent of a lobotomy." Whether the metaphor denotes cleansing, erasure, or emptying, every single move in this process reflects the power play taking place. O'Brien replaces Big Brother as an apparently all-seeing agent who can detect, for instance, when Smith is lying, and who seems to possess a limitless knowledge of the latter's innermost fears. So successful is O'Brien that by the novel's coda Smith has been brought to love Big Brother and to desire his own death: "the long-hoped-for bullet was entering his brain."[44]

The austere consistency of Orwell's narrative grew out of an objection he took to a possibility raised in *Darkness at Noon* that the totalitarian state would publish the true facts at some future date. For Orwell the mistake here was to superimpose a liberal concept onto the totalitarian presumption that history was something to be made, not recorded. This means in turn that the problem of narrative provenance becomes even more acute in Orwell's novel since Smith is a figure of only symptomatic significance to the party (a "flaw") whose complete placing within the state immediately predates his own demise. Indeed the truly chilling aspect of Orwell's narrative lies not so much in O'Brien's treatment of Smith as the latter's expectation of and then yearning for his own death, and the resultant identification of ideological inscription with the erasure of the subject. Christopher Norris has attacked Orwell's "homespun empiricist outlook" for ignoring the way ideology operates in non-totalitarian regimes; but *Nineteen Eighty-Four* demonstrates clearly the Althusserian notion that "the individual subject is a fiction . . . held in place by a process of imperative socialisation."[45] Norris glosses Orwell's projection of such a view onto an "alien" regime as a defensive, not to say evasive tactic, although here again Orwell makes a complex interplay or the familiar and unfamiliar, reflecting in the discontinuity between the general London scene and the pyramidal structures of the state ministries.

No sooner had *Nineteen Eighty-Four* been published than it was situated within the emerging Cold War context. Philip Rahv for one had no doubt that Big Brother was "obviously modeled on Stalin" and warned that cases like that of Cardinal Mindszenty gave the novel an immediate urgency that the West was all too reluctant to face: "The truth is that the modern totalitarians have devised a methodology of terror that enables them to break human beings by getting inside them. They explode the human character from within, exhibiting the pieces as irrefutable proof of their own might and virtue." Correspondingly, Marxist reviewers took the novel as yet another attack on the Soviet Union and therefore a mere part of "cold war propaganda."[46]

From whatever political angle it was approached, critics agreed that Orwell's novel had become part of the cultural landscape of the 1950s. Cold War terms of reference inflected such commentaries as Isaac Deutscher's 1955 attack on the novel for following the "plot of a science-fiction film of the cheaper variety, with mechanical horror piling up on mechanical horror." For Deutscher, Orwell's incapacity to grasp the historical complexities of the Moscow trials means that his novel encourages readers to think in black-white polarities pandering to contemporary fears of the atom bomb. Deutscher waxed indignant over the assimilation of Orwellian terms into political discourse and Orwell's demonization of Communism; both factors had rendered the novel a fictional equivalent to the bomb, a "sort of ideological super-weapon" in the Cold War.[47]

The 1954 BBC TV adaptation of *Nineteen Eighty-Four* by Rudolph Cartier plays directly to the apocalyptic fear identified by Deutscher in the repeated shots of nuclear explosions that introduce the drama. There Cartier shifts the focus to the paranoia surrounding internal security with a voice over warning viewers to beware the "enemy within." Despite Cartier's faithfulness to Orwell's novel, the BBC received threatening phone calls, and he had to be given a bodyguard because many viewers took the drama to be pro-Communist.[48] The adaptation predictably makes more extensive use of visual images than the novel, even adding "facecrime" to the list of offences. Smith's ordeal at the hands of O'Brien is telescoped into a number of brief scenes, the most striking of which shows the former lying in a coffin-like container and then cuts to a hand turning dials on a machine. The array of methods described in the novel—hypnosis, drugs, and so on—are here simplified to a technologically induced transformation of Smith. In late scenes from this section he is shown trapped in a bright pool of light from overhead, signifying the interrogation process, with no clearly visible background against which his self can be defined. The drama concludes austerely with an image of Smith in his convict-like tunic where his identity has become minimized into a state cipher: WS KZ-6090. This makes a logical preliminary to Smith's final displacement by the image of Big Brother.

■ Although the novels just examined deal with comparable situations of arrest and "correction," their methods vary considerably. Zamyatin depicts a process of abstraction where characters become totally identified with their state functions; Koestler presents a realist exposé of the Soviet purges; and Orwell transposes Soviet processes onto the British political scene of the imminent future. Shortly before the term "brainwashing" was coined a number of notorious trials in Eastern Europe prepared the way for public recognition of the startling relevance of *Nineteen Eighty-Four* to current Soviet practice. The most famous was the imprisonment and trial in Budapest of the Hungarian Catholic leader Cardinal Mindszenty, whose fate was dramatized, in the words of one early commentator, as part of the "most stupendous spiritual battle of world history," that between religion and materialism. The Mindszenty story, according to Gilbert Seldes, was based on a prediction in the *London Tablet* that the cardinal would be drugged and tortured, which was rapidly converted into fact and made the basis in the American press of a "campaign of hysteria and falsehood," although it has since been asserted that the CIA had a top-level spy in Mindszenty's prison who reported the application of drugs, something not even Mindszenty himself would have realized.[49] Although U.S. agencies had been experimenting on hypnosis and the use of drugs as early as the Second World War, the Mindszenty case galvanized the CIA into intensifying such research and was an important trigger to establishing the MK-ULTRA program on mind control.[50]

Important as it was, the Mindszenty case lacked the special resonance of Robert A. Vogeler's, since the latter was an American. As a supervisor of IT&T in Austria, Czechoslovakia, and Hungary, Vogeler had to make numerous visits to those countries, where he was involved in the construction of radio and telephone facilities. In addition he helped a number of refugees find safety in the West. On one of his visits to Hungary in 1948 he was arrested and imprisoned. At his trial in February 1950 he pleaded guilty to espionage and sabotage. In his subsequent account of his experiences Vogeler asserted that "the purpose of the trial was not to establish guilt or innocence, but to teach a political lesson at the expense of the defendants," the lesson being that all Westerners were to be regarded as enemies of the state.[51] But Vogeler had become a pawn in Cold War politics, and his case brought about a crisis in Hungarian-American diplomatic relations. Hungarian consulates were closed, and the State Department forbade American citizens from traveling to that country. Eventually Vogeler's release was achieved at the cost of these measures being reversed and the halting of Voice of America transmissions to Hungary. After his return to America, in 1952 Vogeler presided over the opening of the American Liberation Center in New York, which was an organization dedicated to encouraging dissent in Eastern Europe.

Vogeler's description of his experiences in *I Was Stalin's Prisoner* (1951) is strikingly similar to Koestler's narrative. He is questioned by "No. 1" at length and given his first "confessions" to sign. At no point is he subjected to physical violence himself, although he hears the screams of a prisoner in a neighboring cell and hears reports of the use of the bastinado. Like Rubashov, he is confronted with confessions by associates that implicate him in fantastic conspiracies (for these to be true he would have had to serve simultaneously as an officer in all three armed services). And again like Rubashov, Vogeler realizes that he has been caught up in a ritual where at his trial he has to play the role of the imperialist villain. Vogeler's torture consists of extreme fatigue, sleep deprivation, and the discomfort induced by having a lamp trained in his eyes during interrogation. While he plays down any novelty in the methods used against him, Vogeler nevertheless recognizes the insidious attraction in his prescribed role:

> "Here," No. 1 was saying, "just sign this and you'll be given a nice, comfortable bed."
>
> It was yet another typed confession. A new personality that was prepared to do everything that No.1 suggested. But my old personality — or perhaps it was merely the instinct of self-preservation — still held its ground.[52]

Typical of such accounts, the self becomes a battleground where the discourse of conquest is internalized, although the strategies followed in the "battle" alternate bewilderingly between threat and inducement. The Mindszenty case has already been digested by Vogeler as an ominous indicator that he himself will certainly submit, as he eventually does.

The Vogeler case convinced John Dos Passos of the "existence of a conspiracy of assassins" and was used as the basis of Paul Gallico's 1952 novel *Trial by Terror*.[53] This takes place in the immediate aftermath of the imprisonment of an American businessman in Hungary. Despite warnings, an idealistic journalist from the *Chicago Sentinel* enters the country illegally and is arrested, brainwashed, and tried. He is freed only after tortuous negotiations by his enterprising editor, who blackmails a Hungarian minister into striking a deal. Gallico's purpose is made clear in a note omitted from British editions of the novel that it presents a "portrayal of the thinking and tactics of government behind the iron curtain and the means by which public confessions are elicited in the iron-curtain countries." The opening description of the Hungarian minister who promises to hang all subsequent Western "spies" establishes the novel's ideological credentials in its over-determined detail:

> [He was wearing] a shapeless ill-fitting coat of the type affected by Moscow-trained government officials who want to give the impression of belonging to the proletariat. . . . [T]here was an overlaid expression of cynicism in the mouth and the lines about it as though he had lived too long exposed to the inner and outer atmosphere of brutality. [Despite his peasant fingers] he had country lawyer, politician-come-to-power, written all over him.[54]

The passage is focalized through a hypothetical Western journalist attending the minister's press conference. The vast majority of the few Westerners permitted to be present would be sympathetic to the Communist line, whereas this description is obviously heavily critical. And this is its whole point, since Gallico uses the minister to personify a brutalized and opportunistic regime directed from Moscow. His very appearance substantiates in advance the process of arrest and trial that he threatens.

The predictable sequence of arrest, interrogation, and trial, however, contains an enigma. How could Frobisher (read Vogeler) and Mindszenty have made their confessions? And we start too with the problem of how American journalists can cope with the political circumstances of Cold War Europe. Gallico shrewdly demonstrates the overlap between journalism and politics that constantly complicates the process of reporting. So one story on how a Czech Catholic helped another cross the border will compromise the former's safety; another will embarrass the State Department and strain relations with the newspaper. Indeed the editor Nick Strong combines the roles of diplomat, Mr. Fixit, and political commentator in the novel. It is he, for instance, who recognizes the dangerous irrelevance of comparisons with World War II where characters yearn to take decisive action. "What had remained," he reflects, "of all the beautiful courage, sacrifice, and adventuring?"[55]

This is the context entered by Jimmy Race, an ex-paratrooper who personifies to the point of parody a crude, macho courage that leads him to attack anyone demonstrating a shortage of "guts." His determination to open up the Frobisher story is expressed as a sexual boast whereby he will lay his report in the "lap" of Paris. Despite repeated warnings, Race sets out on his quixotic mission, only to find himself locked up in the Andrassy Prison in Budapest. Race's self-image as "unconquerable"—a personification of national pride based naively on physical superiority—leaves him totally unprepared for his treatment as a kind of human specimen being "studied and examined" by his captors. The first phase is isolation. Next he is infantilized and humiliated, being questioned naked before a panel of officials. His interrogator tells him: "You look and are behaving like an ugly little child."[56] This brief criticism attacks Race's three points of pride: his good looks, his physical size, and his male pride. This humiliation is then followed by sleep deprivation (he is denied a bed and kept in a brightly lit cell) and degradation, the process reaching its climax with Race's spell on the "glockenspiel." This is Gallico's equivalent of Room 101, the worst phase, which is at first not described apart from its effects on Race: puffed-up features, a staggering walk, and glazed looks. The device proves to be nothing more imaginative than a common pail placed over Race's head, which is then beaten with broom handles.

The weakening of Race forms an elaborate preparation for his indoctrination or conditioning. The prison psychiatrist directs his "education to guilt," initially administering a drug that "unhinged the moral values of the patient confused and unsettled his mind and made it completely amenable to outside suggestion." This is the point where the consciousness of the "patient" is reshaped: "if the seeds were properly sown, the ideas and emotions grafted on the personality of the patient at the moment of his greatest weakness would become a part of him and remain in his consciousness."[57] Race is trained like a performing animal to deliver the required lines in his trial, and once he has been returned to the West his friends see him as an "empty shell" rather than possessing a new personality. Anticipating what was to be called "menticide" later in the 1950s, Gallico stresses that at his lowest point Race "died mentally." The result is a total disabling, only partly offset at the end of the novel by a colleague's decision to act as his permanent nurse.

The sequence of events experienced by Race confirms his editor's perception of historical crisis: "There had never been a time when huge and evil forces were playing more desperately for keeps than the years of '49–'50 with the pressure ever increasing."[58] The novel is caught awkwardly between confirming this image of superpower confrontation and dramatizing the practice of investigatory journalism. Jimmy Race's purpose in finding out how forced confessions are produced is ironically realized in his own experience. In one sense therefore he becomes an object lesson in complacent ignorance, but Gallico does not make the slightest gesture toward explaining how Race's experiences could be conveyed to a third party. He is so severely crippled mentally that there is great doubt as to whether he would ever be able to tell his own story. Accordingly, all the criteria of journalistic enquiry—checking facts, communicating them via telephone if necessary, and so on—must be suspended in the case of Jimmy Race. By the end of the novel the reader has been granted privileged access to a process that can only be surmised in broad outline by Race's colleagues.

Nevertheless, the narrative voice throughout the Race chapters ignores the problem of provenance and negotiates between Race's (and, by implication, the reader's) ignorance and the combination of threat and opportunism being exerted by the system's practitioners. Gallico foregoes the immediacy of Race's perspective in order to identify the phases of the process he undergoes. Thus we are told: "He was being trained like an animal being put through a scientist's maze in order to learn what things could win him a moment's respite from the daily routine of planned horrors. His subconscious was carried along with his physical and conscious being. Here was the real deviltry of the Red torture pattern, for it led man to the wholly unconscious betrayal of himself."[59] The first sentence implicitly points to an application of Pavlovian techniques, and then Gallico follows the examples of Koestler and Orwell to deny that any area of the self is exempt from attack. While he might deny that this method is totally new, he nevertheless demonstrates how Race's subjectivity can be totally unraveled to the point of an infantile dependence on his "therapist." Race's buried insecurity, which he subdues through macho bravado, comes to the surface in a kind of induced neurosis that, according to Western doctors, could easily lead him to suicide. The conclusion also underlines the utter impotence of the national self-image embodied in Race: a complacent confidence in his strength and size, and an assumption that direct action can be taken on the model of World

War II. Cold War Europe, however, needs the combination of diplomacy, realism, and political shrewdness represented by Race's editor.

Trial by Terror draws on the fiction discussed earlier in this chapter, but diverges from Koestler and Orwell in describing a Westerner's venture into a totalitarian regime. The division of locations between Budapest and Paris means that only in the former can Gallico capture an Orwellian claustrophobia. There remain escape routes and a place of freedom. Gallico presents the Hungarian interrogation methods as part of a larger Moscow-directed system. This same strategy was followed by the Hungarian writer Lajos Ruff, who was arrested in 1953, interrogated, subsequently escaped to the West in 1956, and testified to the U.S. Senate committee on brainwashing. Ruff's 1959 account of his ordeal, *The Brain-Washing Machine*, demonizes the method of interrogation as an alien procedure coming "somewhere from the steppes of Asiatic Russia" and focuses it on the surreal "magic room" of his prison. Here a psychological analogue of splitting the atom takes place, where the Communist technicians "penetrated the infinitely finer construction of the human soul [finer than the structure of the atom], but only to destroy the soul's hidden forces after discovering them."[60] The repetition of "soul" forms part of Ruff's anti-Communist discourse by implying a perspective on brainwashing as a simultaneous sacrilegious violation of the secrets of Nature and of the spirit. Ruff writes with the full consciousness of Mindszenty's precedent; indeed the Cardinal was interned in the same prison.

The "magic room" proves to be a kind of ultimately controlled environment where hidden projectors could throw disorienting images onto the walls.[61] Although Ruff is administered drugs, the room seems designed to simulate their hallucinatory effects so that internal and external space collapse together. Film sequences accelerate and decelerate, splicing together erotic scenes and surreal shots of men walking in midair; "in among these pictures," Ruff continues, "there were running lines and colour slides, abstract figures, out of any context." The destabilization of his sense of the real is achieved by the authorities' exploitation of sound as well as visual effects: "the shadows wandered, the sea murmured and the feminine weeping could be heard regularly, and the beam followed me with a slow movement."[62] Nothing is distinct here except a beam of silver light that metaphorically represents the process of surveillance to which Ruff is being subjected. It cannot be avoided and, by implication, can penetrate his innermost self. The "magic room" represents an astonishingly elaborate combination of cell and psychiatric laboratory presided over by Dr. Nemeth who justifies his practices with the conviction that modern culture has lapsed into schizophrenic dissociation. There is thus a certain consistency in Ruff's subsequent transfer to an insane asylum.

There is a consistent line of argument from Koestler through Orwell, Gallico, and Ruff, where the techniques of mind alteration are seen as part of a monolithic state machine directed toward its own self-maintenance. The processes of interrogation are, by implication, part of a centralized culture organized on a war footing to combat internal and external enemies. This was the central argument of George S. Counts and Nucia Lodge's 1949 account of Soviet mind control, *The Country of the Blind*, which used an epigraph from *Darkness at Noon* to establish its theme. In the Wells story from which they took their title, a race has been isolated so long within an Andes valley that a disease brings about a general loss of sight. Substitute Iron Curtain for mountain barrier and the loss of sight can be glossed as a political myopia for Counts and Lodge's purposes. Both they and the novelists considered here described different variations on what, by the mid-1950s, had become known as brainwashing. The paradigm had been established. The time was ripe for the term to be coined and promoted. Exactly how this happened must be our next consideration.

two

Brainwashing Defined
and Applied

"Brainwashing, the word and the technique, burst like a bombshell upon the American consciousness during the Korean War," noted a reviewer in 1956.[1] The expression was coined by Edward Hunter in 1950 to describe the thought reform methods being used by the Communist authorities on Chinese citizens and was then applied to the treatment of U.S. captives in the North Korean prison camps set up along the Manchurian border. By the end of the decade it had become "associated with all Communist efforts to extract confessions and indoctrinate captive audiences, as well as with their internal educational and propaganda efforts."[2] There are indications that the term was promoted by the American authorities specifically to counter Communist allegations that the United States had been using biological weapons in Korea and as a stratagem in the ongoing propaganda war of the 1950s. In 1953 a CIA official met with the U.S. ambassador to the United Nations and reported that the ambassador was "seeking a very dramatic word which would indicate horror and would condemn (by its sound) Soviet practices of attacking people's minds." "Brainwashing" was ideal for this purpose because "by identifying a clear enemy, [it] reaffirmed the necessity of Americans banding together to fight against an insidious and underhanded foe."[3]

By 1950 Edward Hunter, a journalist with a Far East expertise and an interest in psychological warfare, as well as a former member of the OSS (the

Office of Strategic Services, which served a role during World War II that the CIA would assume in the cold war), had become a CIA aide. Hunter produced two books and a number of articles on brainwashing, was active throughout the 1950s in the cause of refusing UN membership to Communist China, and between 1964 and 1975 edited *Tactics*, which he described as a "Psywar" journal. The term thus entered the language during one of the most ideologically critical periods of the Cold War and was to play a key role in the Western demonization of the Communist conspiracy. Hunter brought the term "brain-washing" into the English language as a translation of the Chinese *hsi nao*, originally in tandem with the expression "brain-changing," distinguishing between them as follows:

> Brain-washing is indoctrination, a comparatively simple procedure, but brain-changing is immeasurably more sinister and complicated. Whereas you merely have to undergo a brain-cleansing to rid yourself of "imperialist poisons," in order to have brain-changing you must empty your mind of old ideas and recollections.[4]

The latter term described the procedures leading up to a show trial, for instance, while the former designated the government-directed collective process of reduction that Hunter documented in *Brain-Washing in Red China* (1951). During the fifties "brain-changing" dropped out of the language and "brain-washing" took on both meanings. *Brain-Washing in Red China*, which was approved for distribution among the troops in Korea (although this never actually happened), assembles information culled mainly from refugees on the changes taking place in Communist China: the group criticism sessions, the control of propaganda and media information, and so on. Although his focus falls on China, Hunter stresses the origin of brainwashing in the Soviet Union, citing the Robert Vogeler case early in the book. The state-orchestrated Hate Week, when abuse is directed against effigies of Uncle Sam, closely resembles the corresponding episode in *Nineteen Eighty-Four*, though the comparison is left implicit.

Hunter's purpose in promoting the term "brainwashing" was blatantly partisan from the very start. One of his earliest reports on China, published in September 1950 against the background of the Inchon landings in Korea, opens with the stark declaration: 'Brain-washing' is the principal activity on the Chinese mainland nowadays."[5] Playing on the precarious geographical position of Hong Kong as an embattled outpost of Western democracy, he evokes the looming threat of a Red China mobilized for militant expansion. His sweeping generalization suggests a total centralized organization of society that confronts the West with something unprecedented. "This is psychological warfare," he declares, "on a scale incalculably more immense than any militarist of the past has ever envisaged."[6] Hunter exploits the novelty of brainwashing to reinforce an apocalyptic perception of the Cold War that he was to develop later in the 1950s. Brainwashing for him functioned as the identifying sign of an implacably hostile ideology. From the very beginning, Hunter had moved significantly away from reportage on developments in China in order to contextualize the process by including the cases of Cardinal Mindszenty and Robert Vogeler. The coinage of the term becomes a political act in breaking the silence of Communist regimes, making manifest a secret technique. "Brain warfare" (subsequently publicized by the CIA director Allen Dulles) is presented as a covert analogue for nuclear war, in a way even more sinister because it is only partially glimpsed and certainly not understood in the West. The aim is a planned confusion of the mind where "shadow takes form and form becomes shadow."[7] The Communists normalize this process by presenting it as education. Indeed, Hunter and his successors alert their Western readers to decode the discourse of "learning," "democratic discussion," or "turning over" that had to be learned in relation to the desired political conversion of citizens after a preliminary softening-up phase.

Like Howard Fast and Arthur Koestler, Hunter satirized Communism as a kind of political church with its own scripture (Marx's writings and their commentators) and power rituals. Thus, when an individual makes a confession of guilt this enacts a gesture of submission to party authority since the Communist aim is to "win converts who can be depended on to react as desired at any time anywhere." In a later edition Hunter made the same point even more forcefully: "The intent is to change a mind radically so that its owner becomes a living puppet—a human robot—without the atrocity being visible from the outside. The aim is to create a mechanism in flesh and blood, with new beliefs and new thought processes inserted into a captive body."[8] The unity of the self is ruptured by a dissociation of inner from outer, of mind from body, so that the individual becomes a mechanism. The speech of one returning American POW from North Korea seemed "impressed on a disc." Another is quoted as stating that "the words were mine . . . but the thoughts were theirs." Thus the "mental automaton becomes the ideal of education."[9] By this point there has emerged the fantasy figure of an individual drained of identifying characteristics and transformed into the passive tool of party policy. We shall see how this robotic figure recurs in invasion narratives of the 1950s and reaches its culmination in the "sleeper" assassin, the Manchurian Candidate.

Hunter's version of brainwashing was underpinned by the special status enjoyed in the Soviet Union by Pavlov's theories. He records how he went with the novelist Ayn Rand to see a documentary film called *The Nervous System*, which in its full version contained scenes of experimentation on human subjects. Hunter describes how Lenin gave Pavlov the specific assignment of looking into how his theories of conditioned reflexes might be applied to humans. The latter produced a four-hundred-page manuscript that was enthusiastically received. From that point on Pavlov's status rose to the extent that the Soviet scriptwriters presented him as a "sort of master magician with occult like powers over men's minds, the Merlin of dialectical materialism."[10] Pavlov emerges as a scientist striving not so much for an understanding of the brain as for means of controlling it. One commentator suggested that his theories were attractive to the Soviet authorities because they could be put into practice so easily and also because, if impressions were integrated into reflexes, this would seem to confirm Marxist environmental determinism.[11]

Hunter pursued his anti-Communist campaign in *The Black Book on Red China* (1961), which contained a chapter on brainwashing and genocide. Here Hunter rehearses the history of a practice applying Pavlov's theories to create "new Soviet man." The Chinese Communists further developed this method in their crusade against freedom and transported hundreds of POWs who subsequently disappeared across the Korean border into Manchuria "for special handling." Then, extrapolating the traditional trope of the body politic, Hunter continues: "The effect on an entire population of a concentrated program of brainwashing would inevitably create a national neurosis. The mental upset caused in a single individual is duplicated on a national scale. A nation afflicted with brainwashing would be a mentally sick country, made deliberately so as a national policy."[12] By thus appropriating the 1950s discourse of mental health Hunter manages to turn on its head the metaphor within brainwashing so that it becomes a means of inducing illness, not health or purification. The trope of the health of the body politic extrapolates from the individual to the nation, a move we shall see repeated in depictions of the fate of the American POWs in Korea.

Through the 1950s Hunter established himself as such a specialist in psychological propaganda that on March 13, 1958, he was consulted on that subject by the House Un-American Activities Committee. Here Hunter expresses pride in his coinage of the term that he explains as meaning "mind attack": "brainwashing was the new procedure, built up out of all earlier processes of persuasion, using the Pavlovian approach to make people react in a way determined by a central authority, exactly as bees in a hive."[13] Hunter based all his remarks on the dual premise of total warfare and a goal of take over rather than destruction: "The Objective of Communist warfare," he declared, "is to capture intact the minds of the people and their possessions, so that they can be put to use."[14] Hunter's blurring together of mental and social spaces equally vulnerable to take over helps to explain why fantasy narratives of mind invasion should have become so popular in the 1950s. In the course of his meeting with HUAC Hunter variously criticized the lack of leadership from American intellectuals, the failure of the U.S. government to properly brief troops in Korea, and the suppression of information about brainwashing until late in the Korean War. The latter was particularly dangerous, he insisted, because it promoted a misperception that brainwashing was only applied to POWs, whereas it was being used generally for social control throughout Communist regimes.

Hunter's early accounts of brainwashing informed a rare public statement on that subject in 1953 in an address to Princeton alumni by the CIA director Allen Dulles. In this classic statement of "two worlds" Cold War policy, where the Eastern bloc is methodically depopulating its border zones (an "impenetrable barrier"), Dulles conflated the concept of an ongoing "battle for men's minds" with Hunter's coinage to produce the phrase "brain warfare" to identify a concerted campaign being waged by the Communist counties against external and internal foes. Dulles drew on *Brain-Washing in Red China* to repeat Hunter's distinction between "brain-washing" and "brain-changing," and warned that the Communists' ultimate aim was to produce robotized, acquiescent citizens: "Parrotlike the individuals so conditioned can merely repeat thoughts which have been implanted in their minds by suggestion from outside. In effect, the brain under these circumstances becomes a phonograph playing a disc put on its spindle by an outside genius over which it has no control." Dulles applied the brainwashing metaphor literally in his worst-case scenario as a total erasure of thoughts followed by the creation of "new brain processes."[15] Through a rhetoric of polarized opposites—American pluralism vs. Soviet conformism, freedom vs. collective imprisonment, and so on—Dulles delivers a grim warning of a monolithic aggression emanating from behind the Iron Curtain and targeting the very center of the free self.

Among the accounts of imprisonment by the Chinese, Dries van Coillie's *I Was Brainwashed in Peking,* published in 1969, incorporates the term within his description of the day-by-day torture and humiliation he received. During his time in prison, van Coillie, a Catholic missionary, was put under constant pressure to "confess" to being an "international spy" and was told in effect that he could leave his prison "when you can gladly take part in brainwashing, when you are able to 'kill' your own personality with enthusiasm."[16] Although the term would not have been in English currency when van Coillie was imprisoned in the early 1950s, he is probably weaving it into his account in the Chinese sense (he was a fluent speaker) of purifying change. A key moment of insight comes in his account when he realizes the ramifications of Chinese surveillance: "the spy is the grand master in this form of government. He is everywhere. He has all kinds of tricks. It is he who alters people's minds, hearts and consciences. *The eyes of Big Brother are watching me,* says George Orwell in his book '1984.' Here the eyes, and the ears of Big Brother communist are everywhere, in a microphone in the room perhaps."[17] Van Coillie experienced the divisive effect of the Chinese system of informers, which induced total mistrust of fellow prisoners. He even speculated that he might have so internalized surveillance that his subconscious was monitoring the workings of his conscious mind.

Hunter's account of Chinese brainwashing was partly challenged in the memoir of a Belgian Benedictine who was subjected to extended indoctrination by the Communists. Eleutherius Winance's *The Communist Persuasion* (1959) drew on the author's knowledge of Chinese culture and made a real effort to relate brainwashing to the Chinese practice of trying to bring about the "slow transformation of minds" by collective criticism.[18] The scenes Winance describes are very similar to the "accusation meetings" that appear in the memoir of a Chinese Christian journalist ghost-written by Edward Hunter, *The Story of Mary Liu,* published in 1957. The difference is that Winance projects a far shrewder sense of an overall cultural process at work without understating the psychological pressures involved. Thus he recognizes the Communists' assault on the inner self and implicitly sees an analogy with religious conversion running from the guilt and self-accusation induced by indoctrination sessions, through a confessional phase, and finally to a "scientific conversion." Unlike most commentators on this subject, Winance drew on the writings of Mao Tze-tung and contemporary Communist pamphlets to show that brainwashing had its roots in Chinese culture, and he concludes: "To my mind, any effort to explain brainwashing exclusively in terms of Pavlov's conditional reflex is completely off the track." Brainwashing therefore involved a program of "thought reform" through which the Chinese Communists were trying to convert a whole generation of youth to the new ideology.[19]

■ By the mid-1950s brainwashing was well established within the public discussions of mind control. Although the American public would not have known this, brainwashing had taken on such importance in the intelligence community that Allen Dulles commissioned a special report from the CIA, which was completed and passed on to J. Edgar Hoover in April 1956.[20] In the public domain three writers endorsed and elaborated Hunter's account of brainwashing, thereby consolidating the grand narrative of which it formed a part. The first, Joost Meerloo, former chief of the psychological section of the Netherlands Armed Forces and a naturalized U.S. citizen, was called in as an expert witness during the trial of Colonel Frank H. Schwable, an ex-POW who had "confessed" that the United States was using bacteriological weapons. Meerloo tried to disperse the serviceman's guilt into a general human vulnerability by arguing that no one could resist the process of brainwashing, and he made one of the most emotive interventions in the debate with his study, *The Rape of the Mind* (1956). As early as 1951 Meerloo had coined the term "menticide," to mean by analogy with "genocide" an "attack on man's very mind, on his will and conviction," citing the Mindszenty case as an example of individual menticide and Nazi propaganda as demonstrating social menticide. By 1956 he had developed the notion of assault into the crime of mind murder, where a "powerful dictator can imprint his own opportunist thoughts upon the minds of those he plans to use and destroy." Drawing numerous parallels with the Nazis, whose methods Meerloo had witnessed first hand during their occupation of the Netherlands, he followed the Hunter line in identifying Pavlov as the theorist of a newly systematized attack on the individual citizen. Again noting precedents in Nazi practice, he stresses how the media can be marshaled into the purpose of causing menticide: "there is scarcely any hiding place from the constant visual and verbal assault on the mind."[21]

Meerloo assimilated Hunter's description of how the mind can be transformed into an automatism within his larger perception that "in the totalitarian master plan for world control, conditioning of behaviour and its different techniques have become most important." In 1954, through the pages of the *New York Times*, he directed his attack more forthrightly against the Soviet

Union: "through a continued repetition of indoctrination, the Soviet man becomes a conditioned reflex machine, reacting according to a prearranged pattern imprinted on him." Through this irresistible process the human mind is brought into a "condition of enslavement and submission."[22] Reactions to this article were mixed; one correspondent thought Meerloo's understanding of Pavlov was crude, while another praised him for identifying the political applications of posthypnotic suggestion. One reviewer of *The Rape of the Mind* went even further and described Meerloo fulsomely as "one of the great spokesmen of the democratic world."[23]

Meerloo's 1956 study is simultaneously aware and unaware of his chosen language and therefore is important for drawing our attention to the key metaphors embedded in terms like "brainwashing." The latter, unlike the vaguer expression "brain-changing," combines two familiar words in a problematic new context. How is it possible to *wash* the brain, after all? The term risks confusing an organ with a function and is further complicated by commentators' tendency to discuss one metaphor through another. So we find the mind-as-vessel trope used in a parodic summary of the popular image of "Communist efforts to break an individual prisoner . . . and then to empty him of his old beliefs and attitudes and pour in new Communist beliefs and attitudes." Or the psychologist J. A. C. Brown might exchange "wash" for the electronic metaphor "wipe," which William Burroughs was later to use, when Brown objected that "literally washing the physical brain could not remove memory traces in any way comparable to the demagnetising of a recording tape."[24] Brown concluded, prematurely, that "brainwashing" was a misnomer, whereas Hunter, William Sargant, and others showed how the process was comparable to narratives of spiritual conversion with their traditional discourse of cleansing to express the transition of the self from sin or error to a new faith. The metaphor of the purge, given its sinister connotations from Stalin's show trials of the thirties, similarly connotes an internal cleansing of the body politic. Undoubtedly one reason why the term "brainwashing" caught on so quickly was that it harmonized easily with already existing metaphorical discourse.

Meerloo shrewdly highlights the limitations of a key term in behaviorist theory, "reflex," which retains Cartesian analogies between body and machine: "According to the old mechanical view, actions are associated only with the part of the body which performs them, and they have no relationship whatsoever to the purposeful behaviour of the organism as a whole."[25] We shall see that Thomas Pynchon's 1973 novel *Gravity's Rainbow* similarly burlesques the application of Pavlovian methods from a standpoint of organic holism. But, even as Meerloo is questioning the thinking within one metaphor, he is investing another with emotional force. His very title *The Rape of the Mind* follows Hunter in relocating the discourse of warfare. Hunter's phrases like "mind attack" and "mind warfare" (the latter synonymous with "total war," he tells us) imply that the individual self is a besieged citadel, reactive to external aggression. Meerloo similarly presents the self as a private space liable to be "violated" or subject to "enforced mental intrusion." His own term "menticide" was clearly designed to identify a collective crime against the individual, a new form of murder where the victim paradoxically lives on.

The emotional force of Hunter's coinage lay partly in its vagueness. Hunter himself admitted that by the mid-1950s it had taken on two quite distinct meanings: indoctrination and the softening-up process preparatory to indoctrination or confession. "Brainwashing" entails two factors—agency (who does it?) and method (how do they do it?)—that tantalize the reader with implications never made clear. Born of the perceived secrecy of Communist regimes, "brainwashing" became a catchword that constantly expanded its meanings and that trailed suggestions of physical torture, the forced administration of drugs, and—as Hunter admitted, the most difficult point to prove—posthypnotic suggestion. Ironically, Meerloo describes a Pavlovian system of verbal conditioning through "daily propagandistic noise backed up by forceful verbal cues" without realizing that he was contributing to that very effect by strengthening the term "brainwashing," which became one of the keywords of political discourse from the early 1950s onward.[26]

Meerloo demonstrates an awareness of the narrative that supports the practice of brainwashing, tracing it back through Orwell to Huxley and Wells. Here again he paradoxically questions and reinforces Cold War pieties, however. As an account of despotism "this myth of an imaginary world conspiracy aims at bringing the fearful citizens of Totalitaria into a concerted defence against non-existent dangers."[27] In other words conspiracy could form part of the Soviet bloc's collective brainwashing of its citizens. At the same time, conspiracy becomes an explanation (not a symptom) of how the West views Communism. Diagnosing a contemporary need to invent an enemy, Meerloo strengthens the demonized view of the Communist bloc.

The second writer to promote Edward Hunter's line was a London physician in psychological medicine who had been doing work on war neuroses and who was appointed by the British government to liaise with U.S. agencies pursuing mind control programs.[28] William Sargant's *Battle for the Mind* (1957) was completed while he was recovering from a bout of tuberculosis in Majorca. There he met Robert Graves, who enthusiastically revised ("Englished," as Graves put it) the manuscript and even contributed a chapter on "Brain-Washing in Ancient Times." Sargant draws on a broad range of instances taken from American POWs, Koestler, Orwell, and others to demonstrate that physiological conversion mechanisms exist. Sargant's account of Pavlov is detailed and not demonizing since he finds the latter's theories useful in treating war neuroses. Indeed Sargant approaches a Pavlovian position in identifying a physiological process whereby beliefs could be implanted after the brain has been subjected to accidental or deliberate disturbance. Whether the individual is participating in the Eleusinian Mysteries, an Evangelist meeting, or Stalinist indoctrination, the process remains basically the same whereby assent to beliefs is not brought about by cool rational scrutiny so much as by isolation, sleep-deprivation, and endless questioning. Sargant's conclusion helpfully glosses the apparent mental–physical oxymoron in "brainwashing" and also looks forward to later accounts of brain modification. Sargant recognizes a similarity between the functioning of a dog's brain and that of a human, noting that humans "are gifted with religious and social apprehensions, and they are gifted with the power of reason; but all these faculties are physiologically entailed to the brain."[29]

Sargant draws suggestive parallels between the group dynamics of religious revivalism and political meetings, identifying patterns of collective behavior that produce otherwise inexplicable changes in subjects' beliefs. It was the latter that provoked criticism from J. A. C. Brown, who accused Sargant of promoting the notion "that an idea is a 'thing' located in the brain which can be planted there or dug up at will. . . . If Sargant's thesis be correct, there is no reason why any idea should not be implanted and retained regardless of circumstances."[30] In other words a false reification was at once further promoting the view of the mind as a container and also understating the complex process of maintaining beliefs. More recently, Sargant has been questioned for recognizing neither the cognitive, learned dimension to confessions nor their dependence on a reinforcing environment.[31] Sargant's linkage between brainwashing and religious practice was echoed by O. John Rogge, who identified a specific tradition of interrogation that dated back to the medieval Church. For him the Communist interrogators "used the inquisitional technique backed by the power of modern totalitarian states to make the alien part of the minds of their victims their ally."[32] Rogge stresses two points of particular importance here. First, that the victims have, if not a predisposition to confess, then at least psychological needs that could be exploited. And second, with the exception of a brief period in the 1930s, physical torture was hardly ever used by the Communists. Their techniques were overwhelmingly psychological in their strategy.

The most famous writer to promote Edward Hunter's version of brainwashing was Aldous Huxley (*The Devils of Loudun* was cited by Sargant), who in 1958 devoted a whole chapter of *Brave New World Revisited* to that subject and who, along with Bertrand Russell, endorsed Sargant's study as an important contribution to psychopolitics; a "very remarkable book," he declared to Humphrey Osmond, whose implications left "very little hope for our unfortunate species."[33] Throughout the postwar period Huxley wrote on the possible risks in applied technology. As early as 1936 he reflected on the political abuse of drugs, like scopolamine, which could alter behavior. "A system of propaganda," he speculated, "combining pharmacology with literature, should be completely and infallibly effective."[34] By 1949 Huxley had begun registering postwar developments that appeared to confirm the dystopian insights of *Brave New World*. That year he wrote to Orwell to point out—urbanely—that *Nineteen Eighty-Four* had already become an anachronism: "I believe that the world's rulers will discover that infant conditioning and narco-hypnosis are more efficient, as instruments of government, than clubs and prisons, and that the lust for power can be just as completely satisfied by suggesting people into loving their servitude as by flogging and kicking them into obedience." Huxley had been reading George H. Estabrooks on the military applications of hypnotism and later accounts of M. N. Eagle's "tachistoscope," which flashed microsecond images onto a screen. In short, Huxley was all too aware of the growing technology of mind control. In 1949 he wrote to the novelist Philip Wylie, citing the case of Cardinal Mindszenty to demonstrate how the barrier of the conscious will could be overcome: "the scientific dictator of the future—the near future," he warned, "will not have to rely on machine guns. He can make people do what he wants and (more important) make them like it, by getting at the deepest layers of the psyche through childhood conditioning and through the narco-hypnosis of recalcitrant individuals in later life."[35]

Huxley was torn between a growing interest throughout the 1950s in the mind-expanding possibilities of hallucinogens like mescaline and recognizing the possibility for political abuse that these substances opened up. By the end of the decade he had come to view one of the defining characteristics of

Soviet Communism as its willingness to "permit technicization to go to the absolute limit." Peering grimly into the imminent future, Huxley estimated that the techniques were virtually in place where dictators could "make their subjects actually *like* their slavery." The net result would be a kind of political anesthesia, a "painless concentration camp."[36] Speaking as the only man of letters at a 1959 conference on pharmacology and the mind, Huxley struck an apocalyptic note in arguing that the "Final Revolution" was the "application to human affairs, both on the social level and on the individual level, of technology." This could imply a millenarian confidence in a new era opening up, but Huxley's examples show anxiety rather than confidence. Linking the notion of hidden persuaders to propaganda, he states: "the technicization of the means of getting at the human unconscious presents an enormous danger to our whole traditional conception of democracy and liberty." Brainwashing formed one part of this broad process and, to judge from reports of the Korean War, was "exceedingly efficient, and probably going to become more and more efficient as time goes by."[37] For Huxley the signs of this ominous development lay both in the Communist regime's brainwashing and in the "hidden persuaders" of U.S. advertising.

Huxley knew of Donald Hebb's experiments at McGill and of John C. Lilly's at the National Institute of Health on sensory deprivation. He met Lilly in person and also visited the UCLA laboratories in 1956 to observe experiments on animals with electrodes planted in their brains. The latter provoked the science fiction writer Fritz Leiber to protest against "invading the human brain." Leiber speculated that human subjects could be "bugged" to follow transmitted orders; and even a "midget bomb might be implanted in the flesh, set to explode at the proper signal." We do not need the image of brainwashing, he insisted, to be repulsed by such techniques of thought control.[38] In light of subsequent revelations of these projects, Huxley's declaration in a letter of 1957 reads as startlingly naive when he declares: "What men like Hebb and Lilly are doing in the laboratory was done by the Christian hermits in the Thebaid and elsewhere."[39] Maybe so, but the statement ignores Huxley's numerous public expressions of unease at this time over the institutional abuse of the developing technology of mind control. In one of his 1959 Santa Barbara lectures Huxley returned to these "limited environment" experiments where he drew comparisons with the Indian mystics, once again avoiding the issue of control and concentrating instead on the hallucinations that were triggered by sensory deprivation.[40] Huxley knew of Wilder Penfield's use of electronic brain stimulus on epileptics to induce recall, and the above experiments brought him to a position very close to Edward Hunter's, where new technology could reinforce totalitarian regimes.[41] Huxley drew an approximate distinction between Soviet and American science: the latter was potentially dangerous, the former actually so. Hence Huxley's ambiguous joke in his 1956 essay "The Desert" about caterpillars in the California desert resembling Soviet agents "parachuted from the stratosphere, impenetrably disguised, and so thoroughly indoctrinated, so completely conditioned by means of post-hypnotic suggestion, that even under torture it would be impossible for them to confess, even under DDT."[42]

Huxley's ambivalent fascination with scientific experiments that had a potential application to mind control did not prevent him from refusing any form of environmental determinism. However, he recorded his recognition of Pavlov's investigations of external conditioning, especially of subjects under stress.[43] Huxley expressed particular indignation over the position of behaviorists toward the individual: "There are preposterous utterances in J. B. Watson's earlier writings, and even today you will find eminent psychologists, like B. F. Skinner of Harvard, solemnly coming out with statements that 'modern science' makes it clear that the achievement of the individual (as opposed to the group and culture) approximates zero."[44] Huxley rejected this view as unscientific, because it ignored the biological uniqueness of each individual and also was symptomatic of a "Will to Order," which in other contexts he had attributed to dictatorships.

Brave New World Revisited was designed as a report on certain aspects of the postwar scene read through Huxley's earlier novel. He documents a depressing series of ways in which the human mind can be manipulated: through the media and advertising, drugs, subliminal persuasion, "sleep learning" (hypnopaedia in *Brave New World*), and posthypnotic suggestion. Ultimately he paints a picture of a world where reason is constantly being circumvented in the name of commercial or political expediency. Huxley's chapter on brainwashing describes the various methods of applied behaviorism, drawing on Sargant and other works. Indeed, Sargant's study had so depressed Huxley that he made the other's conclusion explicit by declaring that "the effectiveness of political and religious propaganda depends upon the methods employed, not upon the doctrines taught."[45] This grim possibility confirmed in Huxley's writing a certain hostility to the masses as a suggestible mob. In his appendix to *The Devils of Loudun*, for instance, he had waxed eloquent against a "crowd-delirium" that could be exploited through rhythmic sound or the mass media by dictators bent on stifling individual thought. Now the situation is even worse because there appears to be no defense against brainwashing techniques. Echoing his letter to Orwell, Huxley extrapolates a political regime where "whispering machines" and "subliminal projectors" are used in schools and hospitals. This technology might be extended into the whole social environment "where audiences can be given a preliminary softening-up by suggestibility-increasing oratory or rituals."[46] In a 1958 interview for WABC-TV Huxley again warned against the abuse of "powerful, mind-changing drugs" and of subliminal messages in the media that might be extended to political campaigns.[47] Huxley speculates throughout *Brave New World Revisited* on consequences and adaptations. These, he insisted, were imminent; "tomorrow" is one of his recurring terms. Ignoring the death of Stalin a few years earlier, he argues in effect that whatever is technically feasible will be put into practice. Huxley recognizes that "brainwashing" is a mixed term, but attributes this to the scientific inadequacy of the historical moment: "Brainwashing, as it is now practised, is a hybrid technique, depending for its effectiveness partly on the systematic use of violence, partly on skilful psychological manipulation. It represents the tradition of *1984* on its way to becoming the tradition of *Brave New World*."[48] Huxley's political gloom arises from a reversal of faith in progress. Science, he implies, carries its own momentum that he predicts with pessimistic assurance. Exclaiming to Humphrey Osmond in 1957 about the use of subliminal visual projections (discussed in the following chapter)—a "new horror," as he calls it—Huxley dons the role of a Jeremiah predicting the demise of freedom: "But what an appallingly effective tool for the dictators! Combined with drugs, brainwashing, and straight conditioning, it will rob the individual of the last shred of free will."[49]

Huxley's friend Arthur Koestler was altogether more skeptical about the notion of brainwashing and also expressed grave doubts about Huxley's faith in drugs as opening an avenue toward enlightenment. When he reviewed Sargant's *Battle for the Mind* he scathingly accused the author of ignoring whole areas of knowledge like psychosomatics with all the "bias of a Pavlovite convert."[50] In 1960 Koestler joined Huxley at a symposium on "Control of the Mind" organized by the University of California Medical Center in San Francisco.[51] He subsequently recorded how the conference reversed his expectations of how the mind could be controlled by drugs, brainwashing, and other means: "by the end of the Symposium, the one consistent lesson that emerged was the astonishing control of the mind *over* the physical impact of drugs, brain-washing, and other forms of coercion."[52] Koestler was

particularly impressed by the fact that figures like Wilder Penfield were arguing for a nonbehaviorist conception of the mind, and he argued strenuously
against a passive view of the mind that tended to creep into much discussion
of brainwashing. In contrast, he drew the reader's attention to the mind's
complex activity to which the behaviorists' conception of the self "as a bun-
dle of conditioned reflexes" could not begin to do justice.[53]

■ In 1955 there appeared one of the strangest publications of the Cold War,
a brochure, *Brain-Washing: A Synthesis of the Russian Textbook on Psychopolitics*. One edition purports to have been compiled by Charles Stickley
over a period of ten years to refute attacks mounted by the Communists
against Dianetic and Christian Science. Partly because of this purpose, it
has been suggested that the work was a hoax written by L. Ron Hubbard or
that Hubbard produced the booklet to set up his claims that Scientology
could reverse the effects of Communist brainwashing. Another edition carries a note by the ex-Communist Kenneth Goff identifying the brochure as
used in the party underground schools for training in "psychopolitics," that
is, the "art of capturing the minds of a nation through brainwashing and fake
mental health." Goff combines horror at reports of brainwashing in Korea
with suspicion of domestic mental health reform into a single paranoid narrative of Communist subversion, a strategy "authorized" by the preliminary
address to American students by Beria.[54]

Brain-Washing purports to be a summary of methods of "psychopolitics"—virtually what would come to be known as "psyops"—that is defined
as the "art and science of asserting and maintaining dominion over the
thought and loyalties of individuals, officers, bureaux, and masses, and the
effecting of the conquest of enemy nations through 'mental healing.'" The
brochure falls into three main sections: a demonstration of the need for harmony in the Communist state, and therefore of the need for dealing with
dissidents; a justification of the use of force and Pavlovian methods generally; and an account of subversive techniques for conquering the will of citizens. Its premise is the ultimate goal of Communist world conquest. In order
to establish the prime need for political harmony in the state, the brochure
weaves variations on the traditional trope of the body politic. Thus the individual resembles a political entity: "man is already a colonial aggregation of
cells;" and the state conversely resembles a body where "the political entities
within the State lest the State itself fall asunder and die."[55] The twin purpose
in this argument is at once to politicize the concept of the individual and

also to naturalize the state as an organism so that ultimately the concept of the individual disappears. Indeed the brochure targets that cherished national- al ideal of America, rugged individualism, as being totally at odds with the state. The expression the "constitution of Man" accordingly links health with political order as an unquestionable ideal of harmonious functioning.

The simple analogy between body and state becomes complicated by the figure of the surgeon and his implicit analogues. Despite the heavy emphasis on the organic, the model used for behavior is rather mechanistic and if "the individual must be directed from without" an immediate division occurs be- tween the tractable masses and an elite of directors, a caste of technicians who, as Huxley noted, would themselves need to be brainwashed or liquidat- ed once their purpose was accomplished. The following passage will demon- strate the brochure's bizarre combination of politics and therapy: "a heart, or a kidney in rebellion against the remainder of the organism is being disloyal to the remainder of the organism. To cure that heart or kidney it is actually only necessary to bring its activities into alignment with the remainder of the body." As we have seen in Koestler and Orwell, the trope of heterodoxy-as-illness is used to deny political difference and encode dissidence as a kind of mental disease. Since the individual has been reduced to an organ, that is, to a part with no meaningful function apart from the whole, the necessity is opened up for "alignment," an abstractly sinister term for an unspecified process. Once it has been established that obedience is a natural and desirable state, we are then told that "obedience is the result of force." This is where brainwashing comes in as a political technique since, "in moments of expediency . . . the personality itself can be rearranged by shock, surgery, duress, privation, and in particular, that best of psycho-political techniques, implantation, with the technologies of neo-hypnotism." Here we approach the heart of the brochure, which purports to describe actual Soviet strategy once the ideological euphe- misms have been stripped away. The effect is rather like approaching and entering the cells of the secret police where the physical brutality of the re- gime is finally revealed. So the Stalinist principle of relentless force is first described (man is "hammered and pounded again and again, until . . . his only thought is direct and implicit obedience") and then elided by the meth- ods of psycho-politics, where such violence need only be suggested.[56]

The final section of the brainwashing brochure deals with the techniques of mental subjection necessary for political conquest. The model method is a Pavlovian stimulus-and-response sequence since this is rapidly internalized by the subject as a "police mechanism subsequently monitoring that subject's behaviour." Although the brochure claims a materialistic view of humanity, this emerges as a desired end rather than a premise, for ease of manipulation: "Thus, the first target is Man, himself. He must be degraded from a spiritual being to an animalistic reaction pattern." The brochure follows the practice of the earliest accounts of brainwashing by shifting the discourse of warfare into the domain of the mind and describes a process of subversion where psychotherapy functions as a screen concealing psychopolitical operations. The identity of this unlikely fifth column is made explicit later when we are told that "every chair of psychology in the United States is occupied by persons in our [Communist] connection."[57] Psychiatry becomes the point of entry to the culture. This ideology can then spread into areas like the armed forces and eventually must confront Communism's true enemy—the church. Political subversion is thus described as needing a vocabulary of concealment and as playing both on the status of science and on public fears of insanity. The latter can become a pretext for political "therapy" and a convenient charge to level against any enemies of the process. Ironically, the brochure reverses the perception, identified later by Albert D. Biderman in writings on brainwashing, that "Communist doctrine per se is ego-alien, . . . fundamentally alien to human nature and social reality." Here *anti*-Communism is neutralized as insanity. Not only does the brochure anticipate revelations about the Soviet psychiatric hospitals, but it ingeniously thematizes its own paranoia as a cover story that actually strengthens the basis for that paranoia. Thus, "the by-word should be built into the society that paranoia is a condition 'in which the individual believes he is being attacked by Communists.' It will be found that this defence is effective." Finally, the brochure confirms the widespread perception in the mid-1950s that the purpose of brainwashing was to robotize its victims. By using a simplistic "building-block" model of the personality, it maximizes the ease of changing an individual's ego. And by drawing on the currency of lobotomies and electrotherapy, it attempts to normalize institutional violence, to condition the public to "tolerate the creation of zombic conditions to such a degree that they will probably employ zombies, if given to them."[58]

The brochure plays cleverly on fears of the time: that there was a Soviet master-plan, that Communist agents would sacrifice life if necessary for the greater goal, and that the movement was militantly anti-religious. Although its origin was suspected as soon as it appeared, nevertheless the brochure was taken seriously enough to warrant an evaluation for the Operations Coordinating Board of Eisenhower's National Security Council. The evaluator declared:

"if the booklet is a fake, the author or authors know so much about brain-washing techniques that I would consider them experts, superior to any that I have met to date."[59] The concluding recommendation was for politicians to take great care how the booklet was used, not because it was intrinsically fantastic, but because the public would not believe it and because the Communists were so expert at ridiculing such revelations.

In 1955 and 1956 copies of this booklet were sent to the FBI, in the first of these years by L. Ron Hubbard, and it was evaluated by the Bureau's Central Research Section. Their conclusion was that the booklet's authenticity was "of a doubtful nature" because it lacked "documentation of source material and communist words and phrases." Therefore "the author is expressing primarily a dissatisfaction with methods of treatment of mental patients in this country."[60] If anything, this conclusion is even more bizarre than the booklet itself, which exploits a whole series of alarmist tactics to whip up fears of the Communist threat. For that reason, a more recent evaluation of the pamphlet by an anonymous book dealer concludes that it is a "dystopian romance, a work of fiction that presents itself as fact to give urgency to its theme."[61] The authorship of this work is usually attributed to Hubbard.

The 1955 booklet combined accounts of strategy and methodology that by implication minimize the capacity of the subject to resist the processes. In October 1954 the science fiction writer and editor John W. Campbell devoted an editorial to this subject, describing brainwashing as "psychiatry-gone-wrong." In answer to the issue of how we might defend ourselves, Campbell replies starkly: "nothing remotely human can resist brain-washing." With a certain grim relish he spells out a process that quite simply bypasses the faculty of judgment in such a way that heroism becomes irrelevant. The human subject is no different from an animal: "Any organism using a bio-chemically powered brain can be affected in this way [by using physical discomfort as a prelude to implanting new orientations]; courage and determination are meaningless terms at the level of biochemistry."[62] Campbell gives an extreme version of biological determinism that relates to early accounts of brainwashing as a triumph of technological know-how. Although given a more benign purpose, there is a close similarity between the perceptual processes described in the 1955 booklet, Campbell's essay, and L. Ron Hubbard's *Dianetics* (1950), which Campbell praised for its application of the stimulus-and-response mechanism. Hubbard wanted to promote a "science of mind" based on the analogy of a computer. According to Albert I. Berger in a 1989 article on the origins of Dianetics, Hubbard was attempting to realize a utopian harmonization between science and psychology in this new system. Memory was described by Hubbard as an "engram bank," a kind of mental data storage, which could be retrieved through Dianetic training. Posthypnotic suggestion was only a pale version of what the new science could achieve. Coincidentally, a 1955 government report on brainwashing made use of Hubbard's key term. Describing the bombardment of words and images "always converging on the same idea," it continues: "The suggestions and words become strong engrams, work their way into the brain cells, become part of the subject's thinking and therefore a power in the Land of the Evil controlling the propaganda."[63]

■ From 1949 through to the mid-1950s U.S. government agencies pursued with increasing urgency research into every aspect of mind control, fearful that there might be a "brainwashing gap" between East and West. This new process so alarmed the government that during the early 1950s it initiated a number of projects to investigate—and hopefully counteract—methods of mind control. The 1956 CIA report on brainwashing made it clear that one of the major factors under consideration was public perception in the West of Communist power at manipulation. The report declared that brainwashing had "created the belief that our opponents are mysteriously formidable," whereas in fact "there is nothing mysterious about personality changes resulting from the brainwashing process."[64] One purpose thus emerged as a kind of damage limitation exercise rendered problematic, according to one CIA psychologist, by the "ingrained belief on the part of agents that the Soviets were 10 feet tall, that there were huge programs going on in the Soviet Union to influence behaviour."[65] It was obviously crucial that such convictions should not reach the general public and so we find that official statements on the subject of brainwashing play down its demonic aspects.

A number of reports that minimize the originality or efficacy of brainwashing had an institutionally vested interest in doing so, since they were produced under the auspices of sections of the U.S. Army or government. The Department of Defense report, the unclassified version of which was published in 1956, went to considerable pains to question the public perception of brainwashing as an "esoteric technique" and described in detail the police interrogation methods of China and the Soviet Union. At every point they stressed that these were developments of known practices. Even the Mindszenty case, the popular prototype of brainwashing, followed the same pattern and did not include any use of drugs. Those American POWs who actively collaborated with their captors usually had a background of disaffection and had thus "lost their identification with the society in which they originated." The report therefore concluded: "there is no need to assume that the Communists utilise occult methods in managing their prisoners." Similarly Albert D. Biderman's research group for the U.S. Air Force concluded: "there was nothing new or spectacular about the events we studied."[66] The U.S. government would have had a self-evident vested interest in demystifying brainwashing, which is exactly what the Hinkle and Wolff report did. Not only did it question the accuracy of the term, it even denied its use in Communist China where other expressions described thought reform. If this was true, "brainwashing" takes on an even more problematic status as signifier, for the 1956 report did nothing to reduce its circulation in cold war discourse.

The dispassionate detail of the 1956 report contrasted markedly with a secret 1955 paper, "Brainwashing: The Communist Experiment with Mankind," presented to Eisenhower's Operations Coordinating Board. This document pulled no punches in describing an amoral malign system that was a "perversion" of Pavlov's experiments. Instead of minimizing the novelty of brainwashing, the paper stressed that for prisoners of the Communists "atrocities and brainwashing will be the rule, not the exception." Further, the Communist authorities will continue to "practice their theory that Communist indoctrination can change the complex of human consciousness."[67] All was not lost, however, for one important consolation lay in the fact that such indoctrination passed as soon as the prisoner was returned to his home environment. Also in 1953 the Department of Defence issued the U.S. Fighting Man's Code specifically in response to events in Korea. Here again brainwashing was not denied, but limited to a smallish number of GIs. The Code further reinforced the perception of the Cold War as a "total war for the minds of men" and presented a number of principles for the GI to remember, like keeping faith with his fellow soldiers, the intention being to strengthen the collective will of the U.S. Army.

As we might expect in this period, published information on the Korean POWs was selective and angled toward different institutional purposes, like limiting damage to the army's image. The New Yorker correspondent Eugene Kinkead was given access to the participants in the army study and published his own account of Korean POWs in 1959 under the title In Every War But One (1960, U.K. title, Why They Collaborated). Kinkead quoted an army official to warn his readers against using the term "brainwashing" to suggest that the Communists were applying "something magical, something beyond the reach of man's power of comprehension"; however, at the same time he grimly warned that interrogation and indoctrination formed the "total psychological weapon" in Soviet world conquest.[68] Kinkead was criticizing the vague popular applications of "brainwashing" as being both ignorant and dangerous because the sinister implications of the term itself could undermine any will to resist. He also followed the army's conclusion that no specific practice was used by the Communists that could be called brainwashing, by which they meant a "process producing obvious alteration of character," but their actual methods proved effective to the extent that one in three of the POWs collaborated in some way.[69] Kinkead reinforces the grand narrative of Soviet conspiracy and presents an exceptionalist account of the Korean War (and therefore the cold war) as unique in American history because the enemy was attempting to manipulate the minds of POWs, whose subsequent behavior then became a national problem. In effect Kinkead disperses the sinister aura of "brainwashing" throughout the whole Korean War, which is itself explained as a three-power collaboration: the Chinese directing the North Koreans' treatment of POWs and the Soviets directing the latter's indoctrination program.

■ Throughout the 1950s and beyond treatments of brainwashing could be divided into two broad camps: the "hard" meaning of a special method of psychological manipulation for political ends, and the "soft," where the unique and often general meanings of the term were refused. This division was summed up by Paul Linebarger, whose work will be discussed in the next chapter, as follows in a letter from June 1962 to the managing editor of *Orbis: A Quarterly Journal of World Affairs*:

> There are two basic schools on the effectuality of propaganda. The liberals, with Lifton and others, hold the propaganda is slight, that mass communication cannot re-structure culture or change individual character, and that "brain-washing" is Right-wing hooey. The realists hold that Soviet psychological warfare techniques are universal, effectual, and just about permanent in their effects.[70]

While the realists tended to support hawkish positions in relation to Soviet Communism, the liberals, primarily psychologists, attempted to demystify brainwashing and assimilate its practice within known theories. This was the thrust of the special 1957 number of the *Journal of Social Issues* devoted to brainwashing, where it was categorically denied that the Soviets were applying Pavlovian methods and where the subject could be understood through stress theory.[71] In September of that same year the closing session of the American Psychological Association proposed the "DDD syndrome" as constituting the conditions for brainwashing, such as debility (induced by fatigue among other things), dependency, and dread (chronic fear of not being returned home and other things). Two studies of 1961 further consolidated this view. *Coercive Persuasion*, part-written by Edgar H. Schein, who had participated in the rehabilitation for returned POWs, denied that the popular image of brainwashing fitted the experience of prisoners and argued that they had basically been subjected to "unusually intense and prolonged persuasion."[72] Robert Jay Lifton, who based his 1961 study *Thought Reform and the Psychology of Totalism* on interviews with Chinese refugees in Hong Kong, identified a totalitarian pattern of controlling the environment and inducing confessions with specific relevance to the practices of Chinese culture.

Lifton, in common with other commentators, attacked the popular catch-all meaning the term had developed, especially its "lurid mythology" as a "mysterious oriental device," or the general image of brainwashing as an "all-powerful, irresistible, unfathomable, and magical method of achieving total control over the human mind." Surveying the applications of the term "brainwashing" in 1962, Albert D. Biderman complained that its meaning had been determined by journalists and victims; in contrast, scholarly studies had denied that there was any special method involved. Broadly speaking, perceptions of brainwashing had been shaped by the "diabolical view of Communism and the racist basis of reactions" when the process was applied to Americans.[73] In 1963 he returned to this charge in his rejoinder to Kinkead's *March to Calumny*. Here he complained that "brainwashing" had come to be perceived as a "unitary, super-potent gimmick based on an original patent, secretly registered at the Kremlin by I. Pavlov, with major modifications by cunning Oriental scientists." The term had expanded to become a catch-all reference to the "attempts of Communist functionaries to coerce, instruct, persuade, trick, train, delude, debilitate, starve, torture, isolate (and to use various other means of manipulating individuals and playing members of a group against one another for which our language has not yet evolved one-word verbs)."[74] The few voices noted by Biderman as criticizing the term were confined to scholarly journals or monographs, whereas the two hundred articles on the subject listed in appendix 6 to the U.S. *Fighting Man's Code* appeared in mass-circulation journals like *Time* and *Life*. Biderman writes primarily as a scientist criticizing methodological shortcomings in earlier accounts, while the very attraction of the term "brainwashing" was its vagueness, so that different expanding meanings could be projected on to it. If it is defined as a mystery, this had the advantage of allowing an expansive series of meanings to accumulate around it. Also the rational objections of Biderman, Lifton, and others paid no attention to the emerging technology of brain control through pharmacology, conditioning, or electronic means.

We should recognize the real cultural anxieties expressed by writers like Hunter and Meerloo in their discussion of brainwashing. The more the process was demonized, the more vulnerable its victims seem and the weakest sections in early documents on the subject deal with how to resist brainwashing. Descriptions of Communist manipulators could be read as a strategy of defense by displacement: "A single American soldier converted to Communism could arouse feelings of anxiety and guilt over one's own repressed ideological doubts. Hence, our eagerness to attribute such conversions to the demonic machinations of the Doctors Pavlov and Fu Manchu."[75]

Last, the Cold War would have made it next to impossible to take up an objective stance toward the issue of brainwashing since any public statement on the matter could be used within the propaganda war of words between East and West. The public debate over brainwashing, which ran through the 1950s and into the early 1960s, brought out anxieties over national purpose and fears of what was widely perceived as an alien practice. As we shall now see, the political debate ran in tandem with a series of imaginative enactments of brainwashing in the fiction of the same period.

three

Dystopias, Invasions, and Takeovers

It remains one of the main ironies of the history of brainwashing that, although the concept was formulated as a devilish alien practice, its representations in fiction and film presented it as primarily a domestic issue. The institutions responsible for maintaining national defense and civic order prove to be most vulnerable to threatening change. Again and again those figures concerned with local order or health are in the front line of the targeting agencies. Fiction of the 1950s applies the concept of brainwashing through narrative contexts of conspiracy, investigation, and invasion. One rare exception to this general tendency is Richard Matheson's "The Waker Dreams" (1950), which describes a man's heroic battle against predatory monsters in the city, only to reveal that this sequence was suggested through a drug that produced "loosened brainways."[1] The story presents a repeated fantasy compensating for humanity's entropic decline and is thus not situated in any political context. More characteristically, the fate of the individual protagonist is shown to represent the imminent fate of the nation as a whole. Although the earliest narratives describe alien aggression against the United States, the majority internalizes the alien to pose the disturbing question, how can you distinguish alien "converts" from right-thinking fellow citizens?

Walter M. Miller's "Izzard and the Membrane" (1951) extends *Nineteen Eighty-Four* into a Cold War confrontation between power blocs focused on an individual captive technician whose presumptions about reality the Communists subvert through the exploitation of different media. It describes the experiences of an American cyberneticist captured during a Eurasian invasion of Western Europe. Planning his "conversion," the officials smile "with their Oriental eyes" and rig up an elaborate set of cinescreens in his isolation cell. On these they project a series of scenes alternating between his wife having sex with another man and shots displaying the Soviet unity of purpose: "the same picture over and over again, interspersed with Russian newsreels showing troops on the march, factories turning out war planes, high leaders at the conference table. Then the howl of jazz again, and the awful horror."[2] In time, Scotty comes to believe that both his wife and country have betrayed him, attempts suicide, and is then taken to a psychiatrist for indoctrination, assenting to prescribed phrases like the accusation that the United States is a "degenerate imperialist nation." He then willingly designs a war machine for the Soviets, at which point it is revealed to him that the film of his wife was a simulation. Despite the destruction of Scotty's ego ("His will lay dead at [his conscience's] feet. He pleaded guilty, and surrendered all desire"), he paradoxically retains the single purpose of avenging himself on his captors by sabotaging the planned invasion of America.[3] Miller's eagerness to demonize the Eurasians as single-mindedly cruel and aggressive prevents him from giving even a basic explanation of how they could have constructed so convincing a simulation of Scotty's home that he was fooled. In effect the story tries awkwardly to combine the individual assault of personal interrogation with the general impact of propaganda films; and Miller shies away from the logic of the brainwashing process in retaining a single purpose in Scotty's ego so as to ensure a triumphalist conclusion.

We can already discern a narrative application of the "hard" view of brainwashing that will recur throughout this fiction: the transformation of an individual into the functioning part of a military–political machine. In Miller's story Scotty risks becoming not just a traitor but a key mover in the demise of his nation, whereas in Pat Frank's *Forbidden Area* (1956) the human weapons are four Soviet-trained saboteurs who are landed on the coast of Florida with instructions to plant pressure bombs in the latest U.S. bombers. These agents form part of a long-term plan for achieving world supremacy. One has become transformed from Stanislaus Lazinoff to "Stanley Smith":

He and his companions were very special people, the end result of a scientific experiment utilizing the Pavlov-Lysenko theories of conditioned reflexes. A new environment had been painstakingly grafted on personalities of unquestionable and fanatic loyalty to the state. An American body and mind had been synthetically created, while the heart remained Russian.[4]

Smith's very name suggests that he has been de-individualized into an anonymous and passive instrument of Soviet foreign policy. Trained at a special facility in Ukraine known as "Little Chicago" because it simulates an American town, Smith, too, has become a simulation indistinguishable from authentically American citizens. So far it might seem that he is a precursor of the Manchurian Candidate, but Frank deals only cursorily with his training, remarking merely that "on orders, when you entered Little Chicago you forgot your past."[5] Smith's group are not the unwitting assassins of later fiction but rather agents with a consciousness layered, so that they never forget their ultimate identities as officers in the Red Army.

Frank did not linger over the training of these agents because he wanted to dramatize the debate within the U.S. military establishment over the nature of the Soviet threat. Forbidden Area demonstrates a whole series of instances where information is ignored or not passed on (the landing of the agents is witnessed by a courting couple). At the heart of the Pentagon a secret Intentions Group assembles evidence of an imminent attack by the Soviets, which is blocked by their director, a general whose World War II experience disables him from recognizing the new kind of conflict. Similarly, in Frank's An Affair of State (1948), the director of the U.S. legation in Budapest plays war games that exclude the atomic bomb because it "spoils the fun." This admiral feels excluded from an alien world of circulating rumors and media propaganda: "The heretics talked of psychological warfare, and political warfare, and battle by radio."[6] Both novels describe a ritual purging of such figures from the U.S. establishment because, in the case of Forbidden Area, their refusal to recognize the paradigm shift in strategy triggered by the use of nuclear weapons in Japan actually threatens the survival of the nation. The conditioned agents come from a culture lived under surveillance into one of freedom, but Frank's demonstration of the laborious discovery of their conspiracy actually dramatizes the danger within that freedom. The spatial title of his novel reflects its central theme of attempted invasion; danger comes from outside.

For Frank and Miller mind alteration was the technique of demonized Communist regimes; it was firmly distanced as an alien practice. However, Robert Heinlein's 1956 novel Double Star takes a more ambiguous purchase on this same subject. Set in a post–Cold War future where conspiracies are rife, the novel is narrated by a professional actor who is called in to play the part of a political leader kidnapped by terrorists. When the leader is released he is found to be in such poor psychological shape that the performance must continue to the point where, upon the leader's death, the actor literally becomes his role. The actor contextualizes the mental destruction of the leader Bonforte as follows: "'Brainwash' is a term that comes down to us from the Communist movement of the Late Dark Ages." This originally denoted wearing down by physical torture and then "brainwash-by-drugs," but both practices have since been replaced by a much quicker method: "simply inject any one of several cocaine derivatives into his frontal brain lobes." While Bonforte's destruction is reported but never seen, the actor-narrator undergoes an apparently more benign form of mind-alteration in being reconditioned by one Dr. Capek to not be repulsed by Martian body odor. So, although he loftily declares "there is something immoral and degrading in an absolute cosmic sense in tampering with a man's personality," the novel contradicts this categorical statement. Not only is he fascinated by that technology, but he undergoes a milder version of the process himself in the good cause of winning out against terrorism.[7]

Miller, Frank, and Heinlein were writers who knew of brainwashing only through public accounts. At this point we encounter a figure unique in the history of representations of brainwashing, who combined the careers of novelist, sinologist, and consultant to U.S. Army Intelligence. In the early 1950s Paul Linebarger held a chair in Oriental Politics at Johns Hopkins University and at the same time was playing a lead part in the U.S. Army's psychological warfare section that was being consolidated at that time; Truman, for instance, established the Psychological Strategy Board in 1951. As the author of a seminal work on this subject (*Psychological Warfare*, 1948), Linebarger was brought in to lecture at the Naval War College, where he recommended *Nineteen Eighty-Four* for the light it could shed on Stalinism, as an "example of what the breakdown of language can do." Speculating on the direction "psychiatric warfare" could take, he asks: "What would happen if total war could be geared to an understanding of the privacy of the enemy's individual personalities and the enemy's group life?" Citing the Mindszenty case, Linebarger somewhat contradicts his reassurance that this new kind of warfare hadn't yet arrived by declaring: "Somehow they took his soul apart."[8] Essentially Linebarger gives his audience the grim warning that the Soviets have stolen a lead over the west in the military use of "psychosomatics" and that Communist Chinese practice is mounting an "attack on identity."[9] Linebarger was a close personal friend of Edward Hunter, a fellow specialist on Asia, and wove the latter's account of brainwashing into his 1954 expanded edition of *Psychological Warfare*. He endorsed the term itself as "correct" and defined it as a "frontal attack on all levels of the personality, from the most conscious to the most hidden." Once the old identity has been broken down, the Communists then "rebuild the personality, healing their victim into Communist normality."[10] For Linebarger this new technique represented a threatening development of total war.

Under the pseudonym Cordwainer Smith, Linebarger developed these perceptions in a series of science fiction stories revolving around a future regime called the Instrumentality of Mankind. As the first term suggests, Linebarger examined ways in which humans might be used for political ends. One of the earliest of this series, "No, No, Not Rogov!" (1959) is the most trenchantly anti-Soviet and describes a secret government project to design a "brain-equivalent machine" capable of "jamming" thoughts. The ultimate aim is a kind of long-distance monitoring: "the machine itself could obtain perfect intelligence by eavesdropping on the living minds of people far away."[11] The project is based on two overlapping premises: that the mind is the property of the state and that the brain is a weapon. In the event, however, the mind proves to be too unruly to be controlled by the Soviet authorities and the project fails.

This story is characteristic of the series in that Linebarger foregrounds the mind as an agency of conflict but describes its extended faculties through analogies drawn from electronics. It becomes quite standard for his stories to contain cases of telepathy that can be used for good or ill. In one tale "pin-sets," i.e. helmets anticipating the virtual reality of the 1980s, can be worn to "amplify" telepathic capabilities. The dystopian regime of the Instrumentality contains key features of the technology Linebarger feared had already been developed by the Communists. If any emotional contacts take place between the elite and the underclass, "the underpeople were always destroyed and the real people brainwashed."[12] In his novel *Norstrilia* a routine state punishment consists of "oblivion and reconditioning" whereby subjects are "brain-scrubbed," just one of the many lexical variations on the central term of this study.[13]

The bleakest of Linebarger's dystopian stories is "A Planet Named Shayol" (1961), where the eponymous planet is used as a cross between a gulag and a biological facility where the inmates are used as hosts for endemic life forms.

A man named Mercer is tried for an unnamed crime while "wired and plugged in to the witness stand." Sentenced to transportation, before landing on Shayol a doctor offers him the option of oblivion: "I can destroy your mind before you go down."[14] The very fact that this is an option marginally softens the description of Shayol as a surreal Hell-like expanse of desert by suggesting a survival of consciousness prior to the liberation of the facility.

Frederik Pohl's 1960 story "Mars by Moonlight" uses the same convention of a planetary penal colony, this time on Mars, where Earth's government practices a method of "mind-washing." As one character explains, "instead of putting someone in jail and keeping them there . . . they wipe out the parts of the mind that has the criminal pattern in it. They go back erasing memory, until they come to a past that is clean and unaffected."[15] Pohl applies the by now traditional aspect of brainwashing as purification but gives it an ironic twist in that memories of crimes are erased and with them any specific explanation of why characters are on Mars. The second twist turns the story into a dramatization of reality management when the protagonist discovers that "Mars" is an illusion maintained by posthypnotic suggestion. The dystopian fiction actually screens an alien invasion by the "skulls," an intelligent life form who have set up a test farm on Earth to simulate Martian living conditions.

Where Pohl uses the analogy between memory and a tape recorder, which will be developed further by William Burroughs, Linebarger constantly reifies the personality as an "imprint" that can be transferred from brain to brain. This figure somewhat resembles L. Ron Hubbard's use of the mind-computer analogy in *Dianetics*, where "complete recordings" of perceptions or "engrams" are stored in the mind's memory "banks." Such metaphors reflect a critical problem of expression in fiction dealing with brainwashing. Although these narratives engage with the fate of the mind, they often resort to awkwardly concrete or mechanistic figures to articulate the action. John Roeburt's *The Long Nightmare* (1958; also published with the title *The Climate of Hell*), for example, weaves brainwashing into a tortuous *noir* thriller where the very repetition of the term "brainwashing" in the opening pages is clearly designed to impress the reader. The narrator Larry Stevens has been rescued from arrest for killing his wife's lover by a gang who impose a new identity on him (Kirk Reynolds) so that they can use him to carry out an impersonation and thereby help them seize money from a rich businessman. In fact, the plot really functions as a pretext for tracing out the process of implanting this new identity through means—beating, drugs, repetition, and so on—that we associate rather with a political, not criminal, situation. Roeburt's narrator expresses this process variously as "demolition" or erasure of the old, followed by a "filling" with new information: "my brain opened up and these stocks refurbished."[16] It is as if a lid were taken off a store room in a metaphor that reifies the mind as a static container and this effect is directly contradicted by the busy workings of the narrator's mind as he struggles to understand his experiences. Roeburt is evidently not too concerned with plausibility when it is finally revealed that the narrator really was Kirk Reynolds brainwashed to believe that he was someone else impersonating his own identity.

The transformation of human subjects into means or, as Linebarger would put it, instrumentalities, comes out clearly in his 1958 story "The Burning of the Brain," which describes a space voyage that almost ends in tragedy when the vessel gets lost. Eventually it returns to the home planet by "reading" the star charts mapped on the captain's brain. "Imprint" suggests a process brought about by an external agency, an unspecified other, which finds its most terrifying expression as the revelation of ultimate helplessness experienced by travelers in deep space. *"We felt that we had been made the toys or the pets of some gigantic form of life immensely beyond the limits of human imagination"* (italics in original). [17] This perception of being turned into an instrumentality has its physiological counterpart in the insertion by technicians of electronic connections directly into the brain and its political equivalent in the loss of mental space by the citizen. Linebarger appropriates the verb "peep" from Alfred Bester's *The Demolished Man* to denote a similar process of mind-surveillance by the authorities. All these instances demonstrate the regime's self-perpetuation through techniques of separation and control. However varied the technologies of mind control might be in Linebarger's dystopias, he always preserves the possibility of liberation through empathy in his narratives. As a practicing Episcopalian, he refused absolute status to any material conditions of servitude.

■ The narratives just considered imply rather than describe elaborate regimes of surveillance and investigation. Examining the "visibility of control" in relation to state punishment, B. F. Skinner explains how the desire to avoid the punishers leads to secrecy. However, he continues, "a state which converts all its citizens into spies or a religion which promotes the concept of an all-seeing God makes escape from the punisher practically impossible, and punitive contingencies are then maximally effective."[18] We have already seen in *Nineteen Eighty-Four* how strategic cameras, helicopters, and telescreens were used for surveillance and demonstrated the constant monitoring of citizens by Big Brother's regime; but Skinner is here describing a kind of ultimate surveillance where the conviction of visibility overrides the need for any physical manifestation.

Alfred Bester conceived *The Demolished Man* (1953) as an "open-murder mystery" where "the protagonist does not really know his own motivation. It is concealed within himself and we are now deeply involved in psychiatry."[19] The novel thus combines social and psychological surveillance. It foregrounds the trope of God's all-seeing eye in its epigraph, which draws apparent attention to the limitations of human perception: "what may appear exceptional to the minute mind of man may be inevitable to the infinite Eye of God."[20] In fact the novel dramatizes the capacity of a future regime to penetrate even the most deeply repressed areas of consciousness. Set in the twenty-fourth century, *The Demolished Man* describes a regime where social orthodoxy is maintained by the Guild of "Espers" or "peepers," a kind of telepathic security force that combines therapy with enforcement. The elite of these agents who possess an ESP facility can even see into a person's unconscious. Like Philip K. Dick's *Eye in the Sky* (1957), Bester's novel secularizes the divine gaze into a system of surveillance that attempts a total monitoring of behavior. Those who break the law, even slightly, are "adjusted" (we are never told what exactly that involves); and those who commit serious crimes are "demolished." Alan Scheflin has pointed out that Bester's notion of controlled infantile regression followed by a "rebuilding" of the personality closely parallels the erasure ("de-patterning") and reconstruction of personality ("psychic driving") being practiced in the 1950s by Ewen Cameron in Canada.[21]

Bester's protagonist Ben Reich, the director of Monarch Utilities and Resources, kills his commercial rival D'Courtney when he refuses to accept a merger bid. Like many postwar American dystopias, *The Demolished Man* identifies political with commercial power. Reich's very surname signals an impulse to rule. When he plans his murder it is like a military campaign: "I'll have to invade first . . . cut through the defensive network surrounding D'Courtney"; and when his guilt is reaching crisis point toward the end of the novel, Reich dreams a series of negative imperatives that ironically predict his own ultimate fate: "ABOLISH THE LABYRINTH . . . EFFACE . . . EXPUNGE."[22] The aggressive impulses of Reich's id resemble the imperialistic drive toward monopoly in Monarch. The novel turns into a bizarre murder mystery where an extended struggle takes place between Reich and the chief investigator. The key revelation that D'Courtney was Reich's father as well as rival has led one critic to read the novel as an oedipal conflict where Reich schizophrenically plays out the dissociated roles of business leader and the eraser of his own hated paternity."[23]

"Demolition" can thus be taken as the ultimate consequence of the investigation of Reich, which is at once legal and psychological. The Espers perform a "Mass Cathexis," a concentration of psychic energy that blanks out key aspects of Reich's world and forces him to realize his illness. By the end of the novel he has become depersonalized into an anonymous instance of a general practice:

> When a man is demolished at Kingston Hospital, his entire psyche is destroyed. The series of osmotic injections begins with the topmost strata of cortical synapses and slowly works down, switching off every circuit, extinguishing every memory, destroying every particle of the pattern that has been built up since birth. . . . But this is not the pain; this is not the dread of Demolition. The horror lies in the fact that the consciousness is never lost; that as the psyche is wiped out, the mind is aware of its slow, backward death until at last it too disappears and awaits the rebirth.[24]

Paradoxically, this description is both powerful and irrelevant. If the crime investigation follows a quasi-Freudian progression, the forcing of the suppressed material into the subject's consciousness should carry its own therapeutic purpose. The process Bester describes above recapitulates this regression pharmacologically and occurs too late in the novel for him to weave into the drama. It makes a climax but, as George Turner has argued, Bester leaves the demolition process carefully vague. In answer to the question, what is being demolished, Turner replies: "In a haze of words we never find out. But it makes a nice sadistic close to the action and gives the detective an opportunity to think up some completely pointless blather about the future of re-educated humanity."[25] At the end of The Demolished Man Bester awkwardly tries to conflate three concepts: ECT or electrocution, erasure of the mind, and regression to infancy. But he does not indicate how Reich could develop after this. Accordingly the horror of the mind witnessing its own deconstruction remains dissipated and general, whereas in novels like David Karp's One we witness the reshaping of an individual as well as his "demolition."

■ Published in 1953, *One* describes a regime in an unspecified future where the benevolent state has created not only a general situation of suburban well being but also has induced a collective introspection: "The preoccupation with the outer world had fallen off. There was more looking inward."[26] Although one reviewer described the novel as a "new approach to the American witch-hunt," Karp describes his future state as emerging from a pervasive process of Americanization, and his novel combines a perception of the "Indifferent Generation" as "security-minded, cautious, and uncontroversial" with the totalitarian methods Karp associated with Communist regimes.[27]

Karp's protagonist is one Professor Burden, who for years has been combining his academic career with the function of a state spy, sending in daily reports on those around him. When one of these reports is randomly selected he is diagnosed as possessing "integrated heresy" that must be rooted out. Accordingly, the investigator—the very personification of the organization man—becomes the investigated, and most of the novel describes his gradual breakdown at the hands of the Department of Internal Examination. The recurrence of the term "heresy" to denote political deviance can be read toward either end of the political spectrum. On the one hand, the witch-hunt analogy, which is made explicit to Burden as if he is possessed, was revived during the period of McCarthyism. Marion L. Starkey, for example, introduced *The Devil in Massachusetts* by noting that theological disputes had been replaced by ideological ones. On the other hand, comparisons between the Communist Party and the Church had become commonplace by the mid-1950s, informing such works as Howard Fast's *The Naked God* (1957). When toward the end of *One* Burden's identity is transformed, the plot follows the paradigm of a specifically Communist version of transformation. The protagonist of Karp's later novel *The Last Believers* (1964), is told just before he is received into the Communist Party: "you must be reborn"; he subsequently has to swear an oath and his entry is signaled by him being given a new name. Exactly the same process takes place once Burden has been "cured" of his own "heresy."[28]

The regime in *One* has abolished the concept of, or more precisely the word, "punishment," substituting "therapy" in line with its supposedly benevolent ideology. However, the reader's discovery that heretics are usually scheduled for "destruction" gives a hollow ring to professions of benign intent. Burden himself demonstrates from the very beginning of the novel disequilibrium between the lexical traces of an older punitive system and the official discourse of the regime: "*Punishment.* Burden shook his head

again at his own stupidity. There was no punishment. Punishment, punitive — odd the way the concept kept cropping up in his thinking. That was all
done with. It no longer existed as a socially accepted concept." Like Koestler's Rubashov, Burden has internalized state ideology in such a way that he
attempts to censor the language of his thoughts. Burden's unfocused sense
of oddity reflects a failure in the state's fiat that does not address the collective memory embedded in the language. Karp draws on Orwell for his depiction of the state "psychosemanticists" who view linguistic alteration as a form
of mind control. As if in recognition of the link, both novels were cited in
the 1963 CIA bibliography on brainwashing (see appendix). As in Newspeak,
the process is primarily one of erasure, since "a man without words is a blank"
on which the state can reinscribe the desired mind-set.[29]

Burden's prolonged interrogations are directed toward this end. The complex stages to his investigation are as follows:

1. A preliminary interview with Conger to disturb his self-confidence.
2. A hearing before a panel, observed through a two-way mirror.
3. A "reassuring" interview with Richard.
4. Questioning under drugs.
5. Two extended dialogues with Lark.
6. Investigation of sexual fantasies under drugs.

This process is guided by Lark, the Dostoyevskian inquisitor of the regime,
the subject himself of a Pavlovian experiment in conditioning, and Burden's
antagonist. As the investigation proceeds, the action turns into a struggle
between the two men. Much the same thing happens in the 1955 film based
on the Mindszenty case, *The Prisoner* (adapted from a 1954 play by Bridget
Boland with the same title), where a prolonged battle of wits takes place
between a cardinal (played by Alec Guiness) and his zealous interrogator
(played by Jack Hawkins). Lark also combines the psychological sophistication of Orwell's O'Brien with a fanaticism, which, as we shall see, puts him
in a paradoxical relation to the regime. It is Lark who belies the ideology of
therapy with statements of aggressive intent: "I'm going to pulverise this
man's identity. I'm going to reduce him to a cipher, from one . . . to nothing."[30] Despite the dramatic opposition between Burden and Lark one reviewer complained that "both hero-victim and his inquisitors are the merest
pawns."[31] This charge, which, together with the opposing claim that Burden
retains individuality that has been made by more recent critics, misses the

point of the novel by merely reasserting a concept of discrete, stable identity that the novel throws into question.

The true protagonist of the novel is the investigative process itself, which carries its own inner logic and momentum and which constantly resituates Lark and Burden in their shifting roles of investigator and subject. One of the first ironies of the novel emerges when the analytical skills Burden has been using in his reports are turned against him. Indeed the self-censoring strategies we have seen him using in his own thoughts are now developed into self-accusations by Lark and his colleagues, starting with his very first interview where Conger invites the anxious Burden to consider why he has been brought in for the interview.[32] The 1956 CIA report on brainwashing stressed how helplessness was induced in prisoners by an "impersonal machinery of control," and this happens to Burden, for example, when he is told that the addressees of his reports were simply official fictions.[33] The disorientation this produces is further reinforced by the very layout of the DIE building, which consists of a labyrinthine network of concentric circles. As in Orwell, the hearings are designed to undermine the subject's self-confidence by arbitrarily shifting their methods so that Burden never knows what to expect. Thus a reassuring session with Richard, where he lets Burden in on some of the secrets of the regime, forms the prelude to his first questioning under drugs, which starts at 4:00 A.M. This is a purposeful echo of the arrests in *Darkness at Noon*, the text acknowledged by Karp as his main model for *One*.[34]

In this novel Karp depicts the strategies of interrogation with great skill, tracing out the shifts in the relationship between Burden and his interrogators. The resemblance between the processes depicted in the novel and the pattern outlined in Harry Stack Sullivan's *The Psychiatric Interview* demonstrates the seepage of discourse from one area of experience to another. Sullivan calls the interview an "interrogation" at several points and outlines the strategic shifts in role that are played out by the psychiatrist. Although Sullivan's subject is psychiatry he constantly slides into the language of political interrogation, where the patient's suppressions are protected secrets. Sullivan conceives the interview entirely in informational terms, where the patient comes increasingly to resemble a spy: the interviewer "may be able to discover that in addition to the immediate activation of the security operation, there has been a covert operation" that will reveal more of the patient's motivation.[35]

The typographical arrangement of dialogue in Burden's sessions, where one voice has no speech-marks, suggests that the interrogators are gaining access to the very ground of Burden's consciousness, just as Sullivan's psychiatric interrogators try to uncover deep-level omissions and are forcing the first confession from him:

> "Are you a heretic?"
> No. I told you there is no heresy and hence no heretics.
> "Within the present meaning of the term—are you a heretic?"
> The present meaning of the term is in error.
> "Within the present erroneous meaning of the term—are you a heretic?"
> Yes, of course.[36]

One describes a process that can be read not only as political but also as an investigation into layers of the self. The writer Clifton Fadiman's promotional statement for the first edition predicted: "It can be read, of course, as a political parable. More probably it will be read as a spine-chilling psychological detective-story."[37] Burden has to identify his own crime as the interrogations proceed intermittently along the lines of psychoanalysis, where transference takes place between himself and Lark. Unlike psychoanalysis, however, the interrogations are ideological performances designed to break down Burden's confidence in his own individuality and to induce a desire to remerge into a new collective. The lowest points of this process are thus reached when he finds himself in a huge bare grey room and when he is moved into a ward for the insane. The first totally disorients him and starves him of sensory perception; the second brings a hallucinatory crisis as if Burden is living out a waking nightmare. His reeducation can now begin.

Huxley's Fordist rituals emerge in *One* through the Church of State whose members always refer to themselves in the third person as if they didn't exist, or in the first person plural, as we saw in Zamyatin and Ayn Rand. The secularization of the concept of heresy implies a contemporary idealized notion of the state that the term "church" makes explicit. When Burden-Hughes attends one of their services the liturgy recapitulates Lark's formulation of the utopian future "where all feel a part, take a part, are a part." The incantatory repetition of the key term—"part," signifying role and synecdoche—anticipates the same rhetoric used in Burden's reeducation tapes: "The State is your family and your fellow citizens are your brothers and your sisters. . . . You must only believe in it. You must only trust it. You must only love it."[38]

Burden's conditioning continues into his participation in the ritual where recitation enacts the consolidation of the collective summed up in the slogan "all is one and one is all." The title of Karp's novel plays constantly on the semantic slippage of the term "one" between singularity and union. However, the two meanings never quite converge as Lark's agent reports, since Burden stands apart from the Church of State, refusing commitment. Thus Lark's experiment fails and Burden is marked down for execution. The trope of conversion-as-rebirth whereby Burden receives a new name and identity similarly fails. Although he responds to the outside world with a rapt eagerness ("just as if I had been born all over again"), his inability to identify his possessions makes them resemble the "belongings of a corpse," which, proleptically, is exactly what they are.[39] The novel opens with Burden registering puzzlement as forbidden thoughts pass through his consciousness and closes with his continuing perception of oddity. One reviewer declared that "it is the conflict between the helpless, insignificant man and the demoniac forces against him" that gave the novel its power but there is no point prior to Burden's participation in those forces.[40] To posit a drama of the individual against the system would totally distort the novel, since Burden from the very start participates willingly in the institutions of ideology maintenance. He starts with an invitation to the DIE and finishes entering a different office; in other words his narrative is institutionally framed and the failure of Lark's project is not due to heroic resistance on his part so much as to the technical inefficiency of his conditioning. Anthony Burgess's praise for the novel because a "man is cussed enough, under all the circumstances, even when he's brainwashed, to hang on to this spark of opposition to the corporate, to the imposed" does not quite fit the narrative progression of *One*, though Burgess does identify an opposition that Karp himself valued.[41] He praised Ernst Pawel's 1957 novel *From the Dark Tower* for its portrayal of an organization man's rejection of conformism. Pawel's protest against the "reign of the clerk in all its variations, from the Tower on the Square, to the Superstate on the Volga" is described through the experiences of a business executive who becomes ostracized because he will not make a "small symbolic gesture of surrender."[42]

Burden's impending death is only one of the novel's aspects that led critics like Cyril Connolly to compare *One* with *Darkness at Noon* and *Nineteen Eighty-Four*.[43] However, unlike those novels, *One* does not limit its perspective to that of the victim. Virtually as many scenes are focalized through the investigators as through Burden, and for that reason the process becomes protagonist, imposing its own deterministic pattern on events. At this point we can now identify a paradox at the heart of the novel. The regime is geared toward a utopian end-point where individual and state interests converge, but the novel's present is a pre-utopian situation where heresy persists. In fact the regime needs heretics like Lark and others precisely to expose heresy, but once heresy has disappeared, Lark—who prides himself on being a spokesman for the regime—will no longer exist, nor will the DIE. Because we only apprehend the regime in *One* through its enormous system of surveillance, it is literally impossible for the reader to imagine how else the state might figure. The failure of Burden's transformation suggests a deferral of utopian realization; but it does not necessarily contradict Lark's assertion that "human nature is a myth."

■ The fears of mind control stoked during the 1950s by the debate over brainwashing resulted in a national state of mind identified as follows in 1957 by a contributor to *Commonweal*: "Americans are haunted by the threat of having their brains brutally washed by politicians and their desires stealthily manipulated by advertisers." And that same year Vance Packard warned the American public that the "most serious offence many of the depth manipulators commit . . . is that they try to invade the privacy of our minds."[44] These fears emerge in narratives of invasion by alien forces throughout the decade where political and psychological anxieties run together.

Robert Heinlein's *The Puppet Masters* (1951) describes mind and territorial invasion in virtually the same terms. A parasitic life-form that reproduces by fission is dropped on Earth, hence a character's conclusion that "we are going to have to learn to *live* with this horror, the way we had to learn to live with the atom bomb."[45] The parasites have the form of slugs that attach themselves to the backs of their subjects, transforming them into passive automata. Heinlein here draws on traditional representations of possession as a kind of physical leeching, as does Emma Bull in her 1991 novel *Bone Dance*, which figures mind control as a state of being ridden by "Horsemen." Heinlein deploys terms like "recruit" and "securing" (key locations) to describe a war conducted stealthily from within America. The slugs represent a kind of species politics whereby a parasite takes over its host, a concept that was to be further developed by William Burroughs and that is explained in *Bone Dance* as follows: "A Horseman seals up the host personality and uses the rest of it: memory, conscious and unconscious motor control, learned skills."[46] Under the surface of narrative fantasy Heinlein telescopes together a number of period fears: loss of autonomy, Communist takeover, and estrangement from familiar communities. Much of this subtlety was lost in the 1994 film adaptation of Heinlein's novel, which concentrated on the element of suspense in the action. Even the metaphor in his title was politically grounded. In the 1951 propaganda film *Face to Face with Communism* the soldier–protagonist tells a judge during his trial: "you think that you can make people act like puppets." The slugs show no sign of feeling and operate according to the principle of a hive mind where each individual creature functions as part of a collective. Their subversion of America necessitates a universal surveillance, "everybody watching everybody else," and, as in *Invasion of the Body Snatchers*, involves the takeover of local police forces and the manipulation of the news media. This is a process that takes place secretly (the slugs are always hidden by their subjects' clothes), rapidly, and irresistibly. Heinlein evokes the same state of emergency as the first *Body Snatchers* film and at the same time satirizes the U.S. authorities for being so slow to act.

Heinlein gave literal expression to the Cold War slogan of the "battle for men's minds." The preamble to the third periodical episode of *The Puppet Masters* declares: "Beaten in every battle with the ghastly invaders, man has one single weapon left—his mind! But will that prove enough?"[47] The slugs' manipulation of the media, police, and other agencies suppresses public knowledge of their presence. Even transformed citizens seem indistinguishable from those left unscathed. Thus Heinlein evokes the same paranoid vision as *Body Snatchers* where Americans lose trust in their common identity.

Until, that is, Heinlein's narrator–protagonist moves into action. Sam is a member of an elite intelligence agency run like a nationally representative family presided over by the paternal figure of the "Old Man." He narrates events in a clipped professional idiom reminiscent of detective thrillers as he plays out the roles of investigator, sacrificial guinea-pig, and national guardian. He is helped by a fellow agent named Mary, who alternates between sister and romantic partner and who supplies the only apparently reliable test of characters' identities: if they—the men, that is—do not react to her flirtatious overtures, this proves that they have become zombies. And so it seems that the very destiny of the nation depends on Mary's fluttering eyelashes.

Because Miles Bennell is the narrator of the novel and the focalizer of the first film adaptation, we are never given access in *Invasion of the Body Snatchers* to the consciousness of any victims. We simply infer changes from differences in behavior, appearance, and speech. A similar thing happens in *The Puppet Masters*. For example, after Mary and Sam marry, the main sign that she becomes possessed is the traditional feature of vitality—her eyes—that "were no longer wells of horror but merely dead." Luckily, possession is not irreversible as in *The Body Snatchers*, but it falls to Sam as hero in the struggle for survival to enact that survival in person. Not that his consciousness becomes a site of struggle. Rather, Sam bears witness to mental takeover that can then be combated by the collective mind of the Old Man's group.

When Sam is taken over by one of the slugs, Heinlein describes the transformation of his consciousness as a seminarcosis where he retains perceptual clarity but loses all volition:

> I saw things around me with a curious double vision, as if I stared through rippling water—yet I felt no surprise and no curiosity. I moved like a sleepwalker, unaware of what I was about to do—but I was wide awake, aware of who I was, where I was, what my job at the Section had been. And, although I did not know what I was about to do, I was always aware of what I was doing and sure that each act was the necessary act at that moment.
>
> I felt no emotion most of the time, except the contentment that comes from work which needs to be done. That was on the conscious level; someplace, more levels down than I understand about, I was excruciatingly unhappy, terrified, and filled with guilt, but that was down, way down, locked, suppressed; I was hardly aware of it and not affected by it.[48]

Sam becomes the perfect agent of subversion by immediately and unquestioningly following directions that are never vocalized, simply presented as a scripted sequence of actions. The hints of suppressed fears could be a feature of Sam's professional training or a suppression induced by his "master." Certainly Sam perceives himself as a totally passive implement: "I had no more to do with words spoken by me for my master than has a telephone. I was a communication instrument, nothing more."[49] Sam has to repeat exactly the same function when the slug is questioned through him so that information can be gleaned on their purpose.

The Puppet Masters then describes a new kind of conflict that Sam explains as follows: "War with another race is psychological war, not war of gadgets."[50] A war, that is, of commitment and intelligence; but one that will act as a prelude to the more direct combat with the puppet masters' power source predicted in the novel's coda.

Heinlein extends the action of his novel too rapidly to follow the pattern followed by science fiction films of invasion, particularly the targeting of the small town for the starting point. Sand Rock, Arizona, in *It Came from Outer Space* (1954; screenplay by Ray Bradbury) is typical in being a community where everyone knows everybody else. Whether a blob, pod, or series of flying mechanisms, the alien invader functions as a device to divide towns-folk from each other and separate members of families through a process of transformation that leaves the victims unchanged outwardly. The newly wed wife in *I Married a Monster from Outer Space* (1958) exclaims that her hus-band resembles a "twin brother from some other place." The visual clichés of such a change were quickly established as a verbal monotone, wooden movement, and the recurring image of a "loved or trusted person staring coldly into the camera or into off-screen space."[51] Less commonly, duplica-tion might occur instead of transformation; several scenes in *It Came from Outer Space* show characters gazing in horror at their own replicants. This pattern is reflected in the 1962 Department of Defense film *Red Nightmare* (an alternate title is *The Commies Are Coming, The Commies Are Coming*) that shows an idyllic small town family being turned into unfeeling appa-ratchiks by a Communist takeover.

The transformation of human subjects carries with it a change in their relation to each other since they all become selfless agents in a collective cause. *Invaders from Mars* (1954) ingeniously combines sabotage thriller with alien takeover when Martians implant tiny control devices in the base of their victims' necks so that they will unquestioningly bomb parts of a Califor-nia rocket installation. When their function is complete, the devices explode, killing the now redundant agents. This film is focalized through the most vulnerable member of a family, a small boy, whose perspective exaggerates the height of the male authority figures, most of which let him down.[52]

The most famous of these films, *Invasion of the Body Snatchers* (1956), has been linked by critics with contemporary fears of brainwashing and de-scribed as an "imaginative visualisation of the national security state."[53] Cer-tainly the drama played out in Santa Mira, California, has implications for the United States as a whole through a series of expanding spatial identifica-tions between body, home, town, and nation. Hence the calculated pun between organism and political subversion when a character declares: "They're taking you over cell for cell."[54] Although the term "Invasion" was a later addition to the title, the concept was already central to Jack Finney's original serial, where we are told: "Santa Mira is virtually complete. Now we're making a systematic invasion of the county."[55]

Typical of the subgenre, the takeover starts with figures in positions of authority: policemen, psychiatrists, and so on. This immediately problema-tizes the form resistance will take. *Body Snatchers* is more complex in this respect than, say, *Invaders from Mars*, where the U.S. Army finally restores the status quo. In Finney's serial, a phone call to the FBI produces a last-minute intervention when Dr. Miles Bennell and Becky are captured by the "pod people." For the novel Finney removed the FBI and presented the final departure of the pods as a reaction to planetary hostility.[56] During the making of the film the studio imposed a narrative frame to establish a condition of emergency from the very beginning. The ironic inversion where the doctor has become the patient suggests in itself a disruption of social order, and only the convenient coincidence of a traffic accident confirms Bennell's story. In the famous final frame scene where he shouts at indifferent motorists "You're next!" this functions as an extra-diegetic warning to the audience, for the film avoids the closure of Finney's narrative, halting at the point where the authorities are about to swing into action.

The cinematic frame also foregrounds skepticism that is thematized throughout Finney's novel as a running dialogue between the narrator Bennell and a familiar but doubting companion. The opening lines foreground this issue: "I warn you that what you're starting to read is full of loose ends and unanswered questions."[57] Producer Walter Wanger originally intended to address the narrative's credibility by having Orson Welles introduce the film as if during a news broadcast with a warning to the viewer not to dismiss the account as fantasy because "strange things are happening all around us, some visible, and some not."[58] In the final film, this deliberate echo of the *War of the Worlds* broadcast was dropped and the question of credibility fed into the dialogues in the first half of the film. The strange changes in Santa Mira are described as a "malignant disease spreading through the whole country" and a "contagious neurosis." These phrases straddle categories, problematically linking mental and physical illness. And a further complication arises from the fact that the town psychiatrist who dismisses events as a group delusion is himself a pod person. Similarly, the biologist Professor Budlong, who plays a major role in the novel by categorically denying the possibility of reconstituting a human body, is also one of the "changed." In other words, the strongest voices of reason become the most discredited. *Body Snatchers* thus dramatizes a clash between perception and understanding that is played out through the narrator–focalizer Bennell. As the town doctor, Bennell tends to interpret strange behavior pathologically, and a local psychiatrist strengthens his diagnosis by identifying a "strange neurosis, evidently contagious, an epidemic mass hysteria" spreading through the town.[59] The metaphor of illness naturalizes the process of change taking place but also encodes it as biological, therefore making it unsusceptible to reason. Finney distracts the reader from searching for an exact account of the transformation by focusing instead on the time of such transformations and their consequences. The change always happens at night and so, as Michael Rogin has pointed out, "self-surveillance in *Body Snatchers* makes sleep itself impossible."[60]

Bennell unconsciously establishes that the alien manifests itself linguistically as an absent or deferred referent. All of these narratives draw on pronominals like "it" and "them," as can be seen in Bennell's description of the Becky replicant. This is his second visual crux in the narrative and occurs in the basement of Becky's house and at night. Note in the following how Bennell defers visual identification as long as possible:

> There it lay, on that unpainted pine shelf, flat on its back, eyes wide open, arms motionless at its sides; and I got down on my knees beside it. I think it must actually be possible to lose your mind in an instant, and that perhaps I came very close to it. And now I knew why Theodora Belicec lay on a bed in my house in a state of drugged shock, and I closed my eyes tight, fighting to hold on to control of myself. Then I opened them again and looked, holding my mind, by sheer force, in a state of cold and artificial calm.
>
> I've watched a man develop a photograph, a portrait he'd taken of a mutual friend. He dipped the sheet of blank sensitised paper into the solution, slowly swishing it back and forth, in the dim red light of the developing room. Then, underneath that colorless fluid, the image began to reveal itself—dimly and vaguely—yet unmistakably recognizable just the same. This feeble orange glow of my flashlight, was an unfinished, underdeveloped, vague and indefinite Becky Driscoll.[61]

Running through this passage is a reluctance to admit that the form before him is a displaced and altered image of the most familiar figure in his life. The liquid metaphor in brainwashing is here applied to the coming-into-definition of the image while the transformed town librarian has "washed out" eyes, as if some vital principle had been erased. The second operative metaphor here of photography implies a flattened out simulation and another loss of an original.

In between such moments of visual crisis the suggestions of gradual changes taking place induce in the viewer of the film a kind of paranoia that

Vivian Sobchack has skillfully summarized: "We are seduced by the minimum activity and novelty of what's on the screen into an attentive paranoia which makes us lean forward to scan what seem like the most intentionally and deceitfully flat images for signs of aberrant alien behavior from the most improbably of suspects."[62] Forced to scrutinize every movement or gesture, we are implicitly participating in Bennell's gradual estrangement from a long familiar environment. This change is registered powerfully within the small town but totally lost in the 1978 remake of the movie, which starts from a premise of general urban alienation in San Francisco.[63] The 1956 movie extends the dissociation between apparently normal exterior and unknown interior into chiaroscuro effects where the sheer difficulty of seeing reflects corresponding problems of understanding. Many scenes take place at night, as when Bennell peers into a little pool of light from his flashlight surrounded by the unknown dark spaces of basements. Traditionally evocative of mystery and suspense, shadow now suggests a metaphorically "darker" side to mundane acts, as when the meter man emerges from a basement where he has placed new pods. The most complex play on light occurs in the scene in Bennell's greenhouse, where the canted camera angle implies a disruption of the real. Barred light falls diagonally across the actors, anticipating their later captivity, and throws a surreal perspective on the juxtaposition of the pods' "birth" to Bennell's "murder" of his replicant self. This play on shadow introduces a dimension of threat into the most familiar mundane settings. The sheer difficulty of seeing change in this film generates much of its tension. Individuals do not turn into zombies, as happens in the more melodramatic films on this theme, but rather generate a new single-minded group consciousness.

The use of pods as an alien agency was a clever choice because *Body Snatchers* thereby avoided monster clichés or the awkwardness of the "bubble" perspective in *It Came from Outer Space*. The pod is a magnified image of a familiar object suggesting uniformity and incipient proliferation, but not danger. Director Don Siegel pointed out in an interview that "to be a pod means that you have no passion, no anger, the spark has left you." The suggestion was therefore of an emotional emptying and Siegel added: "there is no real physical threat from the pods. The threat is from sleep."[64] The narrative relocates horror in one of the most mundane (and unavoidable) daily processes and adds an extra dimension to the endemic paranoia that characters have to monitor themselves to stave off the dreaded change. Exactly what that change signifies has remained a matter of critical dispute.

Before his death, Jack Finney repeatedly denied any symbolism, insisting: "the book isn't a cold war novel, or a metaphor for anything."[65] Opinions differed even between those involved in making the film. Walter Wanger intended it to be a "plea against conformity," while director Stuart Gordon who worked on the second remake has stated: "The first movie was really about the Cold War and the fear of communists being among us, some of our friends being not really who they say there are."[66] Critic Peter Biskind has more helpfully proposed two levels of significance, taking pod possession as an overt metaphor for Communist brainwashing and a covert metaphor for "pluralist therapeutic authority, which operated by entering the mind and directing behaviour from within."[67]

Despite the importation of malignity to the aliens in these narratives, they explain their own purpose as utopian and benevolent. The possessed professor in *The Brain Eaters* (1958) describes the aliens in the following terms: "Our social order is pure, innocent. It has the exactitude of mathematics. We shall force upon man a life free from strife and turmoil." In *Body Snatchers*, too, the pod people promise a compulsory liberation into a stress-free utopia, rationalized through the social diagnosis that "the whole world's sick." The use of pods as the transforming agency injects a note of Darwinian determinism since they are only following a biological imperative. The signs of the change are all absences, losses, and erasures: life going out of eyes, loss of emotional inflection. Hence the accuracy of the prediction "there'll be no more tears." The film uses the trope of rebirth that we find in Karp's *One*, encouraging reading the narrative as a conversion process. In the novel, however, Professor Budlong attempts to explain the transformation through the notion of the "intricate pattern of electrical force-lines that knit together every atom of your body to form and constitute every last cell of it."[68] This concept of pattern, a kind of ultimate organic blueprint, anticipates the fiction of William Burroughs and raises a different anxiety that the personality might be reducible to an electronic formula and quantifiable as information that can be transferred at will.

We have seen how surveillance was related to the all-seeing eye of God. Correspondingly, all three narratives of mind invasion under consideration here take their different bearings from the New England witch-hunt that for Arthur Miller, introducing *The Crucible* (1953), constituted a "perverse manifestation of the panic which set in among all classes when the balance began to turn toward greater individual freedom."[69] *The Puppet Masters* describes mass possession as a state of being "hagridden," a deliberate anachronism evoking the legend of being ridden by the nightmare. In *Body Snatchers*, the psychologist Mannie Kaufman cites the Salem witch-hunt as a precedent for the mass delusion occurring in Santa Mira, but conversely Bennell notes ominously in his voice-over that "something evil had taken possession of the town."[70] Frederik Pohl makes the most extensive use of this analogy in the opening sections of *A Plague of Pythons* (1965), where sophisticated technology jostles the routine sale of amulets to ward off demonic possession.

Pohl foregrounds the irony of the irrational within society by depicting what is apparently a "pandemic insanity" or "planetary lobotomy," spreading through all levels of society and manifesting itself in outbursts of wild behavior that induce panic. Clearly a force is at work of unknown origin: "Demons? Martians? No one knew whether the invaders of the soul were from another world or from some djinn's bottle."[71] Partly, Pohl uses the notion of possession in order to describe nuclear war as an irrational convulsion. H-bombs have been launched by East and West, causing massive destruction but without anyone understanding why the war happened. In the aftermath "possession" continues and is used by the protagonist Chandler to defend himself against the charge of having attacked a young girl.

Chandler represents a typical instance of the general fate befalling the population. Soon after his trial collapses he experiences once again a dissociation of mind from body, where the latter performs functions prescribed from elsewhere: "The gun went flying, Chandler's body leaped after it, with Chandler a prisoner in his own brain, watching, horrified and helpless." The power of such passages is damaged somewhat by Pohl's lack of coherence over what kind of possession is taking place. Here, for instance, Chandler's consciousness remains intact while he loses physical autonomy. Later in the novel we are told: "once again an interloper tenanted his brain."[72] This time he finds himself speaking a Slavonic language he does not know. And here lies one of Pohl's difficulties. Even in his most extreme possession Chandler's consciousness never becomes confused; so, while his mental space is invaded in one sense, Pohl essentially conveys a physical state of servitude. He revives Heinlein's puppet metaphor as a distant power source "pulling the strings."

The force controlling Chandler is described at one point as an "occupying power," and this suggestion of territorial aggression is substantiated by the gradual revelation of conspiracy. What starts out in the novel as a supposedly terrifying and irresistible force is scaled down to a secret weapon devised by neo-Stalinists in Russia. The device is a kind of radio transmitter that "controlled the minds of men. The "receiver" was the human brain. Through this little portable transmitter surgically patch-wired to the brain of the person operating it, his entire personality was transmitted in a pattern of very short waves that "could invade and modulate the personality of any other human being in the world."[73] Technologically, Pohl's device relates to the use of ultra-low frequency radio waves and José Delgado's experiments in the 1960s on the electronic stimulation of the brain. What makes his description hyperbolic is that the novel describes specific messages being transmitted to subjects, not an entire personality transfer, and nowhere does Pohl even begin to explain how the encoding or quantification of the personality could take place.

Although *A Plague of Pythons* is set after the Cold War, it perpetuates a view of the Soviets we have seen promoted by Huxley and others, of that regime as being aggressively expansive and indifferent to the technological manipulation of human subjects. Indeed the radio technology can be read as a long-distance form of brainwashing, hence Chandler's comparisons between himself and American POWs forced to make radio broadcasts in Korea. Pohl reinstates the ideology of individualism by having Chandler singlehandedly outwit the malign oligarchy (the "Execs") ruling the world. Although he succeeds in this, the technology still exists; the miniature denotes their potential use for world dominance that is not closed off by the narrative.

■ In 1957 New Jersey cinemas began showing microsecond advertising slogans that appeared to be effective, and the subsequent public controversy led the Institute of Practitioners of Advertising to set up a commission of enquiry into the practice. That same year Vance Packard's bestseller *The Hidden Persuaders* made the startling claim that the "chilling world of George Orwell and his Big Brother" had already arrived in the United States, since mass marketing and political agencies were applying the behaviorist theories of Pavlov and others.[74] The use of motivational research had resulted in the construction of covert messages within advertisements (what Huxley called a "campaign in favour of irrationality"), some of them using "subthreshold" effects from split-second images. The invention of a "tachistoscope," created to experiment with images so rapid that they occurred below the threshold of conscious perception, led Aldous Huxley to prophesy grimly that such a device "might well become a powerful instrument for the manipulation of unsuspecting minds" and in a 1958 BBC "Brains Trust" program identified motivational research with Orwellian subliminal advertising.[75] Packard's study transposed perceptions of Soviet institutionalized manipulation onto the American scene. A note to the British edition declared that "Americans have become the most manipulated people outside the Iron Curtain," and Packard even reported that some agencies were making Pavlov's lectures on conditioned reflexes required reading.

In 1958 the CIA began experiments into the operational value of subliminal messages, taking as their cue the advertising executive James Vicary's trials in New Jersey. Their in-house journal *Studies in Intelligence* issued a report in 1958 that concluded that subliminal techniques were interesting but unreliable and not very useful because they needed precise controls and the right kind of messages. Nevertheless, there is some evidence that subliminal techniques were incorporated into the CIA's MK-ULTRA project.[76] More importantly for present purposes, the CIA was unconsciously anticipating fictional treatments of subliminal messages in their enquiries into the political applicability of such techniques. At that time these experiments were secret. Any disclosure of them would have further fueled public anxieties about covert manipulation.

Out of this controversy grew the perception that brainwashing was a function of the media, which we will see in *The Manchurian Candidate*. Much of the impact of *The Hidden Persuaders* lay in its linkage between advertising and politics, and in the way it played on cold war paranoia by suggesting that secret processes were at work. The novelist Frederik Pohl, himself a former advertising executive, anticipated the debate over subliminal practices in his story "The Tunnel Under the World" (1954) where the inhabitant of a small American town reflects on the ad men, "maybe they hypnotise us. . . . They pour advertising into us the whole damned day long . . . and then they wash the day out of our minds and start again the next day with different advertising."[77] The truth turns out to be even more bizarre in that, following a massive industrial accident, a local company has reconstructed a miniature simulation of the town and townsfolk. The "takeover" is total. The tunnel of the title symbolizes the attempt at concealment in the simulation whereby the townsfolk are distracted from enquiring into causation by an environment packed with advertising promotions.

Pohl concretizes the metaphor of warfare routinely applied in the discourse of commercial competition. "The Wizard of Pung's Corner" (1959) makes this even more explicit. In the wake of World War III the reconstituted central government is attempting to take back Pung's Corner and bring it back into the nation, which it does through the fifth column activities of an agent named Coglan who possesses a "devil's smile and a demon's voice." His malignity is confirmed when Coglan inserts momentary images into the local television programs and his strategy becomes recognized for what it is, namely subliminal compulsion, appealing to the "basic sex drive; you don't know you're seeing it, but the submerged mind doesn't miss it."[78] These images are speedily demystified, whereas in Cordwainer Smith's (Paul Linebarger) "Angerhelm" (1959) the subliminal section of a taped message, apparently from outer space, cannot be located or its origins identified. Rather than presenting an enigma, Pohl shows how advertising functions as a kind of internal warfare, literally so since Coglan's actions are reinforced by national troops besieging the town. The characters identify rather than experience a loss of control "when the [ad] agency had you in its sights and the finger squeezing down on the trigger."[79]

Where Pohl's story narrates economic activity as an attempt to impose power from the center, J. G. Ballard's "The Subliminal Man" (1963) thematizes semiotic deconstruction. The story draws extensively on *Invasion of the Body Snatchers* in focalizing on a doctor and attaching the panicky warnings that open that film to a separate character named Hathaway. His first question—"Have you seen the signs?"—is a pun that establishes a note of urgency that might just be paranoia. In place of pods, Hathaway is alarmed at the construction of enormous signs by the side of the local expressway. These signs can be read as messages pointing toward consumer goods or as objects in their own right. On the face of it Hathaway's claims appear ludicrous. "They're invading your brain," he shouts at Dr. Franklin, "if you don't defend yourself they'll take it over completely! We've got to act now, before we're all paralysed."[80] The ironic transposition of an alien threat onto American commerce amounts to a satire on accelerated production that might lead ultimately to a monopolization of waking hours by work.

Hathaway's outburst represents a call to look beyond the restricted guidance of the highway, which stands as a metaphor of induced consumerism, and Franklin acts on it by keeping a record of all purchases made by himself and his wife. He comes to an astonishing conclusion: "*Not once had he actually decided of his own volition that he wanted something and then gone out to a store and bought it!*" On his way home one day Franklin sees that Hathaway has broken open the front of one of the enormous signs confirming his earlier discovery that "they've got hundreds of high-speed shutters blasting away like machine-guns straight into people's faces and they can't see a thing."[81] Hathaway's sabotage literally makes the hidden sign ("BUY NOW

BUY NOW") visible and at the same time signs his own death warrant since he is shot down by a police machine-gun. The weapon analogy thus points to the deadening narcosis induced by the signs and then is actualized in the institutional maintenance of the system. For Bruce Franklin, "The Subliminal Man" is one of Ballard's most important stories because it dramatizes the contradictions within capitalism and shows how "in the present stage advertising uses a variety of means to get round rational thinking, which would reject its message, in order to jam that message into our unconscious processes."[82] The confirmation of the process in Ballard's bleak story changes nothing at all.

The hidden signs in Ballard's story induce desires totally separate from any felt need. Although it is a commerce-oriented process, it could easily be applied to other fields of experience. Ewen Cameron's "depatterning" experiments, for instance, concluded with positive phrases from patients' interviews being played back to them through speakers concealed under pillows while the patients slept. This "psychic driving" led the historian John Marks to conclude that Cameron "carried the process of 'brainwashing' to its logical extreme."[83] Though carried out in the name of therapy, his system had political applications that Aldous Huxley did not hesitate to spell out: "The scientific dictator of tomorrow will set up his whispering machines and subliminal projectors in schools and hospitals . . . and in all public places where audiences can be given a preliminary softening up by suggestibility-increasing oratory or rituals."[84]

■ This survey of early treatments of brainwashing cannot fail to include an unusually comic adaptation of the theme by Kurt Vonnegut in *The Sirens of Titan* (1959). Vonnegut has recognized the influences on him of Huxley (for the plot of his first novel *Player Piano*) and Orwell. Of the latter he has declared: "Spiritually, I feel very close to Orwell; politically I feel very close to Orwell."[85] But these influences do not prepare us for the method of Vonnegut's novel. *The Sirens of Titan* describes a ludicrous attempt on Mars to create a perfect army by wiping clean the memory of its members. The following quotation from the Director of Mental Health on Mars apparently strikes a suitably clinical note:

We can make the centre of a man's memory virtually as sterile as a scalpel fresh from the autoclave. But grains of new experience begin to accumulate on it at once. These grains in turn form themselves into patterns not necessarily favourable to military thinking. Unfortunately, this problem of recontamination seems insoluble.[86]

We have already seen how brainwashing was perceived from the very beginning as a means of converting the human subject into a means or passive agent. Here the scalpel is displaced as an implement for human use into a metaphor of the "purified" individual, but this statement of intent is significantly qualified by misgivings over "recontamination," which, decoding the terminology, signifies for the speaker a lapse back into humanity. Instead of integrating these statements into his narrative, Vonnegut places them as an epigraph, inviting the reader to speculate about the implementation of this practice.

Vonnegut transforms the blatantly bogus claims of the Martian authorities to therapy into a parodic account of militarism focused on the hapless figure of Unk ("uncle"), an older soldier who has orders to become a model soldier. Unk has to be cured of "mental illness" that makes his mind "almost a blank":

> At the hospital they even had to explain to Unk that there was a radio antenna under the crown of his skull, and that it would hurt him whenever he did something a good solider wouldn't ever do. The antenna also would give him orders and furnish drum music to march to. They said that not just Unk but everybody had an antenna like that—doctors and nurses and four-star generals included. It was a very democratic army, they said.[87]

Vonnegut draws on the repertoire of science fiction devices used in *Invaders from Mars* in order to dramatize an ironic gap between intention and result. Unk is reduced to an automaton, even strangling a fellow soldier during training. In the more melodramatic contexts of Korean War fiction and *The Manchurian Candidate*, such an act would trigger horror, but Vonnegut constantly foregrounds Unk's position as victim. The Martian authorities are promoting military discipline as an ideal model of human behavior, but, as Joseph Sigiman has shown, Vonnegut applies textual discontinuities (analogous to quantum jumps) in order to undermine any clear continuity between cause and effect.[88] If the military ideal represents an ultimate form of control, which in turn implies an undemocratic elite of controllers, the total inefficiency of Unk and the Martian army in general demonstrates the failure of this mechanistic dream. And the failure does not come as a surprise to the reader since the gossipy version of the authorities' medical claims reads as altogether less neat: "*When they clean out a man's memory on this place called Mars, they don't really clean it completely. They just clean out the middle of it, sort of. They always leave a lot of stuff in the corners.*"[89] This popular version denies the process dignity and efficiency, presenting the medical technicians as incompetent "housekeepers" of the mind.

Vonnegut creates black humor over a potentially chilling issue — the erasure of an individual's subjectivity — and locates this action on a near planet so as to give the reader a bizarrely estranged version of a militaristic tendency perceived on Earth. We shall see in more recent fiction how the failure of such medical experiments becomes a constant theme, together with the breakdown and, in many cases, death of the experimental subjects involved.

■ By the 1960s brainwashing had become established as a staple ingredient of conspiracy narratives. Len Deighton's first novel *The Ipcress File* (1962) contains the subject within a rigid espionage thriller paradigm. The novel is narrated by a member of military intelligence who constantly distracts the reader from the central subject by ridiculing his class-bound superiors and supplying "insider" details of the intelligence services. Initially, the investigatory narrative works quite well at uncovering glimpses of a secret project being pursued in a London house where one floor is divided into cubicles and another contains a large water tank possibly used for sensory deprivation. When the narrator is captured and taken to be interrogated at length by the plotters, his ordeal is presented as a displaced rerun of Hungarian brainwashing conducted by an Eastern-looking official he nicknames "Kubla Khan." The process is a composite deriving from Orwell and descriptions like Vogeler's and Gallico's, where beating, drugs, and meaningless questions reduce the narrator — potentially — to the point where he will be ready to stand trial. The most surreal moment in the novel comes when the narrator makes his escape, only to find himself in a north London bean-patch. The "detention camp" proves to be a house in Wood Green.

With the exception of his brief imprisonment, the narrator's account totally understates the impact of brainwashing. The "Ipcress" of the title is an abbreviation for "Induction of Psycho-neuroses by Conditioned Reflex with Stress," designating a process being carried out by an organization directed by the evil genius of the novel, Mr. Jay.[90] Mr. Jay has devised a way to plant brainwashed figures in positions of authority and, through an experimental "synthesized environment" in Switzerland, to supply continental factories with docile workers. It is he who states a bold rationale for conditioning by appealing to social efficiency: "One of these days, brain-washing will be the acknowledged method of dealing with anti-social elements. Criminals can be brainwashed. I've proved it. Nearly 300 people I've processed. It's the greatest step forward of the century."[91] Jay describes brainwashing in contradictory terms both as a means of bringing the antisocial within norms and as a means of conquest ("another terrible weapon" even worse than nuclear bombs). Jay's practices are described as being congenial to Communism although his organization is notionally independent and the defeat of the latter becomes a purging of the British establishment and therefore its consolidation. Because Deighton's chosen method of narration only allows him to give cryptic glimpses of Jay's activities, the reader has to wait for the narrator to explain brainwashing in the concluding chapters. Deighton's *The Billion-Dollar Brain* (1966) shows similar difficulties in weaving mind control into the main narrative. Here the crazed right-wing General Midwinter has built a massive installation in Texas where a "streaming" of rapid-sequence photographs is used to induce the cover stories of his agents.

The 1965 film adaptation of *The Ipcress File* gives more space to the theme of mind control, especially in showing its effects on a scientist. As this specialist in nuclear fusion begins his lecture in London he freezes in mid-sentence and repeats his last phrase with a blank stare. The effect is mechanistic as if a tape recorder has jammed; and the Ipcress tape used for conditioning confirms this model of mental processes. The protagonist, now named Harry Palmer, sets off on an express toward Eastern Europe, is knocked out by a "ticket inspector," and regains consciousness in prison. The process of brainwashing as disorientation, sleep deprivation, and near starvation is enacted in far more detail than in the novel. Palmer is a captive subject under observation. Like the experimental subject in the film *The Terminal Man*, the camera identifies the viewer's point of view with Palmer's as he—and we, the viewers—see guards observing him through the cell spy-hole. Once physically weakened, Palmer is then strapped into a chair suspended in a metal tank where psychedelic sounds and images pulse before a voice begins to repeat: "Listen to my voice. Nothing but my voice. . . . You will forget all about the Ipcress file. You will forget your name." The use of the trigger phrase "now listen to me" is almost identical to that quoted by George Estabrooks of an operator hypnotizing a subject while asleep.[92] Palmer resists the hypnotic conditioning by gouging his palm (surely a tacit play on his name) to maintain a painful self-awareness. As the electronic voice repeats "no name," he insists over and over "my name is Harry Palmer." The conditioning is thereby enacted through a kind of dialogue between anonymity and individual selfhood, where Palmer's only resource is his willpower. This is crucial to the action of the film, which mounts a drama of attempted betrayal by Palmer's superior, who seems the very personification of the British establishment.

The questioning of this establishment is symptomatic of how the theme of mind control became applied in narrative. Even when the source of control is external, its effects are usually played out on domestic sites. And the nature of that control is investigated and debated within the narratives. In chapter 2 we saw that the Korean War occasioned the emergence of the term "brainwashing" and in some of the narratives just considered Korea had become a reference point. We now need to ask how Korean War fiction itself dealt with the issue of brainwashing.

four

The Impact of Korea

T he Korean War was the first time U.S. soldiers engaged in open combat in the Cold War but was one of the least conclusive military actions in modern history; early U.N. victories gave way to a protracted stalemate after the Chinese intervention. In comparison with World War II or Vietnam, this war has received far less attention in fiction or film.[1] Partly for that reason it has been labeled the "forgotten war." More importantly, severe doubts about army morale were induced by reports of U.S. prisoners collaborating with their captors and, in a few cases, even refusing repatriation.[2] The problem of how to receive the returning GIs was a serious one. Sometimes they were viewed as virtual traitors, sometimes as returning heroes. A sympathetic report in 1955 viewed them as the victims of a disparity between army and air force policies on military behavior.[3]

"I was forced to be the tool of these war mongers and made to . . . do this awful crime against the people of Korea and the Chinese Volunteers."[4] Thus "confessed" U.S. Air Force 1st Lt. John Quinn and this act symbolized the traumatic effect of the Korean War on national morale. For one contemporary reporter Korea was the site of the first overt clash between East and West where the new techniques of mind manipulation, the "total psychological weapon," were being used toward a goal of Communist world domination; and this war is regularly described as the first where combatants tried to convert POWs to their own ideology.[5] The Korean conflict had a covert psychological dimension where each side bombarded the other with pamphlets and tried to undermine the other's purpose. In addition, the United States carried out extensive psychological monitoring of its troops, but without preparing them for the ordeal of the prison camps.[6] The "confessions" that the United States was using germ warfare in Korea have been described by one historian as the "only true case of a man's mind being turned to his captor's will" since there is no evidence that such weapons were ever used.[7] These "admissions" complicated a cherished national myth of triumph. As Tom Engelhardt puts it, the debate over the confessions "reflected confusion over the location of the real enemy. Was the enemy out there, or was it some aspect of the American self?"[8] For Engelhardt the Korean War brought into question one of the grand narratives of American culture, that of the nation's progress from triumph to triumph. Certainly from the mid-1950s onward, debate over brainwashing centered on weaknesses in American policy. One naval commentator, using the term "brainwashing" in the loose popular sense of wearing a captive down psychologically until he breaks, argued that the Korean War was a propaganda coup for the Communists that the United States had helped by following a hesitant and contradictory policy. How to treat the ex-POWs was one sign of this uncertainty, and as a remedy he proposed a blanket assurance to military personnel that they would not be held to account for anything they said in captivity.[9] Although the view that many POWs became collaborators has been increasingly challenged, this anxiety can be seen in the way that every narrative considered in this chapter has a double subject: military and political conflict becomes a cue for cultural self-examination. The situation of captivity internalizes conflict into an extended crisis of cultural identity where the protagonist's deepest values and feelings are brought into question.

The widespread public perception at the time was that a general breakdown of morale had taken place among U.S. POWs as a result of manipulative pressures being applied by the Chinese captors. This view was questioned as early as 1963 in Albert D. Biderman's *March to Calumny* where he took Kinkead to task for not recognizing the Communists' use of the traditional exploitation of terror and for reinforcing the popular perception of Communist methods as being part of a "well-planned program." Biderman insisted, following Lifton and Schein, that the treatment of POWs was no worse than comparable treatment of political prisoners in China or Eastern Europe. He demystifies the concept of brainwashing by dispersing it among familiar methods of totalitarian treatment to "coerce, instruct, persuade, trick, train, delude, debilitate, frustrate, bribe, threaten, promise, flatter, degrade, starve, torture, [or] isolate." What was original, he insists, was the "singular and total character of the ideological objectives of the Communists," rather than any unique new means. Biderman thus rejects the whole image of the Manchurian Candidate zombie, ready to be triggered by his Communist masters and with it the allegation that "among American war prisoners [there were] fellow travellers or guilt-ridden expatriates working off sins of their past wealth or of their nation's past imperialism."[10]

Biderman's voice was a lone scientific one, based on his research for the U.S. Air Force (as discussed in chapter 2). It could not reach the extensive mass audience of a journal like the *Saturday Evening Post*, which published a number of combat stories on the Korean War and also an article on brainwashing by Rear Adm. Daniel V. Gallery. In the latter Gallery confirmed the popular image of brainwashing as a "devilish new process." Gallery directed his main indignation at the political and military establishment for trying to play by the book and not recognizing that "we are in a life-and-death struggle with a godless system bent on world domination."[11] He did not blame POWs for cracking under the strain, since brainwashing could induce them to invert their beliefs. The tragedy was that the POWs' heroism had gone for nothing. Gallery's version of brainwashing was embodied in Sidney Herschel Small's "The Brainwashed Pilot" (1955), which polarizes the stark cultural opposition between political blocs. Here the wife of a pilot shot down over North Korea is acting as a nurse at a medical post on the Hong Kong border when she hears from a refugee of a stranger, possibly a Westerner, living in his village. When the refugee persuades the stranger to cross the border, Anne recognizes her husband but the recognition is all one-way. His eyes are "unfathomable" and he has taken on a totally Chinese identity, explaining: "I look as I do because my father must have been a foreigner."[12] He has become so totally estranged from his own culture that he speaks only Chinese and, when he hears his name Johnny, he "orientalizes" it into "Yan Hai." Thanks to his wife's patience, a small crack appears in his false memory when he recalls that "many men screamed" at him. The Cold War battle for men's minds plays itself out in miniature when a Red Chinese raiding party is driven off by Hong Kong guards. The story says virtually nothing about what happened to the pilot and exploits a topographical contrast between the named features of Hong Kong and the vast unknown terrain ruled by the Communists. The pilot, we are told, has been subjected to a process called brainwashing, but the narratives discussed here follow their protagonists into Communist captivity in order to conflate the psychological and political dramas that result.

Hold Back the Night (1952) by Pat Frank (who served in the U.N. mission to Korea between 1952 and 1953), is one of the earliest novels to dramatize the capture and interrogation of an American officer as a crisis of faith. The action takes place during a retreat from the north of Korea before a Chinese offensive. The immediate literal significance of the "night" of the title is the time of day appropriated by the enemy for its movements, but the term takes on darker connotations of the irrational forces opposed to freedom. The sheer number of Communist personnel ranged against the Americans (the British play a supporting role, other U.N. contingents are hardly mentioned) is scarcely imaginable, hence a deep-lying anxiety of defeat that runs throughout the novel. Within this context Marine Lieutenant Raleigh Couzens is captured and questioned at length by Colonel Chu, a Chinese political officer. The situation is introduced as an interrogation but Chu removes all overt signs of threat, offering Couzens American cigarettes and whisky. Couzens's expectations are thwarted when Chu demonstrates a complete knowledge of American military positions. The questioning then revolves around Couzens's political attitudes and is carried out in a perfect, if formally British, verbal register. Frank totally distinguishes Chu from the "fang-toothed barbarians" (his own phrase) of propaganda. He pays only brief attention to Marxism and at no point tries to indoctrinate Couzens.

If all this is the case, how can such informal questioning induce a crisis? Chu lulls Couzens into a feeling of false security, whereupon he criticizes with considerable frankness the president and the United States. In between these outbursts Chu makes telling criticisms of American racism ("your treatment of the Negro has been our most consistent weapon") and materialism: "You are oppressed, although perhaps you don't know it. You have been hypnotised, drugged by material things." At this point Frank anticipates later writers such as Richard Condon who, as we shall see, transpose the concept of brainwashing onto domestic American culture.[13] The fact that Couzens has no real answer to these charges suggests that he is insecure about his relation to his own culture, which peaks, ironically, after he has been returned to the American lines. It was all suspiciously easy and he imagines his incautious words being broadcast to the West as part of the Communist propaganda effort: "He had failed his country. Why else would the Communists release him?"[14] Couzens imagines himself facing a tribunal of enquiry virtually accusing him of treason, although the novel was written before the "confessions" of biological warfare. This is the second and more unsettling sense to "night." Although the novel describes infantry combat in considerable detail, the deepest focus of fear is the psychological one. What might follow capture? Couzens's ultimate challenge is how to contain his own darkness, which implicitly raises questions about the American national nerve in commitment to the anticommunist cause.

Reports on returned Korean POWs stressed a crisis in articulation as if the experience of the prisoners was literally indescribable. Thus they "could not explain clearly" what happened to them. The 1956 film *Toward the Unknown* dramatizes this predicament and is based loosely on cases like that of Col. Frank H. Schwable who was tried by a military court for signing a "confession" in Korea. As noted earlier, at his hearing he claimed "the words were mine but the thoughts were theirs."[15] The film describes the attempts of a U.S. test pilot to pick up his life after imprisonment and the signing of a similar admission. When Major Lincoln Bond (whose very name suggests a relation to his nation) returns to his U.S. Air Force test center, he is a walking enigma to all who meet him. The brainwashing process remains the "unknown" of the title, a referent he himself suppresses and one that is incomprehensible to others. When a supporting officer makes out a case to his commander he explains that Bond had "held out for fourteen months of brainwashing and gone through—well, who knows what they go through."[16] His girlfriend begs him to tell what happened in Korea, but he retorts: "It would be like two people trying to communicate with each other, each in a different language." To his commanding officer he merely states that mental torture is "something entirely new." In short, Bond's traumatic experience remains inexpressible throughout the film and his prospects for reintegration into American life look bleak indeed.

The situation is saved by the procedures of the air force, which represent an ideally organized version of the nation. Bond enters the film in civilian dress and walks around the mess looking at the signs of its history—portraits and the handprints of former pilots. His commander draws on explicit analogy between Bond and an experimental aircraft, agreeing to test him out gradually. In this way Bond's self-examination and self-testing become dovetailed into air force practice, a combination of physical and mental trial with ready medical backup. The implicit defeat and humiliation of Bond and his fellow prisoners in Korea can thus be symbolically overcome by reconfirming his status as a test pilot in the larger military effort of the Cold War. It seems at one point that he has failed. In a brawl with an officer, Bond's arms are pinned back and the associations with Korea make him lose control. Bond describes his trauma in quasi-mechanical terms: "The Reds hammered me to my limit and broke it. I put a patch over it and hoped it would hold." "It" here designates a fracture in the self, analogous to those Bond had been locating in experimental planes. Once again his commander contains the notion of psychological failure within the key analogy; the Communists had merely pushed Bond beyond his "design limit." So when Bond identifies a design flaw in a new model he is flying he is in effect re-enacting his own credibility and externalizing his inner wound into a fault that can be remedied by military-industrial cooperation. The therapeutic process and his reintegration into the air force coincide with test flights of x-2 rockets, the weapons of the future.

Toward the Unknown dramatizes the symbolic reintegration into his culture of a pilot accused of treason, which is also the subject of Frank G. Slaughter's *Sword and Scalpel* (1957). This novel alternates a court hearing with extended flashbacks in the memory of the accused. Captain Paul Scott, a medical officer, is charged with treason for having made an apparently voluntary admission in writing that the U.S. had been using bacterial weapons. Scott remains largely silent during the trial, which is focalized through a TV commentator determined to find out why Scott collaborated. The silent, personal reason emerges gradually from the flashbacks as a desire to save the life of a captive priest, which was unsuccessful, and a singer. Two conceptions of confession likewise emerge that sharpen the East–West contrasts in this novel. The camp commandant tells Scott: "a confession obtained by any means is still valid, in our eyes," the "means" including torture.[17] The captive priest, on the other hand, has kept a confession book that details exactly what went on in the camp and that has found its way into the hands of the bishop of San Francisco. In a finely managed piece of courtroom drama the bishop reads out this account that shows that others collaborated, not Scott, who is thereupon acquitted.

Once again the accused is reintegrated into his culture, but this time with a religious *deus ex machina* that implies real doubts about whether the legal system could have found out the truth. There is no suggestion that the Communists used any methods other than physical torture, solitary confinement, and sleep deprivation. However, Scott uses sodium pentothal on the priest in Korea to reveal his suppressed guilty feelings. This "neurosynthesis" is "based on the fact that the conscious mind could not always be controlled by the will."[18] Does this make Scott himself a brainwasher? Certainly it opens up a gap between action and conscious motivation that the novel never addresses. But it does not clear up the status of the evidence (photographs of casualties, fragments of shell casing) of biological weapons shown to Scott. In short, the novel raises more questions than it can answer and concentrates instead on saving the protagonist from performing the role of scapegoat for the nation's humiliation in Korea. Although Scott is absolved, that absolution can only come through a religious medium outside a legal, political, and military system shown to be tainted with populist hysteria and personal malice.

Nevertheless, Scott is absolved. The same does not happen in the 1956 film *The Rack*, where a returned officer, played by Paul Newman, is tried for collaboration. The film opens with a flawed welcome-home ceremony where his father, with unconscious irony, boasts of his son's heroism. Most of the film shows the officer's trial where his defense lawyer mounts a general indictment of Communist interrogation methods as a departure from generally accepted morality. Alerting the viewer to the symbolism of the film's title, he argues that the Communists were practicing a "new moral perversion where the mind can be placed upon the rack and made to suffer agony for which there is no measure." The details of Edward Hall's supposed collaboration gradually boil down to the question of his breaking point and in the process reveal how his family had produced the loneliness that induced his collapse, specifically the early death of his mother and the remote authoritarianism of his father. In the trial Hall's lawyer draws the following distinction: "It isn't brainwashing. It never was. No attempt was made to eradicate the mind, but every device was used to make it suffer."[19] The court martial verdict is guilty, but this is offset by Hall's symbolic reunion with his father who had wanted to disown him. *The Rack* thus problematizes Hall's return and refuses any harmonization of military, legal and domestic, or emotional judgments on his actions.

Such films as *Toward the Unknown* and *The Rack* obliquely interrogate the values of American society through their protagonists. As Susan L. Carruthers has shown, these films reflect how "public attention shifted from Communist brainwashing to flaws in the American character which, by extrapolation, suggested that America itself was an unfit competitor in the Cold War."[20] Similarly Charles Young has declared about the same films: "America's inability to prevail was transferred to the prisoners' failure to do the same."[21] The viewer's judgment of the protagonist therefore delivered a verdict indirectly on the nation itself.

■ POW novels usually gain their dramatic immediacy by a concentration on the local circumstances of captivity, a logical reflection of the POWs' own experience. One unusual exception to this is Duane Thorin's *A Ride to Pan-munjon* (1956), which combines personal memories with general reflections on the POWs' situation and how it might be perceived in the West. The protagonist Sergeant Wolfe not only observes first hand the isolation of prisoners from each other but also realizes shrewdly that the very promotion of the idea of brainwashing was acting in the Communists' favor by sowing seeds of distrust at home. Once again, the language of psychological warfare is turned against America: "Communist victories in the battles for the minds of men depend on the weakness of the opposition, rather than the strength of communism."[22] A tension runs throughout Thorin's novel between such general perceptions and the day-to-day drama of captivity. Wolfe realizes that the point of the "confessions" the GIs are pressured to write is to force a commitment from them to the Communist point of view, and he documents in close detail the isolation, use of repetition, and physical humiliation to produce these confessions. The Chinese interrogation triggers a number of internal questions in a process of self-examination that often lacks answers. Particularly he asks himself "why had he come to Korea?" and is then mocked by his captor for being obliged "to suffer so without a cause."[23] Interrogation gradually induces an extended crisis of subjectivity that we shall see in other POW novels.

The Chinese use of "repetition, harassment, and humiliation" in interrogation was designed to break down any group allegiance, hence the divisions promoted by the "confessions" system.[24] As the subject of interrogation becomes isolated, the interrogation takes on the quality of a duel between the interrogator and the prisoner. This pattern recurs constantly through POW fiction and memoirs. It happens between the captured radar officer Purdick and his Chinese political officer Chung in Charles Bracelen Flood's *More Lives Than One* (1967), for instance, and this opposition focuses the central drama of Francis Pollini's *Night* (1960).

Indeed, the internalization of interrogation lies at the heart of Pollini's novel, which depicts the behavior of American POWs in Korea as not merely unheroic but as a collective comment on weaknesses in American culture. Pollini could not place the novel initially with any U.S. publisher, partly because of its sexually explicit language and partly because "the setting was not very comforting for American readers."[25] Eventually it was issued by the Olympia Press in Paris in 1960 and the following year by the London publisher John Calder and in New York by Houghton Mifflin, who added the subtitle *A Truthful Novel of the Nightmare Called Brainwashing*. The cover to the first edition presents the novel as a virtual companion to Eugene Kinkead's *In Every War but One*, and there are many points in the novel where Pollini dramatizes the kinds of events and practices described in Kinkead. The novel records the experiences of an infantry sergeant named Marty Landi, born (like Pollini himself) into a Catholic family in a Pennsylvania coal-mining town. He is taken after capture to a prison camp on the Yalu River, where he is interrogated at length by a Chinese officer (the Communist military personnel in *Night* are virtually all Chinese) and begins a series of classes in political indoctrination. When the authorities decide that he is unredeemable, Landi is transferred to the Reactionaries' hut where a POW organizes the murder of the U.S. collaborators in the camp. This officer is subsequently caught and beheaded. On his return to the United States, Landi has been so traumatized by his captivity that he commits suicide.

Pollini uses Landi as a figure positioned between the extremes of compliance and total resistance, whose conflicting impulses suggest that he is "torn between the natural urge to survive and his conditioning from infancy." Each prison hut contains a pressure exerted on him by other prisoners: to submit or to resist. Unlike Pat Frank, Pollini does not situate the point of Landi's capture geographically. Instead it is an existential moment of surrender, the first in a whole series of defeats making greater and greater inroads into his psyche. Pollini probably drew on the model of *The Naked and the Dead* to focalize the action through different soldiers—although Landi remains the protagonist—and to show their behavior as revealing weaknesses in U.S. culture. Thus one prisoner remembers how starkly the filth of actual combat contrasted with popular fiction about World War II. In this novel, however, the main threat is posed to the mind and to morale. When Landi arrives at this prison camp he finds that rank and therefore discipline have totally collapsed, in contrast with the Chinese. From Kinkead Pollini took the two categories of "Progressives," meaning prisoners who have been indoctrinated; and "Reactionaries," those who resist indoctrination. In Landi's camp by far the largest category is the first, suggesting that the vast majority of prisoners have become either active collaborators or acquiescent to their captors. This again was characteristic of the Korean War since the Chinese (directed by the Soviets) introduced indoctrination after their entry into the war with a striking reduction in the summary killing of prisoners. The location of Landi's camp on the Yalu River was again typical of those chosen for this treatment.[26]

Landi's protracted interrogation forms the narrative spine of *Night* and again exemplifies the generality that "the chief interrogator at each Communist camp . . . was a well-educated, polished, expert officer and a fluent conversationalist in English."[27] Very little mention is made of specific military information. Indeed, from the very beginning Ching asks for—but does not demand—general thoughts from Landi, as we saw in *Hold Back the Night*. Ching quietly and with infinite politeness tries to worm details out of Landi about his home background, setting up a dialogue that he can scarcely resist participating in. Ching contrasts forcibly with a brutal officer whom Landi strikes, and the officious camp commandant. First Ching subtly disorients Landi by discussing apparent irrelevancies to assess his susceptibility to indoctrination and to set up a relation of trust between them. Or rather, he asks for trust but at the same time keeps Landi guessing by denying any kind of routine to his questioning and by asking for details on his (probably fake) Red Cross form. He makes the routine professions of a "lenient policy" and infantilizes Landi into an errant child ("you've been a bad boy") who must be punished for his own good. This induced regression was recommended in the CIA's 1963 KUBARK Interrogation Manual to break down resistance and bring about new dependence.[28] Unlike Pat Frank's political officer, where tiny flaws in his English reveal the masquerade of concern, Ching proves to be a master of tone and innuendo, constantly drawing Landi into a common predicament of cooperating with an irresistible system. He punctuates his questioning with the insistence "we're not savages" and from the very first pages of the novel Pollini distinguishes his Chinese from the apelike caricature "gooks" of anti-Communist propaganda.

As one reviewer noted, *Night* has a double subject. The "ostensible theme" is the brainwashing of the POWs, but the second subject is more disturbing: "what breaks the spirit of man are well-aimed thrusts at some psychological weakness within himself that he is dimly aware of, but has never been forced to face."[29] Like O'Brien in *Nineteen Eighty-Four*, Landi's interrogator combines different roles, but the first resemblance is with a priest; indeed one returning POW recalled that his political instructor was like a "sort of father confessor." In his survey of Korean War fiction Arne Axelsson argues that *Night* marks a divergence from the pattern because the "hero is no longer a religious man."[30] However, Landi implicitly situates Ching within his own cultural background through the priest analogy that gives a double meaning to the confessions that take place within the novel.

One of the crises in *Night* confirms Edward Hunter's claim that when the Communist authorities insisted on "confessions" they were using the term not to mean admission of guilt but rather "agreement with the rules laid down and hence submission to the existing hierarchy." The ritual of confession therefore enacts "submission to the domain." During one of the interminable reeducation sessions Landi allows his mind to wander and is suddenly pulled up by the instructor, who demands an acknowledgement of guilt ("Confess that you are filled with Rotten Bourgeois Ideas") and purification ("You must Cleanse yourself!"). These demands fall on deaf ears. It is the group of POWs who put the maximum pressure on Landi, since all are forced to stand for his fault. In the account of such an episode in Kinkead, the prisoner bowed to peer pressure and "capitulated," but Landi's nonsubmission leads to physical brutality.[31] The Chinese tactic of isolating him from his fellows leads them to beat Landi unconscious. In contrast, when a collaborator gathers POWs to produce a camp newsletter and hears a sarcastic comment from one, he successfully forces the other to confess to error caused by traces of "Capitalist Flotsam." Pollini uses the simple device of capitalization to draw visual attention to the Communist catch-phrases that are incorporated into a hybrid discourse where the main register remains colloquial American English. The confession performed here and earlier refused by Landi is a ritual submission to the authority of the prisoners' captors, which is the ultimate goal of Landi's adversary Ching, since it undermines what little group solidarity remains among the Americans.[32]

Clearly Ching also performs the role of a travesty psychotherapist whose goal is exposure and humiliation, not therapy. He declares disingenuously: "We believe in the mind and have respect for it," then, more ominously, he promises: "Your mind will be straightened out."[33] Cleansing, purging, and then rectification, Ching is an adept with the tropes of mind alteration and deploys them within a verbal arsenal that finally breaks Landi down.

Pollini draws on cognitive psychology to depict Landi's collapse, in particular on memory schemata as formulated by Frederic Charles Bartlett in *Remembering* (1932), to mean a "postural model" of the self constructed through the act of recall, then later extended to internalized models of the world.[34] *Night* traces out a process of deconstruction where the different groups—military, national, and so on—underpinning Landi's identity are stripped away. A metaphorical rhythm soon establishes itself of a repeated fall into the black void of nothingness. This is Landi's night, a more ultimate and terrifying concept than anything we encountered in Pat Frank. The following example is typical, a description of Landi's semi-consciousness after being set upon by the other prisoners: "Night descending and taking him, suspending him a moment, then releasing him, sending him plunging in an endless, timeless fall." Falling can denote collapse from exhaustion or physical violence; but it can also suggest, remembering Landi's Catholic background, spiritual and moral guilt. In effect, Landi endures a series of deaths where the syntax of his consciousness fragments. He loses the sense of time and place, his memories blur together, and he can no longer distinguish between internal and external voices. One POW recalled that the constant repetition in the indoctrination classes induced mental confusion: "I felt my thinking processes getting tangled, my critical faculties getting blunted. I could not think, and I was afraid."[35] In *Night* this process concentrates dramatically in Ching who should be thought of as the personification of a system, his words being echoed by other officials. When the Chinese tell Landi and others that they must have "cognition" of the true situation in Korea, Pollini is playing on the simultaneous senses of recognition (involving admission of national guilt) and re-cognition, that is, the rebuilding of their cognitive models of the world.

The trigger to Landi's collapse is Freudian. As happens in Richard Condon's *The Manchurian Candidate*, Pollini gradually reveals a suppressed oedipal feeling in Landi for his mother complicated by internalizing her chronic dissatisfaction with home life as a guilt in himself. What Edward Hunter would call the "siege" of Landi's mind is figured as a quasi-physical invasion with Ching "pushing into" his deepest feelings. Gradually Ching brings to the surface a hatred between Landi's parents so severe that the mother was yearning for the father to be crushed in the coalmine to liberate her from family bondage. Ching's capacity to hone in on small details of expression from Landi confirm the general perception that emerged after the Korean War that silence was the best defense. Talk in itself was positively dangerous because "those who yielded were forced to yield more and more. The Communists never stopped pumping them, because their own system never stops pumping *them*." Landi's willingness to participate in any dialogue with Ching gives the latter a foothold on the other's consciousness that he exploits so cleverly that at times he appears to penetrate Landi's thoughts. One reviewer recognized that this internalization transforms the opposition between the two men: "In the most brilliant parts of the novel we listen from within Marty's mind as his interrogator, Ching, the only man with whom he can make any really human contact, converts their dissentious relationships into an epitome of all Marty's human intercourse."[36] The revelation of Landi's mother's suicide denies the psychological support of the nuclear family, one of the most heavily promoted values in U.S. domestic propaganda of the Cold War. This exposure therefore has an implicit political significance as well as bringing Landi's self-image to crisis point.

It is hardly surprising that Pollini could not find an American publisher for *Night*, since it presents such a relentlessly unflattering portrait of American GIs. Every detail of their behavior, Landi's included, reveals weakness and an inability to cope with their circumstances of captivity. After initial examples of beatings, Pollini demonstrates that the POWs are their own worst enemy, in their lack of survival skills and in their redirection of violence against their fellows. The leader of the Reactionaries' hut declares bravely: "My weapons are words and fists. . . . My objective . . . to smash the Enemy's plan to capture their minds."[37] Pollini sardonically demonstrates that old-style military heroism in this context is both suicidal and murderous. Phillips is less interested in de-converting the GIs than carrying out a death sentence for dereliction of duty, and in so doing demonstrates a greater brutality than the Chinese captors.

In the course of his dialogue with Landi, Ching utterly condemns American society and the prisoners. Just as their behavior confirms his charges to Landi, so the thought-sequences of different GIs make it virtually impossible for the reader to shrug off Ching's accusations. Landi describes the Chinese treatment as sadism: "You play hell with their weakness;" to which Ching retorts: "Listen, there is absolutely nothing inside them worthwhile—shallow, hollow, infantile, that's it."[38] Diagnosing a national pathology licenses, indeed necessitates, Ching's "cure," which Landi privately caricatures as the adopted role of ward doctor. However, another prisoner recalls equally cynical treatment by medical "humanitarians" of the inmates of a mental ward. Here memories of the electroshock therapy are triggered by an association between the screams of the inmates and those caught in the midst of battle, which in turn draws an implicit and unflattering analogy between U.S. and Chinese practices. Such crisscrossing between domestic America and the prison camp makes it impossible to demonize the latter as barbaric and alien.

Ching's most forceful criticism of America virtually silences Landi who can only mumble sarcastic comments but not answer the indictment. Ching locates a collective avoidance of reality by Americans:

They are buried under the avalanche of mass entertainment—infantile or at best adolescent to the extreme—and mass advertisement—corrupt, cynical as can be. Ad-Mass, someone has called it. . . . The reality is: most tyrannised people in the world. . . . Infantile character structure, marked by masked envy and greed.

Ching inverts the national ideal of freedom in order to displace the notion of brainwashing on to the very commercial system that was being promoted throughout the 1950s as helping to guarantee freedom. Unlikely as it may seem, he quotes J. B. Priestley to align himself with Western critics of cultural materialism. Both within the novel and elsewhere Pollini links commercialism with sexual infantilism. In his play *All Mine* (1967) a Korean veteran and a Vietnam draft dodger both ridicule patriotic images of the United States, the latter asking: "What do you think of American Civilization, Fran? Is it contemptible? Beneath contempt? Is it near the end? . . . Will the Adman triumph."[39] In *Night* the brainwasher turns diagnostician to reveal a culture pathologically fixated on death while the utopian goals of the Communists—unity and integration—serve to foreground the fragmentation of the American captives. Landi first approaches death at the hands of other GIs and then embraces death in his suicide.

The general hallmark of Pollini's fiction is to make extensive use of dialogue while contextual description is reduced to a minimum. This privileging of mimesis over diegesis means that Ching's insiduous power is concentrated in his voice and many of their exchanges read like a drama with a rapid momentum that contrasts strikingly with the physical immobility of the two men. The following exchange is typical:

[Ching has just mentioned Marty's mother.]
    Marty's heart leaped suddenly.
    . . . . *Because I have told him. When? I don't know. Most certainly must have . . . how much more? How much? . . . you'll see . . .*
    "Yes," came the Ching-voice, quiet, knowing.
    Mary said nothing, tried meeting his gaze.
    "Your mother," said Ching, softly.
    "Your grandmother," said Marty.
    Ching's voice, pressing, "Perhaps so—but it's *your mother.*"
    Marty said nothing. He puffed the cigarette, blowing smoke upwards, watching it billow, hover . . .

He was frightened.

Ching gently launched another.

"When did she die?"

He swallowed the smoke abruptly, and only through great effort kept from choking, coughing. His heart was hammering.

He kept quiet.

Ching, sipping coffee, waited.

He began to calm down.

"She's not dead," he said quietly.

"Oh yes she is. Don't lie. Why do you lie to me?"

"You are the world's worst bastard."

Ching sipped more coffee.

"Yes. Yes. A bastard. But you lie to me. How many lies have you told me? Can I believe anything you've told me? Do I keep things from you? Think a minute. Have I lied to you? Don't you feel guilty? You're covered with guilt. When did you last tell the truth?"

"Oh, for Christ's sake!"

"Yes, we are back at that again—Christ—only now, slightly different: *you've* taken all her sins upon yourself, and now you are Christ in *that* way—"

"She had no sins! She was sick!" he blurted out, and in the next moment, amazed, wondering how it had happened, hating himself, and Ching.[40]

In effect, two dialogues overlap here: the external one between Landi and Ching, and an internal one within Landi's consciousness where his reactions to Ching's shrewdness are phrased within an incredulous voice. Note also that Ching becomes disembodied into a "Ching-voice," which seems to possess an unnerving ability to identify Landi's evasions. The physical business of the scene, the smoking and coffee drinking, offer opportunities for pauses within a verbal sparring where Ching dismisses each delaying tactic in a psychological offensive clearly signaled in the phrase "Ching gently launched another." What is at stake here is not political information so much as Landi's assumed prerogative of keeping certain details of his private life hidden.

Ching in effect becomes internalized as a psychological catalyst. Something similar happens in Sanford Friedman's *Totempole* (1965) where a GI serving with the military police in a South Korean internment camp profits from a relationship with a Korean to acknowledge his own homosexuality.

Friedman reverses the normal captivity pattern by presenting Korean anti-Communists from the North and by showing his protagonist as captor, not captive. In fact the latter can only achieve sexual liberation by discarding the authority-structures of the army. Friedman rather easily reduces the political division of Korea to a metaphor for Stephen's psychological "partition" and shows the "gooks" and "fairies," as a redneck MP calls them, to be more enlightened than any contact Stephen has in the United States.

Both Pollini and Friedman use the supposedly alien setting of Korea as the site for an extended interrogation of their protagonists, which leads to unwelcome discoveries about their psyches. Pollini's novel is by far the bleakest, however, in tracing out a gradual displacement of Landi from any military, national, and family ties. To argue that his interrogation has no limits is not to point out Ching's lack of scruple so much as to indicate the self's loss of defining boundaries. The last section, when Landi has returned to the United States, is curiously featureless; it is as if he has not regained any purchase on his home country. As a result of this ideological and psychological displacement, Landi's suicidal walk into a black void only actualizes a mental process that has already taken place.

■ To turn from Pollini to A. E. Van Vogt is to turn from ultimate psychological doubt to an unquestioned belief in positive thinking. Van Vogt's writings have centered from the beginning on systems of self-development or of maximizing the potential in the individual. In 1950 he published a handbook on hypnotism and soon afterward began receiving correspondence from L. Ron Hubbard, who convinced him to become head of the California Dianetics organization. Van Vogt was drawn to Dianetics because it opened up a means of greater control of the self: "A basic theory of Dianetics," he wrote in 1955, "is that it is possible for an individual to free himself from the effect of the shock experiences and self-negation of a lifetime."[41] Despite the hostile press Scientology had already attracted as a cult brainwashing its initiates, Van Vogt saw the theory of Dianetics as essentially liberating and he wrote his belief in self-empowerment into his fiction.

The Mind Cage (1957) describes the aftermath of a third atomic war, the ultimate consequence of the rise of Communism, the "first important Authoritarian group movement."[42] The planet is now ruled by an enormous electronic brain—administered by the "Great Judge" on dictatorial lines where the utterance of heterodox opinions can be punished by death. The "group idea" is in the ascendant and results, at the opening of the novel, in the death sentence being given to a scientific genius. This man has discovered a means of mind transference and frees himself by exchanging bodies with the protagonist David Marin. Necessity thus forces Marin to use his mind to the full in order to avoid impending death, and it is only when he realizes he must think "without boundaries" that he can realistically wage a struggle against his antagonist, the Brain.

In practice, this boils down to a struggle within Marin between his conditioned allegiance to the group and the new creed of super-individualism put forward by the scientist. Since Marin is a security director, he can witness first hand how the regime deals with political opponents that it does through a kind of brainwashing: inducing mental collapse by sentencing the individual to death and then performing forceful indoctrination. Once Marin joins a subversive movement he finds himself on the receiving end of interrogation and he resists questioning through synthetic rage: "His sustained rage began to affect his interrogators. . . . The very inner violence which had drawn each of these men into Control was an unsuspected weakness, stimulated now. The barriers of outward calmness went down, one by one, before that most dramatic of emotions."[43] The result is that the others are reduced to gibbering wrecks. *The Mind Cage* suffers from a weakness common to Van Vogt's other writings, namely that his emphasis on mind-power leads him to wish away the physical obstacles to his protagonist's self-realization.

When he was working on *The Mind Cage* Van Vogt also began preparing his nonscience fiction novel about Communist China, *The Violent Man*, which was not published until 1962. His research was so intensive that during the period of composition he consulted around one hundred works on China and Communism, many of which were listed in a bibliography at the back of the first edition. This novel grew out of his interest in personality types fostered by Dianetics. In his autobiographical *Reflections*, Van Vogt describes *The Violent Man* as his "ultimate achievement," although it remains relatively unknown, perhaps because he attempted to combine his psychological and political interests. "As I studied more and more of the tactics of the Communists in taking over China," he recalls, "I presently saw a pattern of skill in what they did, that no one in government authority here — or apparently anywhere — observed." That pattern was crystallized when Van Vogt read Lenin's *The State and Revolution*, which opened his eyes to the strategy of Communist takeover. Here Engels discusses the obligation of the transitional proletarian state to use violence against its opponents, and it was against the background of mass executions in China that Van Vogt set his novel.[44]

The Violent Man describes the experiences of an American "man of action," Seal Ruxton, and twenty-two other Westerners who are taken to an experimental prison in the north of China in order to convert them to Communism. The novel focuses specifically on an extended battle of wits between Ruxton and Major Mai, and Van Vogt explained: "By selecting a fixed location like a prison, I avoided the kind of complication that can result from taking in a lot of territory in a foreign culture."[45] The choice of a prison recapitulates the setting of narratives of Korean POWs but now uses the situation of captivity as a site for an ideological contest between representatives of Eastern and Western cultures. As in *The Mind Cage*, the novel's starting point is a death sentence, against which Operation "Future Victory" might offer the captives a reprieve. The prison combines a number of different functions. The main premises, a hotel, offers by Chinese standards luxurious accommodation; it contains a reading room where the inmates are to study Communist texts and a theater where they can witness new Chinese art; and it also contains a kind of torture chamber with a treadmill. It is, in short, a hybrid environment, but one totally under the authorities' control.

Seal Ruxton personifies an idealized combination of improvisatory skill with self-analysis. It very quickly becomes evident in the novel that he operates according to a method of analysis that reads like applied Dianetics, especially the concept of "clear" that Van Vogt has described as follows: "Hubbard stated on several occasions that he intended the term to be an analogy with a computing machine being cleared of its past problems, so that the new problems could be set up without interference from the past. But there is no doubt that the word became identified with supermen." This admission bears directly on Van Vogt's protagonist, who has anticipated Communist surveillance by monitoring every aspect of his behavior. Again and again he asks himself questions and engages in a "study of himself" that gives an impression of him standing apart from situations of great personal danger while participating in them. It was said that American POWs in Korea suffered because they did not know what to expect, but Ruxton represents a totally different state of mental and physical preparedness. He analyzes his own behavior and that of those around him according to a number of psychological categories that, we shall see, results in "diagnosis" of Chinese Communism and that also, most ludicrously, suspends the drama of his escape from the prison while he writes an essay with his "mind pen," "summing up his observations, objective and subjective."[46] Although Ruxton is not the narrator, his insistent analysis invests him with the privileged authority of a narrative voice and suggests that he acts as a surrogate for Van Vogt's own views within the novel.

Van Vogt undermines Ruxton's prowess in these ideological debates by attributing the latter's success to his irresistible sex appeal; or rather, he firmly situates the debates within the domain of male experience. Just as in *The Mind Cage* the transmission of the techniques of mind control takes place from fathers to sons, so in *The Violent Man* the Western subjects of ideological pressure are all male. Ruxton takes two lovers, both from the orient: Tosti, a Japanese spy masquerading as a servant, and Madam Mai, wife of the project director, who serves to confirm that the "male-female problem" is universal when she succumbs to Ruxton's charms. In neither case do the women play any important part in the discussion of ideas. Instead they bear special sexual witness to Ruxton's force of personality.

Van Vogt overemphasizes Ruxton's personal qualities no doubt because *The Violent Man* is a revisionist novel attempting to compensate for the reports of American GI collaboration in Korea. In his bibliography to the novel Van Vogt acknowledges debts to Edward Hunter, William Sargant, and other writers who had described the collective collapse of morale in Korea. Brainwashing thus starts out as a subject embedded in the historical past of the novel and then gradually emerges into the foreground of the action. Project 'Future Victory' starts out as a new, and apparently more humane, form of brainwashing, where the Westerners have two years to convert to Communism. A turning point is reached when the Frenchman Lemaine asks Mai where the brainwashing methods are, whereupon the latter retorts: "Your task in 'Future Victory' is to brainwash yourself."[47] Mai had already put forward a related metaphor in declaring that Communist pamphlets should "erase" the older concepts from the prisoners' subconscious, prior to indoctrination.

The confrontation between Mai and Lemaine, however, moves the action from debate to blatant physical threat in the Russian roulette he forces them to play. This is "brainwashing, old style," a reversion to methods reported from Korea, and possibly even an allusion to the film *The Manchurian Candidate* where one GI is hypnotized and made to shoot another. At this point Mai makes an astonishing admission: "Brainwashing does not work. Not as it has been practised up to now." True, the majority of GIs collaborated in the Korean camps, but the vast majority returned home to the material comforts of the United States, whereas the Chinese want total commitment: "The man must give himself to us all the way." The hapless Lemoine is chosen for the brainwashing experiment in this novel. The other prisoners see him reduced to total physical collapse after days of "fatigue treatment." Then, drawing on William Sargant (see chap. 2) and the political commentator Richard L. Walker, Van Vogt describes a Pavlovian process of removing inhibitions before Lemoine is reconditioned to perceive the Chinese as friends. As a priest notes, "the mind is destroyed," and when Lemoine rejoins the group his manner has transformed into belligerence and hyper-talkativeness.[48]

Lemoine's fate seems to demonstrate that the older methods of brainwashing persist, but throughout most of the novel the exact nature of the Communist experiment remains an enigma, and this issue is sidetracked by the battle of tactics between Ruxton and Mai. In the course of this struggle Ruxton and the reader encounter an alien discourse made up of Communist catchphrases and, as Paul Linebarger noted, the metaphors common to Chinese thought. The term "correct" emerges as signifying "consistent with the Communist revolution"; similarly "cut all your tails" denotes a radical disruption of behavior patterns caused by breaking all ties with the subject's past. Ruxton learns this discourse as a kind of protocol of political argument that is applied to historical questions like the Opium Wars, Chinese emigration to the United States, or the relation of China to its "big brother" the Soviet Union. Ruxton participates in these debates and takes the initiative in questioning Nationalist Chinese captives, earning grudging respect from Mai in the process. There is a historical point involved in this process, however. A U.S. soldier explains how the Chinese destroyed the "buddy" system in the Korean camps, sowing the seeds of distrust among the captives. Ruxton, in contrast, starts from a position of distrust and by testing out the different European nationalities in the group, helps to maintain a precarious *esprit de corps*. He counters the Communist narrative of the revolution by drawing parallels with the Nazis, noting Lenin's debt to Russian terrorism, and arriving at an Orwellian conclusion of power for its own sake: "All totalitarian revolutions were a waste of time, and a complete tragedy. Communism, like other total control systems, had taken the exact form it had because it was a means whereby compulsive terrorists expressed their irrational need to kill and dominate."[49] "Control" is the key term here. Ruxton constantly alerts the reader to the tactical dimension of every historical and political debate that takes place in the novel. The façade of rational discussion thinly masks a perceived purpose in Mai to enact a series of defeats of his prisoners where conviction becomes less important than submission. The power terms in these confrontations become crucial. Not knowing how to submit to Mai can and does lead directly to the shooting of some of the prisoners.

Since Ruxton acts as the leader of these prisoners he too must be put to a physical test. His resultant fatigue from a spell on a treadmill leads to temporary mental collapse as if he has been administered drugs. His consciousness becomes dissociated from his voice (he hears himself saying that the Japanese woman is a spy), and he regresses to the childhood trauma of his parents' separation. What in similar narratives takes chapters to describe is here telescoped so that Van Vogt can confirm his protagonist's credentials for endurance. One of the main points of the novel is that Ruxton does not break under pressure and that he escapes. *The Violent Man* can thus be taken as a fantasy corrective to the national humiliation of Korea. Unlike Pollini, Van Vogt does not deflect Cold War issues onto the protagonist's own cultural values. *The Violent Man* is far less claustrophobic and far less radical a novel than *Night* partly because the debate over contemporary politics between Mai, Ruxton, and other prisoners never quite leads to psychological exploration. It is used by Van Vogt to probe behind the inscrutable surface of Communist Chinese practice and discourse so as to reveal its racism and then to show the hidden purpose behind Project "Future Victory." For if the point was to convert a selection of Westerners, how could Mai kill a number of them so casually? Ruxton finally realizes that the purpose was not conversion but manipulation, so that each member of the group could be turned against the others. This applied terrorism plays out the tactics Van Vogt (and Ruxton) found in Lenin for taking over a state, but the novel replaces utopian goals with the model of an expansive terroristic system running under its own momentum. The grand strategy of Communist world domination is reconfirmed in *The Violent Man* as a means having become an uncontrollable end in itself.

The Violent Man paradoxically combines a questioning attitude toward the capabilities of the mind with a conventional acceptance of Cold War ideology, pointed up in the dustcover to the first edition that states that Seal Ruxton is a "highly intelligent and resourceful American man of action who is confronted by a peculiarly 20th-century dilemma—to become Red or dead." In idealizing his personal qualities Van Vogt uses him as a representation of the United States's most flattering ideological self-image, the nation as active and decisive in unflattering contrast with the wavering of the Europeans (America's NATO allies in miniature?). Unfortunately, by so doing he throws Ruxton into relief against his surroundings, inducing a conviction in the reader that he will win through whatever physical and psychological weapons the Communists use against him. In that respect his struggles come to resemble those of James Bond against SMERSH, without the Bond stories' self-mockery; and his successes constantly reconfirm Van Vogt's premise of superlative qualities. Ruxton's actions therefore can be read as the fantasy compensations for the political stalemates of Korea and other episodes of the Cold War.

The Australian writer Russell Braddon's *When the Enemy Is Tired* (1968), published in the year that the U.S. intelligence ship *Pueblo* was attacked and seized by the North Koreans, also mounts a counternarrative to reports of Western POWs cracking under pressure and collaborating with the Communist enemy. Set in the 1970s, the novel describes a transformed Asia where China has invaded Thailand, taken over Malaya, and is planning an invasion of New Guinea. In this respect it endorses the premise of Communist expansion that informed Western perspectives on Korea. It presents an autobiographical narrative framed within a situation of captivity. Colonel Anthony Russell, an Australian like Braddon himself, has been captured by the Chinese and imprisoned in Changi jail in Singapore. The ironic similarities between Chinese and Japanese imperialism are heavily stressed. The narrative consists mainly of Russell's life history, which his captors are forcing him to write with the eventual goal of publishing reports of his collaboration to distract the Western media from the New Guinea invasion. Parallels with the Korean War abound. Russell has to undergo repeated indoctrination sessions in Communist theory and is isolated from the rest of the men in his group who have been fed the story of his collaboration. The nearest Russell comes to brainwashing is when his captors drug him and through nighttime posthypnotic suggestion convince him that at a given trigger he will imagine that his friends are being executed by the worst means he can imagine.

The central conflict in Braddon's novel takes place between Russell and his Chinese interrogator Major Lim, whose name makes a possible pun on *limn* (to describe). The latter tries to isolate him completely from the outside world by convincing him that he has no rights as a spy and no longer a country to call home because the Australian government thinks he is dead. Lim's boast is: "We're going to make a new man of you," but Russell ridicules him for "trying to brainwash an old has-been."[50] All the artillery of totalitarianism is deployed against Russell. His cell is bugged, monitored by CCTV, his writing is analyzed by computer for weaknesses, and drugs are secretly mixed with his food. He has been forced to sign letters published in Australia but disguises his handwriting deliberately. In a similar way the captain of the *Pueblo* signed letters in ludicrously stilted English where the style was intended as a give-away.[51] In an appreciative review that drew parallels with Koestler and Orwell, Martin Levin argues that the basic method to "restructure Russell's personality" is through "compulsory reminiscence."[52] Russell's memoir therefore offers him the only refuge against Lim's probing: "Misled by the tidy paragraphs and unagitated hand, his enemy would detect in them [his paragraphs] none of the intricate gossamer strength of carefully woven words: he could hide from Lim, deep inside the woven words."[53] The standard Communist procedure of compulsory self-examination through written autobiography is here transformed into a means of covert resistance by Russell. However, neither in this memoir nor in the dialogues between Lim and Russell, which take up only a minor part of the novel, does Russell's subjectivity ever seem in real danger of collapsing. Lim is clever rather than demonic, but ultimately not quite clever enough. His aim is to persuade Russell to make a broadcast similar to the admissions of germ warfare in Korea, but Russell's will proves too strong for him. The final twist in the novel comes when Lim has Russell repatriated, since this gives the Australian military the problem of proving whether he was a genuine POW or a collaborator or even a spy. At the end Russell laughs at the irony that the Australians are asking him to write his story just like the Chinese. His response reflects a lack of anxiety over his homecoming although the hero's welcome is replaced by solitary confinement and a fresh sequence of interrogation. However, the point has been made to the reader, who has been granted a unique access to his consciousness, that he never did give in. And so he is spared the stigma of collaboration. A further account of the Pueblo Incident was the memoir written by the boat's commander. *Bucher: My Story* (1970) was essentially yet another captivity narrative describing the commander's resistance to his Korean captors' attempts to make him sign a confession to spying.

■ Later Korean POW fiction continues the search to understand what happened to the POWs and continues to interrogate how the United States comes to terms with that war. Jack Lynn's *The Turncoat* (1976) combines political thriller with psychological narrative to explore why a POW would have refused repatriation. The eponymous turncoat is Corporal Gerald Hawthorne, who endures years of captivity but who returns to the United States only in 1961. The attempts of Washington-financed mobsters to keep him silent gradually bring to light a cover-up (the novel was published only three years after Watergate) of the fact that highly placed members of the government and army had been selling military secrets to China in the 1950s. The arrival of

Hawthorne in the West thus carries a national symbolism: "Journalists were treating the event cautiously as though Hawthorne were an ugly thought which had been hidden away and forgotten." The last term suggests that Hawthorne personifies the whole Korean War insofar as he carries the memory of national betrayal from that period, and as a carrier of secret information he is perceived to pose a potential threat: "He might have been programmed by the Chinese for a delayed explosion. It's been done before," a senator warns.[54] The allusion to *The Manchurian Candidate* is clear, but the only "explosion" that occurs is an outburst of sexual not political violence, since Hawthorne, like Raymond Shaw, proves to have an oedipal attachment to his mother so severe that it amounts to psychosis.

The protagonist of *The Turncoat* was not actually brainwashed. Instead, his lenient treatment in Korea contrasts ironically with his experiences in the United States before and after captivity. The novel is punctuated with moments of ideological repositioning by its main characters. Hawthorne becomes Chinese in many respects but retains U.S. citizenship. The senator who champions his cause and reveals the conspiracy declares: "*I have decided to declare war against the United States.*"[55] The enigma of why Hawthorne apparently collaborated, narrated through flashbacks as in *Sword and Scalpel*, is thus not only a personal issue but also shades into a larger question of national betrayal. Hawthorne's suicide is synchronized with political revelations, and both events mark a collective purging of the recent American past.

The main irony of Slaughter's *Sword and Scalpel* lies in the critical light the novel sheds on the very institutions attempting a literal interpellation of the protagonist as traitor. Throughout the novel's present Scott remains a quiet, even acquiescent figure, like Benjamin Beer, the protagonist (also a medic) of Stephen Becker's *Dog Tags* (1973), where the charge of fraternization is leveled by other POWs in situ. Beer is not only passive but also unclear about his own experience. Pushed and pulled by the rival groups in his prison camp, he can only ask himself questions (after the armistice, "had he been purified?" for instance) that never take the form of institutional investigation. One reason may be the late date of Becker's novel, which inevitably suggests a distance from the Korean War. This distance has assumed the dimension of a generation in Frederick Busch's *War Babies* (1989), where a symbolic rapprochement between POWs who died and those who collaborated is sought through a love affair between the daughter of one of the former and the son of one of the latter. The romantic treatment sits awkwardly with such a complex subject and leaves the one description of psychological torture hanging in a vacuum. Rather like the "glockenspiel" described in Paul Gallico's *Trial by Terror*, the result is a radical disorientation: "The repeated thudding became for the men inside the sound of time itself, abstracted and refined, perfected. [The released] found the world a silent place in which time grew slow and soggy, unmarked."[56] By this stage in the novel the narrator Pete Santore has taken it upon himself to write out the forgotten story of the prisoners, concentrating on their hardships and performing the function of historical witness.

Korean POW fiction demonstrates the sheer difficulty of writing such stories because in this context narrative coherence would imply that the author has arrived at a lucid sense of events. Instead, these novels focus on investigatory plot sequences or on local interrogation scenes where the protagonist's deepest assumptions about his relation to his culture are brought under pressure. This chapter has deliberately avoided any more than a brief mention of the most famous novel and film to engage with the Korean subject— *The Manchurian Candidate*, which in its own right forms the subject of the next chapter.

five

The Manchurian Candidate

The *Manchurian Candidate* (novel 1958; film 1962) has become a classic of the Cold War in its depiction of a Communist-programmed assassin gunning down an American politician. It capitalized on a number of incidents from the Korean War, for instance, alluding in its title to the holding camps across the Manchurian border where the indoctrination of POWs was particularly intensive. A 1953 CIA report stated that POWs leaving North Korea via the Soviet Union "apparently had a blank period or period of disorientation while passing through a special zone in Manchuria."[1] Glossing this passage after researching the military use of hypnosis from World War II onward, Alan Scheflin has stated that "by 1953 . . . the notion of the Manchurian Candidate in almost those exact terms, had been theorized by the CIA."[2] Eugene Kinkead reported the U.S. Army's discovery that a number of American prisoners had been trained to return to the United States as "sleepers" (dormant agents) and then refrain from spying for a period of years.[3] The title phrase passed into general usage after John Marks published his 1979 study *The Search for the "Manchurian Candidate."* Although he could not find a specific instance after examining thousands of declassified documents, Marks concluded that such an assassin was possible. Subsequently a Manchurian Candidate has been defined as a "person who has been hypnotized to the extent that he/she is willing to perform atrocious crimes, such as assassinations, without fail, and against the 'candidate's' own will. Manchurian Candidates are set into motion by 'trigger' phrases, hand signals, tone combinations or sequences."[4]

There is no suggestion in Eugene Kinkead's *In Every War but One* that hypnosis or any other mind-altering process was used on Korean POWs. For that possibility we have to turn to George H. Estabrooks, a specialist in applied hypnosis. Estabrooks served during and after World War II in U.S. Army Intelligence. It has been argued that from as early as 1942 (years before the term "brainwashing" was coined) Estabrooks was engaged in producing Manchurian Candidates for military purposes. He himself has recorded how his wartime activities included preparing "hypnotic couriers" to carry secret information that could only be accessed by those who knew the relevant trigger phrases.[5] John Marks has rightly drawn attention to Estabrooks's 1945 novel *Death in the Mind* (written with Richard Lockridge) as a precursor to *The Manchurian Candidate* in its treatment of the hypnotically conditioned assassin.[6] The novel is set in the United States in 1942 and establishes a context of inexplicable acts by Allied personnel who have apparently willfully destroyed their own boats in suicidal actions. This opens the mystery dimension to the plot, which extends into the problematic allegiances of American Germans now that the United States has entered the war. In tandem with this investigation goes a gradual explanation of the possible military applications of hypnosis and a relentless questioning of the commonsense position stated by one character that "You can't—psychologize a man into treason."[7] The related conviction that no hypnotic subject can be persuaded to do anything against his will is quietly questioned, and the reader receives instruction on hypnosis even through footnote references in the text. To counteract the distanced reports of military action (and to add a romantic interest) the girl-friend of the investigator receives a record in the mail containing a strange voice repeating over and over the words "forward" and "falling." This is later explained as the "sway test" to identify potential subjects for hypnosis. And indeed she is subsequently conditioned to act as a courier. The operating of this process, triggered by the phrase "I want you to listen very carefully" (exactly the same strategy is used in Len Deighton's *The Ipcress File*) produces an unusual tension between inner and outer modes of description. When Madeline feels the influence of her German director, "it was as if a memory of something unpleasant had welled up, through the pleasant moment." The key effect is one of bewilderment, but the novel can best convey this through a hypothetical observer. Thus lines like "there seemed to be anger in her eyes" convey a minimal external effect. The novel attempts to prove its own plausibility but at the same time demonstrates the difficulties of expressing its subject. One character glosses the title by declaring: "It—it's a kind of death in their minds. Only what *results* is tangible."⁸ Consequence replaces direct representation and the unusual grammar of the novel's title spatializes the mind as a living area within which a segment dies and at the same time leaves the door ajar to perceptual error, only an imagined death.

Death in the Mind shows saboteurs being prepared for single tasks, but in his monograph on hypnotism Estabrooks explains how the "Super Spy" can be produced by inducing layered personalities. Aware of the fantastic nature of his subject, Estabrooks introduces his chapter "Hypnotism in Warfare" with denials that his account was taken from "mystery novels," but insists that his "Super Spy" would have a layered personality whose complexity would actually defy fiction. Thus, Personality A (the waking one) might be rabidly Communist while Personality B is the very opposite. Although B might include memories of A, the converse will not be true, and a shift from A to B would be triggered by a code phrase. Such spies would have a special advantage: "Convinced of their own innocence, they would play the fifth column role with the utmost sincerity, and . . . this conviction of innocence would probably be their greatest protection." Estabrooks presents the subjectivity of suitable candidates as a *tabula rasa* on which different personalities can be imprinted. What he calls a "synthetic hypnotic spy with a dual personality" would be virtually undetectable, and the induction processes could be used to prepare men to be "completely immune to this so-called brainwashing technique." Estabrooks conflates Pavlovian research with posthypnotic suggestion and even boasts, after glancing at the Moscow trials and the Korean "confessions": "We have definite ideas as to how these ends are attained and undoubtedly could do just as well in this matter of brainwashing as our communist friends, if we so wished."⁹ After conducting research into Estabrooks's papers and CIA documents from the 1950s, the Canadian psychiatrist Colin Ross concluded that Estabrooks participated extensively in secret programs that attempted to use a combination of sodium amytal and posthypnotic suggestion to induce amnesia barriers and implant false memories as a method for controlling secret agents.¹⁰ In short, without Richard Condon being in a position to know it, the experimental procedures were in place by the late 1950s to produce exactly the programmed assassin he was to describe in his novel.

According to Condon's friend Walter Bowart, who published *Operation Mind Control* in 1978, Condon read the works of Pavlov and the hypnosis specialist Andrew Salter (who viewed hypnosis as part of conditioned reflexes), then "invented the rest because it was a pretty basic premise." Also, William Jennings Bryan, the California hypnotist, was brought in as technical consultant for the movie adaptation of Condon's novel. Bryan had served as director of an air force survival project and coined the term "Powerized" to suggest that the U2 pilot Gary Powers had been brainwashed.[11]

As we shall see, events took over the fortunes of this film since the Kennedy assassination led to the withdrawal of *The Manchurian Candidate* from circulation for some fifteen years. Debate over its premises overlapped into hypotheses about the Kennedy killing. George Estabrooks admitted in 1968 that Oswald and Ruby "could very well have been performing through hypnosis" and earlier the ex-FBI agent Lincoln Lawrence's *Were We Controlled?* (1967) hypothesized that methods of behavior control could shed light on the event. Thus Oswald could have been directed by Radio-Hypnotic Intracerebral Control (RHIC) activated by a radio signal.[12] According to Lawrence (a pseudonym), Oswald gained insights into Soviet research on electronic brain stimulation and was then programmed as a sleeper to infiltrate the United States. Meanwhile, the same process was applied to Jack Ruby to ensure he killed Oswald. Lawrence produces a fascinating conspiracy narrative centering on unnamed individuals referred to simply as "The Group" who wanted to engineer the assassination to make a massive stock market killing. A similar case to Lawrence's has been made by Frank Camper who argues in *The MK/Ultra Secret* (1996) that the assassination was carried out by a team of disgruntled figures on the political Right and that Oswald could have been a subject in the CIA mind control project of the 1950s. This cannot be the place to consider the proliferating explanations of the Kennedy assassination. Suffice it to note that speculation went down a path suggested by *The Manchurian Candidate*. Indeed, Richard Condon himself was to make his own contribution to the conspiracy fiction, relating to Kennedy's death in his novels *Winter Kills* (1974) and *Death of a Politician* (1978).[13]

■ Condon's most famous novel combines three elements in its title: the threatening Chinese alien (Fu Manchu), American politics, and specific allusions to Korea. Condon deploys a number of Chinese references throughout *The Manchurian Candidate*. In particular, his oriental conspirator Yen Lo is compared to Fu Manchu at one point, and in fact one of Sax Rohmer's novels uncannily anticipates the theme and treatment of Condon's novel. *President Fu Manchu* (1936) describes a right-wing plot to install a "coming

Hitler" in the White House. Fu Manchu presides over an underground network of agents, and he drugs the half-brother of the presidential candidate to
shoot the candidate at Carnegie Hall on hearing a trigger-word. The use of a
process that seems to combine drugs with posthypnotic suggestion to inter-
fere with the U.S. presidential campaign clearly anticipates *The Manchurian
Candidate* and suggests that the Cold War themes merely continue those of
an older Yellow Peril tradition.

During the Korean War, POW camps designed for intensive interrogation
and "reeducation" were built along the Yalu River, either within Korea or
across the border in Manchuria. And it is now certain that these interrogations were conducted primarily by the Chinese under Russian supervision.
The Manchurian Candidate (1958) tapped into fears that had been circulating throughout the 1950s that the Communists had developed irresistible
techniques of mind alteration, embodying them in a narrative where the
public celebration of military heroism in a returning GI and the promotion
by that same soldier's family of impeccably right-wing politics prove to be
masking a Communist conspiracy. The fact that Raymond Shaw has been
betrayed by his mother, who further manipulates the political career of his
McCarthy-like father substitute John Iselin, carries a particularly pointed
political irony, since throughout the 1950s the nuclear family was promoted
as a cultural bulwark against Communism. The Department of Defense
film *Red Nightmare* specifically dramatizes the Communist takeover of a
small American town as a subversion of the family unit where children and
mother turn informer against the "deviationist" father. In Condon's novel
the family itself has become the source of Communist subversion.

The narrative opens with an episode of public celebration when the "war
hero" Raymond Shaw returns home from Korea; but then Condon, as Joe
Sanders has pointed out, characteristically "works backward into the past."[14]
In effect we have two diametrically opposed narrative processes at work that
are counterpointed against each other. There is the Communist plan, growing out of a 1936 dream of Beria's and targeting the Republican convention
of 1960—the imminent future when the novel was first published. Against
this there is a series of retrospective segments revealing the nature of that
plan and the personal past of Raymond Shaw's mother. Throughout the
novel melodrama alternates with political satire, the latter merging initially
in Shaw's perception of a distance between feeling and behavior ("I am playing the authentic war buddy"). This sense of performing a required role signals a disparity between personal and public that progressively widens as the

novel unfolds. Far from being the expression of a purely personal predicament, his words introduce a radical dissociation between public events and concealed planning, which ultimately gives the novel its melodrama.

The second chapter suspends the initial narrative in order to describe the Russo-Chinese plan of creating a "perfectly prefabricated assassin." "Prefabricated" also describes the Research Pavilion erected in North Korea where the brainwashing will take place. The pieces of the building metonymically encapsulate the efficiency of the plan in fitting together like a jigsaw puzzle. Condon uses an anonymous third-person narrator who introduces the novel's technical theme thus: "Conditioning, called brain-washing by the news agencies, is the production of reactions in the human organism through the use of associative reflexes."[15] When Shaw's patrol is captured, Condon only goes through the form of describing the brainwashing they receive. We are told of "implantation" and "originating processes" that function through suggestion and implication. Once this subject has been introduced, Yen Lo, the Chinese director of the project, takes over explaining to his audience the feasibility of inducing in the subject the necessity of "submitting to the Operator's demands." He performs a necessary expository function in disposing of the reader's objections to the possibility of brainwashing by quoting chapter and verse from Eastern and Western experts. Shortly after the novel was published Condon wrote to Henry Morgan in terms that directly echo Yen Lo's statements: "For years people have been telling us that it is impossible to hypnotise anyone into doing anything that was against their best interests or (b) contrary to their moral natures. Poppycock it is. . . . Brainwashing and hypnosis are handmaidens. . . . There is a full literature on brainwashing in our public libraries and all procedures I outlined in *The Manchurian Candidate* have been authenticated."[16] Condon gave the process plausibility within the novel by describing the aftereffects rather than the programming itself and by his insistent use of technological terms as if Yen Lo were constructing a machine. Indeed the most powerful moments in this scene occur when Shaw kills two of his platoon without batting an eyelid on Yen Lo's orders. Yen Lo's ideal is a conflation of engineering and psychiatry to achieve "precision in psychological design" and his plan involves periodical services where his subject will be "refueled"; that is, the subject's conditioning will be tested and if necessary reinforced.

Condon borrows the discourse of mechanism from contemporary discussions of brainwashing and Pavlovian psychology to underline the total malleability of his subjects' sense of reality. So the soldiers in the captured American platoon imagine they are staying in an American hotel, drinking Coca-Cola, when actually they are drinking Chinese tea. Walter Bowart has written that Condon "brought the Fu Manchu myth up to date," but Yen Lo also combines elements of Svengali in demonstrating his hypnotic prowess through acts performed on a stage.[17] In a letter of 1959 Condon stressed the centrality to his novel of brainwashing and insisted that it had become a routine social process because "people act against their own best interests every day." Similarly, as if he had read Estabrooks, he declared: "Brainwashing and hypnosis are handmaidens."[18] If the ideal aim of brainwashing is total control of another, the subject inevitably approaches the robotic. However good a simulation Shaw may be, he still remains just that, an imitation man. His eyes give the game away years later to his sole friend from Korea, Ben Marco: "The only fault with the lighting circuit was behind his eyes. Raymond may have believed that his eyes did light up, but unfortunately they could shine only within the extent of his art as a counterfeiter of emotions."[19] Ironically it is Marco who comments on this motif when Shaw expresses amazement at his pick-up routines, complaining to the latter "what do you think I am—a zombie?" But it is Shaw who is encased in a "suit of stifling armor," not Marco.

Two terms in this novel are twinned and foregrounded: "brainwashing" and "assassin." Indeed the main epigraph to *The Manchurian Candidate* is an encyclopedia entry on the Order of Assassins. This term, however, is not exclusively attached to Shaw. From a routine fact of Stalinist political life, it is then applied to Shaw, Chunjin (the Communist "guide" who sets up the platoon's capture in Korea and who then resurfaces in New York as Shaw's home help), and Senator Iselin, who is described as an assassin of character. Of course it is primarily a term situated within the Communist covert operations and loaded with connotations of secrecy, fanaticism, and the technological exploitation of human subjects. In the same year as the novel's publication there appeared a study of Trotsky's assassin that concluded that the killer "turns out to be the prototype of the coming race as seen from Moscow in her universalist role of the mother of all nations. It is a race in which man and machine alike will be harnessed twins. . . . Beneath the mask of the prisoner in Mexico lurks the Kremlin's happy robot of the future."[20] Shaw too is described throughout as a masked figure who can never quite gain access to his true feelings because quite simply he is being directed by impulses screened from his own control. This notion clearly gave some reviewers problems with the novel. The writer Pat Frank complained that, though the initial idea was good, Condon "drifts into the implausible and the incredible," and Thomas B. Sherman stated defensively that "this novel is so fantastically macabre as to be acceptable only as science fiction."[21] In fact, *The Manchurian Candidate* shifts between a number of different genres, including melodrama and satire, and it approaches science fiction particularly when Condon conveys the extent of Shaw's self-alienation.[22] To Marco he seems at times like a Martian, probably an allusion to the 1953 movie *Invaders from Mars*, where the invaders implant devices in the base of their victims' skulls and thus transform them into obedient zombies. When his mother speaks to him, it is "like trying to have a whispered conversation with someone on a distant star."[23]

Shaw's isolation would be total were it not for the arrival of Ben Marco, whose recurring nightmares of Korea push him to the brink of total collapse. Marco's seizures represent the symptoms missing from Shaw. Indeed memory becomes a crucial defining factor of humanity in the novel since it involves recalling Shaw's "experimental" killings under orders.[24] Marco's nightmares also have an important political symbolism in that they suggest the posthypnotic amnesia in the brainwashing has been less than successful.[25] Therefore, in his comparisons between *The Manchurian Candidate* and Condon's other novels, Joe Sanders is only partly correct to state that "each novel focuses on a device of control, a tool that a character in the novel has managed to systematise until it can be used with scientific precision."[26] Whether "device of control" means brainwashing in general or the trigger-phrase in particular, Shaw demonstrates his humanity by being an inefficient tool in his manipulators' hands; he is induced to jump into a Central Park lake by taking an American colloquialism literally. Furthermore Shaw never ceases to be a self-conscious subject, however alienated. He understands that his self is a private space liable to invasion. When he first hears of brainwashing he rejects the notion because he cannot "abide the thought of anybody tampering with his person." Shaw's extended dialogue with Marco throughout the novel involves Marco trying to persuade him that this personal space was violated long ago. So Marco declares: "They made you into a killer. They are inside your mind now, Raymond, and you are helpless. You are a host body and they are feeding on you."[27] He expresses Shaw's brainwashing as a kind of parasitism where he is being slowly consumed, implicitly aligning this process with earlier 1950s narratives of takeover like Heinlein's *The Puppet Masters* (1951) or *Invasion of the Body Snatchers* (1956). In all these cases the visible signs of the subject acting under the influence are identical: acquiescence and obedience, physical automatism, and a loss of individuating color from their speech. Shaw internalizes this metaphor as an invasion of his bodily space but only registers fear when he experiences a memory lapse. This void in his consciousness and the related figure of his deep mind being "sealed off" from the American investigators both pave the way for the final revelation of his psyche.

Raymond Shaw's loss of autonomy is expressed stylistically through passive verbs or through an evocation of other forces acting on him. So the queen of diamonds, a visual cue, begins to open up controlled memories: "They began to order him, through Marco, to unlock all the great jade doors which went back, back, back, along an austere corridor in time to the old, old man with the withered, merry smile who said his name was Yen Lo and who promised him solemnly that in other lives, through which he would journey beyond this life, he would be spared the unending agony which he had found in this life."[28] This process of recall resembles the gradual uncovering of the repressed in Freudian psychiatry and leads up to an acknowledgement to Marco of the truth, not in any way similar, however, to the forced confessions described in *Darkness at Noon* or *Nineteen Eighty-Four*. As we have seen and will see again in brainwashing narratives, the individual subject is so radically estranged from the induced psychic material that he or she could cooperate, as does Shaw, in the process of investigation because it appears to be happening to another. The real crisis of subjectivity comes when the individual begins to doubt cherished beliefs about the self, like autonomy or continuous memory.

In a publicity statement for *The Manchurian Candidate* Condon explained that the novel "tends to point out that life without love is pointless" and the two significant female figures other than Shaw's mother both perform the role of therapist.[29] During his teens, Shaw meets Jocie Jordan, the daughter of a Democratic senator, just after he has been bitten by a snake. Jocie then sucks the poison from the wound, a metaphor of the "poison" instilled in him by his mother. Similarly when he is on the brink of collapse, Marco meets Rosie Cheyney, who takes an immediate liking to him and who starts the healing process by enabling him to sleep for the first time in months.

Both these young women act as foils to Shaw's mother, the real villain of the novel. At about the time when Condon was beginning to plan the novel, his wife started an early morning television course on Greek literature. From watching this Condon conceived the purpose of writing a "classical tragedy in the classical form."[30] As a result, Shaw's mother is introduced into the novel as a Clytemnestra, with Shaw playing Orestes avenging his betrayed father. Stanley Friedman has identified a similar grouping of characters but related it to a Shakespearean original: "Shaw acts as a debased Hamlet, while the villainous Mrs. Iselin is an extremely degraded Gertrude. Shaw's stepfather, who seeks to gain the presidency through murderous means, serves as a lesser Claudius; Senator Jordan and his daughter become parallels to Polonius and Ophelia; and Bennet Marco, Shaw's friend, the man who helps him achieve his victory, is a dim reflection of Horatio."[31] These analogies and resemblances shift from section to section of the novel. For a time Shaw and Jocie act out the roles of Romeo and Juliet, the lovers crossed by feuding families. In all these cases, however, Shaw's mother's role stays consistently autocratic and manipulative. She personifies the "destroying mother" that Philip Wylie made notorious in his indictment of shifted gender roles in American society, *Generation of Vipers* (1942). What Wylie designates "momism" involves an emasculation of men and a possession of sons through a power play masquerading as maternal love.[32]

Raymond's mother, whose title is used as an insistent designation throughout the novel, embodies all the negative predatory traits in Wylie's account.[33] Condon is so eager to confirm this role that he overloads her with negative significance, describing her as a female Fu Manchu (wearing a brightly colored Chinese housecoat), witch, "mail-order goddess," morphine addict, and sexual predator. She reduces her husband to impotence and forces Raymond to fill the sexual gap left by her father, with whom she had been having an incestuous relationship. Families are central to Condon's fiction and it is revealing that he opens his foreword to Walter Bowart's *Operation Mind Control* by describing acts of parental betrayal by the father of Grock the clown and by "our Father who art in the American secret police."[34] In *The Manchurian Candidate* the materialistic psychology of Pavlovian conditioning is counterbalanced by a Freudian drama playing itself out within Shaw's family group. He is obsessed with his absent father, projecting his feelings of love and hate onto the mother. At the beginning of the novel, Shaw seeks out the father of a soldier he has unwittingly killed and briefly performs the role of proxy son to the grieving mother. He then finds a replacement father in Senator Jordan (whose wife is dead, significantly) only to be directed to shoot him. Finally, at the party convention that concludes the novel, Shaw has broken sufficiently free from his conditioning to kill Iselin and his mother before turning the rifle on himself. Condon composed the novel from the ending forward to the beginning. The presidential nominating convention was to be the "terminal point" where the brainwashing and the tensions within Shaw's family drama erupted into the most public violence.[35]

Condon himself classified his novel in the following way: *"The Manchurian Candidate* is a political adventure story. This has been a highly popular novel form for many hundreds of years."[36] Within this subgenre he cites Sinclair Lewis's 1935 warning of the rise of fascism in America, *It Can't Happen Here*, Robert Penn Warren's novel about Huey Long, *All the King's Men* (1946), and William J. Lederer and Eugene Burdick's *The Ugly American* (1958). Having established these precedents, Condon built *The Manchurian Candidate* partly around satirical parallels between Senator Iselin and Joe McCarthy. The point was, as he explained to a reviewer from the *Detroit News:* "My book devoted 311 pages to loathsome characters presented larger than life in an effort to suggest an imperative idea which cannot be expressed in any form too often: that we must re-examine our homogenous condition of national political gullibility: that we must cease this insistence upon being governed by inferiors."[37] As we shall see, Condon extends the notion of brainwashing to include the vulnerability of the electorate to media exploitation.

McCarthy is represented in the novel by Senator John Yerkes Iselin (named after the Chicago speculator Charles Yerkes, whose career gave Theodore Dreiser the plot for his *Trilogy of Desire*) and Robert Shaw's mother. Condon split McCarthy into two roles: "the male to be satirised and understated, the female to be melodramatised and overstated."[38] Iselin then personifies the bluster and the physical resemblance while his wife represents ambition, strategy, and political PR. Her role throughout the novel is to be the power behind the scenes, manipulating Iselin, who supplies the public face of right-wing causes. Among the Richard Condon papers at Boston University is a special issue of the *Progressive* for April 1954, *McCarthy. A Documented Record*, which supplied Condon with most of his factual data for the Iselin–McCarthy parallels. From this record he selected mainly the details that would trigger the reader's recognition, such as his early wheeling and dealing as a judge, the fact that he wore built-up shoes, and the fraudulent claim in McCarthy's campaign literature that he had seen combat in World War II. Condon transposes the field of action from the South Pacific to the Arctic, where Iselin's only wounding is being bitten in the foot by an Eskimo woman during a sexual fracas.[39] Condon nimbly combines elements of farce and threat in describing the activities of Iselin and his wife. Shaw's mother is never named and emerges therefore as the personification of a particular kind of political activity, even as a force, which she had been planning from the age of sixteen at the very least. Iselin only enters the novel's account when she takes him over. In other words, he is her stooge, being instructed at every turn by her. Their dialogue "behind the scenes" comes straight out of gangster movies and implies a hard-bitten cynicism about the democratic process that the narrator makes explicit as a "conviction that the Republic was a humbug [and] the electorate rabble."[40]

It is suggested again and again that politics is a kind of theatre. Shaw's mother is a consummate actress, knowing exactly how to use her sexuality for political favors. The blundering Iselin, however, has to be coached at every step. So the McCarthy catchphrase, "point of order" (which he used constantly in committees), is suggested by Iselin's wife as a means of making a dramatic exit when all he wants is to relieve his bladder. The theatrical dimension reaches its high point toward the end of the novel in a fancy dress reception on Long Island, where the Iselins don the guises of "honest dairy farmers," a facetious glance at McCarthy's campaign among Wisconsin farmers for election to the Senate.

In a novel focusing heavily on espionage and conspiracy, we might logically expect Condon to stress disguise and the untrustworthy nature of appearances, but this question bears specifically on the reception of McCarthyism. McCarthy's opponents repeatedly drew two analogies: with Hitler (most famously by Eisenhower's brother) and with the very Communists he was attacking. To cite only one from many possible examples, the atomic scientist Harold C. Urey declared: "I don't believe the U.S.S.R. has a better agent in the country than Senator McCarthy."[41] This was scarcely hyperbole, because the same complaint was voiced so widely within America and abroad. By weakening the links within the Western alliance McCarthy was unconsciously realizing the aims of Stalin's foreign policy. Condon built this perception into the novel by literally making Shaw's mother one of the top Soviet agents in the United States. In this way Condon demonstrates a bizarre identification of political positions from the extreme right and left. For this reason it has been argued that he was parodying Robert Welch's *The Politician* (circulating in manuscript since 1954), which claimed that Eisenhower was a Communist-directed pawn constantly working against U.S. interests. Welch, a pioneer of the John Birch Society, saw containment as a "crime" and appeasement as "folly" since the Soviets had constantly bested the United States in situations like the conclusion of the Korean War.[42] *The Manchurian Candidate* could thus be read as melodramatic fantasy on the failure of containment where the innermost parts of the American political establishment are penetrated by Communist conspiracy. Robert Shaw's fate enacts in individual terms just such a penetration of the body politic.

In *The Manchurian Candidate* satire and melodrama meet. Condon articulates the absurdity *and* danger in McCarthy by making Iselin both a fool and the darling of the American extreme Right and by having Shaw's mother express anger at her son when he falls in love with the daughter of a Democratic senator. This anger emerges through a pastiche of McCarthy's rhetoric characteristically prefaced by an accusation that the senator is a "Russian agent": "Well, we *are* at war. It's a cold war but it will get worse and worse until every man and woman and child in this country will have to stand up and be counted to say whether or not he or she is on the side of right and freedom."[43] This harangue is named a "filibuster" in the narrative appropriately because it blurs the domains of public and private rhetoric.

The melodrama of *The Manchurian Candidate* is shot through with irony, especially in scenes that contain Iselin or Shaw's mother. Condon gradually reveals the latter's cynical manipulations of the American political system and then late in the novel presents a cryptic dialogue between a Soviet agent and a figure who is referred to simply as "Raymond's operator." Of course, this figure proves to be his mother, and Condon achieves an internal plausibility in this identification by representing her as a single-trait character who exists through power functions. Raymond's mother embodies the contradictions of the American Right in their most stark form. Driven by an obsession to "save" the United States from its enemies and to wage a "holy crusade" against national betrayal, she actually adopts the role she projects on to supposed left-wingers. She evokes crisis when she addresses Shaw like an Old Testament prophet: "Blood will gush behind the noise and stones will fall and fools and mockers will be brought down. The smugness and complacency of this country will be dragged through the blood and the noise in the streets until it becomes a country purged and purified back to original purity, which it once possessed so long ago when the founding fathers of this republic—the blessed, blessed fathers—brought it into life."[44] Briefly, she composes a jeremiad on the shortcoming of the United States reminiscent of the Christian nationalism of the extreme Right.[45] Her lines are heavy with irony, however, since she was responsible for killing Shaw's father. Within the context of a largely secular novel, the agency of this retribution is left unspecified but the style itself expresses nostalgia for the certainties of manifest destiny. In his analysis of the confrontation between McCarthy and Ed Murrow, Robert L. Ivie argues that the senator lost the exchange because of his insensitivity to a substructure of metaphor (where Communism was equated with darkness, for instance).[46] Quite simply Mc-

Carthy was a linguistic incompetent, whereas Shaw's mother can "put on" any rhetoric she chooses.

The crowning irony here is that this spokeswoman for the extreme Right is acting out the role of a Stalinist agent—her peroration just quoted is prefaced symbolically by her putting "steel" into her voice. This melodramatic coincidence functions consistently within Condon's satirical perspective on the rise of the American Right by combining within a single person both extremes of the political spectrum. Condon himself wanted *The Manchurian Candidate* to evoke a set of circumstances "where the purposes of the Soviet Union, as they regarded the United States, and those of a U.S. Senator much like the late Joe McCarthy were seen to be identical."[47] The broad outlines of McCarthy's career could be taken as read so Condon only needed to supply a parodic summary of Iselin's antics. What is more important is to notice the dovetailing of the Communist conspiracy (dated from 1936, the year when Shaw's mother starts her relationship with Iselin) with Iselin's rise to power. Shaw's mother in short performs a crucial linking role between these two sequences, and in her split role represents the charges of McCarthy's opponents made flesh. The divisions within her role bear no possibility of resolution and Condon ends his novel in a violent burst of melodramatic irony. Trained to assassinate a presidential nominee, Shaw instead turns his rifle on his step-father, mother, and then himself. The final shot is described as "short, sharp, and clean," as if to suggest that Shaw ultimately acts on a conception of military honor that restores the status quo intact.

■ *The Manchurian Candidate* is of course equally famous as a movie. It seemed initially that its political subject might present a serious obstacle to the film being made. Reportedly James Mason told Frank Sinatra that a main role should be his, perhaps because he had starred in the 1954 thriller *Suddenly*, where he played the leader of a gang out to assassinate the U.S. president. The director of United Artists initially refused the project because, as Richard Condon explained, "the novel's plot somewhat revolved around a character not unlike the late Senator Joseph McCarthy who had been well patronized by the President's father and brother." In the event Sinatra approached Kennedy directly and the president told him he "admired the novel and had no objections to a film being made of it."[48]

The 1962 adaptation of *The Manchurian Candidate* combines as many genres as the novel. Its prologue seems a straightforward war action; the first scenes after the credits appear to show a quasi-documentary account of a war hero coming home; and the film combines elements of a murder mystery with the twist that the murderer has no idea that he is the perpetrator of the deeds. The central subject of brainwashing functions here to destabilize these genres by gradually revealing a dislocation between public and private similar to that we have seen in the novel.[49] There is scarcely a glimpse of this in the first scene after the prologue, which shows Raymond Shaw's return home shot as a news item. The commentator announces solemnly about the medal of honor: "this nation guards its highest award for valor jealously." This voice articulates a collectivity that comes under pressure immediately as personal animosity is revealed between Shaw and his father-in-law. As we shall see, the ironic gap between the returning "hero" and the ballyhoo his mother has organized encourages the viewer to question the authenticity of such ceremonies.

Up to this point, however, the real has remained intact. The first challenge to the viewer's presumptions of stable normality takes place in a brilliantly managed scene framed by two shots of Ben Marco having a nightmare where Shaw's platoon are demonstrating their submission to conditioning by the Communist authorities. The shooting script for the film establishes the "nightmare" as a women's gardening society meeting in a New Jersey hotel. The chairlady is being watched by Marco. Then "as he looks at her a curious thing happens. The chairlady changes slowly into an elderly and rather sinister-looking Chinese gentleman."[50] The film avoided such potentially awkward transformations. As Greil Marcus noted, "the sequence is set up as a dream, but it doesn't come off the screen as a dream, doesn't come off as a blur, with soft edges, dissolves, milky tones—it's severe, mathematical, a fact, true."[51] All the images are crisp and clear, and the whole scene revolves around incongruities, starting with why a group of U.S. soldiers should be sitting with the chairlady while she holds forth on hydrangeas. The camera does a slow 360-degree pan, coming to rest this time on a Chinese speaker in a small lecture theater. As the panning continues the speaker's statements about brainwashing are taken up by the chairlady in her same genteel idiom, by which time a total mismatch has been established between words and appearances. John Frankenheimer explained that the dream sequences were crucial because they would show what really happened: "What I had to do here was really *show* the brainwashing."[52] On the release of the film he had made the same point: "I've tried to tell this story to friends verbally several times and always failed . . . [t]o make this wild plot believable—and I want people to believe it and take it seriously—every scene had to be done with the utmost reality and clarity."[53] The method he chose was to have a slow-paced scene apparently shot from a circling camera that took the characters in at least six combinations: the POWs on the New Jersey stage, the women delivering the lines of the Communists, and so on. This method produced what Frankenheimer described as the scene's "surrealistic quality." Then the same scene was replayed with black actresses performing in the dream of the black member of Shaw's patrol. In the first dream the killing of the GI is represented by that soldier falling violently backward, but in the second Frankenheimer introduced the symbolic detail of the GI's blood splashing the huge portrait of Stalin in the background. The maintenance of the decorum of the women's meeting becomes the chilling context for Shaw to kill another member of his platoon. The viewer is presented with a paradox: how can two totally dissimilar situations occupy the same scenic space? The answer is, only if we understand we are watching a depiction of the brainwashing process. By keeping the details of these shots naturalistic, Frankenheimer disorients the viewer and blocks our capacity to draw back from the whole concept of brainwashing.

A second scene framed as a nightmare by a black soldier in this same platoon follows a similar procedure, this time showing black women in the meeting. By avoiding the visual cliché of dissolves, the film makes it difficult for the viewer to encode these scenes safely as dreams, and instead they function like warps in the reality of American life where any citizen can speak as a Communist agent. Metaphorically this process is expressed through the visual motif of circles: helicopter blades, bicycle wheels, fans, and so on. These circular images suggest the endless repetition of the brainwashing process. Edward Hunter, for example, comments on the "mental convolutions and circuitous thinking that the communists set in motion to break down minds."[54] The circles also reflect on how Condon's original narrative closes the political loop so that extremes meet from the Right and Left. Scenically it emerges through an interplay between scenes confirming the brainwashing conspiracy and others depicting American political or domestic life. From an early stage in the film it is crucial for the viewer to lose his or her sense of the Korean War having ended. Instead, a conspiracy is ongoing that manifests itself through the most familiar American settings, whether in a bar, a press briefing, or a garden society meeting. When the film was released, Condon wrote an article that stressed that "beneath the surface it hopes to illuminate the condition that all of us have been brainwashed and that it is possible that 'free will' has been educated out of us in many important areas."[55] He continues to extend the concept of brainwashing into as diverse areas of American life as consumerism, the space program, and civil defense: "we have been brainwashed into believing that economic prosperity can be equated with something called happiness; that there is proof of superiority in superlatives; that dying is unnatural; that all scientists possess a deep and abiding moral sense; that we must put a man on the Moon or Pluto 'first'; that bomb-shelters can preserve the ecology and should be built instead of preventing war."[56]

Condon foregrounds the television as a medium for publicizing the performances of Iselin, and in his later satire *Emperor of America* (1990) he described post-1950s Americans as a "visual generation . . . which television had conditioned away from thinking into reflexive watching, the generation which had only seen Ronald Reagan, his fine figure . . . but had never heard what he was a saying." Here Condon echoes commentators on the 1950s like Vance Packard, who saw a Pavlovian process taking place in the media. Although he did not weave this into his dystopian novel *One* (see chapter 3), David Karp has put forward an equally jaundiced view of a medium only saved from political exploitation by financial considerations: "That it [television] has not fulfilled Orwell's prediction that it would be used to 'brainwash' citizens is simply due to the fact that brainwashing doesn't seem to have a ready sponsor to pay for the time." When *The Manchurian Candidate* was released, John Frankenheimer was quoted as making the even more sweeping claim that "we live in a society that is brainwashed by television, commercials, advertising, politicians and a censored press."[57] The provocative energy of the film was thus directed against those cultural media responsible for the promotion and circulation of politically charged images.

This array of social targets named in the preceding paragraph is too diverse for the economy of the film's action, which must of necessity focus on a specific conspiracy and, unlike the novel, limit its chronology to the years 1952–1954. The futuristic dimension to the novel is lost, but without any damaging consequences to the convictions of particular scenes. The interplay between Laurence Harvey's cold wooden acting as Shaw and Sinatra's extraordinary range of emotional expressiveness through repeated close-ups maintains a tension throughout, especially as Marco fractures into two distinct roles—victim and investigator. Yen Lo, the Chinese expert on brainwashing jokes knowingly about the term being a "new American word," but the film takes the process very seriously. As in the novel, it does not linger over how the conditioning was achieved, only its results.

The most obvious and predictable sign that brainwashing has occurred is a quality of automatism that comes out when members of Shaw's platoon repeat their prepared lines about his sterling moral qualities or when Shaw is carrying out any actions under orders. Briefly identifying the existence of a Soviet-run spy network within the United States, the film cuts down on the number of Shaw's operatives, logically so because his orders come from a single composite source through his mother. Shaw is referred to as a constructed function and represented visually in the sanatorium as a figure connected to weights and pulleys. Toward the end of the film Marco returns to this metaphor by claiming that Shaw has been liberated through dismantling: "the wires have been pulled." Even the claustrophobic interiors that make up most of the film's settings have a metaphorical as well as social resonance, suggesting different areas of the mind. Marco appropriately figures Shaw's deconditioning as a process of "unlocking doors." The most repeated scenic theme that expresses Shaw's manipulation is the synecdoche of disembodied hands shuffling card decks, carrying a pistol (when Shaw shoots Jordan and his daughter), or assembling the rifle for the final assassination. In all these cases, character has been reduced to function, and the carrying out of functions is presented in a consistently understated matter-of-fact style established in the early brainwashing scenes. The elision of the head from visual representations of agency consistently implies that brainwashing involves a loss of mental faculties. When Shaw is in the sanatorium, Yen Lo discusses his case with a Russian operative as if Shaw were a scientific specimen, stressing that he is a "normally conditioned American who has been taught to kill and then to have no memory of having killed."[58] Just at this point Shaw removes a false head bandage, a good example of the unobtrusive visual symbolism in scenic details. Shaw is here acting the role of a physical casualty (supposedly victim of a hit-and-run accident) when he is actually a *mental* one. The white bandage at the same time functions as a metaphor of what Yen Lo jokingly describes as Shaw's mental "dry-cleaning."

The film reinforces Condon's ironic view of American politics and public life in general as theater. Figures therefore are constantly going in and out of guises. We have just noted Shaw playing the hospital patient. At the beginning of the film we see him in combat and then dress uniform, in civilian dress, and finally disguised as a priest for the assassination. Again, as in the novel, the Iselin fancy dress party makes this most apparent with Iselin himself wearing the costume of Lincoln (with the beard askew), the mother as a shepherdess, and Shaw as a cowboy (as befits a sharpshooter). Dress becomes an important visual index of Ben Marco's changing situation. As he heads toward breakdown he becomes increasingly disheveled, but once his nightmare has been corroborated he immediately returns to his military role in impeccable full uniform. Chunjin first appears in South Korean uniform, then in Communist uniform, and finally in civilian dress. This fluidity of guises helps to support the paranoid implication that all meaningful political activity is going on *behind* appearances and without citizens' knowledge.

The film then manages to maintain this sinister possibility and to introduce bizarrely comic touches at the same time because appearances are so malleable and untrustworthy. A good example of this comedy can be seen in the Secretary for Defense's press briefing. Inevitably the film had to cut out the expository material on Iselin's career, which was always a worry to Condon's editor at McGraw-Hill. Instead the film dramatizes a number of scenes centering on Iselin as a performer. Greil Marcus has rightly noted that the press conference breaks down into chaos: "the event is dissolving; even as it proceeds, all that's left are its representations."[59] The decorum of the event is the first to go, and as the hubbub rises we see the mother watching the scene through the television monitors, obviously assessing its impact. Marcus's point about representations therefore applies to the media packaging of Iselin's charges, which are themselves unsubstantiated "representations" in a different sense.

The depiction of Iselin as an inept actor constantly fumbling his lines and bawling "point of order" into the camera is the most prominent example of a whole series of comic touches that have led one critic to claim that the movie's "cynical, absurdist tone was itself 'sick.'"[60] The black humor of such works as *Catch-22*, *Dr. Strangelove*, or Jules Feiffer's cartoons grew out of disillusionment with public statements on nuclear or foreign policy and repeatedly singled out officialdom for its targets. Similarly in *The Manchurian Candidate* the dignity of the highest congressional medal and of Congress itself is ironically undermined. As we have seen, even the leading conspirator Yen Lo enjoys a good joke. This comic dimension grows out of a self-consciousness of dialogue in scenes like the meeting between Marco and Rosie on a train where pick-up routines are commented on explicitly before the characters exchange information. Indeed, one of the most glaring ironies lies in the fact that the most vociferous defender of American national integrity should turn out to be a pawn in a Communist conspiracy.

The characters in *The Manchurian Candidate* are repeatedly posed against political portraits or national symbols. The spread eagle, it has been suggested, is "correlated with death and the military," but it is also a visual echo of Norman Bates's stuffed birds in *Psycho*, difficult to miss since Janet Leigh, who here takes the role of Rosie, starred as the victim in the earlier film.[61] The American flag even more ironically is reduced to its lowest level as a commodity at the Iselins' party, where a stars-and-stripes cake made from Polish caviar is consumed. Because Senator Jordan is seen against a background of these two symbols, his "test" murder by Shaw becomes an overtly political assault on the republic, whereas the Iselins' possession of a portrait and bust of Lincoln suggests the grotesque (and unconvincing) mimicry of political engagement by Iselin.[62]

The film constantly exploits similarity to imply a blurring of differences. Neither American party is identified by name (unlike in the novel), and Communist and American political portraits appear to be interchangeable. A principle of substitution is at work here, indicated in any early piece of business as when Iselin enters his private plane, replacing his hat with a military cap. Such substitutions might involve reversals, as when Chunjin gives Shaw a left-handed salute, or an exploitation of screen space. When Shaw is remembering his love affair with Jocie, his head occupies the left-hand side of the screen, whereas his mother instructs him on Cold War ideology from the right. The most subtle and complex instance of substitution, however, occurs in the Iselins' library and revolves around the symbolism of the queen of diamonds, Shaw's second trigger. His mother's solitaire routine is interrupted while Shaw's lover Jocie watches from the terrace through a lace curtain. Once the mother leaves, Jocie enters the library, at which point the viewer sees that she is wearing a queen of diamonds costume like a magician's assistant. The lover here replaces the mother, and Shaw and Jocie elope, leaping behind the giant card that is the sign of the mother. After his marriage Shaw returns to confront his mother, and in a brief reprise of this scene the viewer once again sees the scene from Jocie's viewpoint shortly before her husband murders her. The second scene reasserts the dominance of the queen of diamonds when the camera closes on the mother's hands getting out a deck of cards. Similarly, when Shaw is given his final instructions, it is against the background of the same giant card. The mother is thus sometimes replaced by her sign as the "red queen," a pun on her political commitment and the fantastic resemblances in the film to Wonderland.[63] The playing card becomes surcharged with meaning, at different points signifying character type, the drive for power, or the chancy nature of conspiratorial stratagems.

The brief romantic relief provided by Shaw's elopement could not last without destroying the conspiracy that is taken throughout with absolute seriousness. The film heads from an implied but never seen primal act of brainwashing toward an inevitable climax involving death and political destruction as prophesized in the mother's key speech to her son:

> I know you will never entirely comprehend this, Raymond, but you must believe I did not know it would be you. I served them; I fought for them; I'm on the point of winning for them the greatest foothold they will have had in this country, and they paid me back by taking away your soul from you. I told them to build me an assassin from a world *filled* with killers and they chose you because they thought it would bind *me* closer to *them* [close up: takes Raymond's face in her hands]. But now we have come almost to the end. One last step and then when I take power they will be pulled down and ground into dirt for what they did to you and what they did in so contemptuously underestimating me [kisses him].[64]

Since Shaw is sitting in a zombie-like state, these lines are really addressed to the audience with the mother briefly playing chorus. Shaw is mentally absent despite her physical gestures, and she proudly threatens destruction of "them"—probably but not certainly her Communist directors—for their attempt to take over filial allegiance.

The power play that we have witnessed throughout the film builds up to a climax of suspense, since we cannot be sure until the last minute whether Shaw's conditioning has remained intact. There is a tragic but also symbolic consistency in Shaw's death. In the split second before he pulls the trigger of his rifle he vanishes from the screen to become an absent figure commemorated in the epilogue through contradictory public and private representations: as war hero and as political victim. The pathos of that epilogue lies as much in the impossibility of reconciling those two accounts as in the fact of Shaw's death.

Opinions have divided over the politics of this film. Greil Marcus attacks it for representing characters from an exclusively political standpoint so that "everyone acts as a citizen of the republic, or as an anti-citizen."[65] However, in a more nuanced analysis, Susan Carruthers argues that the film condemns the far Right, preserves a notion of the Communist peril, "but also refuses to accept the power of political ideas."[66] The claim that *The Manchurian Can-*

didate makes national allegiance a clear positive ignores the ways in which the novel and film problematize claims of patriotism. Condon made a number of statements to the effect that his target was the gullibility of the American public and his satirical emphasis on the means of persuasion inevitably tended to minimize the content of political agendas. Frankenheimer followed Condon in this respect, shifting the satire more onto the media and onto national imagery.

The Kennedy assassination in 1963 might have been one reason for Sinatra's withdrawal of this film from circulation, after buying the rights, although another reason given is that the film was bringing in less and less income. Ironically, when the film was first released it was picketed for being pro-Communist and too right-wing. It was subsequently re-released in 1988. By the 1960s *The Manchurian Candidate* had become assimilated into discussions of mind control. In a 1964 essay, the novelist Philip K. Dick declared dramatically: "We have entered the landscape depicted by Richard Condon in his terrific novel *The Manchurian Candidate*: Not only can delusions and hallucinations be induced in virtually any person, but the added horror of 'posthypnotic suggestion' gets thrown in for good measure."[67] Most of Dick's own fiction concerns itself with reality manipulation, but *Lies, Inc.* (1984) explores the panic of a subject who is convinced that his thoughts are being implanted by a malign corporation.

■ It is a measure of how rapidly *The Manchurian Candidate* became a central text in discussions of brainwashing that Richard Condon should have been asked to comment on related public events. In the year when Gary Powers was brought to trial (1960), Condon was invited by the manager of the *London American* to write an article about the sort of conditioning Powers might expect from the Soviets, but Condon responded that, since the outcome of Powers' trial was never in doubt, brainwashing was scarcely relevant. He returned instead to the home scene, insisting that it was far more important to examine the effects of national advertising, McCarthyist demagoguery, and the whole ethos of the "Age of Overcommunication."[68] The assassination of Kennedy appeared to be a case of life realizing art, and, when asked by a journalist whether he felt responsible for the killing (on a copycat logic), Condon dispersed the blame through American society as a whole. Noting many similarities of personality between Oswald and Raymond Shaw, Condon concluded that they were both produced by their culture:

When the fanatic is the assassin he steps out of the fabric of the people and is seen. This American fabric has been woven by the overcommunications industry which is uniquely American. Its minute-to-minute offering is programmed violence of fact and fiction until they intertwine and form a most overpowering, scarring educational system. Our extraordinary overcommunications industries have brainwashed our people into appetites and even cravings for being diverted and instructed by every form of violence.[69]

Condon's extension of the concept of brainwashing virtually identifies it with every kind of social conditioning and thereby risks losing its individuality as a political process.

By the 1970s Condon had revised his initial contrast between the dispersed conditioning through the American media and politically directed Communist mind alteration into a realization that both blocs were pursuing similar covert strategies. In his foreword to Walter Bowart's *Operation Mind Control* (1978) he warned the American reader: "Please keep fearfully in mind that the astonishing information published in this seminal work of investigative reporting, concerning avenues taken to decision and execution by our secret police to fracture or dissolve human minds, then to operate those minds as a small boy might operate a Yo-Yo, for purposes of counterintelligence military 'efficiency,' . . . was drawn directly from federal records."[70] Condon implies that the real shock of Bowart's revelations about what he calls the American "cryptocracy" is that it forces the reader to reassess demonized interpretations of Communist conspiratorial practice. Suddenly the United States stands revealed as a bizarre mirror image of the very regime it has been insistently labeling the enemy.

Condon wrote this revised perception into his 1976 novel *The Whisper of the Axe*, where a Chinese guerrilla camp for training subversive agents has its counterpart in the CIA's Behavioral Activities Department. In this novel the conspiracy involves smuggling nuclear devices into the United States and the triggering of guerrilla warfare in key American cities. Once again we have a narrative of aggression, but Condon now makes extensive play on the mirroring of activities by both Chinese Intelligence and the CIA. The novel was published at the time of the Senate investigations of the CIA, when the extent of its own mind control program was becoming evident. Condon weaves the covert CIA involvement in the Asian opium trade into his narrative and goes into much more detail on techniques of mind control than was explained in *The Manchurian Candidate*. A brother and sister team working within the CIA is described as "classical products of the greatest achievements in brain-washing."[71] By introducing these characters before any Communist agents, Condon avoids demonizing the process as alien and ironically praises the ex-Nazi Dr. Baum as the CIA's best brainwasher.

On the other side of the political divide a group of American mercenaries is taken to a Chinese training camp and, in an underground facility, put into a chemically induced state of trance reminiscent of *Brave New World*:

> Feeding tubes leading to bottles containing Chinese-developed preparations (some perfected over centuries, some in recent years), which opened the doors of consciousness and led the interrogators to the truth locked inside the minds of each of the men, shadow-thin layer upon shadow-thin layer, were inserted into the nostrils, into veins at wrist, thigh, and ankle so that the saturation of the unlocking mechanisms could begin.[72]

Condon sticks close to the original paradigm of brainwashing, presenting it as the work of political technicians and alluding in the passage to the 1950s experiments with mescaline (the subject of Huxley's *Doors of Perception*) and LSD. After this first phase, the Americans are subjected to an extended interrogation of their whole lives, until finally they undergo the "re-educative process." By the end of the whole sequence the individual has merged into a new manipulable group: "They adored Authority, Discipline, Service and the Team. They were one intricate, self-involved body."[73]

In *The Manchurian Candidate* characters' presumption of a single stable ego meant that any threat to the self was met with surges of vertiginous horror. The later novel uses an almost deadpan prose style to suggest that it has become a matter of routine for an ego to be constructed (the mechanical metaphor concluding the quoted passage above is symptomatic) to play a part in the political struggle between East and West. The result can be a fractured self performing totally dissociated functions. An American woman undergoes the kind of "counter-brainwashing" conditioning recommended by Estabrooks, which is so thorough that capture by the Chinese presented no danger: "she could be split precisely into two halves and loyally serve both masters without conflict." This conditioning has been performed by a Dr. Baum, the wizard of an Oz-like world where the most literal induced schizophrenia has reversed the humanistic ideal of sanity. The subject who has undergone this process has been depersonalized and degendered into a mere function:

> The agent was in a sense changed into a true schizophrenic; one part an agent of the United States Army, not only assigned to the task of saving the future of the United States of America but *locked* into that concept by Dr. Baum with neither voluntary nor involuntary means of evasion; the other part a convinced, cold-blooded, violently murderous revolutionary re-educated to help direct the execution of the Teel Plan against the United Sates. By the most advanced technological procedures of military psychology, the agent had been rendered insane.[74]

This technology has become so sophisticated that sanity and even political commitment have been rendered virtually meaningless. The self in passages like the one just quoted becomes a site for psycho-technicians to inscribe responses or future actions. Condon limits his pessimism to susceptible individuals with very low self-esteem who are the ideal subjects for brainwashing. Such an agent is like an actor who is simultaneously playing out diametrically opposed scripts whereby the politics of East and West have been reduced to alternating polarities within a consciousness.

Condon's concept of the establishment figure trained by his nation's enemies to assassinate his compatriots was even applied to James Bond. *The Man with the Golden Gun* (1965) resembles *The Manchurian Candidate* in that Bond returns to the West after "treatment" in Leningrad by "Colonel Boris," unconsciously programmed to kill his superior M.[75] But the job has not been done very efficiently. Discrepancies in his behavior and an "odd sort of glazed, sort of far-away look" make the British authorities suspicious and the assassination fails. To regain his healthy hatred of the KGB, Bond has to undergo deconditioning, a kind of benign brainwashing through ECT and pentathol, which restores him to psychological and political health.

Condon's revision of the notion of political conflict was matched, though in a different way, by another political thriller from the same decade. Walter Wager's *Telefon* (1975) presents a modified retelling of *The Manchurian Candidate* within Cold War circumstances that make such a conspiracy dangerously inappropriate. In the immediate wake of the U2 spy plane incident of 1960, the Soviets set up project Telefon whereby 136 deep-level "sleepers" with bogus identities take up residence in the United States. Their purpose is to sabotage the nearest military target once they receive a trigger phrase over the telephone. "They were to infiltrate and burrow deep, waiting patiently for the strike signal," a Soviet official explains. Wager does not linger over how the agents are programmed, suggesting drug-assisted hypnosis as one method. The efficacy of the plan, which recapitulates Pat Frank's *Forbidden Area* as well as *The Manchurian Candidate*, presents its real danger in the 1970s. When a Stalinist coup fails in the Soviet Union, a disenchanted cipher clerk named Dalchinski flees to America with a copy of the code book and begins triggering the saboteurs. At this point the KGB orders one of their troubleshooters, Tabbat, to hunt him down with the help of a resident Soviet agent. Most of the narrative therefore, as a reviewer of the 1977 movie adaptation noted, consists of a "good old-fashioned chase thriller."[76]

More than that, however, *Telefon* describes how an earlier Cold War project comes to haunt the transformed present. The narrative subject is a blatant anachronism but dangerous nonetheless. Wager presents the Cold War as a status quo where each superpower covertly helps the other. The true oppositions thus realign themselves as between the defenders and opponents of that stability. One of the first ironies of the novel emerges when a KGB security director cites *Nineteen Eighty-Four* to explain how the authorities will erase the Stalinist plotters. The elusive Dalchinski could therefore be read as a personification of the militant Soviet old guard whose elimination is in the interests of Americans and Soviets alike. The second irony, which Wager labors somewhat, is that the Soviets have themselves become consumers. He writes explicitly against the Hollywood-promoted image of the KGB as Communist thugs, presenting Tabbat as a Frank Sinatra fan, an American in all but name. We are told at one point that the "KGB agent responded with his finest All-American grin. It was pure country boy, worthy of a shaving cream commercial."[77] In the context of the 1950s and 1960s such comparisons would trigger a paranoid fear that enemy agents could totally simulate Americans. Here, although Tabbat has received such training, he is no longer the enemy, but—paradoxically—the defender of the United States in his chase to prevent a renegade from causing a nuclear holocaust. The movie makes this point even more strongly since Tabbat and his helper are played by Charles Bronson and Lee Remmick. Bronson, who usually takes the role of a loner, is now acting to preserve the Soviet establishment with elegant assistance from Remmick. The final twist comes after Dalchinski's death, when Remmick reveals that she is a CIA agent. By this stage the layers of masquerade have totally blurred our sense of political sides. The two protagonists demonstrate total ease with all aspects of American life. Furthermore, each character's security agency is shown to be a mirror image of the other: bureaucratic, hierarchical, and riven by internal rivalries. The KGB even dispatch a second agent to kill Tabbat.

But what of the working of Telefon itself? Both Wager and the film revamp the stereotypes of automatic response when the sleepers receive their triggers. Considering how he might preempt Dalchinski, Tabbat reflects:

> He would have to speak the trigger-phrase, utter the coded message that would destroy the fiction—and life—of Conrad Bernard Temko. Once these words were spoke, that character would vanish as if written out of the script of some soap opera series. But . . . once this man reverted to his identity as a KGB commando, he'd be motivated by a tremendous compulsion to complete his assigned mission. They'd built that into him when they programmed him so expensively and thoroughly all those years ago.[78]

Telefon is based on the most mechanistic model of human programming and draws a clear distinction between the saboteurs who are dehumanized into remote-control weapons, and the operators who demonstrate resourcefulness and improvisation. The former are wrenched out of domestic contexts with a speed that denies the transformation any pathos. Where the saboteurs are totally scripted, Tabbat and Barbi, his assistant, act out their roles with a comic self-awareness, and retain a prerogative to vary them if necessary, changing costume to suit the needs of each occasion. The film increases the impression of the saboteurs' uniformity by having them all be triggered by the same lines from a Robert Frost poem.

The novel alternates sequences focusing on the protagonists, with sections focalized through Dalchinski that present him as a paranoid puritan misreading America as a Stalinist dictatorship. These sections draw attention to one of the novel's implausibities: that a character should be so familiar with American life and yet not know anything about its legal and security systems. This disparity, together with Dalchinski's largely irrelevant discovery of his sexual appetite in America, are dropped from the film, which centers primarily on the protagonists. Here Dalchinski functions in a more sinister way as a mechanism at large, only apprehended through the "accidents" that result from his telephone calls. The film thereby presents the Telefon project as a kind of collective superweapon that misfires. Dalchinski proves to be a Soviet Strangelove attempting to compensate for presumed political betrayal, but distinctions between the Soviet Union and the United States constantly blur. The last scene of the novel shows an internment camp containing the last of the Telefon sleepers guarded by a sentry who reflects: "this was the kind of thing they did in Russia."

Both the melodramatic embedding of opposite roles like hero and traitor within a single character and, even more importantly, its conspiracy plot-line where political appearances are totally untrustworthy, helped to establish *The Manchurian Candidate* as a key narrative of the Cold War. We turn now to a writer whose works make up a positive encyclopedia of conspiracy, covert action, and mind-altering technology—William Burroughs.

six

William Burroughs

Control Technologies, Viruses, and Psychotronics

n October 1956, while he was working on *Naked Lunch*, William Burroughs wrote to Allen Ginsberg: "Brain-washing, thought control, etc., is the vilest form of crime against the person of another."[1] Ginsberg, for his part, returned the point by arguing in 1968 that "Burroughs provides counter-brainwash techniques and leads the reader to examine conditioned identity."[2] Throughout his career Burroughs explored the different technologies of mind control that were emerging during the Cold War. These technologies were for him ultimately linked with death and with the fallen state of the United States after detonating the atomic bombs over Japan. In Burroughs's private mythology Hiroshima occupies a special symbolic status. As he wrote in his later journals, "the earth has been violated by the atom bomb. No longer innocent. It was the Apple, and the Pentagon slobbed it down."[3]

Technological power cannot be imagined in separation from the agencies that exercise it. *Ah Pook Is Here* (1979), for instance, begins its meditation on death with the Hiroshima bomb blast and speculates about the "secrets of fear and death," wondering: "is this terrible knowledge even now computerized and vested in the hands of far-sighted Americans in the State Department and the CIA?"[4] Burroughs maintained a consistent vision of how the autonomy of the individual self was being threatened by bureaucratic agencies. As early as *Queer* (published in 1985 but written in the 1950s) a character warns against "automatic obedience, synthetic schizophrenia, mass-produced to order. That is the Russian dream, and America is not far behind. The bureaucrats of both countries want the same thing: Control. The superego, the controlling agency, gone cancerous and berserk."[5] Among the numerous forms of addiction Burroughs identifies, none is more potent than the pursuit of power. We shall see how the concept of control recurs throughout Burroughs's writings.

When asked to do a profile on William Burroughs, J. G. Ballard recalled a meeting where Burroughs kept glancing at the door and windows. "The CIA are watching me," he confided. "They park their laundry vans in the street outside."[6] This meeting strengthened Ballard's conviction of Burroughs's paranoid imagination. Conspiracy was central to his writing, hence the special symbolic importance he attached to the Order of Assassins and its founder Hassan-I-Sabbah.[7] In a 1965 interview Burroughs admitted being influenced by the evocation of conspiracies in the final volume in C. S. Lewis's Perelandra trilogy, *That Hideous Strength*. These were so apposite to that historical moment that Burroughs concludes: "Actually 1984 seems a bit cosy over this point, I think. Rather out of date."[8] Orwell remained a major reference point for Burroughs in situating his own dystopias. For example, at the opening of his *Blade Runner, A Movie* (1979), set in 2014 Manhattan, we are told that extended government control of U.S. citizens "has not produced the brainwashed standardized human units postulated by such linear prophets as George Orwell. Instead, a large percentage of the population has been forced underground."[9]

The self exists within a network of controlling structures from the earliest of Burroughs's writings. He explained to Allen Ginsberg in 1955 that *Naked Lunch* described "vast Kafkian conspiracies . . . between the East—representing spontaneous, emergent life, and the West—representing control from without, character armor, death. . . . But it is difficult to know what side anyone is working on, especially yourself."[10] The grand conspiracy of Communist world conquest is ridiculed in *The Wild Boys* (1971), where a parody of a U.S. general explains the flight of American youth from their families in the following terms: "All over America kids like Johnny are deserting this country and their great American heritage suborned by the false promises of Moscow into a life of drugs and vice."[11] However, it is not the world of drugs that Burroughs presents as a disease but rather institutionalized control.

Conspiracies require a directing elite, hence the recurrence in Burroughs of "evil scientist" figures like Dr. Benway in *Naked Lunch* (1959), who is introduced as a "manipulator and coordinator of symbol systems, an expert on all phases of interrogation, brainwashing and control."[12] Modeled on Dostoevsky's Grand Inquisitor, Benway acts as spokesman for different dystopian possibilities, like the totally bureaucratized state Annexia where the citizens are not permitted to do anything without the appropriate documents, or his Reconditioning Center in Freeland. In an echo of the tour that opens *Brave New World*, Benway proudly guides the astonished narrator around the center unconcerned with the impact of his words as he identifies himself as a Fordist, a "pure" scientist, and an expert on the manipulation of his subjects, especially of how they perceive their own experience: "The subject must not realize that the mistreatment is a deliberate attack of an anti-human enemy on his personal identity. He must be made to feel that he deserves *any* treatment he receives because there is something (never specified) horribly wrong with him."[13] Psychological assault is screened by procedures that Eric Mottram has summarized as evoking a "condition of advanced state bureaucracy operated through obscene and insane controls."[14]

The model of political interrogation is extended into all forms of investigation as if humans are the carriers of information. So, when he is weighing up the efficiency of scopolamine, Benway comments that it impairs the memory: "an agent might be prepared to reveal his secrets but quite unable to remember them, or cover story and secret life info might be inextricably garbled."[15] Like Unruh von Steinplatz in *Cities of the Red Night* (1981) who produces lethal viruses by irradiation, Benway is a technician far more obsessed with ways of doing than any end product. He applies a combination of cybernetics and behaviorism in controlling the citizens of Annexia who are subject to constant monitoring and who spend their lives rushing from one state bureau to the next. Here Burroughs's Kafka influence becomes evident. The obsessive state search for subversives results in agents carrying cover stories that cannot be distinguished from authentic selves. Indeed the self in Burroughs's dystopia becomes flattened out into a space where the authorities can inscribe identities. The second technician of the self in *Naked Lunch* is Dr "Fingers" Schaeffer, the Lobotomy Kid, whose designations reflect an absurd combination of doctor, criminal, and cowboy. In a burlesque conference on "Technological Psychiatry" he unveils his master creation, Clarence the "Complete All American De-anxietized Man." No sooner has he been displayed than Clarence metamorphoses into a giant centipede (Kafka again), to the horror of the delegates, and the conference breaks down in chaos. Benway, Schaeffer, and Burroughs's other technicians collectively embody what two critics have called "instrumental rationality," a discourse and set of

practices that underpin control and that are repeatedly satirized and burlesqued in Burroughs's works.[16]

In *Naked Lunch* Burroughs's narrator comments: "Americans have a special horror of giving up control, of letting things happen in their own way
without interference."[17] The concluding phrase sounds oddly utopian within
the context of Burroughs's constant fascination with the technology of mind
control. In an interview he named only a small number of science fiction
novels that he admired. One of these, Henry Kuttner's *Fury* (1954), which
Burroughs quotes substantially in *The Ticket That Exploded*, describes a war
on Venus between the survivors of a nuclear war on Earth, where a technique
of "psychonamics" is used against opponents. This involves a series of posthypnotic suggestion treatments from childhood, each session followed by a
memory erase, so that the subjects, like the Manchurian Candidate, will be
conditioned to obey commands but have no idea that they were influenced.
Such techniques recur throughout Burroughs's writing. To name only a few
instances, at various points in his writing he refers to CIA-backed experiments
on LSD and other drugs, Electronic Stimulation of the Brain, scramblers used
to implant information in subjects' minds, sensory deprivation, and psychotronics (Burroughs wanted to construct a psychotronic generator but did
not have enough time).[18] Again and again Burroughs adopts the role of an
insider supplying the reader with secret information. It is an important biographical detail in this context that Burroughs volunteered for the OSS during
the Second World War but was rejected. One reason why he paid such close
attention to this technology was that it confirmed the mind's dependence on
the body and its physical environment. He dismissed Freudian psychology as
mysticism for not paying adequate attention to the physical ground of consciousness and even declared in interview: "The whole of Western psychiatry
has been sidetracked from the way it should have gone. It should have gone
along the lines of Pavlov and the conditioned reflex."[19] This assertion strikingly distinguishes Burroughs from the vast majority of writers discussed in
this volume who demonize Pavlov into a cynical exploiter of responses. In
chapter 9, for example, we shall see how Thomas Pynchon depicts a Pavlovian psychologist in *Gravity's Rainbow* as self-mystified and morally dubious.
Burroughs appears to have rejected the Freudian unconscious because it
understated the effect of capitalism on the psyche and because it ignored a
possible physical location in the brain for the unconscious.[20]

One of Burroughs's most important essays, "The Limits of Control,"
points a warning finger at the covert technology being developed in the

United States: "Brainwashing, psychotropic drugs, lobotomy and other more subtle forms of psychosurgery; the technocratic control apparatus of the United States has at its fingertips new techniques which if fully exploited could make Orwell's 1984 seem like a benevolent utopia."[21] Burroughs uses shock tactics here to startle the reader into wondering how a totalitarian regime could ever come about in America and at the same time points out a paradox in the existence of control agencies. The latter are ostensibly devoted to eradicating dissent and subversion, but if this process were ever fulfilled the agencies would cease to exist. Institutionally then, these agencies perpetuate themselves by contradicting their stated purpose. Burroughs's other main nonfictional statement on mind-control technology, "In the Interests of National Security," discusses the working of the CIA's Special Operations Division and describes José Delgado's Electronic Stimulation of the Brain (ESB) as the "ultimate form of behavior modification." Delgado's dependence on implanted electrodes, which Burroughs described elsewhere as "a little cumbersomer," might be superseded by direct transmission to the brain and Burroughs speculates with a certain relish: "Could directed auto-stimulation by the administration of a drug? Could a virus directed to certain brain areas serve as a terminal for electrical impulses delivered by radio control?"[22] Burroughs's questions implicitly challenge any presumptions the reader may have that the individual mind is autonomous or that U.S. agencies operate in a benign way, and he grimly warns that the end result of such experiments may be the destruction of the planet.

In "The Limits of Control" Burroughs admits that "words are still the principal instruments of control" despite the increasing sophistication of mind-control technology. This is by no means a reassuring statement because, Burroughs explains elsewhere, "it is generally assumed that speech must be consciously understood to cause an effect. Early experiments with subliminal images have shown that this is not true."[23] Words, then, become symbolic counters, lexical triggers for associations that can be manipulated at will. In 1939 Burroughs attended a series of lectures by Alfred Korzybski whose *Science and Sanity* he was to cite repeatedly for its discussion of semantics; from Korzybski Burroughs took the principle that "a word is *not* the object it represents."[24] Separation of word from referent replaces meaning with effect and that in turn leads Burroughs to stress use, or rather exploitation. In *The Job* Burroughs wrote: "Verbal techniques are now being used to achieve more reliable computer-processed techniques in the direction of opinion control and manipulation[,] the 'propaganda war' it's called." The first stage in this process is that a "population segment" is "conditioned to react to words rather than word referents" through the use of imageless prose that functions purely to instill conditioned responses.[25] In *The Ticket That Exploded* (1967) Burroughs evokes an ironic version of Scientology, called the "Logos group," which practices a predictable science of human behavior directed by certain word combinations. This kind of automatic predictable response is the direct opposite of what Burroughs aims for as a writer. His constant shifts of register and genre jolt the reader out of habits of response to verbal pattern and invite us to think skeptically about the associations of words. Burroughs saw a role for the underground press here in subverting the order of conventional media messages and reducing their impact by damaging their verbal consistency. Burroughs expresses skepticism about the stability of verbal meaning in *Nova Express* and other novels through the trope of reality as a film, which suggests that there is no precultural reality and also that reality itself might be scripted. Who or what is the hidden director?

Burroughs's main concern within the area of control was that government-funded agencies were secretly working against the interests of American citizens. It is unusual for him to give much attention to Communist regimes, which he explains as a relation between mental states and political environment. A character in *Interzone* (1989) is deported to a country behind the Iron Curtain and experiences a "complete relaxation" because of the equilibrium between inner fears and outer circumstances.[26] The worst has already happened, whereas the United States is less centralized and allows for an underground as well as free-acting agencies. The processes that Burroughs cites with ambiguous fascination are those dealing with different kinds of mind control. CIA-funded experiments in sensory withdrawal were being conducted by Dr. John Lilly (see chapter 9). Burroughs cites Lilly by name in a footnote to the "Smorbrot" episode of *Nova Express* (1964), where immersion tanks more benignly induce pleasure and even orgasm in subjects.[27] A far more sinister instance occurs in *Naked Lunch* where a warning is given against the Senders, cynical technicians of bio-control who might implant miniature radio receivers in the brain soon after birth.

At this stage the device is only presented as an imminent possibility, but Burroughs was to become familiar with the experiments of José M. R. Delgado, who used ESB "stimoceivers" implanted in the brain. Delgado was a proponent of modifying central activity through physical and chemical technology and carried out numerous experiments on monkeys and human subjects using electrodes implanted in their brains. Delgado carefully distinguished his own work from the images of popular fiction: "Science fiction has already imagined men with intracerebral electrodes engaged in all kinds of mischief under the perverse guidance of radio waves sent by some evil scientist. The inherent limitations of ESB make realization of this fantasy very remote."[28] Exactly this kind of device was used in Frederik Pohl's *A Plague of Pythons* (1965), where a renegade Soviet scientist uses low-frequency radio waves picked up by tiny implants to induce servility.[29] When Allen Ginsberg asked Burroughs what filled him with fear, he answered: "possession," explaining that he meant loss of control through some form of bodily invasion. He continued: "Imagine that the invader has taken over your motor centers," and he described how it might feel for the mind to be helpless before the body's actions.[30] The "death dwarfs" in *Nova Express* (1964) are fantasy control agents that Burroughs explained as "parasitic organisms occupying a human host, rather like a radio transmitter, which direct and control it."[31] The technology devised by Delgado made a very deep impression on Burroughs. He saw it as the realization of what was speculation in *Naked Lunch* and as making possible ultimate control of human minds. "There's no limit to what they can do," he warned in 1974.[32] He used a device similar to Delgado's experiments for a satirical political sketch set in Chicago in 1968. Burroughs had described Mayor Daley as a throwback to turn-of-the-century boss politics and "In Last Resort the Truth" (in *Exterminator!* 1973) draws on Robert Ardrey's *African Genesis* to depict a former Supreme Court justice as an ape miming to a political script transmitted by a technician off-stage. Homer the ape mouths a series of right-wing clichés, trying to whip up support for the Vietnam War as a "holy crusade against the godless forces of international Communism."[33] The satire against the mindless audience responding with Pavlovian promptness to all the trigger-phrases is allowed to take form only shortly before the whole scene degenerates into chaos as the technician induces frenzy in the ape. In the ensuing fracas the ape is shot down and subsequently receives a hero's funeral as a defender of the American way.

The notion of the radio-controlled assassin was applied to the shooting of Kennedy in an account by a former FBI agent. Lincoln Lawrence's *Were We Controlled?* (1967) extrapolates on Delgado's research and gives us a recessive conspiracy narrative. We are reading insider information drawn from a secret report that in turn refers to the most secret text of all, a small black diary of the assassination plot. Lawrence bases the credibility of his account largely on the plausibility of the technology involved. First he establishes the possibility of posthypnotic suggestion induced by radio control (RHIC);

then he makes his key assertion: "Lee Oswald was to be utilized as . . . (and now you must clear your brain and put aside your preconceived notions of what espionage and sabotage are *today*) . . . a RHIC controlled person . . . somewhat like a mechanical toy."[34] Lawrence classifies Oswald as a "sleeper" to be operated at will by distant triggers, like those in *The Manchurian Candidate* and *Telefon.*

Ken Kesey admitted that Burroughs's *Naked Lunch* had helped in the composition of *One Flew Over the Cuckoo's Nest,* but it was in Kesey's later film script, *The Further Inquiry* (1990), that this influence can be seen most directly. The subject is a trial of Neal Cassidy with many references back to the 1960s trip of the Merry Pranksters. Kesey introduces a Benway-like voice over, a Dr. Knot, who explains a method of "psychochemillogical breakdown" by applying Wilhelm Reich's notion of character armor: "First a person is chemically disarmed and dis-armored, then bombarded psychologically." Like Burroughs, Kesey draws on the imagery of disease to express the stultifying effects of thought patterns. These harden into a screen that spreads like an illness: "The infection had gained a stronghold in the plumpest parts of the American spirit. The situation was *bound* to become—still *might* become—terminal, unless that cancerous screen is blasted away, like scales from the eye, tartar from the tooth—obliterated!—so the healthy new impressions are allowed to pour in."[35] Kesey appropriates Burroughs's imagery of disease but lacks the latter's conspiratorial claustrophobia. The process of purging outlined in these lines owes more to a libertarian ethic of cleansing the doors of perception than to Burroughs's evocation of malign agencies, and this marks a further difference between Kesey and another novelist who has acknowledged Burroughs's influence.

Kathy Acker shared Burroughs's heightened awareness of conspiracy and, like him, used references to the CIA as a way of designating a power operating behind the visible. Just as Burroughs stated that "political conflicts are merely surfaced manifestations," so Acker took Watergate as a symbolic moment revealing hidden agencies at work. In interview she stated: "Everybody now knows what's happening. . . . People know that the CIA has done a lot of chemical warfare testing, they know how things work now; they just don't give a damn."[36]

Her 1988 novel *Empire of the Senseless,* like Burroughs's Nova trilogy, describes an attack on patriarchal authority as an attempt by terrorists to penetrate the CIA library—archive and computerized power center—in their search for the code of a "certain construct." Burroughs has his Dr. Benway,

Acker her ex-Nazi scientist Dr. Strughold, who hires Sidney Gottlieb to conduct the MK-ULTRA project, "designed to cause total human amnesia" in its guinea pigs after their use has ended. He in turn delegates the running of sub-project "Midnight Climax" to an agent named Black, who organizes special brothels in Paris where LSD is covertly administered and its results observed through two-way mirrors. Acker explained such episodes as reflecting her perception of her own present: "I live in a world which is at least partly defined by the multinationals, the CIA, etc. . . . So the CIA kept invading the Paris in *Empire*."[37] Acker has taken the factual details of part of MK-ULTRA and transposed them from San Francisco to Paris, which is used as the site for a power struggle in her novel. Gottlieb was the project director, but he delegated to George *White*, a federal narcotics agent. Acker changes the name to increase its demonic symbolism while retaining allusions to White's notorious extravagance.[38] Acker's narrator is implicated in the project by occupying a vantage point behind the mirror that would only have been available to an agent and experiences a shock of recognition when he sees a lobotomy: "I was watching when the sailor's cerebral cortex was chopped. I knew death when I saw death. I knew, in the brothel of lobotomies, I was a dead man seeing my skeleton in a mirror, the land of the CIA, or a dream character who knew that he lived only in the darkest region, of himself, a land or face which he didn't recognize when he was awake."[39] If the self is defined by agencies like the CIA, any victim becomes an alternative self, hence the complex recognition that takes place here. The mirror is used to encode a self-cognition and at the same time to hint at the Carroll-like fantastic dimension of what is seen. Observer and observed collapse together, just as the distinction lapses between what is internal and external. The circularity of the gaze is symptomatic of a general ubiquity of control, which Patrick O'Donnell finds in *Empire of the Senseless*. For him, control lies at the center of information systems and identity constructs to such an extent that Acker's future Paris simply reproduces the control systems of the past.[40]

■ Burroughs has never wavered in his conviction of the interdependence between mind and body. He has insisted that "morality . . . ethics, philosophy, religion, can no longer maintain an existence separable from facts of physiology, bodily chemistry. . . . Psychology no longer exists."[41] In other words, for Burroughs, value and politics are bodied. This in turn explains the complex symbolism of the virus, which assumed greater and greater importance in Burroughs's works from the early 1960s onward. Here he ran together at least four different concepts. From science fiction he took the notion of alien organisms; from the drug subculture addiction as a form of contagion; from the nuclear age radiation as form of disease; and from Wilson Smith's *Mechanisms of Virus Infection* he took his biological data. In the latter work Smith identifies a basic process as follows: "For all viruses the infection cycle comprises entry into the host, intracellular replication and subsequent escape into the external environment."[42] Burroughs attributes an ultimate purpose to a virus in *The Western Lands* (1988) as follows: "A cancer cell, a virus has no destiny, no human purpose beyond endless replication. . . . The ultimate purpose of cancer and all virus, is to replace the host." In other works he transposes the concept into an attack mounted by forces elsewhere: a "time bomb left on this planet to be activated by remote control."[43] The narrator of *Ah Pook Is Here* warns the reader: "Remember the life cycle of a virus . . . penetration of a cell or activation within the cell, replication within the cell, escape from cell to invade other cells, escape from host to infect a new host."[44] Here the replication of the virus offers Burroughs a cyclical narrative of invasion that underpins a politics of the body as well as of the individual.

The virus signifies a kind of organic warfare with extermination as its end and signifies too a process that conflates disease, subversion and liberation: "fight cell by cell through bodies and mind screens of the earth."[45] This passage from *The Soft Machine* (1968), the second volume in Burroughs's 1960s trilogy, deploys the discourse of revolution to articulate challenges to ideologically inflected representations of the real—what he calls here the "Reality Studio"—as if ontological certainty will in itself confer political power. "The Mayan Caper" sketch in the same novel similarly describes an adventurer's penetration of the room where the "codices" (for which read "control codes") are kept. Once he finds them, the control machine of that society can be sabotaged and dismantled. The title of *The Soft Machine* signifies a biologically based paranoia where the "human body [is] under constant siege from a vast hungry host of parasites."[46] The virus thus opens up for Burroughs a multiple analogy that he can vary at will. At one point he can describe love as a virus, at another Christian teaching or even death, which could be taken either as meaning death wish or a consciousness of mortality. *Naked Lunch* describes bureaus as cancerous cells turning away from evolution; in other words in the most literal sense bureaucracy becomes a life-denying force.

From science fiction novelists like Eric Frank Russell, Burroughs took the convention of articulating viral threat as an alien invasion. Russell's *Three to Conquer* (1956) describes how three astronauts return to America from a secret space flight to Venus carrying with them an intelligent virus that takes over hosts by direct transmission through the blood stream. The novel's action therefore consists of attempts to stem at once an invasion and an epidemic: "The invader was a horde multi-millions strong. Each capture of a human body was victory for a complete army corps represented by a few drops of potent goo in which the individual warrior was—what?"[47] Here the discourse of military conquest is displaced onto a process of quasi-sexual infection where the agencies of the process are so minute they can scarcely be identified.

In *Nova Express* Burroughs similarly introduces "death dwarfs" from another world, who are "parasitic organisms occupying a human host, rather like a radio transmitter, which direct and control it."[48] This is not presented as an occasion for simple horror or defensive measures, as happens in earlier invasion narratives, but makes a satirical comment on the numbed acquiescence of the general public. *The Place of Dead Roads* (1983) shows aliens planning a parasitic takeover, confident in the knowledge that they have millions of stupid human "hosts" at their disposal. Robert Heinlein's 1951 novel *The Puppet Masters* had already described an invasion by intelligent slugs that fasten on to the backs of their hosts and gradually subdue whole areas of the Earth to their rule. Burroughs appears to draw a similar analogy between the organic, demonic, and politically maligned in *The Western Lands* (1987) when we are told: "demons must possess human hosts to operate."[49] One crucial difference, however, between Burroughs's accounts and earlier narratives is that he never allows a single analogy to determine his narrative. The reader must therefore constantly read between double and triple meanings within foregrounded terms like "cell" and "operate" to negotiate between different levels of discourse. Most obviously Burroughs anthropomorphizes the simultaneous operation of aggressive and ally viruses as the "tough cop and the con cop" routine.[50] In short, virus functions in Burroughs's works as an open sign combining different dimensions of meaning and carrying traces of its connotations in the 1950s of the alien. Its characteristics of invisibility and irresistibility link the virus with Cold War tropes of Communism as a malignant parasite and the threat of the pods in *Invasion of the Body Snatchers*. There Miles Bennell describes the transformed humans in the following metaphor: "Their bodies were now hosts harbouring an alien."[51] The very notion of being taken over "cell by cell" conflates, through a pun, biological invasion and political subversion by Communist cells. These tropes of contamination and infection form part of what Andrew Ross has described as the "Cold War culture of germophobia" and Michael Rogin has explained as an identification of Communism with disease, already manifest in the diplomat George Kennan's 1947 description of Communism as a "malignant parasite."[52]

Burroughs uses the trope of the virus to combine physical and political horror. It can be read in two complementary directions. On the one hand, no part of the body or of the mind—since Burroughs stresses their interdependence—remains inviolate; on the other hand, political takeover is given the most visceral expression that radically "others" the invading agency. Barbara Rose has argued convincingly that a shift of paranoia takes place in Burroughs's 1980s trilogy: "What is scandalous about *Cities of the Red Night* in the context of Burroughs's previous texts is its acknowledgement that there is no neutral space or ideological clean slate." She then describes the experiments with a virus to wipe out unwanted populations and continues: "But unlike the viral agents of the previous texts, this virus has no alien source."[53] Indeed, it may have no cause at all, nor may it be any longer possible to distinguish between virus and host, at which point the potential drama of the takeover process lapses.

Burroughs stated in his *Paris Review* interview that his writings have one general aim: "All of my work is directed against those who are bent, through stupidity or design, on blowing up the planet or rendering it uninhabitable."[54] The threat might come from outside, like the Venusian virus of *Nova Express*; or it might come from within. Burroughs was all too well aware of secret government program of research on narcotics. Commenting on the supposed suicide of the biochemist Frank Olson in 1953, Burroughs's skepticism led him to the conclusion that the CIA admission that Olson was researching into LSD was just a smoke screen, and his suspicions were further confirmed by the Rockefeller Commission revelations of 1975.[55] Burroughs wove this awareness into two sketches for hypothetical films. "Twilight's Last Gleaming" (collected in *Exterminator!*) describes a conspiracy to blow up a train carrying nerve gas. The cliché of a last-minute triumph by the forces of law and order is suddenly reversed by an explosion counterpointed against lines from the "Battle Hymn of the Republic," the context giving a grim new irony to the line "He hath loosed the fatal lightning of his terrible swift sword." Divinely endorsed military triumphalism is replaced by a secular wasteland of dead cities across the country. Similarly "Beauty and the Bestseller" (in *The Adding Machine*) concerns a writer's attempt to sell an idea for a horror movie. At first it goes well. According to the movie pitch, the viewer would be taken inside a secret biological research establishment (the lure of penetrating a forbidden area) but then it is discovered that an infected rat has escaped, spreading a deadly virus. Millions fall victim to this blight, which peaks in outbursts of putrefaction and sexual frenzy. The sketch has a twist in the reason why the scenario is refused. Its proposer wants to commodify catastrophe as spectacle but "the reader likes a menace to keep its distance."[56] This is exactly the effect that Burroughs's own fiction tries to prevent by introducing the most graphic descriptions of disease and frenzy, and by subverting the reader's sense of the narrative form such a "menace" might take.

It is dangerous to oversystematize Burroughs's writing, but in general the term "image" carries positive connotations of vitality: "image *is* organism."[57] The word in contrast can become the capitalized Word, the sign of an authoritarian reality structure. Although he does not unpack the virus metaphor, Brent Wood rightly argues, "What Burroughs terms the viral function of language is its ongoing ordering of reality toward the limit of total control, the opposite of anarchy."[58] Thus in *Nova Express* Burroughs expresses apocalyptic disruption as physical violence against the Word itself: "Word dust drifted streets of broken music car horns and air hammers—The Word broken pounded twisted exploded in smoke."[59] Here the word at one and the same time collapses into noise and is reified into an object to be destroyed. The syntax flattens out into a paratactic sequence of items without hierarchy. Paradoxically Burroughs cannot get away from the verbal medium, but then there is no reason to suppose that he is attacking the medium itself. Instead he is surely attacking an authoritarian instrumentalist use of language, a recurrent target in twentieth-century dystopias.[60]

Burroughs sums up the different dimensions to virus in the sketch "Technical Deposition of the Virus Power" included in *Nova Express* and *The Third Mind* (1978). For Burroughs "deposition" regularly implies the statements of a witness at a trial or official hearing; in other words, exposition is supplied within the fictional context of an investigation. The "deposition" starts as follows:

> Gentlemen, it was first suggested that we take our own image and examine how it could be made more portable. We found that simple binary coding systems were enough to contain the entire image. . . . Our virus infects the human and creates our image in him.
>
> We first took our image and put it into code. A technical code developed by the information theorists. This code was written at the molec-

ular level to save space, when it was found that the image material was not dead matter, but exhibited the same life cycle as the virus. This virus released upon the world would infect the entire population and turn them into our replicas, it was not safe to release the virus until we could be sure that the last groups to go replica would not notice.[61]

Although the term "image" is employed here, the speaker is using depersonalized, imageless prose to describe the transmission of representations. The encoding of information and the whole "deposition" play on a combination of familiarity and its opposite. On the one hand, the official terminology suggests the conventions of a formal report; on the other hand, these words are delivered by a spokesman who situates himself outside humanity. The origination of the project is left unknown by the anonymous passive formulation "it was suggested," and the term "image," traditionally linked to the sense of sight, is now paradoxically associated with a transformation of humanity both fundamental and imperceptible. Through key terms like "code," Burroughs's speaker conflates computing, virology, genetics, and covert political operations. The ultimate code is the genetic one, which was being theorized during the 1960s, for example, during Burroughs's formative years as a writer, whereby organism could be defined only in informational terms. Thus the gene was the "smallest unit of genetic information encoded in the genetic material."[62] That a code implies encryption can never be imagined in Burroughs's fiction separate from an institutional agency, so it was only a matter of time before a DNA police force was described. Sure enough, such a force appears in *Cities of the Red Night*, patrolling an international zone called Portland (named after the British government biological research facility at Portland Down), and serving as "authorities on every disease and drug in the galaxy."[63] If DNA is a "code," Burroughs plays with the term's institutional meaning, as if it represents a civil legal system, to hypothesize a fantastic regime of total genetic enforcement. Within Burroughs's notion of the virus it becomes ultimately impossible to separate organism from information. Steven Shaviro glosses this notion helpfully when he explains in a deliberate pun that the colonizing virus is never originatory, self-sufficient or even apprehensible only as an organism: "A virus is nothing but DNA or RNA encased in a protective sheath; that is to say, it is a message—encoded in nucleic acid—whose only content is an order to repeat itself."[64] Every means of describing a virus raises new problems, since "order" suggests an origination that is inaccessible. In linguistic terms, we could say that Burroughs's references to the word *virus* highlight language's biological otherness in existing prior to any individual. The fantastic possibility that words may speak us lies behind Burroughs's constant preoccupation with control.

■ The human subject in these contexts becomes reified into a body of information that is sought for its political potential. One early sketch shows an American in Mexico who learns that he is being sought by the "Bay of Pigs" (the CIA); in fact, agents from leading nations ("all the forces of suppression") have all converged on Mexico to search for the legendary books of the Maya. In Burroughs's mythology the lost books of Alamut in Iran carry the status of ancient blueprints for the training of assassins. Whether they have found them or not, depending on the reader's degree of paranoia, the CIA now uses similar methods: "the operation is mapped out in stills animation and moving film."[65] This typically deadpan statement of apparent fact screens huge assumptions. If the original books are lost, who can know what methods are similar? And who can know the CIA training methods? Putting information at a premium cues in a figure more familiar in Gothic fiction—the seeker. The speaker in a sketch entitled "The Conspiracy" declares: "Since early youth I had been searching for some secret, some key by which I could gain access to basic knowledge." The impossibility of this search is revealed in Burroughs's general refusal to construct extended narrative and in his preoccupation with secret powers at work. The seeker in "The Conspiracy" decides that his quest is futile because there is no secret, but then revises that position: "There *is* a secret, now in the hands of ignorant and evil men, a secret beside which the atom bomb is a noisy toy."[66]

Burroughs's heightened view of how information is mediated led him to characterize the postwar political situation by systematic deception on a massive scale: "The cold war is used as a pretext by both America and Russia to conceal and monopolise research confining knowledge to official agencies."[67] The CIA men who recur throughout Burroughs's fiction are the very personifications of such agencies: featureless men in grey flannel suits whose appearance carries no information. Like the agencies, they are all surface and Burroughs's political vision is a paranoid one of hidden orders working behind the visible. It is not surprising then that Burroughs has admitted that one of his fantasy careers is as a writer of espionage fiction, and a short piece collected in *Exterminator!* can be read as a pastiche of the genre. "The Perfect Servant" takes place within the Pentagon, where an official is confronted with the decision whether or not to release on America a virus that will bring about the "complete, precise and permanent programming of thought feeling and sensory data."[68] His servant Bently *seems* to be the typical self-effacing functionary until a whole series of officials die after contact with him, thanks to devices like an exploding pen. The reader's expectations of who he is are obviously influenced by the Pentagon official who declares: "gotta stay ahead of the Commies" (a recurring slogan of Burroughs's knee-jerk patriots), but in fact Bently wipes off his grey features to reveal none other than Fu Manchu, who watches the death of the whole American landscape. The servant's revelation anachronistically breaks the genre convention preventing a Communist takeover, which, Burroughs implies, would just perpetuate the same power structure, and the sketch slides into a fantasy of national death.

Burroughs draws on conspiratorial narratives to articulate a permanent state of crisis from the early 1960s onward. "These are conditions of total emergency" is a refrain that echoes through *Nova Express* but that applies equally well to the other novels. Against the historical backdrop of revelations of covert government programs, the Vietnam War, and Watergate, Burroughs's attribution of a multifaceted conspiracy to the CIA sets off an extrapolative series that only gradually becomes farfetched. Are they secretly using the methods of Scientology? Perhaps. Are they encouraging a plague against the white race so that they can rebuild the race to their own specifications? Less likely, but this is raised within the context of a fictional narrative. There are some signs that Burroughs took these conspiracies all too seriously; in one interview, for instance, he even admits a suspicion that AIDS is a fiendish plot mounted by the CIA.[69]

The ambiguous allusion to Scientology reflects Burroughs's ambivalence toward that organization. In 1959 he suspected that Scientology was being "used more for manipulation than therapy" and toward the end of his life noted that the movement was "evil and basically ill-intentioned and nasty."[70] In 1968 Burroughs took a course in Scientology and, according to his biographer Ted Morgan, became disgusted by that organization's security checks, which included making Burroughs submit to a lie detector.[71] Indeed he described the Scientologists' E-Meter as a "sloppy form" of ESB technology, something between a "lie detector and a mind-reading machine."[72] Burroughs left the movement but felt it raised such important issues that in 1970 he published a considered statement on its methods. Although he continued to respect its "precise and efficient" methods of therapy, he attacked the institutional practices of Scientology as authoritarian; claimed that L. Ron Hubbard's statements were frequently fascistic, that Scientologists demanded "unquestioning acceptance" from new subjects; and argued too much of the organization remained shrouded in secrecy.[73] Claiming to liberate the subject, Scientology was basically offering a different kind of mental bondage.

■ The most fantastic dimension to mind control was suggested to Burroughs by Sheila Ostrander and Lynn Schroeder's 1970 study *Psychic Discoveries behind the Iron Curtain,* which in the late sixties before the Brezhnev clampdown, gathered a wealth of material suggesting that the Soviet Union was pursuing systematic research into telepathic transmission, distance viewing, and a host of other subjects beyond the orthodox Western limits of physiology.[74] The Soviet authorities revealed that the U.S. Navy was pursuing research into telepathy. Burroughs had decided in the early 1950s that telepathy was a real possibility and so must have viewed sympathetically the Soviet scientists' open-minded approach. Both these scientists and Ostrander and Schroeder warned darkly of a bizarre PSI race that might develop between the superpowers, which Burroughs imagined was a systematic program of black magic being pursued by the CIA.[75] He then wrote the possibility into the last volume of his Western trilogy, *The Western Lands,* in a narrative concerning two Special Operations agents called See (who can project deadly hatred through his eyes) and Prick (who has other skills). Both agents begin to imagine they are being pursued everywhere by a dog until Prick is knocked down by a laundry truck (a detail Burroughs transposes from the report of an alleged CIA killing), and See apparently commits suicide. Their bosses assume that these deaths cannot be accidental, and Burroughs's reader similarly assumes that the agents' hallucinations have been technologically induced by unspecified means.

During the 1970s Burroughs became interested in the psychic dimension to intelligence. In an essay from that period he declared: "I suggest that what the CIA is, or was working on, at their top secret Nevada installation may be described as *computerized* black magic." He goes on to recommend a science fiction novel by John E. Rossmann that contains "some real inside information" on psychic research, particularly on the use of electronic mood-alteration machines. Burroughs quotes a scientist in the novel who predicts the following scenario: although currently different groups are competing with each other in a sort of psychic arms race, "there is a good possibility that they could even now join forces and make a *combined* psychic bid for world control." Burroughs takes this speculation further and imagines the emergence of an "elite of power addicts," concluding with a warning of the dystopia that may result: "There would be no place for dissent or independent research. The troublesome artist would be eliminated or absorbed. The elite lives happily ever after, at the top of a control state that makes 1984 seem cosy and nostalgic."[76]

Burroughs takes a technical possibility and pursues it to its political extreme, whereas in Rossmann's *The Mind Masters* (1974) such a speculation remains limited to the scientist leading the secret project.[77] The novel describes a nightmarish road race between the protagonist Britt St. Vincent, a professional racing driver, and another car that he can neither shake off nor pass. In this race he is led up a mountain in California to the secret Merlo Institute, where the director reveals that the second car was an induced psychic projection. A Vietnam vet and a physiological psychologist, Britt had once worked for this group and assumed that its activities had ceased. Not so. The work goes on in isolating the spirit as an electromagnetic force field that in turn can be manipulated, controlled, or even destroyed. Most of the novel shows the valiant Britt battling with the forces of evil haunting a Sicilian castle and at the same time playing an impressive part in the Mille Miglia race.

The melodrama of the novel's action has only an oblique connection with the early expository sections that caught Burroughs's attention. These contain first of all a brief history of the subject of psychic warfare and mention Project Pandora. Project Pandora was a CIA operation set up after the discovery that the U.S. embassy in Moscow had been bombarded with microwave impulses. Experiments were conducted throughout the 1960s using monkeys as guinea pigs, and the conclusion was reached that the radiation was not dangerous. This was not the end of such research, however, and the CIA Star Gate program pursued investigations into psychokinesis, distance viewing, and related subjects.[78] The research and even the organization of Rossmann's institute are thus quite plausible, and in a self-authenticating gesture he has the institute produce a series of "true-to-fact novels" popularizing aspects of parapsychology. What emerges most powerfully, however, in the principal Dr. Webster's account of this new technology is the unconsciousness of the public. Gesturing though a window to Britt, he explains: "Out there, beyond our mountain, people are going about their daily work unaware that their very minds and souls are in danger of being possessed by powers and for purposes as evil as any that a Satan could conceive. . . . [E]very one of us [is] threatened by hidden, headlong-rushing research into nightmares!"[79] This is a somewhat disingenuous expression of concern since Webster himself is fuelling this research, and it remains ambiguous whether his evocation of historical manipulation is just a projection of his own institutional paranoia. He presents a view of the student riots in the United States as being stage-managed by means of these new devices by right-wing military fanatics presumably hoping to break down civil order and prepare for a coup.

Where Rossmann has serious difficulties integrating his account of the new mind-control technology into his narrative, which gradually slides into a conventional battle between Good and Evil, Whitley Strieber manages such an integration better in his 1989 novel *Majestic*. Burroughs read a number of Strieber's works, including *Communion* (1987), and in 1989 he spent a weekend with that writer, discussing extra-terrestrial visitors. He later recorded in his journals: "I was convinced that the aliens, or whatever they are, are a real phenomenon."[80] Burroughs must also have responded sympathetically to the paranoid dimension to Strieber's writings that, thematically at least, resembles his own.

Although Strieber's first writings lie within the horror genre, *Black Magic* (1982) moves into the same subject area as Rossmann. This novel too describes a conspiracy, but one situated within the starkest Cold War polarities. A top KGB officer called Teplov is promoting project "Black Magic," which involves a plan to set up extra-low frequency (ELF) radio antennas around the United States to take captive the minds of the population. Teplov himself is a throwback to an earlier Stalinist era; now under Brezhnev "he spent his time manoeuvering and lying, keeping the truth of himself secret from the world." Part of his internalized secrecy is a kind of doublethink where he dreams of conquering America but in the name of utopia: "He was bringing paradise to America."[81] Again, as in Rossmann, technology opens up a spectacle of national enslavement that Teplov's opposite number, CIA agent Paul Winter, imagines in the following way: "The devil of it was that the victims of an ELF field could be controlled so completely that they wouldn't know anything was happening to them. A whole nation could be put in invisible chains. . . . It wasn't science fiction. Hell, it wasn't even advanced physics. But it smacked of parapsychology, and that made it junk as far as the American scientific establishment was concerned."[82] Once again we see the disparity being opened up between public unawareness and secret threat. And the allusions to demonic possession resurface once again as early as the novel's opening scene where a Minuteman crew aborts the launch of nuclear missiles when they are seized by a terror so intense it brings their deaths. Strieber describes the effects of ELF radiation as nausea, hallucination, and even out-of-body experiences. The dream of control remains a fantasy because neither the technology itself nor the operating agency can be controlled. Strieber's novel proves to be as conservative in its narrative form as in its politics. The Soviets are demonized as a cynical aggressor and the action simplifies down to a struggle between the Bond-like Winter and the monstrous Teplov.

Strieber's novel on the 1947 Roswell incident, *Majestic* (1989), was read appreciatively by Burroughs for its portrayal of the intelligence agencies. At one point the main character, an intelligence agent named Will Stone, remarks: "When the history of this era is written, it must certainly be called the Age of Secrets. . . . Everything important is classified." In an interview Burroughs expanded on this statement: "Anything of the least importance nowadays is top secret, classified, unavailable."[83] Strieber plays to the reader's desire for inside information by including within the text top-secret memos and interrogation transcripts and by building a premise of skepticism into the method of the novel itself. He assembles sections that center on key figures involved in what went on at Roswell and pieces together a narrative that follows the sequence of events from the discovery of what was apparently an extraterrestrial craft through the subsequent military cover-up. Although Will Stone presents the most articulate interpretation—and therefore the reader cannot help but suspect that he functions as a surrogate for Strieber—the novel does not allow the different views to gel into a single account. Roswell remains an enigma right to the end of the novel. The aliens and their craft have a disorienting and subliminal effect on those who claim to have seen them, and one of the most interesting progressions in the novel is the shifts in Stone's interpretation. At first he sees the aliens as pure but transformed into monsters by the diseased nature of the human psyche. Then recession, one of the operative principles of paranoid narratives, comes into play. He infers a concealed purpose, deciding that the disk and bodies were put there deliberately: "It was the bait. And we had taken it, and were wriggling on the line." Then the purpose becomes more personal for Stone. As his fear mounts, he realizes: "the aliens had isolated me from my peers. They were breaking me, and I knew it. The devils were out to destroy my mind."[84] Strieber demonstrates how difficult it was historically for the people involved in the Roswell incident to avoid projecting a paradigm of malign alien invasion on to the mystery. The explanation of fears, the release of sexual repressions, and odd behavior shifts as the result of alien intervention is double-edged. On the one hand it evokes powerful forces at work behind the visible; on the other hand it binds those affected together into a community of victims.

One unusual twist to Strieber's interest in aliens has emerged with his suggestion in *The Secret School* (1997) that he, while a young boy in the mid-1950s, was subjected to lengthy and unexplained intelligence tests. This fed his suspicion that he might have been the unwitting subject of the CIA's covert experiments on mind control. For that reason he has stated that he has been amassing material about the agency for some time. Strieber has continued to express belief in alien visitations and the use of implants on their human victims.[85]

By the time James Mills's *The Power* (1990) was published, interest in parapsychology, or psychotronics (the latter term a Czech coinage) as it became known, had become so established within the intelligence community that both the Soviets and the Americans were pursuing research projects in this area. The novel sets its action against the upheavals in Russia caused by Brezhnev's death and exploits reports in the West that the Soviets had gained an advantage in research into psychic warfare. Our hero (for once again we cannot avoid the Bond pattern) is Jack Hammond, a scientific intelligence officer who has to investigate the truths of these reports. The embodiment of the power wielded through ELF technology is Darya, a beautiful femme fatale who induces whole-body orgasms in the men she encounters. Schematically contrasted with her is Valentina, a Christian dissident who exercises her benign healing powers on the dying premier Andropov. Once again we see the problems authors experience in giving adequate narrative expression to the new technology of mind control. One question in the plot is whether Darya will defect to the West. A second is whether she is in touch with Satan, as some allege. As in *The Mind Masters,* the novel opens with rapid (and glamorous) action on the French Riviera, then pauses to expound the psychotronics that lie at the heart of its subject, but ultimately it proves unable to make this technology affect the narrative. The real action of the novel concentrates on Jack Hammond's attempts to verify whether Darya will defect and what exactly goes on in her Serbenov Institute in Moscow. When Hammond finally penetrates the Institute he finds evidence of induced psychoses and sexual frenzy that potentially could be directed against the world's premiers. But Hammond's psychic experience of Darya proves to be conventionally Manichean. When she is torturing the captive Valentina, he has the following "dream": "the living room was in gloom. Something alive was moving, something dark but visible, radiating energy. Everything the darkness touched went to blackness. . . . It destroyed light. As he watched in his dream, his head and stomach throbbing, he could

feel the darkness against his skin—a hot, lightless fire, black fire. A low, reso-
nating growl moved with the darkness. Hammond's nostrils filled with the
stink of vomit, feces, decaying flesh."[86] Here Mills simply transforms the
struggle between the two women into a conflict between light and dark, the
spirit and the body. Darya has become abstracted into figurative representations of her qualities: her energy, predatory nature, and (to the male focalizer) sexual threat. The denouement owes more to pragmatic politics than
moral triumph, however, when Andropov offers the destruction of Darya's
project in return for Valentina's healing.

The capacity of ELF transmissions to affect behavior from a distance is
imagined by Burroughs and Mills as a possibility in the imminent future.
Larry Collins's intelligence thriller *Maze* (1989) attempts to realize this possibility in narrative by describing a KGB scheme to induce uncontrollable anger
in the U.S. president over the bombing, by Iranians as he thinks, of an American installation in West Germany and to provoke him into massive retalia-
tion. The means used will isolate and reproduce the electronic signals that
produce anger within the president's brain. As we might expect from a former
journalist, Collins feeds considerable information about the CIA's own research
on ESP (Projects Bluebird and Seashell) into the narrative and describes in
detail the experiments conducted in a Moscow neurophysiology institute that
make this technology possible. The novel implicitly attacks Americans' complacency about their own intelligence technology and dramatizes a struggle
for credibility between the CIA director and Art Bennington, a specialist in
behavioral sciences working for the agency. In order to set up the credibility of
his subject, Collins, through Bennington, ridicules the idea of *The Manchurian Candidate* ("that was bullshit, pure fiction") and of brainwashing. Bennington retorts to a colleague: "Every time we run up against some guys from
the other side whose behaviour doesn't conform to what we would like it to
be, we decide they're brainwashed. . . . Brainwashing doesn't exist and it never
has."[87] The novel as a whole substantiates Bennington's position by concentrating on physiological research carried out in Moscow, whose lineage de-
scends from Pavlov via José Delgado. The discovery of how to isolate brain
waves is hailed as bringing within the KGB's grasp their "long-standing goal of
finding a way to influence human behavior at a distance by remote means."[88]
But the novel leaves the door ajar to ESP in that an American "distant viewer"
who can locate Soviet submarines is perceived to be such a threat by the KGB
that she is assassinated. *Maze* uses a realist mode to demonstrate, as Burroughs
suspected, that a form of mind reading had become technically possible.

So far we have seen many instances of mind control overlapping into psychiatry. From Zamyatin's *We* through David Karp's *One* to Burroughs's *Naked Lunch*, psychiatric institutions and practices are presented as means for enforcing political and social orthodoxies that transform therapy into coercion. Information about many research projects in the 1950s and 1960s, which were covertly funded by intelligence agencies, began to leak out, appearing to validate the processes imagined in the fiction of the period. In short, psychiatry and politics combined to such an extent that control became the dominant subject. This explains why two of the most famous American novels to describe psychotherapy—Ken Kesey's *One Flew Over the Cuckoo's Nest* and Sylvia Plath's *The Bell Jar*—should both identify the practices of therapeutic institutions with the ideological processes of the nation. How they do this will form the subject of chapter 7.

seven

Psychotherapy and
Social Enforcement

We have already seen numerous instances of how behavioral difference can be construed as an illness needing therapy. In the narratives considered in this chapter, primarily *Invisible Man, One Flew
Over the Cuckoo's Nest,* and *The Bell Jar,* treatment for mental illness is
described as an exercise of institutional power tantamount to imprisonment.
Thomas Szasz asserted as much in the introduction of his 1973 anthology,
The Age of Madness, when he stated: "Involuntary mental hospitalization . . .
has been and remains, the paradigmatic policy of psychiatry." For him the
relation between the institutional psychiatrist and the patient resembled that
of master and slave.[1]

In the 1960s reports were filtering out to the West of psychiatric hospitals
being used to imprison dissidents in the Soviet Union, and Valerij Tarsis's
1965 novel *Ward 7* gave one of the very few descriptions of such institutions.
His mental hospital is run in a manner very similar to those we shall see in
Ken Kesey's *One Flew Over the Cuckoo's Nest:* strict regimentation, compulsory medication, and precious little attention to therapy. However, one difference lies in the fact that Kesey presents his institution as a symbolic representation of the United States as a whole, while Tarsis shows that his inmates
achieve a kind of freedom in their ward. Since the worst has happened, the
ward becomes a place of freedom where the most subversive ideas can be
discussed. A further ironic reversal lies in Stalin's legacy of national neurosis.

One character comments: "You could safely diagnose every Russian as suffering from persecution mania."[2] Szasz and Tarsis interpret psychotherapy as social coercion and in what follows we shall see such power play being foregrounded again and again. We shall further see the diagnostic spotlight being shifted from the therapeutic subjects to the state of a society that allows such institutionalized practices as lobotomy or electro-convulsive therapy (ECT) to take place. Descriptions of mental institutions thus turn into diagnoses of society at large.

The prefrontal lobotomy, which was practiced extensively throughout the 1940s and 1950s as a drastic catch-all cure for mental illness, initially figured only in isolated images and scenes in literary works, like Robert Lowell's poem "Memories of West Street and Lepke." Refused the status in the 1940s of a conscientious objector, Lowell was given a year in jail, where he saw the gangster Lepke after his lobotomy: "he drifted in a sheepish calm, / where no agonizing reappraisal / jarred his concentration on the electric chair." Although Lepke is a criminal, Lowell presents his new apathy as a physical symbol of the "tranquilized fifties," of a decade of "lost connections." In Tennessee Williams's *Suddenly Last Summer* (1959) a doctor is seeking funds to support this new technique of surgery but expresses misgivings about its permanency. His potential backer, Mrs. Venable, has no such scruples and is blatantly pursuing her hatred of her dead son's lover who has received insulin and ECT treatment. Mrs. Venable sees a lobotomy crudely as a means of erasing the past by cutting the story out of the girl's brain and thus of preserving her son's reputation as a chaste poet. Robert Penn Warren's 1946 novel *All the King's Men* takes a different tack in combining a consideration of the ethics of lobotomy with the physical details of the act itself. The journalist narrator witnesses an operation on a catatonic schizophrenic that remains one of the most vivid descriptions of a lobotomy. The trepanning of the skull does not bother him too much:

> I did fine until they started the burning. For taking out the chunks of brain they use an electric gadget which is nothing but a little metal rod stuck in a handle with an electric cord coming out of the handle. The whole thing looks like an electric curling iron. In fact, all the way through I was struck by the notion that all the expensive apparatus was so logical and simple and homey, and reminded me so completely of the stuff around any well-equipped household.[3]

The narrator's familiarization of the operating implements is a far cry from later accounts that stress the alien nature of psychosurgery. In fact, the journalist's reactions are more complex than they seem because he is next struck by the smell as the rod cauterizes parts of the brain, which triggers a memory of a horse burning to death in a stable. The memory link suggests that the operation is a kind of killing (the surgeon is frank about the patient's problematic chances of survival), an implication thinly screened by the narrator's ironic comparisons with religious conversion. At the end of the lobotomy he tells the bemused surgeon: "You forgot to baptize him."

These examples present the lobotomy as an exercise of power, where the patient takes second place to the working of the law, wealth, or the need to try out medical technology.[4] It was Bernard Wolfe's 1952 novel *Limbo* that made lobotomy a central part of its subject by applying the theories of Norbert Wiener. In his 1948 study *Cybernetics*, Wiener briefly speculates on how much light the mind-computer analogy might shed on mental illness, concluding that the latter might be a problem of memory primarily. Wiener dryly comments on the lobotomy to the effect that "it has recently been having a certain vogue, probably not unconnected with the fact that it makes the custodial care of many patients easier." He continues sardonically, "let me remark in passing that killing them makes their custodial care still easier." Here Wiener anticipates objections made in Michael Crichton's *The Terminal Man* and elsewhere to the true motivation for lobotomies. He acknowledges, however, that the operations do have a certain kind of success, not by curing the root problem but by "damaging or destroying the capacity for maintained worry, known in the terminology of another profession as the *conscience*."[5] It is difficult to locate exactly where Wiener stands in relation to what later became known as the man-machine interface. On the one hand, he stresses the complexity and sophistication of the brain; on the other hand, he constructs a science out of how machines might simulate mental acts. For some contemporary commentators he seemed to be the prime spokesman for the mechanization of thought. In a special number of the little magazine *Neurotica* devoted to the machine, John Del Torto recognized Wiener's humanistic scruple in passages like the ones just quoted but nevertheless associates him with the general application of mechanics to many spheres, including that of psychopathology:

> Lobotomy (disconnecting parts of the machine), electric shock (snapping up the voltage in the tubes), rest (shutting down the engine),

chemical shock (priming the carburetor), and, doubtless, transorbital leucotomy (best left undescribed) and all the rest of the castrations—actual and symbolic—so dear to modern surgery, are some of the parallel "machine" processes that are used in human therapy.[6]

The total identification of psychopathological treatment with mechanics rules out any possibility of the former, which is presented as an attack on or violation of the self. We shall see how this position becomes reinforced by other writers of the Beat movement.

When Bernard Wolfe applied Wiener's theories in *Limbo* they were situated within a broad diagnosis of Western man (he pays little attention to the female of the species) as being a "self-maiming animal" and in his appendix of sources cites cases of individuals actually seeking lobotomies. The discourse of mechanics is applied broadly here, to human pathology and also to Cold War politics. A nuclear war breaks out between East and West because each bloc loses control of their defense computer. When this anxiety about control is applied to mental health, Wolfe uses imagery very similar to the *Neurotica* article discussed earlier. Like Wiener, he recognizes the complexity and mystery of the brain, which contrasts ironically with the crudity of the applied medical measures. After listing ECT and "narcotic shock," Wolfe continues: "The new fad became lobotomy and related brain operations. Here the principle was essentially the same, mechanical: now the troublemaking cogs and circuits were snipped out of the machine or at least cut off from it." Wolfe speculates on the motives of neurosurgeons who ultimately do not know what they are doing. Their ignorance makes the operations into a kind of magic that benefits the status of the practitioners rather than the patients. Drawing this comparison, Wolfe denies any grand narrative of progress and even suggests that the surgeons view mental disturbance as a possession by evil forces. Hence the operations are designed "to show that they were not endangered by this malignancy but, on the contrary, were in control of it."[7]

Such narrative comments establish a pointedly ironic context for Wolfe's protagonist, a neurosurgeon who has tried to escape from the lunacy of World War III by flying to an island in the Indian Ocean. Dr. Martine is Wolfe's equivalent of H. G. Wells's Moreau, like him seeking refuge on an uncharted island. The parallels between the two figures implicitly question Martine's motives in that he has transformed the island into an experimental area where he tries to purge the local Mandunjis of their "disturbances" and to perfect his surgical techniques on animals by carrying out lobotomies.

The result is a loss of energy so severe that his subjects become zombies: "Heads lolling, mouths loose and hanging open, arms and legs flung like sacks of maize on the pallets." Martine sees a problem but is unwilling to change his practices as a result. The operations may remove aggression, but they also remove the subjects' sexual drive: "How could you be sure that, in allegedly cutting away some of the devils from the brain, you were not at the same time cutting away some guardian angels?"[8] The simple answer is that you couldn't, and Wolfe's stress on the "couplings" of the brain forms part of a rhetorical opposition between joining and separating that runs right through the novel. When Martine returns to postwar America he finds that a pacifist movement is promoting the cause of amputation as a means of removing human aggression. One of the many black ironies in the novel arises from the fact that the new prosthetic limbs turn out to be more efficient than physical ones and, therefore, easier to turn into weapons.[9] The novel opens with a section on Mandunji Island that explores surgical interventions in the brain and, therefore, the mind; later sections describe the application of equally mechanical and equally mystifying operations to the body. In both cases it is assumed that aggression is a physical characteristic that can be quantified or located in specific sections of the brain.

Throughout *Limbo* Wolfe uses puns and other devices to link apparently disparate fields of knowledge. Connectedness is one of the novel's premises. Take the example of brain mapping. This emerging science is referred to early in the novel to help demonstrate that Martine's well intentioned activities on the island constitute a form of colonial appropriation. While he is trying to locate centers in the brain, he places the island on the map and helps it to enter history—Western history that is. Far from having no effect on the community, Martine transforms their sense of illness so radically that they have come to view the operations as a ceremony with Martine playing one of the leading roles. He is never quite described as a ruler, but the analogies with Dr. Moreau suggest that, and at the same time question, the efficacy of the operations because in Wells's novel Moreau loses control of his subjects. Wolfe dramatizes Martine's activities as a massive intervention in the psyches of individual islanders and at the same time in the working of the community as a whole. The power play could not be more blatant.

Where Wolfe discusses both external and self-imposed treatments for violence, Ralph Ellison's *Invisible Man* (1952) establishes electricity as a metaphor for political power in its prologue, which describes the narrator's underground existence as an extended covert battle against Manipulated Light and Power, the nation represented as a utility. This metaphor figures mainly in two critical scenes: the smoker and the aftermath of the accident at Liberty Paints. In the first, the electrified carpet from which the black boys have to retrieve supposed gold coins recalls the aversion conditioning of *Brave New World*, with the difference that now the aim is entertainment, not psychological modification. The episode ritually reinforces the power of southern whites in their conversion of the boys into spectacle. The boys' loss of control reconfirms the whites' power—technological and political. The narrator arrives at the hotel expecting a graduation ritual, in other words a celebration of coming to maturity, and actually experiences a ritual of subjection where his ethic of "social instrumentality" exposes the blatant contradictions between professed ideals and social practice.[10]

The later episode at Liberty Paints is more complex, since the description is packed with ironically inverted allusions to the nation as a whole: its suppression of the black workforce, its racial distortion of equality, and its identification of commercial with national interests. Appropriately for the McCarthy era, Ellison depicts a paranoid fear of unrest running through the company, against which the narrator can protect himself by the ritual recital of company (and so by implication, national) slogans. Immediately after the accident the narrator goes through a rite of rebirth that foregrounds society's imposition of roles for him. This "mechanized parody of the birth process" entails the function of the building as clinic or hospital, but early analogies with the electric chair suggest that a heavily authoritarian "therapy" is taking place. The narrator is strapped into a machine and then subjected to electroshock treatment: "I was pounded between crushing electrical pressures; pumped between live electrodes like an accordion between a player's hands."[11] The first statement suggests a quasi-industrial process as if the narrator were raw material; the second points to an instrumentalization of the self at the hands of racial or political "performers."

In effect the narrator has become an experimental subject for the white technicians who loom ominously over him and who compare notes about the best "treatment" to pursue. Should it be a prefrontal lobotomy or ECT? One even suggests castration. By this point it has become clear that Ellison is exploiting the narrator's semiconsciousness to depict a situation that shifts surreally from resemblances with a hospital to a death cell, experimental laboratory, and so on. The ambiguity of this key episode disorients the reader, partly because the narrator is compared to a criminal. Does his "guilt" lie in his mere social existence rather than in any specific act? From the point of view of the clinicians this hardly matters since they deny his subjectivity anyway, reducing him to a guinea pig for the new machine. Its proponent claims superior efficiency over a lobotomy: "We apply pressure in the proper degrees to the major centres of nerve control . . . and the result is as complete a change of personality as you'll find in your fairy-tale cases of criminals transformed into amiable fellows after all that bloody business of a brain operation."[12] When an official asks about the narrator's mental life he is told that "the patient will live as he has to live," a tautology that thinly masks the prescriptions implied in the technicians' actions. Their discussion of the narrator perfectly exemplifies what Walter Bowart calls the "external" discourse of behaviorism to such an extent that they even talk of "getting [the narrator] started," as if he is a faulty machine.[13]

Not surprisingly, the narrator experiences a total estrangement from his previous experience (his mind is as blank as the half-formed replicants in *Body Snatchers*) and from language itself. The cards the technicians hold before him act like an interrogation, which fills the narrator with panic because he can find no words. Once he emerges from this aphasia, the estrangement continues nevertheless: "I had the feeling that I had been talking beyond myself, had used words and expressed attitudes not my own, that I was in the grip of some alien personality lodged deep within me."[14] Here the novel approaches science fiction, suggesting a kind of technologically induced "possession." More helpfully, we could view this moment as the narrator's first glimpse of the condition of otherness in language. Up to now he has been naively identifying selfhood with his own words. Now and at later points in the novel he realizes that his words have been already scripted. The trope of death and rebirth dramatizes the attendant alienation from his own discourse, which has already been thematized when a total stranger approaches the narrator to tell him he admired the latter's speech. Such estrangement leaves it an open question whether the narrator can ever become assimilated into the collective social "machine."

■ From around 1951 the CIA was engaged in a search to find the ultimate truth serum, a search that involved testing out many substances, including LSD. The latter was covertly administered to mental patients and members of the armed forces under project ARTICHOKE, later more famously known as MK-ULTRA. Aldous Huxley, who numbered among his friends Jolly West, an experimenter on LSD for the CIA, commented scathingly that the CIA scientists wanted to be Pavlovians but "Pavlov never saw an animal in its natural state, only under duress."[15] Timothy Leary tried out LSD on prisoner volunteers at the Concorde Correctional Facility as part of a program from Harvard University and was told later in the 1960s that the "guys who really run things in Washington" wanted to "use drugs for warfare, for espionage, for brainwashing, for control."[16]

Also under this same program, different facilities paid volunteers to act as guinea pigs in the experiments. Two of these volunteers, both coincidentally signing up in California, were writers Allen Ginsberg and Ken Kesey. Ginsberg was put in touch with the doctors at the Palo Alto Veterans Administration Hospital by the psychologist Gregory Bateson (then working at the hospital as "ethnologist") and took LSD under supervision in 1959. Apart from psychological tests, a stroboscope was synchronized to the alpha rhythms of Ginsberg's brain. Ginsberg was deeply disturbed by the experience. "It was like watching my own inner organism," he later recalled; and he developed a fear that he would be "absorbed into the electrical grid of the entire nation." Then he used a metaphor that was to become central to Kesey's first novel: "I thought I was trapped in a giant web or network of forces beyond my control that were perhaps experimenting with me or were perhaps from another planet or were from some super-government or cosmic military or science-fiction Big Brother."[17] This sequence of increasingly fantastic speculations was triggered by the then prevailing culture of secrecy, although it is doubtful whether confirmation of the covert experiments would have lessened Ginsberg's alarm.

Ken Kesey was at this time taking a postgraduate course in creative writing at Stanford University and, on the suggestion of a postgraduate psychology student, took LSD under the direction of Dr. Leo Hollister at Menlo Park, which was then participating in the CIA's drug research program. Then in 1960 Kesey took a job as psychiatric aide at the hospital, cleaning floors and tending to patients. He found his material for *One Flew Over the Cuckoo's Nest* (1962) here, composing the novel "both on the ward and on drugs."[18]

Given the nature of Kesey's subject, it is surprising that so few critics have commented on the psychiatric context of *Cuckoo's Nest*. One exception is a short article by Robert Rosenwein, who discusses the larger issue of insanity as a social problem and the perception in the fifties that "insanity was a form of moral deviance."[19] The resocialization of the inmate involved the prescriptive process of relearning his or her place in society, which also offered a means for society to protect itself from the insane. Rosenwein helpfully alerts us to the play of social values operating within the world of Kesey's novel. Its political dimension can be brought out by juxtaposing *Cuckoo's Nest* with a contemporary examination of mental hospitals, Erving Goffman's *Asylums* (1961). Goffman spells out the negative effects of what he calls a "total institution" by examining its internal politics and procedures. On entry, the inmate undergoes a "series of abasements, degradations, humiliations, and profanations of the self" when his clothes are removed.[20] He then participates in group sessions that remind Goffman of the "Communist confession camps." Institutionalization takes precedence over preparing the inmates for a return to society, and specific rewards or privileges are offered for obedience to the staff. Spaces in the asylum are very closely controlled, some being forbidden, others being under constant surveillance.

Point for point, every characteristic listed by Goffman appears in *Cuckoo's Nest*. Kesey's ironies are repeatedly directed against the asylum as the site for a power play, not therapy. According to his chronicler, Tom Wolfe, Kesey was obsessed by the "anti-cure" that was at work in the psychiatric ward, which consisted of "Keep them cowed and docile. Play on the weakness that drove them nuts in the first place. Stupefy the bastards with tranquilizers and if they get out of line haul them up to the 'shock shop' and punish them."[21] The early parts of the novel describe the routine of a typical day, where time is precisely measured by the kinds of activity taking place. The staff have created a "world of precision efficiency" where the very thoughts of the inmates have been calculated: "after the nurse gets her staff, efficiency locks the ward like a watchman's clock. Everything the guys think and say and do is all worked out months in advance, based on the little notes the nurse makes during the day."[22] These notes are typed on cards fed into a computer-like machine that reinforces the regular functioning of the ward.

Into this context strides McMurphy, who is simply described as an "Admission," a case that confirms Goffman's account of the degradation patients suffer on entry to the asylum. His clothes are removed, and he is subjected to the routine rectal temperature check, but he comically refuses to acquiesce to the uniformity of the regime by retaining his cap, playing games with his uniform, and earning the stigma of "manipulator" from the ward sister, Big Nurse. Many critics have commented on McMurphy's roots in folklore, but Kesey's own explanation ties him in closely with the inmates themselves. He said that McMurphy had no prototype; he was "fictional, inspired by the tragic longing of the real men I worked with on the ward."[23] In other words, McMurphy is a deliberately exaggerated or idealized figure who personifies the vigor and self-esteem the inmates feel they lack.

McMurphy is too active a character to act merely as witness. Thus in one of the key early episodes, that of the group meeting, he reveals the covert power play taking place. This meeting is based on the concept of the Therapeutic Community, which the narrator ironically summarizes as involving supposedly democratic action and the social judgments made in identifying mental illness. The notion of the Therapeutic Community was actively promoted by Maxwell Jones (named by one of Kesey's inmates) in an attempt to remove the hierarchy in the treatment situation. Thus patients were to take on themselves the function of therapist. One commentator has explained that "the therapeutic community is seen as a society, and in that way analogically related to the wider society itself."[24] Exactly this analogy is drawn in Kesey's novel. The doctor tells the group that their intention is to create a "little world Inside that is a made-to-scale prototype of the big world Outside."[25] Despite the benign purpose of the movement, some more confrontational communities were "denounced by some outsiders as little short of brainwashing."[26]

The practice in Kesey's novel reveals the manipulatory nature of these group meetings. The whole situation is tightly controlled by Big Nurse, who apportions time to speakers, shifts the topic of discussion, and covertly empties the situation of any possible therapeutic benefit. The inmates' "confessions" conflate moral guilt with mental illness, hence the narrator's comparison with a trial. As a Korean War veteran, McMurphy is well placed to draw the same analogy as Goffman with the Chinese prison camps and then to compare the situation with a chicken's "pecking party." Far from any group dynamic, the meeting is designed to reinforce Big Nurse's authority. Kesey skillfully describes the oblique challenges to her "protocol" in McMurphy's mock-serious questions and presents the power struggle between the two through gesture and facial expression. At every point Big Nurse's resumption of a mask-like impassivity signals her regaining the power she needs to orchestrate the situation.

But what of the ward as microcosm? Like the factory of Liberty Paints in Ellison's *Invisible Man*, any national analogies in the novel question the practice of democracy. The ward is presided over by Big Nurse in consultation with an ineffectual managerial group of doctors. To one side of them there is the elite group of technicians who administer the ECT and conduct the lobotomies. In the middle there are the patients, themselves divided into Acutes (who might get out) and Chronics (who never will). They act out a pseudo-democratic process of consultation through the Patients Council. There is also a menial underclass of black attendants who actually exercise power over the patients and who are directly answerable to Big Nurse. Any resemblance to democracy is spurious, and Big Nurse wields a virtually absolute power over the ward on the institutional premise that hers is an insane ward.

This power is exercised partly as a control of space. The inmates are denied any privacy, which means that they have no space free from surveillance. Inmates are encouraged to spy and report on each other, and observations by the staff are recorded in a log book. Big Nurse decides what spaces are allotted to the inmates at what times of day, and any sort of recreation needs a special case to be made out for her approval. Control is exercised on the ward from the Nurses' Station, a glass cubicle that the patients are forbidden to enter. The control of space thus reflects the working of the ward rules, and when McMurphy pushes his fist through the glass of the Nurses' Station "by mistake," this is an obvious symbolic gesture of resistance. Where the theory of the Therapeutic Community was to encourage open dialogue, any request for information about the patients' medication is interpreted as hostility, which can be met with the absolute power of the "shock shop." The strict management of space in the ward establishes a context against which the boat trip by the inmates into the unbounded space of the sea seems to represent an excursion to freedom.

The novel, however, does not mount any simple opposition between inside and outside. The narrator's opening line, "They're out there," leaves ambiguous who "they" are and what space is being referred to. A crudely romantic reading would take the asylum as a prison and outside as the place of freedom, but Kesey's use of the microcosm analogy suggests that leaving the asylum would simply mean exchanging one kind of captivity for another. The attraction of the boat trip thus lies in its temporary distancing of the inmates from society. We should also remember the scene where McMurphy discovers to his astonishment that he is virtually the only nonvoluntary inmate on the ward. As Peter Sedgewick points out, here Kesey shrewdly draws out the "problem of internalised, voluntarised coercion in psychiatric treatment."[27] The narrator Chief Bromden (nicknamed Chief Broom and thereby reduced to a function) has internalized these pressures most effectively. Masquerading as a deaf mute, he uses his own body as a refuge from which he can observe the workings of the ward.

■ Before we consider the characteristics of Chief Bromden's narrative, we should note that during the 1950s some Beat writers transformed the very concept of insanity into a privilege as part of a series of protests against the norms of American society. For one, Carl Solomon had contact with the

French surrealists in the 1940s and after his return to America went to the New York State Psychiatric Institute to ask to receive a lobotomy. Solomon drew on his treatment and experiences in this facility for an important essay that was subsequently collected in *Mishaps, Perhaps* (1966). "Report from the Asylum" takes a Kafkaesque stance toward the mental ward and argues that "in the case of insulin-shock therapy, one finds oneself presented with a complete symbolism of paranoia, beginning with the rude awakening [the drug is forcibly administered in the middle of the night] and the enormous hypodermic needle, continuing through the dietary restrictions imposed upon patients receiving shock, and ending with the lapses of memory and the temporary physical disfigurement."[28] Solomon's capacity to stand apart from his most traumatic experiences helps to give authenticity and clarity to his testimony and colors his account with a black humor. One of the few critics to comment on his writings declares that "Solomon treats his paranoid hell in a prose which is without eccentricity."[29] Solomon displaces the charge of insanity on to the doctors themselves, as we shall see in William Burroughs, and blurs the distinction between asylum and outside world. Of the Pilgrim State Hospital, Solomon writes: "It is almost as though the 'real' world were an asylum and the unreal world is a super-asylum . . . for those who have gone insane in the outer madhouse and been placed in this outer void. It is a place where those who don't know they are insane are placed. Those who know they are ill are outside consulting psychiatrists." Solomon quotes from what he calls a leading "manual of arms" on ECT, where the authors admit that the effects of this treatment remain a "mystery," and he shrewdly contextualizes psychotherapy within the broader enforcement of conformity, which is primarily a social, even political issue: "A society which can't defend itself from its internal or external enemies finding a temporary solution only in conformity."[30] Within a very small compass, then, Solomon manages to criticize the practice of shock treatment as the traumatization of inmates by gratuitous cruelty and to question the popular polarization between asylum and outer world.

Solomon went on to achieve fame obliquely as the dedicatee of Ginsberg's "Howl," which celebrates madness as a form of inspiration. Here Solomon's cautious inversions have become complete. Ginsberg's frenzied style is in itself part of his polemic against sobriety, against a boring and mundane "sanity" that is acceptable to society. To counter this he incorporates phrases from Solomon and expands Solomon's notion of bearing witness to comment on a whole generation. Ginsberg pluralizes Solomon into a group perversity of those who "subsequently presented themselves on the granite steps of the madhouse with shaven heads and harlequin speech of suicide, demanding instantaneous lobotomy." What they receive is a conflation of psychotherapeutic treatment: "who were given instead the concrete void of insulin metrasol electricity hydrotherapy psychotherapy occupational therapy pingpong and amnesia."[31] This string of nouns symbolically smothers the creative activity of those cursed—or rather in this context, gifted—with madness.

Similarly, the Beat novelist Seymour Krim recorded his experiences in mental wards after a breakdown and subsequent suicide bid. During his second hospitalization he joined the now familiar mechanistic process of "therapy": "Once again I was on the human assembly-line: electric shock clubbed my good brain into needless unconsciousness . . . and unquestioned Old Testament authority ruled our little club."[32] As the psychiatrists made blatantly social, not medical, judgments, Krim came to see the very concept of insanity as being used to save families embarrassment and enforce social norms, and he defined a vigorous artistic role for himself in opposition to such prescriptions.

In *Cuckoo's Nest* Kesey was clearly trying to find a perspective that would reflect his experiences with LSD. Tom Wolfe quotes an experimenter as saying that "with these drugs your perception is altered enough that you find yourself looking out of completely strange eyeholes."[33] During the composition of the novel Kesey hit on the idea of using a dramatized narrator in order to bring out the bizarre dimension to his subject. To his friend Ken Babbs he recorded his admiration for Alexander Trocchi's novel *Cain's Book* and for Burroughs's *Naked Lunch*, at the same time indicating the direction he wanted to take: "Both have power and honesty, but lack something I plan to try to add—control."[34] He found this formal discipline in a dramatized narrator. Chief Bromden is a mixed-blood American Indian, suffering from traumatic memories of a wartime air raid, who has been diagnosed as paranoid. Bromden's paranoia represents a psychological starting point that reverses into hostility, the official ideology of benign therapy. The hospital staff represent part of a larger threatening group referred to simply as "them."

Cuckoo's Nest could not contrast more starkly with another best-selling psychiatric novel from the same period, Leo Rosten's *Captain Newman, M.D.* (1961), which describes an army psychiatric ward in America during the last years of World War II. Because the narrator is a lieutenant and a medic he establishes a tension between the perspectives on mental cases by the doctors and the army. Authority itself is never questioned, whereas Kesey presents his own narrative from the perspective of a dispossessed victim who has had repeated doses of electroshock treatment and whose account, therefore, has real difficulty in validating itself. Bromden thematizes this problem by anticipating his audience's objections: "you think the guy telling this is ranting and raving my *God*; you think this is too horrible to have really happened. . . . But it's the truth even if it didn't happen."[35]

Through Bromden, Kesey substitutes hallucinatory metaphors for documentary realism. It is Bromden, albeit not exclusively, who establishes the central dystopian metaphor of the machine to articulate the working of the ward and a quality of being. This metaphor entails a distinction between operator (Big Nurse) and technology (the ward), which Bromden describes as follows: "I see her sit in the center of this web of wires like a watchful robot, tending her network with mechanical insect skill, know every second which wire runs where and just what current to send up to get the results she wants." This double trope conflates dehumanization through technology with predatory intent (Nurse Ratched's name suggests a mechanism with teeth), like Ginsberg's description, then continues with a utopian image of ultimate mechanism: "What she dreams of there in the centre of those wires is a world of precision efficiency and tidiness like a pocket watch with a glass back."[36] This metaphor runs together a number of different characteristics. The spider's web suggests conspiracy and entrapment, the robot dehumanization, the insect analogy implies countless others of the same "species," and the wires imply connections, making an obvious play on technological and political power.

In this imagery it is obvious that power is being encoded as malign and female. Timothy Melley rightly points out that *Cuckoo's Nest* shares with *Invisible Man* and *The Manchurian Candidate* a common gendering of power as a female force sapping the vitality of the male protagonists. *Cuckoo's Nest* "places a potentially powerful story of institutional normalization into a gender framework that equates social control with emasculation and female power." This identification arises from Kesey's "commitment to a masculinist version of liberal individualism, a sense that to be 'free' means to be separate from the domestic sphere and protected from a technologically invasive society."[37] In *The Manchurian Candidate* we saw how the hidden power that betrays Raymond Shaw originates in the mother who fills him with oedipal desire as much as hatred. And in *Invisible Man* the protagonist is infantilized by the factory hospital authorities so as to undergo a "re-birthing." Kesey's use of Western folklore to describe McMurphy detaches ("frees") him from any family background; and Bromden's own origins are measured as a humiliation of his tribe and, even more important, of his father.

Bromden's sense of conspiracy leads him to describe mechanisms as they literally exist. So a pill "contains" a miniature electronic device; Big Nurse's words trigger Orwellian recording devices in the walls; and, in his deepest nightmare, Bromden imagines the ward to have been built over an enormous factory where workers themselves are fed into the furnaces like pods. Each image has a local motivation, arising from the circumstances of a particular moment. So when an inmate fights off an orderly his hand temporarily becomes an iron ball, a fetter transformed into a means of self-defense.

More generally, Bromden replaces democratic therapy with the image of the hospital as a factory producing robots for the Combine, a malign nationwide organization resembling the military–industrial complex. In an interview Kesey explained that he had in mind the "inhuman part of American industrialism."[38] In one of his drafts of the novel, Kesey has Bromden imagine the Combine bugging his body: "They put things *in!* They install things. . . . If you're too big you might turn out to be dangerous, a *Communist*, or a *fiend*, or a *gangster!*"[39] The novel only hints obliquely at the political paranoia of the time but briefly hints at a process changing American society as a whole. When the patients leave the hospital on an outing, Bromden registers changes in the landscape as an increase in suburban sprawl through the same conflation of technology and insect images. Where once lay open countryside he now sees a "*train* stopping at a station and laying a string of full grown men in mirrored suits and machined hats, laying them like a hatch of identical insects."[40]

Bromden's view of conspiracy connects at every point with the technology of mind control. In one of the manuscript pages of the novel, he describes how "they spot-welded my skull . . . pried me open and did something spot-welded me shut again."[41] This account—together with allusions to orderlies who press Bromden's "button" or to inmates' eyes resembling "blown fuses"—reads incongruously, as if machines have taken on sentience, but in fact such passages foreground through estrangement the hospital's treatment of the inmates, using external behaviorist methods that virtually deny the patients any subjectivity. Thus Don Kunz argues that "the idea that man responds predictably to stimuli, is shaped by environmental conditioning, and strives in the most economic fashion to achieve homeostasis is for Kesey a nightmarish absurdity."[42]

Bromden's narration forms a basic part of Kesey's antibehaviorist polemic in the novel by privileging his subjective life over physical response, and forcefully articulates the dystopian ironies in *Cuckoo's Nest*, confirming clinical psychologist Timothy Leary's claim that "the average mental hospital in the United States is a Kafkaesque, Orwellian prison camp more terrifying than Dachau because the captors claim to be the healers."[43] The ward is run with military precision; indeed one nurse comments that it is run by "Army nurses, trying to run an Army hospital."[44] The many references to the war and the army suggest a covert state of conflict between staff and inmates. When one inmate uses a hose against the others, as if firing from a fighter plane, he reminds us that the apparatus of therapy can be used as weapons.

The most charged vocabulary, however, is reserved for the electroshock treatment that takes place in a "filthy brain-murdering room," and *Cuckoo's Nest* reaches a dramatic peak at the point where Bromden and McMurphy are subjected to this ordeal.[45] The prison analogy is foregrounded and burlesqued by McMurphy when Big Nurse asks him to sign a "confession" of wrongdoing. Instead he acts out a medley of roles as if preparing for execution and crucifixion, then converting the experience into comic capital as a "supercharged" psychopath or a car that has just gone in for a service. Bromden's view as witness is totally different. He presents the patients as the helpless victims of a robotized technology now operating under its own momentum. A "beam" from the control panel sucks the victims in; ominously McMurphy's watch breaks open on the floor. Does this imply the failure of Big Nurse's ideal efficiency or the imminent assault on McMurphy's self? McMurphy is gagged and therefore blocked from resistance through joking and singing. Then the "treatment" takes place:

> Twist some dials, and the machine trembles, two robot arms pick up soldering irons and hunch down on him. He gives me the wink and speaks to me, muffled, tells me something, says something to me around that rubber hose just as those irons get close enough the silver on his temples—light arcs across, stiffens him bridges him up off the table till nothing is down but his wrists and ankles and out around that crimped black rubber hose a sound like *hooeee* and he's frosted over completely with sparks.[46]

In this account the operatives are elided to give place to a technological process taking its own course. The implements of violence (rubber hose, irons) cut off the key sign of McMurphy's humanity, his voice, and, ambiguously exploiting the traces of the crucifixion analogy, evoke a quasi-religious radiance and a freezing to death. In fact this scene proves to be a false climax because McMurphy has retained his vitality and—more important—his voice. His final lobotomy (actually performed through his eye sockets) transforms his eyes into "smudged fuses in a fuse box" and removes his voice. For all practical intents and purposes he is dead, and when from human concern Bromden smothers McMurphy, he rationalizes it as an action against a body without subjectivity.

The play of metaphor and analogy throughout *Cuckoo's Nest* acts against the precision of official discourse, revealing the latter as euphemism or deception. Electroshock treatment is compared by inmates variously to sleeping pills, the electric chair, torture rack, and crucifixion. The references to the "shadows of a thousand murdered men printed" on the treatment table could be an allusion to the famous photographs of the victims of Hiroshima.

There is an even more unsettling implication to Chief Bromden's narration that relates to all the first-person narratives discussed in this chapter. If he really is ill, then his account could be colored pathologically. If the hospital has been feeding him with drugs and subjecting him to electroshock sessions, then his narration could be radically distorted by the workings of the very institution he is describing. As we found in Orwell, there is no external reference, no hint of a state prior to the narration, and Bromden's status as an already inscribed ideological subject emerges with such pathological immediacy that it becomes impossible to talk of his having a subjectivity exempt from technological interference. Paradoxically, the conviction carried by the description of the techniques of mind alteration further undermines Bromden's credibility as narrator. The more effectively the narrative subject is established, the more doubts are shed on the provenance of that subject.

■ Milos Forman's 1975 film adaptation of *One Flew Over the Cuckoo's Nest* makes a number of radical changes to Kesey's narration, which for one critic produce an "over-all simplification of dimension."[47] Most obvious of the changes are the removal of Chief Bromden's point of view and his resulting emphasis on the visual representation of the ward. Forman declared: "I hate that voice-over, I hate that whole psychedelic 1960s drug free-association thing, going with the camera through somebody's head."[48] Bromden's narration, of course, is not conducted through free association but through the means of key metaphors that articulate fluctuations in his consciousness.

His repeated references to a "fog machine" worked by the staff to induce confusion help to disorient the reader from the very beginning by destabilizing the narrative voice. As early as the first page of the novel we know that minds have been worked on in some sinister way. This is lost in the film, which opens and closes with a still shot of the Oregon countryside. The novel immediately situates the reader within an institutional situation. The film moves from outside, into the hospital, and finally back out again. George MacDonald has argued that the relation of outside to inside is helped by the contrast between the lush greens of the countryside and the watery colors of the hospital's interior.[49] Forman makes a predictable use of white in the ward as the traditional color of medical uniforms but also represents the hospital throughout as a kind of prison. One of the first internal scenes shows an attendant unlocking a patient's shackles, and we constantly see patients either through or against mesh window screens. This is partly an inevitable result of the film's making everything more explicit visually than in the novel. In the novel Bromden perceives the asylum as a labyrinthine and threatening space. The discipline of the ward relies on the proximity of the "shock shop." In the film there is far less mention of the latter but many more images of the barriers to the inmates' freedom. Even these barriers lack a dimension of threat, however. The screens on the windows can be unlocked easily, and, with Chief Bromden's help, McMurphy climbs over the barbed wire fence to hide in the school bus that takes the inmates to their boat trip. In short, the threat posed by the institution in Kesey's novel is reduced to a visible physical barrier. Forman briefly politicizes this theme through a TV news broadcast about the Berlin Wall during the Christmas Eve ward party.

Because the film removes Bromden's perspective, the point of view is dispersed among the inmates. Shot reverse shots with close-ups on their faces spread the viewer's attention around the group, and the action is punctuated by five group meetings dealing respectively with Harding's problems, changing the work schedule, Billy's relation to his mother, committal of inmates, and the return of McMurphy after his shock treatment. On McMurphy's first arrival in the ward, we see one inmate after another looking up at him and then grinning at his antics. Forman's changes mean that "McMurphy's position as hero is uncontested," for one critic.[50] When he enters the ward, McMurphy stands apart from the other men visually because he is still wearing his own clothes. Psychologically this reflects his becoming the center of attention, but, since clothes signify the outside world, his appearance also suggests that he has not become totally dominated by hospital practice. Just as his status has changed in the film, so has the representation of Nurse Ratched. Forman's realist technique excludes the possibility of the monstrous, so Nurse Ratched accordingly becomes a scaled down figure, strict but not conspiratorial. Elaine Safer argues that in the film the subject of the narrative has changed significantly: "In effect, the movie emphasizes only one major part of the book: McMurphy's challenge of the establishment, represented by Nurse Ratched."[51] The film is far more comic than the novel, but it is the comedy of *MASH*, a series of smaller and larger confrontations between McMurphy and Nurse Ratched over hospital procedures. These confrontations sometimes result in farce, like the men cheering a blank TV screen as if it is showing a baseball match, and McMurphy's antics represent an attempt by him to appropriate ward practice for comic purposes. The real start of the Christmas party comes when he usurps Nurse Ratched's position in the Nurses' Station and calls out "It's medication time!" These episodes confirm Forman's general statement about his preferred subjects: "I have always liked stories which deal with individuals in conflict with the so-called Establishment."[52]

This antiestablishment comedy reduces the suspense that gathers around the "shock shop." In the novel this is presented as a serious threat, with the even more ominous threat of lobotomy looming in the background. The film, by contrast, makes ECT the more prominent punishment. After a fight with an attendant, McMurphy, Bromden, and another inmate are taken up to the ECT room. The inmate is dragged away in hysterics while McMurphy and Bromden exchange gum. At this point McMurphy discovers that the Chief can speak and laughs out loud at this triumph over the system. He is then taken into the ECT room, where Forman's close-up minimizes the equipment used and concentrates instead on the sheer number of staff needed to hold the wisecracking McMurphy down. This scene thus dramatizes through physical action the attempt by the institution to break McMurphy. After the shock, we see McMurphy's body jerk in a diminishing series of spasms; then the scene shifts back to the ward where he returns, walking like a zombie. Of course it is pretence, yet another instance of McMurphy converting threat into a comic role.

The conclusion after McMurphy has been lobotomized makes another radical departure from the novel and another reduction of the book's complexity. When he is describing the lobotomies near the beginning of the novel, Bromden presents them as a form of killing, a murder of the psyche. The victims of the treatment are robotized; one in particular has his eyes, the traditional feature that reveals life, transformed: "his eyes are all smoked up and gray and deserted inside like blown fuses."[53] Once McMurphy returns to the ward, the same image recurs as a metaphor of erasure of the self, an extrapolation of routine references in psychosurgery to the "circuits" of the brain. His eyes are "open and undreaming," and look "like smudged fuses in a fuse box."[54] McMurphy's fate represents the culmination of a whole series of threats to the self, which Bromden records. The fact that McMurphy is brain dead licenses Bromden to carry out his mercy killing in the novel, whereas in the film the ending could be taken to signify "McMurphy's transferal of power to the Chief."[55]

■ Surveying the literature on electro-convulsive therapy (ECT), which was being used on epileptics and depressives, Alan Scheflin and Edward Opton conclude that there is strong evidence of ECT being used as a "punishment for breaking institutional rules . . . in mental hospitals and prisons." They cite Kesey's *Cuckoo's Nest* as by no means an exaggeration of this issue and point to a complication of institutional roles that results from this perception: "If electroconvulsive shock is oppression, the shock psychiatrist becomes an agent of social control, a policeman in a white coat."[56] As we shall see in chapter 9, ECT also formed the central procedure of a method being used in the Allan Memorial Institute near Montreal and covertly funded by the CIA. Ewen Cameron specialized in cases of schizophrenia that he treated through "depatterning"; that is, breaking up existing patterns of behavior, both the normal and the schizophrenic, by the means of particularly intensive electroshocks. Then the patients would undergo "psychic driving," which consisted of playing back to them key positive phrases from taped interviews. The speakers were placed under the patients' pillows while they slept, in an unconscious echo of Huxley's hypnopaedia. "Here was a psychiatrist willing," comments John Marks, "to wipe the human mind totally clean."[57] Once again, we encounter the tenacity of key metaphors: the concept of illness as a pollution of the organism that needs purging, and the "memory tape" analogy that figures constantly in the fiction dealing with brainwashing. Oliver Lange's 1971 narrative of the Soviet takeover of America, *Vandenberg*, for instance, contains a "therapy" for political prisoners known as "memory erase."

Sylvia Plath foregrounds the punitive application of electrocution in the opening lines of *The Bell Jar* (1963), anticipating her narrator's own ECT sessions as a punishment for a crime against the state. Esther Greenwood dates her narrative from one of the main public events of summer 1953 (the year when Plath herself received ECT and insulin therapy): the execution of Julius and Ethel Rosenberg.[58] When sentencing the couple, Judge Kaufman made his famous statement that their crime was "worse than murder" and one that took place at a historically unique moment in America's destiny, when the country was engaged in a struggle with a hostile opposing system. When the executions were carried out, anti-Rosenberg protesters gathered outside the White House waving placards that proclaimed "DEATH TO THE COMMUNIST RATS."[59] The case became an issue of public debate throughout the United States and Europe, partly over the fact that one of the condemned was a woman.

References to ECT in fiction repeatedly link it to punishment. The narrator of Janet Frame's *Faces in the Water* (1961) compares the ECT room to the death chamber at Sing Sing and describes her first session there as a metaphorical death by hanging: "I feel myself dropping as if a trap door had opened into darkness."[60] The male narrator of Charles Willeford's "The Machine in Ward Eleven" (1963) becomes so terrified when an inmate compares ECT to the electric chair that he straps his doctor into the machine, leaving him "buckling and jerking beneath the steady flow of electricity."[61] In Charles Wright's *The Wig* (1966) the treatment is given a racial dimension when a small-time criminal and actor is subjected to repeated shocks like Ellison's protagonist, terrifying the white technicians by the thought that he might be "immune." It is also striking that in E. L. Doctorow's historiographic novel on the Rosenbergs, *The Book of Daniel* (1971), a brother flies into a passion when he thinks his sister in a sanatorium is going to be subjected to ECT, which is described in ironically nontherapeutic terms: "a strong electric current is applied by means of electrodes fastened to the scalp earlobes shoulders nipples bellybutton genitals asshole knees toes and soles of the feet, to the nervous system of the patient. The patient does a rigid dance. The current is stopped and the patient relaxes. The current is applied again and the patient dances again. The current is relaxed."[62] There is no indication of the patient's subjectivity here. What makes the system grotesque is its clear suggestion of torture in the placing of the electrodes and the reduction of the subject to a puppet. And of course the blackest irony lies in the fact that ECT anticipates the victims' final electrocution by the state.

Recording the news of the Rosenbergs' impending execution in her journals, Plath recalled an earlier, "sickeningly factual" account of an execution that described the "shocking physical facts about the death, the scream, the smoke, the bare honest unemotional reporting that gripped the guts because of the things it didn't say."[63] This entry, which also gives us a helpful indication of how Plath was to use understatement, is fed into the novel when Esther Greenwood, implicitly identifying with Ethel Rosenberg, tries to imagine the experience of electrocution, "being burned alive all along your nerves." In so doing she part-echoes Judge Kaufman's superlative when she describes the experience as the "worst thing in the world." At the same time Esther projects the fantasy experience on to her Manhattan environment as a condition of physical discomfort so extreme it amounts to torture. Esther thereby simultaneously estranges herself from the site of professional success and from the U.S. state apparatus, appropriating the Rosenbergs' guilt as a punishment-in-advance for not following prescribed avenues of behavior. Unlike Burgess's Alex in A Clockwork Orange, who has actually killed, Esther takes on guilt as a strategy for coping with perceived shortcomings in herself. This process becomes explicit in chapter 9 of The Bell Jar, set on the day of the Rosenbergs' execution, when Esther has a brief exchange with Hilda, another member of her group. Hilda, the mannequin-like personification of elegance, expresses satisfaction at the deaths, whereas Esther's feelings for the Rosenbergs completely skews her from participation in the Madison Avenue ethos.

Plath's identification with the Rosenbergs arose from her realization of a contradiction within U.S. legal morality: kill the givers of secrets so that those secrets can be preserved as a national prerogative to kill a collective enemy. She had addressed this contradiction in her journal for 1950 after the outbreak of the Korean War: "Why do we electrocute men for murdering an individual and then pin a purple heart on them for mass slaughter of someone arbitrarily labeled 'enemy'? Weren't the Russians Communists when they helped us slap down the Germans? And now." Then she continues to speculate on how incapable the United States would be of controlling a bombed Russia since America was already "losing that precious commodity, freedom of speech." Jacqueline Rose has pointed out how Plath constantly criticized the failure of America to live up to its national ideal of democratic freedom while at the same time participating in contemporary attacks on the lethargy of the masses."[64]

The Bell Jar traces out the gradual collapse of Esther Greenwood's self-image, reaching its climax with her attempted suicide and leading into her psychological reconstruction. Teresa De Lauretis argues that her "madness" is "presented as a necessary consequence of, indeed as consubstantial with, the world surrounding her."[65] The density of cultural reference in the novel is never lost, even when Esther sinks into her deepest depression. In that respect the novel makes a very strong contrast with Plath's other prose narrative involving electroshocks.

The title story of *Johnny Panic and the Bible of Dreams* (1977), according to Elisabeth Bronfen, describes "how an inability to control one's dream work can lead to psychic alienation."[66] The story is narrated by a secretarial assistant at a psychiatric clinic who compensates for her humdrum job by privately becoming a "dream connoisseur." A psychic struggle emerges between her cherished author of patients' dream work, Johnny Panic, and the bearded "psyche-doctors" who want to appropriate and rationalize those dreams. This narrative possesses a claustrophobia never reached by *The Bell Jar* because the narrator's growing psychosis leads her to blank out her surroundings. When she is taken by the medical staff for treatment—in other words, when she has crossed over from clerk to patient—the result for her is a displacement into "alien territory." She structures the event as an opposition between true believers (herself and the inmates) and the materialistic medics. Her shock treatment becomes a travesty crucifixion by the "false priests" dressed in white who place a "crown of wire" on her head. The story's climax ambiguously reverses her expectations of "unseating" through an electronically induced vision: "At the moment when I think I am lost the face of Johnny Panic appears in a nimbus of arc lights on the ceiling overhead. I am shaken like a leaf in the teeth of glory. His beard is lightning. Lightning is in his eye. His word charges and illumines the universe."[67] Soon after this episode the story closes with no hint of confirmation whether the narrator is extrapolating physical phenomena in this fantasy crisis. Plath sticks rigorously to her narrative point of view that excludes contextualization. In "Johnny Panic" and *The Bell Jar* Plath represents institutional processes as aspects of male control, whereas Kesey's Big Nurse makes unusually explicit a perception by male writers of institutional power as a feminine force that dominates its male victims.

Psychoanalytical readings of *The Bell Jar* run the risk of blanking out the dense cultural references in the novel. This absence of critical commentary has been addressed by Pat Macpherson, whose *Reflecting on* The Bell Jar (1991) skillfully brings out the political dimensions to Esther's narrative. In particular Macpherson argues that Esther attempts a kind of "containment"— political pun intended—of her dissatisfactions with society by introjecting them as personal problems that can be cured by "self-purging." Elsewhere in her writings Plath showed an awareness of contemporary American politics, planning with almost missionary zeal to live abroad in order to counteract the image of the United States projected by McCarthyism and exclaiming over the "terrifying, mad, omnipotent marriage of big business and the military in America."[68] In 1960 she witnessed with enthusiasm the antinuclear march from Aldermaston to London. *The Bell Jar* focuses its attention on the institutions supporting the ideology of 1950s "normalcy" and describes an extended process of surveillance, both external and internal, where Esther's advisers and she herself alternately inspect her for signs of deviance. Deborah Nelson has included Plath among the confessional poets who were responding to a politicized conception of the suburban home, whose open plan encouraged observation. Nelson argues that "the omnipresence of surveillance in the cold war was converting the notion of confession as a sacrament into the perception of confession as a criminal act."[69] Throughout the novel Esther associates social conformity as a totalitarian imposition on the self. When she remembers Buddy Willard telling—or rather warning—her that marriage and motherhood will remove her desire to write poetry, she transforms this statement as a psycho-political fantasy of losing her selfhood: "I began to think maybe it was true that when you were married and had children it was like being brainwashed, and afterward you went about numb as a slave in some private, totalitarian state."[70] As we shall see, the tacit charge built into Esther's psychotherapy accuses her of what turns out to be a crime of feeling, not action.

The main sign of surveillance throughout *The Bell Jar* is the scrutinizing gaze. Again and again we find Esther being subjected to the observation of doctors, Buddy, and, above all, her mother. When Esther returns home from New York, her journey marks a transition back into an environment encoded with social prescription and maternal authority. The "motherly breath" of the suburbs suggests a face pressed close to the subject's, and for that reason Esther struggles to avoid visibility from implicitly judgmental (and female) neighbors. In Plath's 1962 poem "Eavesdropper" the home is again the site for observation, for seeing and being seen. The gaze culminates reversibly in "big blue eye / That watches, like God, or the sky / The ciphers that watch it." Exactly the same interpellative gaze is figured during Esther's skiing accident with Buddy, when the "great, grey eye of the sky" looks back at her, an unmoving focus of power to throw her own helplessness into relief.[71] This episode is typical of the novel in framing Esther's thoughts as a dialogue between opposing voices. Throughout *The Bell Jar* Esther simultaneously questions social norms and at the same time internalizes those voices of social authority that charge her with deviance. Esther emerges as a deeply ambivalent narrator and her inability to resolve rival impulses within herself leads to her breakdown where, even by herself, mental illness is encoded as wrongdoing.

The process of Esther's psychotherapy follows approximately the same trajectory as an interrogation in the narratives discussed earlier, complicated by her repertoire of media scripts and images that she tries to attach to her doctors. The first, Dr. Gordon, fails to measure up to her idealized sympathetic helper; indeed, his windowless office that contains only the icons of success (medical certificates) and normality (family photographs) infuriates her. Dr Gordon resembles a preliminary interrogator who gives nothing away and who infantilizes Esther by discussing her therapy with her mother out of Esther's hearing. Esther's heightened perception of facades reaches an unconsciously satirical peak when she is taken to a private hospital, where the building appears to be a simulation and the inmates a gathering of "dummies." Similarly, in Plath's 1961 poem "Insomniac" the city crowd is depicted as a mass of zombies: "everywhere people, eyes mica-silver and blank, / Are riding to work in rows, as if recently brainwashed."

The hospital conceals a basement that doubles as clinic and prison. Like *Invisible Man*, the setting is predominantly white, but the windows are barred and all doors have locks. The walleyed nurse who takes Esther for her treatment gives a surreal dimension to the event because her gaze is a split and unidentifiable one. Pat Macpherson points out that "the nurse attaching the electrodes to Esther's skull is disconcertingly double, mother and electrocutioner, relief and torturer, escape and fate." To Esther, the problem involves distinguishing real from false in the nurse's gaze; failing this, the latter comes to resemble a prison guard. The description of the first shock treatment presents it as an act of technological and institutional violence against Esther's body:

> Then something bent down and took hold of me and shook me like the end of the world. Whee-ee-ee-ee-ee, it shrilled, through an air crackling with blue light, and with each flash a great jolt drubbed me till I thought my bones would break and the sap fly out of me like a split plant.
> I wondered what terrible thing it was I had done.[72]

Here at last is the actualization of Esther's identification with the Rosenbergs, immediately moralized as punishment for an unknown crime. Within the interrogation analogy this point would correspond to a physical beating that serves to push Esther nearer suicide.

The second shock-therapy session takes place within a totally transformed context where Esther's us–them categories begin to break down as she encounters two former friends who personify different instances of failed treatment. Valerie's lobotomy has "cured" her anger at the expense of any desire to engage with the outside world, and Joan has been following group therapy but later commits suicide. The biggest change, however, comes with Dr. Nolan, a courteous and respectful woman who treats Esther as an adult and who initially strikes her as an incongruous blend of resemblances: a "cross between Myrna Loy and my mother." She is the one who explains the treatment, and accordingly she is the one who elicits Esther's confession of hating her mother. Thanks to Dr. Nolan's benign offices, Esther can visualize the observers more clearly and de-specifies the equipment fastened on her head:

> Through the slits of my eyes, which I didn't dare open too far, lest the full view strike me dead, I saw the high bed with its white, drumtight sheet, and the machine behind the bed, and the masked person—I couldn't tell whether it was a man or a woman—behind the machine, and other masked people flanking the bed on both sides.
>
> [The nurse] set something on my tongue and in panic I bit down, and darkness wiped me out like chalk on a blackboard.[73]

Although fear is obviously present here, it is not concentrated in a single threatening gaze. Rather, the masked, degendered figures blur together into the equipment that only comes into operation for an instant. In that moment Esther's consciousness, and by implication her old self, is erased, leaving a new *tabula rasa* ready for reinscription, which is, as Eric Fromm was arguing in the mid-1950s, a heavily ideological position privileging environmental factors in the creation of subjectivity.[74]

This is no simple liberation narrative, however. There is no point in the novel where Esther frees herself from "reality instructors." Indeed the novel closes with Esther walking into the hospital boardroom to be evaluated for release and there is no guarantee that the decision will be positive. The situation resembles a prison parole board hearing and the last scene confirms the authority of such an institution. The "tribunal" on female identity held permanently in Esther's magazine has given way to another kind of judgment on the self by a body with a similar ideological function of enforcing the social status quo. *The Bell Jar* is framed institutionally, so Esther's "rebirth" has an ultimate circularity; it "wipes the state clean only to prepare it for exactly the same message."[75]

Plath's satirical perspective on psychotherapy reveals an ambivalence in her protagonist, then, which prevents us from reading *The Bell Jar* as an unambiguous narrative of self-empowerment, even though Esther gradually takes over the process of her own therapy. Plath's perspective on mental illness is not as clear, for example, as that of Doris Lessing, who shared R. D. Laing's hostility to conventional pathological labels like "schizophrenic" or "neurotic." "We were exploring the phenomenon of the unclassifiable experience, the psychological "breaking-through" that the conventional world judges as mad," Lessing stated in interview.[76] In *The Four-Gated City* (1969), her protagonist Martha Quest discovers the frequency of mental illness and comes to question the social (not medical) authority wielded by psychologists. Her dialogues with her flat-mate Lynda make up an extended interrogation of the social norms projected in psychotherapy. *Briefing for a Descent into Hell* (1971) takes this process a step further by privileging the inner world of a professor who suffers a breakdown over the procedures of therapy. There are brief traces of the power themes we have seen in earlier novels of mind control. At one point the professor asks a doctor: "Are you the secret police?" At another he imagines that he has been "brainprinted," and when he changes his style of expression a character compares it to the self-censoring that goes on in a dictatorship.[77] These are, however, only passing moments within an inner process where the subject gradually regains control of his own life. Lessing, Plath, Kesey, and other novelists of this period were exploring the political dimension to psychotherapy, the limitations of which reflected the values of society as a whole. In the next chapter we will consider further the techniques used to eradicate antisocial and violent behavior.

eight

The Control of Violence

n the previous chapter we were considering narratives that exposed the ideological functions of psychotherapy. For the most part these functions boiled down in practice to the erasure of mental faculties. In this chapter, however, we will be discussing attempts to alter the self by interventions in the traditional locus of selfhood, the brain itself. Speculations on the limits to technological control of humans and anxieties over violating the special status of the brain have been staple subjects in science fiction for decades. One of the most famous narratives of brain experimentation is the expatriate Austrian writer Curt Siodmak's *Donovan's Brain* (1943; film adaptation 1953), where Dr. Patrick Cory attempts to preserve the brain of a tycoon after he is fatally injured in a plane crash. Cory ignores the warning of his older colleague against practicing a "mechanistic physiology" and attempts to map out the functions of the brain, anticipating the research of John Lilly in the 1950s.

Donovan's Brain describes an experiment where the detachment of the surgeon from his subject gradually breaks down. His question, "Which chemical reaction creates success?" reflects a materialistic approach that the novel undermines through the fracturing of Cory's consciousness: "I live a double existence. My thoughts retreat into the back of my mind as I observe, detached, the phenomena which Donovan's brain directs. I am then a schizophrenic, a person whose personality is split."[1] Cory's detached view of his own psyche is premature, however, as the preserved brain begins to exercise control over him. The relation between experimenter and subject gradually reverses through a process inexplicable by Cory's mechanistic concepts.

Siodmak's later novel, *Hauser's Memory* (1968), refines and politicizes his earlier subject. Patrick Cory is now trying to extract RNA from the brain in order to isolate the memory chemically. Once again he is warned against a misplaced quantification of emotion: what can the chemical formula be for fear or courage? The new factor is that American intelligence agencies are supporting Cory in order to access the memory of a terminally injured defecting Soviet agent. A member of Cory's team ingests the Defector's RNA and becomes a carrier of information that he can only partly access since his consciousness switches unpredictably between the two selves. Although the technology of Siodmak's novel is biochemical, the action dramatizes a reification of memory content as information. Thus RNA is imagined as the "translation of the DNA message, like a wax impression of a key."[2] Once again, a struggle takes place between the rival selves, which undermines the clarity of the experiment and which plays out Cold War hostilities in miniature. Brain possession had become a recurrent theme in such 1950s movies as *The Brain from Planet Arous* and *The Brain Eaters* (both 1958) where the vulnerability of the brain to assault by alien agencies is explored. By the late 1960s the technology of brain invasion had become more sophisticated but the central issue of control remained unchanged.

The science fiction writer Larry Niven has stated that "new technologies create new customs, new laws, new ethics, new crimes" and that has certainly been confirmed by the debate over how to deal with violence in society that reached a head in the 1970s.[3] Two novels that achieved notoriety in their own right and then as movie adaptations were Anthony Burgess's *A Clockwork Orange* (1962; film 1971) and Michael Crichton's *The Terminal Man* (1972; film 1974). Both describe material interventions in the mind, depicting possible ways of controlling violence through the use of experimental new techniques of aversion therapy and electronic brain stimulation (ESB). Both works became important points of reference in the debate on this subject. A speaker at a 1974 symposium on psychosurgery declared that the "*Clockwork Orange* concept of a simple choice between anarchical behaviour and robotism must be discarded;" and another psychosurgery specialist, in an article called "Science-Fiction Fantasy and the Brain," commented that "Michael Crichton's *The Terminal Man* will probably have a greater impact than Mary Shelley's *Frankenstein* not because of its literary qualities but because it has convinced many people that computerized control of the human brain is possible now, or at least not very far off in the future."[4]

Depending on the commentator's point of view, the strange congruence that was felt to be emerging between science fiction images and technology might be exciting, unnerving, or more importantly suggests a need to revise our sense of plausibility, of what is or what isn't possible. Perry London (in his *Behavior Control*, 1969) felt that the new knowledge of the brain was realizing "all the ancient dreams of mastery over man and all the tales of zombies, golems, and Frankensteins [that] involved some magic formula, or ritual, or incantation that would magically yield the key to dominion."[5] London is so excited by this change that he doesn't pause to examine the implications of the power terms he uses. "Mastery" over whom? "Dominion" by whom? It is exactly these issues that Burgess and Crichton address in their novels. When he was working on his adaptation of *A Clockwork Orange*, Stanley Kubrick realized that "recent experiments in conditioning and mind control on volunteer prisoners in America have taken this question out of the realm of science-fiction."[6] Reports on these experiments had been leaking out through the 1960s and they had already offered a subject, for instance, to Thomas Disch's *Camp Concentration* (1968), which describes the experimental administration to prisoners of a syphilis derivative in a secret underground facility in the Midwest. This novel and related narratives will form the subject of the next chapter.

By his own account, Burgess wrote *A Clockwork Orange* as a protest against the use of Pavlovian conditioning, which was at that time being considered for use against criminals. He states: "I imagined an experimental institution in which a generic delinquent, guilty of every crime of rape to murder, was given aversion therapy and rendered incapable of contemplating, let alone perpetrating an anti-social act without a sensation of profound nausea."[7] Burgess conceived of the novel as a "sort of tract, even a sermon, on the importance of the power of choice."[8] The crucial point he wanted to convey was a principle expounded by the teacher Tristram Foxe in *The Wanting Seed* (1962) and repeated by Burgess's surrogate Professor Enderby in *The Clockwork Testament* (1974): "Men should be free to choose good," which means in effect that freedom of choice is demonstrated by the presence of evil in society.[9] Take away this element of choice, he argued in his 1986 introduction to the American edition, and the subject ceases to be quite human: "If he can only perform good or only perform evil, then he is a clockwork orange—meaning that he has the appearance of an organism . . . but is in fact only a clockwork toy to be wound up by God or the Devil or (since this is increasingly replacing both) the Almighty State."[10] In his comments on *A Clockwork Orange* Burgess locates his own novel within a dystopian tradition, including Orwell, that dramatizes the individual's struggle against the collective, specifically the state. Burgess's novel is premised on a notion of growth in his protagonist narrator and is numerically constructed so that seven chapters are each devoted to a phase of the narrator Alex's experience: violence leading to a killing and his arrest; imprisonment and then treatment at the new facility; release, attempted suicide, and second treatment.

A tension runs right through the novel between Alex's insistence on his own subjectivity, on his self as subject, and the attempts by the authorities to reduce him to a "case." It is through his use of language that Alex maintains his subjectivity. As Theo D'haen has argued, the true opposition in Orwell's *Nineteen Eighty-Four* and also in *A Clockwork Orange* is that "between mindless communal cliché and imaginative individual variation, between conditioned conformity and personal reflection."[11] This argument works well with Alex, who "can change register at will." Far from being the cowed victim of a drab homogenized state, whose physical markers are the polluted industrial canal and the anonymous apartment blocks, Alex is a versatile narrator who can shift effortlessly in and out of the novel's Nadsat slang (a composite of Cockney and Russian), and feed adults the lines he assumes they want to hear. His use of language is complex and duplicitous because he is constantly inventing fictions about himself and deploying Nadsat to screen the physical brutality of his gang's nighttime actions. When they beat up a writer, his face is described as a "litso all purple and dripping away like some very special sort of a juicy fruit."[12] This description shifts the reader's attention away from a human casualty to an object ready for consumption through violence. Similarly in the fight with the Cat Lady, Alex reduces the drama to slapstick at his own expense as he keeps slipping on saucers of milk, yet another distraction from the violence. The police in *A Clockwork Orange* are conspicuous by their absence, only appearing after crimes have been committed, whereas in *The Wanting Seed* (1962), Burgess's Malthusian dystopia from the same period, they carry out spot checks on travelers and maintain a whole surveillance network of informers to prevent illicit procreation.[13]

In *A Clockwork Orange* Burgess's general intention was to make the violence in the novel "more symbolic than realistic." He rejected the accusation of creating a "pornography of violence," which aroused controversy when the film was released.[14] In general, Alex's narrative could be seen as an attempt to normalize his actions and to write himself into a cultural land-scape already marked out by the names of British politicians. In his selection of information, shifts in register and perspective, Alex manipulates his narra-tion to draw his projected male reader into a sympathetic identification with him. Throwaway allusions to Bunyan, Wilde, and Renaissance drama all help to establish an identification between verbal intelligence, artistic aware-ness, and casual brutality in himself.

When Alex is taken from prison to the psychiatric facility he undergoes a shift in subjectivity from convict to patient. Pat Gehrke has helpfully discussed this shift in relation to Foucault's writing on crime and therapy, pointing out that "there is a morbid irony in the fact that Alex's mental health requires his physical illness."[15] The reclassification of criminality or deviance as illness is a major theme throughout this study, and Burgess was well aware of the dysto-pian possibilities in this practice from, for example, L. P. Hartley's novel *Fa-cial Justice* (1960) where a post–nuclear war dictatorship in Britain disperses the guilt for the war throughout the surviving population by having every citizen take the name of a murderer. The citizens are addressed as "Patients and Delinquents," a phrase that conflates the administration of the country as a prison and a hospital. Thus citizens are under constant surveillance and a controlling "therapy" in that they have to consume daily doses of a bromide sedative. In Burgess's satire 1985 a state official makes this conflation clear to the dissident protagonist: "the distinction between the place of penal deten-tion and the mental home must, of necessity, progressively narrow."[16]

Alex experiences this blurring of confinement with therapy through an apparently benign process, which is riddled with ironies. When he undergoes the Reclamation Treatment by negative conditioning, once again the novel hints at an opposition that the narrative complicates. Alex is told that he is going to "be reformed" and the passive verb form persists throughout the treat-ment, suggesting an institutional infantilization of Alex as the recipient of, not cooperator with, the new therapy. One medic tells him (with an uncon-scious pun): "You are being made sane, you are being made healthy."[17] How-ever, Alex's verbal energy, a sign of attention and enquiry, prevents a simplis-tic reading of him as a totally passive subject in this episode. Consider the following lines, from the first treatment scene when Alex is trying to define the room where he is taken. It is a cinema but like no cinema he has ever seen: "But against the right-hand one of the other walls was a bank of like little meters, and in the middle of the floor facing the screen was like a den-tist's chair with all lengths of wire running from it, and I had to like crawl from the wheelchair to this. . . . Then I noticed that underneath the projection holes was like a frosted glass and I thought I viddied shadows of like people moving behind it."[18] The process that Alex undergoes is not chosen by him; it was the Minister's suggestion that he be used as a guinea pig. And clearly the officials want him to submit with the least demand for information. So when he naively assumes that his injections are of vitamins, no one disabuses him. The effect (if not the purpose) of these injections is to make Alex so weak that he has to play the part of an invalid. Thus his role is transformed from that of convict to patient, with a paranoid subtext of mysterious processes that he is trying to understand. So in the quoted passage Alex's gaze ranges round the room, noting the implements of measurement and attempting to soften the strangeness of the chair by comparing it to a dentist's surgery. The slangy repetition of "like" helps this effect because it shows how Alex is struggling to cope with resemblances that do not cohere into a meaningful scene. Later Alex begins to suspect that the machines themselves are actually making him ill. The motions of his eyes, the inferences, the jokes (the pun on "horror-show" and the Russian "horosho," i.e., "good"), and the appeals to the (male) reader ("brothers") all demonstrate Alex's active status as subject.

Of course Alex's mental activity contrasts totally with his physical immo-bility. He is being frozen in a posture of compulsory observation while he himself is observed, and we shall see that in perspective terms this scene becomes even more complex in the movie. The projector of the film show is positioned close to the point of medical surveillance. Although initially Alex tries to maintain a critical distance from the films by assessing their tech-niques (clever cutting and editing), he cannot avoid their aggressive impact: "even if I tried to move my glaz-bals about I still could not like get out of the line of fire of this picture."[19] Alex's aversion therapy could thus be read as a visual assault over which he feels to have little control. Here again, however, we should note two important ironies that emerge. First, Alex's attention to his experiences remains unchanged. His surprise over his bodily reactions involves a bemused recognition of something physical happening to him. His subjectivity remains comparatively intact. This suggests in turn that the treatment is mainly a physical one, so the reader's perception of a threat to Alex's self is somewhat attenuated. Furthermore, Alex protests vociferously against his treatment: "Me, me, me. How about me? Where do I come into all this? Am I just like some animal or dog? . . . Am I just to be like a clock-work orange?"[20] Like the narrator of *The Bell Jar*, Alex insists on his own selfhood through the only means left to him—through words. Ironically, Alex has unconsciously appropriated the title of his older namesake and double, F. Alexander, who writes a protest against the "attempt to impose upon man . . . laws and conditions appropriate to a mechanical creation."[21] Once the treatment has finished, Dr. Brodsky displays Alex as a transformed figure before an audience of governors and politicians, key representatives of the establishment. The intense theatricality of the conclusion of part 2 reflects yet again the power implications of a process that reduces Alex to passive manipulation. Brodsky declares with a flourish: "At this stage, gentlemen, we introduce the subject himself . . . undrugged, unhypnotized."[22] After the obvious pun on "stage," Brodsky implicitly contrasts Alex with the recipients of treatments like brainwashing and uses the term "subject" here to combine abstraction (into a "case") and with subjection to the state authorities that actually involves a denial of his subjectivity.

Ironically, Alex receives two courses of treatment, the second to erase the effects of the first. After his attempted suicide, Alex finds himself once again immobilized and wired up to machines. But repairing his mind is more important than treating his body. Alex himself figures this therapy to himself in a dream as emptying his body of dirty water and filling it with clean water. The root metaphor in brainwashing seems to be applied only to his body, but his dream could be taken as a symbolic displacement since he asks the nurse: "Has anyone been doing anything with my gulliver? What I mean is, have they been playing around with inside like my brain?"[23] This time the method used is "deep hypnopaedia" to erase his previous conditioning, a term Burgess has drawn straight from *Brave New World*. The main irony in part 3 of the novel is reversal. Alex is freed; the writer F. Alexander is "put away." So the therapy to cure a therapy also takes place below Alex's conscious mind through processes that Burgess sums up in the following way: "In both film and book, the evil that the state performs in brainwashing Alex is seen spectacularly in its own lack of self-awareness as regards non-ethical values."[24]

Alex's status as subject and narrator is problematized by the fact that he undergoes two processes of mind alteration. We have seen how Burgess was overwhelmingly concerned with choice as a defining characteristic of individuality. Introducing the musical dramatization of *A Clockwork Orange*, he describes his narrative as a "sort of allegory of Christian free will. Man is defined by his capacity to choose courses of moral action. If he chooses good, he must have the possibility of choosing evil instead: evil is a theological necessity. I was also saying that it is more acceptable for us to perform evil acts than to be conditioned artificially into an ability only to perform what is socially acceptable."[25] The result of Alex's experiences is that his capacity to make such choices becomes impaired. However much self-awareness his language demonstrates, his suspicion that someone has been doing something to his "gulliver" (head) transfers itself as an uncertainty in the reader over the authenticity of his discourse. Like Chief Bromden in *One Flew Over the Cuckoo's Nest*, Alex articulates his subjectivity and therefore his resistance to the authorities through discourse that has been radically inflected by those authorities.

Burgess designed his novel as a "brainwashing primer," which implies a romantic and anarchistic hostility to the state's cynical manipulation of its citizens. He has explained his use of Nadsat as part of a strategic assault on the reader. At one point in the novel a psychologist comments on this slang that "most of the roots are Slav. Propaganda. Subliminal penetration."[26] Soon after he saw Kubrick's adaptation, Burgess explained the desired impact of the language as follows: "You read the book or see the film, and at the end you should find yourself in possession of a minimal Russian vocabulary—without effort, with surprise. This is the way brainwashing works. . . . But the lesson of the *Orange* has nothing to do with the ideology or repressive techniques of Soviet Russia: it is wholly concerned with what can happen to any of us in the West, if we do not keep on our guard."[27] The reader's unconscious acquisition of Russian vocabulary thus appears to be used to warn the reader against passively accepting the discourse and processes of culture, especially a kind of state corporatism that Burgess went on to attack in the fiction section of 1985 (1978). It is rather disingenuous of him to expect the reader—especially the reader of 1962, when the Cold War was heating up during one of the Berlin crises—to blank out the fact that Russian terms have seeped into the language, because the terms cannot help but be associated with the culture of a monolithic centralized state and to be linked in turn with similarly homogenizing processes taking place in Britain.

Burgess attempts to show how Alex avoids the fixity of classification. He was annoyed when the U.S. publisher of *A Clockwork Orange* cut the last chapter, because this was the one full of future indicators, showing Alex as a father-to-be. Burgess felt that American readers were being given a "clockwork" version of Alex, whereas by the concluding chapter Alex "would realize that aggression was just a mode of youthful activity."[28] Essentially, Burgess felt that the concluding chapter showed Alex for once considering the future, which is one meaning of the novel's refrain, "What's it going to be?"[29] He complained that the exclusion "reduced the work from a genuine novel (whose main characteristic must always be a demonstration of the capacity of human nature to change) to a mere fable."[30] Kubrick for his part was not convinced by this and did not take the last chapter into account when making his film, since he found it "unconvincing and inconsistent with the style and interest of the book."[31]

■ The immediate trigger to Burgess's writing *A Clockwork Orange* was the suggestion circulating in Britain at the time that one way to deal with juvenile violent crime would be an "easy course in conditioning, some kind of aversion therapy which should make them [delinquents] associate the act of violence with discomfort, nausea, or even intimations of mortality."[32] Burgess's choice of title reflects his perception of a double subject: the "application of Pavlovian, or mechanical, laws to an organism."[33] The subject in short was applied behaviorism against which the prison chaplain in *A Clockwork Orange* mounts a vigorous protest. Although he is an institutionally confined figure and one ridiculed for his heavy drinking (in the slang of the period "charlie" means "fool"), his objection to conditioning forms an important part of the novel's debate over treatment. When the Ludovico Technique is first mentioned, he tells Alex: "The question is whether such a technique can really make a man good. Goodness comes from within, 6655321. Goodness is something chosen. When a man cannot choose he ceases to be a man."[34] The opposition he proposes here figures repeatedly in comments by both Burgess and Kubrick on behaviorism and especially on its leading U.S. theorist, B. F. Skinner.

Skinner has consistently posited two views of behavior: the scientific one, which he supports, and the traditional view that "regards man as a free agent, whose behavior is the product, not of specifiable antecedent conditions, but of spontaneous inner changes of course."[35] Skinner ridicules the latter view as impressionistic, introspective, and unusable; here we need to note that Skinner's writings have a very strong bias toward the functional. According to Melvin M. Schuster, Skinner belongs in the meliorist tradition of political thought, which speculates about how humanity can improve its lot. Such traditional notions of improvement and cultural survival therefore are not controversial in themselves. The problems with Skinner arise from means not ends, since his critics express the "fear that Skinner's planned world would destroy the sensitivity, the spirit, and the intelligence of man. Skinner's man would be an automaton, a creature of habit."[36]

Such fears are fed by Skinner's polemical assertions like "we assume that no behavior is free," and his apocalyptic declaration of an intention to "abolish" the concept of "autonomous man."[37] In a late work Skinner declares: "a person's behavior is controlled by his genetic and environmental histories rather than by the person himself as an initiating, creative agent."[38] This assertion can be read across a range of possibilities from genetic determinism, like that designed in *Brave New World*, to a less exceptionable statement about the importance of the environment in behavior patterns. Skinner's most frequent term is "control," which shifts ambiguously between signifying the effect of the stimuli of a culture and the managed alterations to behavior, which have brought the most hostile responses to Skinner. In *Science and Human Behavior* (1953) he describes exactly the sort of aversive stimuli that are applied in *A Clockwork Orange*: the inducing of nausea to divert the subject from addictions to tobacco or alcohol. Skinner's utopianism comes out in his attempts to reduce the complexities of human behavior to a set of simple actions.[39] Thus, in *Beyond Freedom and Dignity* (1971) he pleads for a "technology of behavior" that should be feasible if we accept the analogy between culture and laboratory: "a culture is like the experimental space used in the study of behavior. It is a set of contingencies of reinforcement."[40] His utopian novel *Walden Two* (1948) describes a small-scale attempt to apply the experimental method to all aspects of human behavior. This method of "cultural engineering" includes a reclassification of wrongdoing as illness. Skinner's ideologue in the novel explains at one point: "A moral or ethical lapse . . . needs treatment, not punishment."[41] Skinner rarely makes any attempt to prove his premise of the "scientific view," but argues that the latter can at least be applied in society.

In view of the fears dramatized in the works discussed throughout this volume, there are at least three points where Skinner's statements show an awareness of the negative reactions he might provoke. First, in order to get rid of the impression that he views control as a good in itself, he attacks brainwashing as being too obviously manipulative. Second, and this bears on novels like *A Clockwork Orange* or Thomas M. Disch's *Camp Concentration* (discussed in chapter 9), the case of prisoners volunteering for possibly dangerous experiments might seem to exemplify freedom. "Everyone would protest if the prisoners were forced to participate, but are they really free when positively reinforced, particularly when the condition to be improved or the sentence to be shortened has been imposed by the state?"[42] Here Skinner demonstrates a rare recognition of how conditioning can be enmeshed in the apparatus of the state. Elsewhere, reflecting on utopias, he admits the implications of power in control. Design or order are rational goods but "design implies control, and there are many reasons why we fear it. The very techniques are often objectionable, for control passes first to those who have the power to treat others aversively. The state is still identified with the power to punish"[43] Although Skinner puts forward the theoretical possibility of both positive and negative reinforcement working in a culture, he is enough of a realist to recognize that negative, state-controlled instances dominate the popular imagination. Last, he addresses an issue that is central to *A Clockwork Orange* and *The Terminal Man*: the likeness of man to machine. Regularity or predictability of behavior does not mean that humans have become machines, Skinner insists. On the contrary, "man is a machine in the sense that he is a complex system behaving in lawful ways, but the complexity is extraordinary." Far from being a post-humanist, Skinner insists that human complexity far exceeds that of machines and concludes that "if the machines man makes eventually make him wholly expendable, it will be by accident, not design."[44] Skinner's provisos suggest greater caution over the application of his theories than other proponents of the behaviorism with which his name was linked. In 1970, for instance, the psychologist James V. McConnel made no bones about a utopian replanning of society when he declared proudly: "Today's behavioural psychologists are the architects and engineers who are shaping the Brave New World of Tomorrow."[45]

Burgess took a dim view of behaviorist practices, declaring: "to consider hypnopaedia, or sleep-teaching (which also features in *Brave New World*), cradle conditioning, adolescent reflex bending, and all the rest of the behavioural armoury, is to be appalled at the loss . . . of individual liberty."[46] In an interview Burgess described Skinner's *Beyond Freedom and Dignity* as "one of the most dangerous books ever written" because it explains human actions in terms of negative and positive reinforcements, that is, in terms of control.[47] He saw this work as such a dangerous challenge that he accused Skinner of "perpetrating a gross heresy" on the Western Judeo-Christian tradition.[48] Burgess felt so strongly about this issue that in 1973 he published an ironic sketch called "A Fable for Social Scientists," which describes a group of Americans reflecting on Skinner's work near his gravestone. Burgess's use of dialogue enables the speakers to bounce contrasting points against each other without a single view emerging. So one speaker dismisses Skinner as playing the role of a Calvinistic God, the "big behavioral engineer grinning down from the clouds"; another charges him with extrapolating the university as a model of society; and so on. Interestingly, for this context, one of the group more or less predicts *The Terminal Man* by imagining a "new kind of human being, one who'll see nothing wrong in having his aggression trimmed."[49]

When researching for the film of A *Clockwork Orange* Stanley Kubrick read extensively in conditioned reflexes and he too recognized the importance of *Beyond Freedom and Dignity*. Kubrick was particularly uneasy about Skinner's argument that "freedom and dignity have become inconsistent with the survival of our civilization" because it was difficult to refute. He strongly resisted Skinner's reductive account of human behavior but also worried about its political applications: "this philosophy may serve as the intellectual basis for some sort of scientifically oriented repressive government."[50] Although Kubrick's objections are based on far less spiritual premises, he nevertheless shared Burgess's deep suspicion of Skinner's theories. At least Burgess and Kubrick made serious efforts to understand Skinner, which cannot be said of the 1998 film A *Breed Apart* (also called *Perfect Assassins*). Here a demented behaviorist sees himself as the heir to Skinner and dreams of leaving as legacy the definitive proof that "war, murder, violence is conditioned." To prove this in the abstract is one thing. However, his secondary aim of producing a breed of assassins, each with an "aggressive but totally shapeable psyche," leads the U.S. authorities to drive him out of the country. His resulting facility in Mexico resembles a cross between a terrorist training camp and a zoo where his human subjects are kept in cages and so traumatized that they lose the faculty of speech. The connection between this scientist and Skinner proves to be tenuous to say the least.

■ Kubrick's film adaptation of A *Clockwork Orange* greatly reduces Alex's voice and inevitably deploys image to bring out its themes. In one of the best commentaries on the film, Vivien Sobchack has argued that key scenes, like the gang fight, the representation of Alex's room, and the fight with the Cat Lady, all pack the visual space with art objects, making the cumulative point that "Art and Violence spring from the same source; they are both expressions of the individual, egotistical, vital, and non-institutionalized man."[51] For her, art and violence are never opposed but rather linked in a complementary way. Sobchack's argument usefully extends Kubrick's own statements about violence in the film. Soon after it was released, he explained, "The intention is to make the violence satirical," adding, "I've always enjoyed dealing with a slightly surrealistic situation and presenting it in a realistic manner."[52] Violent episodes are carefully orchestrated and choreographed, since for Alex violence is "like some great action ballet."[53]

From the very beginning Kubrick establishes strong links between sex, violence, and the male gaze. In the opening shot in a futuristic milk bar it is the male figures (Alex and his gang) who move in relation to the simulated female nudes in the background decor. In the episode at HOME, wall mirrors multiply images of the scene foregrounding Alex's own obsession with visibility. When his gang is assaulting the writer's wife (the writer himself is a mirror image of Alex), Alex tells him: "Viddy well, brother. Viddy well."[54] Shots of the rape (figured visually as gradual unclothing) alternate with the writer's anguished face, converting the scene into a sadistic performance for the male victim's benefit. In addition to the costume worn by Alex and his "droogs," his props include a codpiece, a baton, and a false nose. When he goes to the Cat Lady's house, Alex is wearing the last of these, a displaced erection, and he kills her with a second phallic object, the ceramic statue of an erect penis. The famous movie poster showing Alex grasping a knife with an eyeball in the foreground draws the viewer's attention to seeing in relation to violence, and the two scenes just discussed extend this linkage to sex. Kubrick introduced the detail of Alex's pet snake to make this symbolism clear; in the masturbation scene in his room we see this snake coiled around an erect baton.

The treatment Alex undergoes transforms his status as subject more radically in the film than in the novel. Kubrick admitted an element of "social satire" in "dealing with the question of whether behavioral psychology and psychological conditioning are dangerous new weapons for a totalitarian government to use to impose vast controls on its citizens and turn them into little more than robots."[55] The brainwashing theme figures almost subliminally in the film through brief shots of news articles on Alex, one reading: "Brainwashing techniques were responsible for the suicide bid of Alex Burgess."[56]

Laura Mulvey's argument in *Visual and Other Pleasures* (1989) that the cinematic gaze tends to be male gendered and the objects of that gaze female, helps us to see how Alex is feminized by his "therapy." In the first part of the film he is choreographed as a sexual dancer, whereas for the aversion treatment he is immobilized by being strapped into a chair.[57] All the symbolic objects of rampant sexuality—his false nose, codpiece, and baton—are removed, and, as if the point weren't obvious enough, one female doctor tells him: "I imagine you'll be feeling a little bit limp by the end of the day." Within the viewing room the figures simply referred to as "shadows" in the novel become clearly visible as an audience and establish that Alex's gaze has itself become the object of medical observation. Above all, let us consider what happens to Alex's eyes. His head is clamped in a stereotaxic frame (Kubrick used an authentic lidlock for these scenes), exactly the equipment that is used for brain implanting in *The Terminal Man*. Alex's eyes are clamped open in a licensed act of medical violence, while an attendant drops liquid in them from a pipette, as if in imitation of the sexual act but with Alex's gender role reversed. This rape of the eye is implied through voice over comments by Alex, such as: "I still could not get out of the line of fire of the picture." He registers the solicitation of the image and even the hyper-reality of film when he comments: "It's funny how the colours of the real world only seem really real when you viddy them on the screen."[58] It is exactly Alex's responses to these video images that we observe in the shots directed toward his face when clamped in the apparatus. At such points the viewer registers Alex as the passive object of our gaze, and we become implicated in the corrective process taking place by the congruence between our angle of vision and that of Alex's medical attendant.

Kubrick's ironic twist to the narrative comes with a second therapeutic sequence after Alex's suicide bid, when he has to be cured of the first treatment and restored to sexual activity. Even here, however, the process is not a straightforward sequence of personal development but rather a fluctuation in the opportunistic policies of the government and as such can hardly be interpreted as liberating. Both Burgess and Kubrick resist an essentializing category of criminality by showing how members of Alex's gang later become police officers. This change does not mean that they have abandoned violence, as Alex finds to his cost, but rather that the sanctioning or criminalizing of violence depends on social roles. Where Burgess imagines Alex's life as a sequence of phases, Kubrick constructs his film around a series of reversals. Thus, when Alex comments at the end of the film "I certainly was cured," he merely signals a return to the earlier status quo.

Kubrick appears to have conceived Alex as an unrepressed "natural man" since he has stated: "When Alex is given the Ludovico treatment, you can say this symbolizes the neurosis created by the conflict between the structures imposed by society and our own natures."[59] This simple Freudian opposition between desire and denial does not fit the social and cultural intelligence that lies behind Alex's behavior in the novel or film. We encounter Alex only as a creature of his culture, manipulating it for his own advantage. Far from being a natural or a primitive, he is living out an alienated relation to his society. One of the main ironies in *A Clockwork Orange* is the stark contrast between Alex's power as narrator and protagonist and his disempowered social position. Indeed, the much-discussed question of his violence could be taken as an attempt to force his presence on to society.[60] Thomas Elsaesser has argued, rather too simply, that "Alex's antagonists, like his victims . . . are virtually without exception physically unattractive or repulsive, emotionally repressed, crazy, vindictive, pathologically violent if given half a chance, and prepared to abuse institutional power for personal ends."[61] Indeed, Alex's very sophistication almost becomes a problem in the narrative. When his brainwashing is reaching its culmination, he shouts out that it is a "sin" to use Beethoven in this context. For Burgess and Kubrick the disruption of a scientific discourse by an incongruously religious term takes priority over the realist question of whether Alex could ever use such a term without irony.

■ The equipment used in *A Clockwork Orange* suggests some kind of electronic intervention in the brain. Even though he isn't sure what has been happening, Alex suspects that the doctors have been "playing around with inside like my brain," and his second treatment includes "deep hypnopaedia," similar to the taped instructions played to sleeping subjects in *Brave New World*.[62] The technology of electronic brain stimulation had been imagined as early as 1953 in the science fiction film *Invaders from Mars*, where captive humans are implanted at the base of the neck with a miniature electronic device through which they can be directed to commit acts of sabotage.

In the 1950s fantasy was approaching fact in the experiments of José Delgado who was to achieve fame by diverting a charging bull through an electronically triggered brain implant, a demonstration subsequently criticized for not proving any control of aggression at all.[63] Delgado explored the ways in which "cerebral activity is essentially dependent on sensory inputs from the environment." In pursuit of the forms of this dependence he hypothesized a number of basic brain "mechanisms" (an awkward oxymoron) producing mental activity that could then be reproduced through electronic implants. Although he speculated that ESB might become a "master control of human behavior," he did admit the difference between fictional and actual applications of this technology, declaring that "science fiction has already imagined men with intracerebral electrodes engaged in all kinds of mischief under the perverse guidance of radio waves sent by some evil scientist." In practice, however, ESB was far too crude to substitute personalities.[64] Delgado was a pioneer of this new technology and speculated on the brain-computer-brain loop that features in *The Terminal Man*.

In *Profiles of the Future* (1962) Arthur C. Clarke expresses enthusiasm about the accelerated learning that could be facilitated by "Mechanical Educator" devices (hypnopaedia by another name) but pauses over the poten-

tial for a more sinister kind of control: "Electronic possession of human robots controlled from a central broadcasting station is something that even
George Orwell never thought of; but it may be technically possible long before 1984."[65] Clarke showed ambivalence over the discovery of pain and pleasure centers in the brain, perhaps because he sensed a new potential for addiction here, a danger later explored in narrative form by Larry Niven, whose
story "Death by Ecstasy" is a bizarre mystery where the narrator's friend is
found dead, his features frozen in a grin of ecstasy. Connected to his skull is
a device called a "droud," which, it emerges, has induced such pleasing sensations that the victim kept the connection too long. Apart from its resemblance to accounts of death from an overdose of the drug "ecstasy," this story
anticipates later narratives of the fatal consequences of entering cyberspace
by Pat Cadigan and others (see chapter 10), and Niven is clearly drawing on
the imagery of ESB implants here. A second electronic device, but one not
really integrated into the story, is called the "Russian sleep," where electrodes
attached to the eyelids and nape of the neck bring on a loss of consciousness.
This once again is a direct fictional application of reported fact, since Clarke
describes exactly this implement, running on low-frequency pulses, being
designed in the Soviet Union for medical use.[66]

As we have seen, such a process formed the central technological speculation of Frederik Pohl's *A Plague of Pythons* (1965), where a Soviet-designed
microwave transmitter can "possess" human subjects and make them commit any act the transmitter instructs. Similarly, the journalist David M. Rorvik saw ESB as a means of surveillance, titling his report on that technology
"Someone to watch over you." Summarizing the research of Delgado and
others, he stresses that this technology is one of mapping and control. The
logical extension of this fitting "terminal devices" under the scalp, he argued, would be to create an "electroligarchy" where ESB could produce
made-to-order citizens. The ruling elite "need only punch buttons and transmit the appropriate signals to achieve every general's, manager's, president's,
premier's dream of the efficient society."[67] Rorvik imagined a stratified society whose citizens are graded according to electronic design as Electrons,
Protons, and menial Neutrons. When he collected this essay in his study *As
Man Becomes Machine* (1971), Rorvik made the dystopian analogy explicit,
declaring that "an electronically contrived Brave New World . . . might actually be easier to achieve" than Huxley's biochemical system.[68] Rorvik notes
applications of ESB, which will figure in *The Terminal Man*, such as its use
for treating epilepsy and the addictive self-stimulation for sexual pleasure. In

1973 Ed Bryant declared sensationally that the "millenium of mechanized mind control is upon us," quoted a U.S. psychiatrist as saying of Jose Delgado's experiments that the "totalitarian potential is beyond belief," and then shrugged off the issues by insisting that the technology was here to stay.[69] Certainly ESB devices have been explained as enabling a "mass telemetric surveillance," which marks a major development from Jeremy Bentham's ideal prison, the Panopticon, where inmates could not escape observation: "But the Panopticon today is not a construction of brick and iron. It is a much more practical complex of electrical circuits."[70]

Such comments reinforced the dominance of science fiction images in the debate, and the suggestion that criminals might be electronically tagged was taken up in Piers Anthony and Robert E. Margroff's novel *The Ring* (1968). In this dystopia a state computer ("Ultimate Conscience") has codified a "presumptive ideal" for that society and measured the extent to which convicted criminals might deviate from that ideal. The electronic ring that is fastened on a criminal's limb "merely enforces adherence — to that imprinted ideal."[71] The eponymous ring represents a technologically "ideal" form of enforcement, constructed on the model of a lie detector, where it is sufficient for the subject to *want* to break the law for him or her to be given a painful shock. The end result is therefore virtually identical to Burgess's aversion treatment. Anthony and Margroff show the limitations of the system in that it doesn't reduce violence in society, nor can it deal with the paradox that in some critical situations it is impossible to avoid breaking the law. *The Ring* exploits the familiar dystopian irony that a supposed technological advance rebounds on the citizens, in this case making the "Ringers" (wearers of the ring) more obtrusive socially and therefore even more liable to violence than they were before.

Commentary on ESB in fiction and nonfiction alike tended to stress the political problems of its application. It is very difficult in practice to use the term "control" without its entailing agency, a controller. And, although researchers on ESB presented it as benign, suggestions that the leaders of inner-city riots might be brain damaged caused indignation in the African American community. A 1973 article in *Ebony* magazine pitted psychologists against each other — and in the process brought out the racial tensions within the slippery concept of violence. One psychiatrist declared bluntly: "These brain studies are racist. They say that black people are so animal and savage that whites have to carve on their brains to make them human beings."[72] Before any operations are carried out, subjects must give their consent, but the article stressed that the most likely candidates—prisoners and mental patients—had already lost so much of their freedom that such consent became an empty form. Once again we come back to the question of power and who exercises it.

By the end of the 1960s and throughout the following decade the public debate over what had become known as psychosurgery was raging. One commentator has explained that "what caused the greatest concern were the suggestions that psychosurgery and other physical manipulations of the brain might be used to change socially (and politically) undesirable behavior."[73] This was the context within which Michael Crichton's *The Terminal Man* appeared.

■ In the late 1960s a group of researchers based in Boston were investigating the feasibility of curing violence by carrying out operations on the brain. Vernon H. Mark and Frank R. Erwin achieved notoriety in 1967 by publishing a letter suggesting that participants in the recent urban riots might be suffering from focal brain damage and in 1970 published *Violence and the Brain*, which tried to explain the mechanism of violent behavior by considering the relation between the brain and violence.[74] Here they argued that there could be as many as ten million Americans suffering from undetected brain damage and discussed the effectiveness of using implanted devices modeled on José Delgado's "stimoceiver" (a miniature transmitter and receiver). Among the cases they cite is that of Thomas R., an engineer whose brain was damaged when his peptic ulcer ruptured and who then received treatment through different electric stimuli. This case suggested a fictional subject to Michael Crichton, who studied under Mark and who graduated from the Harvard Medical School in 1969.

The Terminal Man (1972) frames its narrative with an introduction and bibliography on psychosurgery, which were designed to counter the sensational public images of mind control that Crichton felt were circulating at the time. This documentation alerts the reader to the contemporary nature of his subject, a point picked up by William Burroughs, who declared: "Michael Crichton's not trying to *predict* anything so much as build a story around what we know is possible."[75] Crichton warns us in the introduction, "Many people today feel that they live in a world that is predetermined and running along a fixed pre-established course" and condemns that attitude as a "childish and dangerous denial of responsibility."[76] For his part, Harlan Ellison denied that the subject was fantastic: "If the harnessing of Harry Benson's dream is only a sf [*sic*] dream, it is certainly the next step in mind control experiments that have been proceeding for several decades."[77] The novel introduces the patient Harry Benson first as a case to be debated in the Los Angeles hospital where he is taken. After a car crash he suffers from brain damage that induces dangerous seizures of violence. A neurosurgeon puts the case outlined by Mark and Erwin (whose book is cited in the bibliography) that there may be operable physical causes for this violence.[78] Countering this position a psychiatrist describes an earlier case where surgery failed and the patient committed suicide. The first section of the novel describes in great detail the procedures leading up to surgery, presenting in effect a dossier narrative that includes charts and photographs of Benson. The laconic chapter titles ("Implantation," "Breakdown," and so forth) divide the narrative according to phases in Benson's case, and, indeed, the novel presents itself as a dossier or report on that case, designed to show a direct correlation between brain damage and violent behavior. Following criticism from specialists, Crichton subsequently published "A Note on Psychomotor Epilepsy," where he recognized that such epileptics were no more prone to criminal or violent behavior than anyone else and admitted: "In the face of considerable controversy among clinical neuroscientists, I am persuaded that the understanding of the relationship between organic brain damage and violent behavior is not so clear as I thought at the time I wrote the book."[79]

Countering the cumulative scientific rationality of the hospital staff, and for that matter the hospital environment where much of the action is set, Harry Benson articulates a position similar to that of David Rorvik, arguing that the machines are taking over and predicting a coming war between machines and humanity. Part of his technophobic paranoia is a negative response to his treatment in the hospital. He mythologizes himself as a "fallen man," succumbing to being changed into a machine. Like Alex in *A Clockwork Orange*, Benson complains about his depersonalization into a passive subject for treatment: "I feel like a goddam machine," he exclaims. "I feel like an automobile in a complicated service station. I feel like I'm being *repaired*."[80] This complaint develops into an overt attack on the female member of the team, when Benson's fears become realized in compulsive acts of aggression: "His face was blank, an automaton mask. His arms were still extended toward her. He seemed almost to be sleepwalking as he advanced on her."[81] The culmination of this rebellion of the medical subject comes when Benson attacks the hospital computer, the power source of an environment that is in effect an extended laboratory.[82]

Ironically one of the researchers into ESB appears to have succumbed to a paranoia similar to Benson's. John C. Lilly developed fears that new techniques could be used to manipulate subjects covertly. In his autobiography, *The Scientist* (1976), Lilly reflected, "If this technique got into the hands of a secret agency, they would have total control over a human being and be able to change his beliefs extremely quickly, leaving very little evidence of what they had done." This fear grew into a conviction that, while he was in a sensory deprivation tank, he was visited by extraterrestrials who told him that humanity would be superseded by computer-like "solid-state entities" that would take over the Earth and then link up with other planets.[83]

In *The Terminal Man* the doctors attempt to create a self-regulating process where Benson's imminent seizures trigger a soothing transmission of electricity to the damaged part of the brain, but the one factor they fail to take into account is electronic addiction ("elad"). The doctors fatally miscalculate how far the minicomputer actually does control Benson's brain. Because the soothing discharges induce pleasure, the brain starts inducing seizures more and more often, with the result that it overloads and Benson goes into a breakdown.

At this point a contradiction emerges in Crichton's novel. He wants to defuse the melodramatic connotations of "mind control" through his Doctor Ellis who, like B. F. Skinner, extends the concept into society as a whole: "The truth was that everybody's mind was controlled, and everybody was glad for it. The most powerful mind controllers in the world were parents, and they did the most damage. . . . Newborn children were little computers waiting to be programmed. And they would learn whatever they were taught, from bad grammar to bad attitudes."[84] Crichton's experimenters echo the sentiments of Burgess's Doctor Brodsky, who declares, "We are not concerned with motive, with the higher ethics."[85] Similarly, the surgical team in *The Terminal Man* pay little or no attention to Benson's subjectivity, only to the probable sequence of his treatment.

The novel dramatizes a male-gendered arrogance about medical technology that proves to have links with military hardware. One technician in the team was an expert on guidance systems for rockets in the U.S. Army. Even the terminology of one field seeps into the other in phrases like the "target area" in Benson's brain. Summarizing the experiment, one doctor explains the body–computer link-up as a takeover by technology: "In one area, the computer brain has total control. And therefore the patient's biological brain, and indeed his whole body, has become a terminal for the new computer. We have created a man who is one single, large, complex computer terminal."[86] Once again we can see the utopian attempt to impose order on behavior and society denying not only the individual's subjectivity but even his organism. The use of the term "created" glances briefly at the *Frankenstein* motif in the novel, and it is left to Janet Ross, the only female member of the team, to empathize with Benson and attempt to save him.

The dominant scientific attitude of the team reflects what one reviewer called the "valueless technological outlook which the tough realism he attempts is meant to express."[87] Because Crichton foregrounds the hospital procedures so insistently, he denies Benson the narrative space to develop as a subject. So for this reason the science fiction writer Theodore Sturgeon decided that ultimately the novel failed to engage the reader. It is, as he puts it, Crichton's exploitation of the "interface between fact and invention" that initially catches our interest but that then smothers the interaction between characters because Benson is too remote and the psychologist concerned with his fate too predictable. Ultimately, Crichton's "verisimilitude locks itself to technology, not especially to living."[88] However, the violent denouement to the novel moves it toward the Gothic tradition of experiments where "the scientists fail to control their new creation," the tradition of *Frankenstein*, *The Island of Doctor Moreau*, and *Dr. Jekyll and Mr. Hyde*.[89] Indeed Crichton himself has said: "I've always wanted to rewrite Frankenstein and this is it."[90]

■ The suppressed Gothic theme becomes a major element in Mike Hodges' film of *The Terminal Man* (1974). Two opening shots immediately establish the self as threatened and imprisoned: a police helicopter where the bulbous "head" of the helicopter anticipates the "space helmets" of the surgeons during the operation and, later, the helmet of the police marksman who shoots Benson; and an open spy-hole in a cell door, which situates the viewer as being under surveillance like Benson. The imagistic continuity between cell and hospital reminds us of the power play in the latter and skillfully establishes a link we have already seen in *A Clockwork Orange*; this link gives Benson a more tangible spatial subjectivity than in the novel. The operation scene presents a more disabling spectacle than in *A Clockwork Orange* because Benson is lying prone, under observation from a gallery above, and the use of drilling to force an entry into his skull is made the subject of a black joke from the surgeon who recalls his tutor as saying: "You act like you're breaking into somebody's tomb. It's only a head." The surreal appearance of the surgeons' helmets and the visual echo of the Martian operation in *Invaders from Mars* suggest at once the alien-ness of the procedure (the first of its kind), its ritual dimension (where the female doctor plays acolyte), and its transgressive nature as an invasion of subjective space.

The surgeon's comment suggests a Gothic counternarrative to that of therapeutic restoration, namely the violation of a grave, so popular in the subgenre of mummy films. Benson's white gown and head bandage help to establish this resemblance, and a later scene at his girlfriend's apartment confirms that the operation has in effect turned him into a monster. Consider the visual symbolism of the scene. The girl is painting her nails black, signifying perhaps the presence of evil or a premonition of death. The parrot in the cage suggests captivity. The film showing on the television is *Them!* the 1954 narrative of giant ants roaming the California desert. The scene on the television shows the opening scene of *Them!* in which there is a traumatized little girl whose family has been killed. Two notions are introduced here, or at least made explicit: the unpredictable and jarring nature of violent attack and the threat from another species. Then, in one of the stereotyped scenes from monster movies, Benson opens his eyes (like Frankenstein's creature), staggers to his feet, and moves toward his girlfriend, as if with a sexual purpose. When he stabs her, the scene is not shot as a simple killing, like that of the Cat Lady in *A Clockwork Orange*. Instead, the girl's head moves from side to side in slow motion as if in orgasm, and once again the film manages to make a theme more powerful visually than the novel, where the connection between violent seizure and hypersexuality is only suggested.[91] The supposedly therapeutic process endured by Benson actually turns him into a murderous, then self-destructive monster. The film deploys science fiction and Gothic allusions to dramatize the limitations of the scientists' knowledge and to disrupt their planned sequence of orderly therapy.

In his novel's title, Crichton makes an obvious pun on technological intervention and endings, which the film expresses through fragmented images of Benson in mirrors and reflections on hospital consoles, suggesting the fracturing of his self.[92] And in the final sequence, Benson's own desire for an ending takes him to a place of death. He wanders down an aisle in a funeral parlor, whose white open spaces recall the hospital, and then outside in the cemetery he slumps into an open grave, where he is shot by a police marksman. The pathos in this ending grows out of our realization that Benson is no longer a real threat but, like Frankenstein's creature, has become excluded from society. The film refuses to make Benson's death the final ending. His case may be the first of its kind, but the film implies that it may not be the last. The concluding image resituates the viewer in the position of surveillance by repeating the cell spy-hole image and echoing the conclusion of *Invasion of the Body Snatchers* by having a voice over say: "They want you next." Unlike the novel, which uses the hospital as its setting, the film starts outside this technologically organized space in a police station and ends with Benson's death in a cemetery and with a coda that moves beyond the fictional frame to draw the viewer into a larger situation of threat from socialized medical and legal processes.

Both *A Clockwork Orange* and *The Terminal Man* describe medical processes that are designed to produce social control but fail. Both processes are revealed to be far less precise than their practitioners assume. Just as the lobotomies described in Bernard Wolfe's novel *Limbo* (1952) cannot get rid of aggression without removing desire, in *A Clockwork Orange* aversion therapy removes desire and with it the subject's capacity for choice. In *The Terminal Man* the damage is even more severe, ultimately fatal, because the surgery is based on a mistaken popular premise that "scientists have discovered that all of the brain's functions—the autonomic, the somatic, and the psychic—are susceptible to electrical control."[93] This could be described as the fallacy of misplaced congruence because, as Elliot Valenstein argues, it is quite wrong to assume "that the anatomical locus for each of the behaviors that can be elicited is discrete and well defined."[94] Abstract categories of behavior should not be identified with discrete parts of the brain, he insists, and the terminal man's self-destruction is brought about by an unexpected activity in the brain, in other words by the brain's holistic resistance to the attempted mapping and segmentation by the medical experimenters. The protagonists of both narratives are experimental subjects, the first guinea pigs in processes of technological therapy that go dramatically wrong.

■ We have seen how the treatment of violence becomes a political issue when legal enforcement agencies collaborate with the medical authorities to shape subjects' behavior according to perceived social norms. Marge Piercy's 1976 novel, *Woman on the Edge of Time*, draws on earlier narratives of mental illness in order to debate the politics of hospitalization. Connie Ramos is a thirty-seven-year-old Mexican American who is committed to a mental ward when she defends her niece against brutal beating by her pimp. Piercy blurs the distinction between medical and legal processes by presenting Connie's medical assessment as a kind of trial by disparate authority figures. Like a criminal, Connie has a "record" of previous violence in trying to defend her child. As soon as she enters Bellevue and then later Rockover State mental institution, Connie demonstrates an awareness that all behav-

ior can be read as symptom.⁹⁵ Internalizing surveillance, she carefully monitors the way she walks, her facial expressions, and her speech so as not to
arouse any undue suspicion from the ward attendants. Like *One Flew Over
the Cuckoo's Nest*, Piercy's novel depicts the capacity of behavior to mask
and, therefore, protect inmates; one woman, like Chief Bromden, never
speaks. And like Thomas Disch in *Camp Concentration* (to be discussed in
the following chapter), Piercy identifies incarceration with social injustice
by naming one of her characters Sacco-Vanzetti.

The novel quickly and skillfully establishes an institutional context virtually identical to Kesey's, and it is at this point that the first suggestions start
filtering in of a new experimental procedure that might enable inmates to get
released. Connie is transferred to a more open ward where she sees her first
experimental subject, a woman with "needles in her brain." Piercy's perception of the social invisibility of mental inmates is demonstrated ironically
when the medical team start filming a violent woman who calls out "I ain't
no guinea pig!" only to be tranquillized by ESB a moment later. The leader of
the team, who is compared to José Delgado by a colleague, boasts: "We can
electrically trigger almost every mood and emotion," thereby revealing that
control is as addictive as the drugs that secretly circulate in the hospital.⁹⁶
Connie learns that Doctor Redding's experiments had originally been on
monkeys until public complaints led him to divert his attention to the mental
patients the public ignores — another of the novel's many ironies. At this point,
Connie escapes from the hospital, only to be recaptured two days later. Piercy
is as pessimistic as Kesey when it comes to showing that there is little difference between inside and outside, presenting her mental ward as a "microcosm of the bureaucratic/capitalist system."⁹⁷ As we shall see in a moment,
however, this does not mean that the novel presents a fatalistic narrative.

Even before Connie participates in the experimental process, the novel
describes the possibility of error (one patient suffers brain damage and later
commits suicide) and engages with the issue of consent when a psychologist
tries to persuade Connie that the experiment will be for her good. On the
eve of her "treatment" Connie experiences a period of agonizing suspense:
"Tomorrow they were going to stick a machine in her brain. She was the
experiment. They would rape her body, her brain, her self. After this she could
not trust her own feelings. She would not be her own. She would be their
experimental monster."⁹⁸ The drama of the moment comes out through the
rapid alternation between "she" and "they." In *The Terminal Man* Crichton
denies his experimental subject anything more than a minimum verbalized

consciousness, whereas Piercy uses her narrative voice to offset Connie's isolation, since she has no reliable companion in the novel's present. The narrator thus authenticates Connie's selfhood by showing the coherence of her
thoughts and the shrewdness of her social perceptions. Unlike the protagonists of *The Bell Jar* or *The Terminal Man*, she can fully articulate within her
thoughts her danger in becoming the subject of an unproven technique.
This subjection is figured as multiple acts of violence that culminates in her
loss of selfhood when she fears turning into a plaything, a substitute "chimp"
for the doctors to manipulate at will.

Conflict is the premise of Piercy's novel, and even when her protagonist
is undergoing an operation she never loses her awareness of self and her
capacity to resist the potential for erasure in the process. As they prepare to
drill into her skull, marking the place with dye, Connie maintains her selfhood through a pun ("They were dyeing her and she was dying") whose
verbal play reasserts her continuing vitality. The operation blocks her capacity for physical response, which she deals with by imagining an out-of-body
state: "She wanted to weep, to scream. But she was contained in a balloon
way back though her skull, perhaps floating out through the hole they had
cut in her, floating out there above them, lighter than air. How patient they
were to take so much of their valuable medical time deciding where to push
in."99 Selfhood is constantly expressed through figures of containment. As
one space (her skull) is violated, Connie imagines a lighter substitute that
not only prevents her self from dissolving in the air but also gives expression
to her sense of being a spectator at her own experience. Instead of being the
patient herself, she displaces the term on to the medical team. This "other-
ing" has the advantage of a survival tactic in preserving a tenuous focus for
Connie's consciousness.

Here we need to consider the nonrealist dimension to *Woman on the Edge
of Time*. From an early point in the novel Connie begins to experience contact with creatures from a future America where medicine is practiced on a
cooperative basis with a minimum judgment on the patient. This utopian
future embodies the alternatives that 1970s America cannot even begin to
implement, and Connie's movements to and fro in time sharpen her resistance to the status quo. One critic has suggested that this utopia may "exist
only as a hallucination of Connie's medically drugged—though intelligently
receptive—mind," but Connie is no Chief Bromden.100 In practice, it is impossible to separate her discourse from the expansive explanations of the narrator. The latter's reinforcement of the silent speech of Connie's thoughts

helps to convince the reader of her lucidity. There is, however, a darker future glimpsed where the same medical experiments have become totally institutionalized as routine. Connie encounters a future anti-self named Gildina, who is totally at the mercy of male medical technicians. The process in question is named "SC" (sharper control) and maintained within a dystopian context where the security police use mental scanners to check citizens for seditious thoughts. Tom Moylan has argued that this society uses a "cybernetic technology that makes people less able to determine their own lives and the direction of society, rendering them passive in the face of corporate domination."[101] The "multi" that dominates Gildina's life specifically is designated "Chase-World-TT," an obvious conflation of Chase Manhattan and the multinational conglomerate ITT. Piercy anticipates the cyborgs of 1980s science fiction in having Gildina monitored by a "cybo" named Cash, who has fibers implanted in his spine that transform him into a "fighting machine." This glimpse of a future where big business, medical technology, and male hegemony have all come together acts as a trigger for Connie to declare private war on the present system, and the novel ends at the point where she has put poison in the doctors' coffee maker. Piercy's inclusion of medical documentation on Connie might appear to resemble Crichton's attempts to authenticate *The Terminal Man* as a case record, but actually has the opposite effect in demonstrating the anonymous and destructive bureaucratic processes Connie is determined to resist. Her political self-awareness prevents her ever succumbing to the status of a guinea pig. Indeed, we will now see how narratives of experiments on human guinea pigs are all, in their different ways, narratives of resistance.

nine

The Guinea Pigs

The protagonists of *A Clockwork Orange* and *The Terminal Man* are at least partially informed about the experimental processes they undergo. Again and again in this study, however, we have seen cases of secret experimentation taking place, often without the subjects' consent, and we now need to consider narratives that explore the ethics of such experiments and that dramatize the fracturing of the self that might result.

In 1952 the Defence Research Board of Canada invited academics at McGill University to research into the possibilities of defense against brainwashing. The issue they chose to focus on was isolation from the environment. Dr. Ewen Cameron began elaborating experiments into what he called "depatterning," combining electric shocks with sleep therapy, and playing back to the patients tape recordings of their emotionally charged statements. At about the same time Dr. John Lilly began related experiments into sensory deprivation at the National Institutes of Health near Washington. Both enterprises came to be funded by the CIA as part of an overall program to research the technology of brainwashing. Although a CIA Isolation Group concluded in 1955 that they "could find no evidence the technique [sensory deprivation] is being used anywhere in the Communist countries in interrogation matters or in intelligence work," research continued. Ironically, one report on these experiments found that they were very close to the practices of the "professional brainwasher."[1] Lilly's claim to notoriety was the design of a tank in which subjects floated in body-temperature water, unable to see or hear. Historian John Marks comments that "intelligence agents swooped down on Lilly again, interested in the use of his tank as an interrogation tool."[2] It was not only intelligence officers who considered this application, however. Donald Hebb, director of the McGill facility, reflected anxiously on the transposition of brainwashing to the home scene: "It is one thing to hear that the Chinese are brainwashing their prisoners on the other side of the world; it is another to find in your own laboratory, that merely taking away the usual sights, sounds and bodily contacts from a healthy university student for a few days can shake him, right down to the base: can disturb his personal identity."[3]

Sensory deprivation was situated within a Cold War military context in Frederik Pohl and Cyril M. Kornbluth's story "The Quaker Cannon" (collected in *The Wonder Effect*, 1961). Here the Korean War is retold as a war against the Utilitarians (or "Utes"), who use behaviorist techniques in their torture of prisoners. Lieutenant Kramer was one such prisoner who cracked under the Chinese use of "Blank Tanks" and confessed that the United States was employing viral weapons.[4] Kramer is then retained in the army in a marginal role until an assault is planned on the Soviet Union across the Bering Straits. Posted as aide to the general organizing a bogus attack force, he falls once again into the hands of the Utes and is subjected to another ordeal by deprivation:

> The Blank Tanks are more than deafness. In them a man is blind, even to the red fog that reaches through closed eyelids. There is nothing to smell. There is nothing to taste. There is nothing except the swaddling-cloths. . . . It is something like being unborn and something like never having been at all. There is nothing, absolutely nothing, and although you are not dead you are not alive either.[5]

This description, the centerpiece of the story, can only proceed by negatives, showing an erasure and reduction of identity to a minimal consciousness of being. The hapless Kramer has in fact been exploited twice over, first by the Utes to secure a confession and second by the army to "brainwash" the Soviet commander into believing that the attack on the Soviet Union was a fictitious plan. The actual invasion follows this plan, so Kramer becomes a shattered hero of the hour. The narrative ironically questions the applicability of the term "Utilitarian," implying its equal relevance to America as to the enemy.

The sensory deprivation experiments inspired the Scottish novelist James Kennaway (the pseudonym of James Ewing Peebles) to write his novel *The Mind Benders* (1963), which was used as the basis for the Anglo-Amalgamated film of the same title.[6] Here the experimentation is shifted to Oxford and the narrative describes an investigation into why Professor Sharpey, the director who (like John Lilly) insists on using himself as a guinea pig, should leap to his death from a train. The case he is carrying proves to contain hundreds of pounds sterling, so one question concerns his loyalty. Has he given away secrets to the Communist agents he has contacted in London? Kennaway follows the paradigm of mystery fiction in narrating the investigation of events leading up to the professor's suicide, but there is a second subject that very quickly takes precedence over the professor's fate: the nature of his experiments. The investigator and main focalizer is Major "Ramrod" Hall from the counterespionage section of MI5, a semiparodic figure explicitly differentiated from James Bond, who combines the roles of policeman, intelligence agent, and layman. Hall has been following the professor for some time and it is he who supplies us with the information that Sharpey has been meeting "undesirables" from East European embassies. Hence the suitcase filled with money. These unconfirmed signs of treason obscure another possibility: that Sharpey committed suicide from remorse or because his experiments had unhinged him. The professor remains an enigma because he is denied any voice in the novel other than a recorded cry of terror on a tape or as the very stereotype of an academic scientist speaking on film.

As an experienced military interrogator, Major Hall immediately places Isolation Laboratory A within a political, not scientific context: "It was a place for political police, not for scientists. . . . In fact the tank simply acted as a kind of super-dark cell, in which a prisoner might be put in solitary confinement."[7] Hall cuts through the rationalization of these experiments as being for space travel and sees them as opening up a new form of mind alteration.[8] Hypnotism merely "scratches the surface" and he privately ridicules the traditional view of brainwashing: "the idea of full confession, and subsequent indoctrination, under hypnosis."[9] Just as the political applications remain ominous but implicit, the novel draws attention to these darker aspects through allusions to *Frankenstein* and *Dr. Jekyll and Mr. Hyde*, allusions of course to experiments gone tragically wrong. This motif is made clear when darkness changes the laboratory into a "nightmare torture chamber."

Cameron's use of tape playbacks is conflated with Lilly's immersion tank in the central, most critical episode of the novel, where Sharpey's deputy

Longman undergoes prolonged immersion. The results appear to confirm a materialistic perception of the self: "the soul turns out to be common metal; it has the same properties for all; its dissolution is merely a question of technique. . . . The rack and rubber truncheon can be put away. They are obsolete now." Human difference is reduced to a common species dependence on a stable environment. Remove the latter and the stability of the self becomes severely impaired so that the field of scientific inquiry comes to resemble the "first experiments in the physics of the soul." When Longman enters the tank he goes through a sequence of phases from irritation through melancholy and erotic fantasies to panic. His cries compound the loss of individuation as a typical experimental subject to a loss of species features: "When pain and panic are extended this far there can be no identity. The noise is literally closer to the monkey house than to man."[10] Kennaway's use of the Oxford setting now becomes clearly ironic. In the midst of an ancient center of culture, experimental proof is being produced that the adult human, like other mammals, is "still a function of his sensory environment."[11]

Longman's spell in the tank alerts Hall to the military applications of this technique. In the 1963 film, for which Kennaway wrote the screenplay, Hall makes this explicit by declaring to Sharpey's colleague Tate: "This is an experiment on the fringes of brainwashing, indoctrination." To test out this proposition, Hall and Tate act out the roles of hard and soft interrogators and test the strength of the subject's most cherished belief—his marriage. Longman is browbeaten into admitting that he does not love his wife, but Hall reassures his companion that "the way to unwash a brain is to return slowly and patiently over the same ground."[12] So far the novel achieves its effects by displacing Eastern interrogation methods onto an English setting and tracing out the self-induced dehumanization of Longman. Two further twists take place, however. Longman appears to recover from his ordeal, thereby nullifying the task's political value for inducing collapse. Then in the final section of the novel he is revealed to be treating his now pregnant wife with callous cruelty. Taking a local prostitute back to the lab he combines experimenter with subject by listening to his own tapes, contradicting the paradigm of mind alteration by showing that "tapes played back to brain-washed victims return victims to their previous lines of thought." After the crisis of her premature delivery, the novel concludes by endorsing Longman's wife's pious conviction that "there were instincts in man laid too deep for the most skilful mind-ender to probe."[13] In fact the very need for asserting this conservative moral and the wavering now-it-threatens now-it-doesn't perspective on sensory deprivation suggests an anxiety toward this subject that Kennaway papers over by reconstituting domestic harmony.

A more recent novel dealing with mind alteration experiments is even more conservative than Kennaway's. Michael French's *Circle of Revenge* (1988) describes what happens when a sixteen-year-old answers a notice calling for volunteers in a university psychology experiment. Robbie has to watch videotapes of victims enduring worse and worse torture in a process that the experimenter, one Dr. Salazar explains as "imagery manipulation." When Robbie's girlfriend breaks into Salazar's office and reads Robbie's file, her worst fears seem to be confirmed. "Was Robbie actually being brainwashed?" The Manchurian Candidate script appears to be confirmed when Robbie almost shoots his friend Carlos, at which point he accuses Salazar of bad faith: "I was only your guinea pig."[14] At this point the rationale for the experiments is revealed. In a Latin American country Carlos's father had been responsible for abducting Salazar's wife and son; the experiments are part of an elaborate plan of revenge. The novel places the technology of mind control firmly within a liberal parable. Robbie learns the lesson of political concern but within the context of an assumption—totally unjustified—that such mind control could not happen in the United States. In that respect *Circle of Revenge* falls within a small minority of the works discussed here.

Experimentation itself is the central subject of Kennaway's novel, whereas most narratives place their emphasis on the consequences or the role of experiments within a larger conspiracy. In Ian Fleming's *On Her Majesty's Secret Service* (1963) Count Blofeld runs an exclusive Swiss clinic for the treatment of allergies on surprisingly militaristic lines. How many clinics maintain armed guards with instructions to shoot uninvited visitors on sight? Blofeld's establishment is an elaborate front for the preparation of agents who will plant a deadly virus in British chicken feed. This ludicrous plot is not helped by the gratuitous gendering of the inmates, who are all nubile (and very docile) young women. Fleming totally avoids a major issue in these narratives—the subject's consent to experimentation—by denying his inmates any will at all. Their role is simply to function as the decorative evidence of Blofeld's fiendish machinations that employ primarily a combination of posthypnotic suggestion and hypnopaedia. At night, as the girls lie "on the fringe of consciousness," hidden devices transmit a regular ticking like a metronome after which Blofeld's voice delivers his instructions together with a "self-erase" coda. Bond immediately realizes what is taking place: "Deep hypnosis! . . . The Hidden Persuader!" For every inmate "the message would work on all by itself through the night, leaving her, after weeks of repetition, with an in-built mechanism of obedience to the voice that would be as deep, as compelling, as hunger."[15] Fleming conveniently forgets the Western origins of Vance Packard's phrase so as to associate the process exclusively with his master criminal. The fate of the girls becomes a marginal issue before the central drama to be acted out between Bond and Blofeld.

■ Bond's investigation of the brainwashing process forms a prelude to this larger confrontation, whereas the most powerful narratives on this subject evoke differing degrees of uncertainty about the experiments taking place. In Kingsley Amis's *The Anti-Death League* (1966) speculation is rife about what exactly goes on inside a secret army facility where the research subjects do not know what injections they are being given.

The covert application of mind-altering drugs to prisoners became the subject of Thomas M. Disch's *Camp Concentration* (1968). Once again fiction stands close to fact. In 1952 the U.S. Army signed an agreement with the CIA to conduct experiments on inmates in a number of military installations including the Concord Corrections Facility where, Walter Bowart claimed in a 1995 interview, Timothy Leary was studying behavior alteration through the covert administering of LSD. *Camp Concentration* reveals a deep-seated political pessimism on Disch's part, which can be seen in his other writings on related subjects, particularly in his sardonic applications of Orwell and in his ironic depiction of behaviorist experiments. His "Thesis On Social Forms and Social Controls in the U.S.A.," a fiction in the form of a student's class paper, presents an argument that Orwell's paradoxical slogans ("WAR IS PEACE") anticipate the schizophrenic culture of the twenty-first century, where opposites coexist without resolution. Thus *Nineteen Eighty-Four* is described as the "prototype of our own" world, inescapably America, where the categories of slaves and freemen are manipulated as citizens move between spells in work camps and freedom: "The transition is effected by steadily decreasing sedation in a restful environment after an initial application of insulin and shock treatment."[16] The satire in this narrative emerging from the comic estrangement of a description of America as if it were an alien society and the apparently casual reference to social "therapy" extends into Disch's other fiction. The protagonist of "Displaying the Flag" (in *Getting into Death*, 1976) tries to cure his fetishism for leather by attending a Manchester clinic that, like the experimental facility in *A Clockwork Orange*, specializes in aversion therapy. Massive electric shocks seem to have cured

Leonard Dworkin until, that is, he begins developing a secret passion for uniforms. By this point the story has slid into a satire of the political right in America. A different system of control is described in *On Wings of Song* (1979), where criminals are confined in a prison with no guards or fences. Quite simply there is no need for them because every convict has an electronic lozenge planted in his stomach that will be detonated by a radio transmitter if he leaves the precinct. This device is "hailed as the Model-T of behavioural engineering."[17] Similar devices occur in such science fiction films as *The Running Man* (1987) and *Total Recall* (1990).

The allusion to Henry Ford and the famous Model-T stresses the national origin of this dystopia in no uncertain terms, and, although Disch designed his anthology of political science fiction, *Bad Moon Rising* (1973), as an expression of "concern for the present political scene and the dismal, or dismaying, or downright terrifying direction in which it's been drifting and/or hurtling during the last grim decade," the specific focus of the irony falls on the United States during the Vietnam War.[18] Disch cites *Darkness at Noon, Nineteen Eighty-Four* and—even more significantly in this context—*The Manchurian Candidate* as examples of prospective political narratives. In the collection, Robert Silverberg's "Some Notes on the Predynastic Epoch" uses the device of representing the reader's present as ancient history in a mock-archaeological report. Like Disch, Silverberg closely links the technology of mind control with right-wing fears of social change and the other as enemy. Thus news reports from this epoch are cited that express anxiety over "mind-affecting drugs," which outline U.S. Army psychologists' plan to "brainwash enemy troops with bars of soap that reveal a new propaganda message practically every time the guerrillas lather up" and which claim that rock bands "use the Pavlovian techniques to produce artificial neuroses in our young people" by destroying their inhibitory mechanisms.[19] At the end of his sketch Silverberg breaks his fiction in order to deny the reader any escape from considering his facetious report as a comment on the present. This self-consciousness about modes of expression also informs Disch's novel.

Disch started *Camp Concentration* in the Austrian Tyrol in the company of his fellow writer John Sladek, who was working on his own first novel *The Reproductive System* (both novels were published in 1968). In the latter the military finance top-secret "Project 32" to devise a self-reproducing machine—a mechanism that is so successful it starts taking over other plants. The director of the project admits that he intends to take over the world. The same paranoid secrecy, military–industrial linkup, and expansionist urge informs *Camp Concentration*, which presents a Dostoyevskyan prison journal narrated by Louis Sacchetti, a "figure loosely modeled on the poet Robert Lowell." According to Disch's synopsis when planning the novel, Sacchetti is serving a spell in Springfield prison as a "Conscientious Objector in the futile Southeast-Asian war of the near future."[20] In the finished novel Disch drops virtually all of these identificatory specifics and adjusts the narrative to concentrate on the processes taking place rather than their causes. Sacchetti is taken from prison to a secret underground complex named Camp Archimedes, where the army is funding research on the "first batch of guinea pigs" into an intelligence-enhancing but fatal drug called pallidine.[21] This is administered to him without his knowledge initially, and the deaths of those around him foreshadow his own fate. Disch's subject and his narrative method are close to those in Daniel Keyes's *Flowers for Algernon* (1966), in which a retarded bakery sweeper is, with his consent, given an operation to enhance his intelligence. Keyes's narrative consists of a series of "progress reports" on Charlie's case. At first Charlie shows improvement but then rapidly deteriorates. Two crucial differences between these novels are that Charlie is a willing subject for the pioneering treatment, and the action of *Flowers for Algernon* lacks the political dimension of *Camp Concentration*.

Disch gave glimpses of the subject he was to fill out in *Camp Concentration* in his 1966 story "The Squirrel Cage," which is the monologue of a writer confined within a "cube."[22] This is a place where there is no darkness, a white space open to interpretation as (padded) cell or laboratory. The monologue represents the speaker's attempts to situate himself in place or time without any external means of verification. The only external object he might rely on is that day's issue of the *New York Times*, although even this newspaper might be a complete forgery. His composition of poems and stories thus becomes a means of imaginatively breaking the bounds of his confinement. Otherwise he remains convinced that he is being kept under observation, perhaps by "young crew-cut Army doctors studying various brainwashing techniques. Reluctantly, of course. History and a concern for freedom has forced them to violate their own (privately-held) moral codes." And if he is being observed, he might be an experimental subject: "Maybe I *volunteered* for this experiment!" he exclaims.[23] The title of the story suggests a barrier between the internal observed subject and his external observers that the narrator modifies in a paranoid direction. He expresses a heightened suspicion of there being invisible watchers behind the white walls. Ironically, the scientific ideal of the effaced experimenter proves to be the most disturbing to the subject because he is unable to verify any aspect of his situation. Even more radically than Sacchetti, the disoriented narrator is suspended within an extended present to which only his mortality sets limits.

In *Camp Concentration* it is an important symbolic detail that Sacchetti is taken from his prison by guards wearing unmarked black uniforms, since this signifies his transfer from the known and legal to the unknown and extralegal. Hence Disch's choice of title since in Camp Archimedes, like the concentration camps, there is "no relationship between behavior and re[w]ard or punishment."[24] Sacchetti enters an experimental space separated from the outside world by its underground location and—though he only reluctantly recognizes this fact—characterized by the total surveillance exercised over the inmates. Like the narrator of "The Squirrel Cage," Sacchetti suspects that an inaccessible agenda is being followed by personnel who embody Disch's version of the Military-Industrial Complex: here, a combination of politics, prison, the military, and psychiatry—all supported by undisclosed sources of commercial funding.

The cultural markers in *Camp Concentration* situate the action historically in the period of the Vietnam War. Sacchetti has been imprisoned in Montgomery, presumably as a civil rights protester, and his name conflates Sacco and Vanzetti, whose case became a cause celebre of the 1920s, when many writers joined the demonstration against their execution. Robert McNamara, Johnson's Secretary of Defense, has become president and is using tactical nuclear weapons. The tripartite link between politics, business, and the military is reinforced within the novel through the figure of ex-General Humphrey Haast, whose initials echo those of Johnson's Vice President Hubert Humphrey. Haast prides himself on being a good "R and D" man, yet another echo of the Rand Corporation. In short, countless details in *Camp Concentration* situate Sacchetti within a specifically American administrative structure where his gesture of noncompliance has rebounded in his becoming the unwitting guinea pig in the army's "investigation of learning processes." The novel's history thus describes how military research on preventing or curing venereal disease accidentally throws up the agent pallidine. But this substance is a two-edged sword because it induces mental agility at the expense of the subject, who experiences a nine-month physical deterioration ending in certain death. Like earlier CIA-funded programs, this project is being partly fed by student volunteers.

Like Burroughs (*Naked Lunch* is referred to in passing), Disch extends the significance of the concept of virus as his novel progresses. Sacchetti has seen an expanse of blighted trees that he assumes was caused by an experimental virus gone astray. When he learns about pallidine in the abstract, it is merely described as an "agent infecting the host" quite apart from himself. But it then becomes apparent that pallidine is carried by himself and actually transmitted to the country at large by a female member of the prison staff who has had sex with a black inmate. This act is speculatively glossed as revenge on the "Great White Bitch of America"; it is given a national symbolism that opens up the further signification of the virus as a cultural corruption being fed by a military-industrial war machine. Ultimately pallidine cannot be contained, like the expanding machine in John Sladek's comic fantasy.

Traditionally prison narratives establish a dramatic opposition between the inmates and the prison authorities, which is based on a stability and clarity of role that *Camp Concentration* does not possess. For Camp Archimedes is at once a prison, clinic, and facility for testing secret weapons. The inmates are reified into "material" by the experimenters and the research on intelligence enhancement is explicitly directed toward the national defense effort. It follows that Sacchetti's journal articulates a subjectivity that the authorities are constantly trying to convert into information or experimental data. In one of his early dialogues with Dr. Busk, Sacchetti is told: "You are not, precisely, a subject."[25] Everything that Sacchetti writes in his journal is secretly scrutinized by his monitors, a fact that implicates the reader in the very processes being described. As Sacchetti's speculations become more extreme and as his medley of literary allusions become more florid, any psychological reading positions us close to his captors. Indeed, the act of reading becomes politicized by its inclusion within psychological investigation and in that respect confirms Sacchetti's declaration that "psychology has become the Inquisition of our age."[26]

Far from acting in opposition to the regime, Sacchetti's very function (to "observe and interpret") is prescribed by the authorities. He is then "bugged" in multiple senses of being infected and subjected to total surveillance. His narrative contains glosses by an anonymous "Ed."—an editor—that suggest a constant tampering with his record and that exemplify their full significance in a warning that everything the inmates write is examined by the National Security Agency (the "code boys"). In *Camp Concentration*, brainwashing manifests itself not as "therapy" or a psychodrama between victim and regime, so much as a condition of textual production. There are many suggestions that Sacchetti is being fed information in order to observe how it effects him. This process can be observed textually when prison officials commenting on preceding (supposedly "private") journal entries and the "defective" state of the journal, decide they need a shadowy "Ed." to bring the journal into shape. At a key point Sacchetti is about to reveal the name of the corporation that is secretly funding the facility, but a lacuna in the text is glossed as resulting from two lines being "defaced" from the manuscript. Part Two of the novel opens with an extended editorial commentary on the growing incoherence in Sacchetti's entries. Peter Swirski logically thinks such editorial interventions prove that "the corporation wields sufficient power to preserve its anonymity." The fact that the journal's coherence breaks down demonstrates that the "traditional art-form" is unable to "stand face to face with a totalitarian system." And the absence of news about the final course of the epidemic suggests that the tight control of information within Camp Archimedes operates across the nation as a whole.[27] The text of Sacchetti's journal itself is, by implication, assembled by officials within the very power structure he is ostensibly opposing. Pallidine symbolizes the appropriation by the regime of the subject's very words.

These textual ambiguities contrast Disch's novel with Donald Bain's *The Control of Candy Jones* (1976), the story of an MK-ULTRA victim. Following her success as a model in the 1940s, Candy Jones was recruited for the CIA in the 1950s by Dr. Gilbert Jensen of the University of California, when she seems to have been subjected to the posthypnotic induction of layered personalities similar to those described in George Estabrooks' *Hypnotism.* These were subsequently erased from her memory and, like the sleepers in *Telefon,* she was triggered into action by telephone messages. Apart from performing the role of agency messenger, Bain stresses, "what she didn't bargain for . . . was becoming a human guinea pig in a secret CIA scientific project in which *mind control* was the goal."[28] Bain's account claims to have been reconstructed from hours of taped sessions with Candy Jones and her husband, where it emerged that the CIA had constructed at least one extra identity that she used while acting as courier. The construction, or rather claimed *re*-construction, of Candy Jones's story would determine its plausibility, but Bain's volume takes this process for granted. As Alan Scheflin and Edward Opton point out, the volume thinly disguises the contradiction that if posthypnotic conditioning can seal the mind, how was it possible for her husband to access her "memories" without any training in hypnosis whatever?[29] Disch, in contrast, foregrounds the "contaminated" production of his narrative at every point. From Thomas Mann's *Doctor Faustus*, Disch took the notion of an entire country becoming a "thick-walled underground torture-chamber," with the difference now that the voice of the commentator cannot be separated from the corrupt regime.[30] One reviewer expressed this in character terms, arguing that Sacchetti was the "perfect articulator of the truths Disch is examining [because he] needed a spokesman as corrupt in his way as the villains are in theirs."[31] Sacchetti's tacit complicity in becoming a means to an end denies his Faustian role that has been appropriated and institutionalized by the U.S. government. Nothing reveals the status of *Camp Concentration* as a novel of the nuclear age more clearly than the metaphor of radiation ("today we must have reached critical mass") as if the inmates were potentially dangerous isotopes.[32] The purpose of Camp Archimedes, as expanded by Dr. Aimee Busk before her infection, is thus to investigate, develop, but above all contain.

Sacchetti's narrative accordingly contains suppressions of inferences, especially that he too has become infected by pallidine. Shortly before he admits this knowledge, after which the narrative temporarily breaks down into disordered fragments, he records a dream revelation where a travesty of an Aquinas figure approaches him from the depths of a pit with an unwelcome message. This information is conveyed metaphorically through consuming a sacramental meal brought on a coffee cart—secularized and institutionalized. A cherub offers Sacchetti a host from his diseased genitals covered with an "indecipherable script"; and then the final revelation comes that Sacchetti is playing host to the virus transmitted to him through the medium of food. This nightmare enacts in symbolic terms Sacchetti's passivity before the solicitations of the authorities and conflates information with food in a cycle of deadly consumption. Sacchetti, too, has fallen victim to the corruption of Camp Archimedes.

The conclusion to the novel gives an unexpected twist to the pattern of experimentation and casual human waste when it is revealed that the prisoners have constructed a "mind reciprocator" that has enabled them to exchange bodies with their guards. Critics like Samuel Delany have expressed unease about this reversal because it shows an unclear optimism.[33] This ending could be read as a literalization of the seepage between the categories of inmate and prison staff that has been taking place from an early stage. Disch himself has explained the reversals as demonstrating that "the way to survive is to accept being in complicity with a social structure that is evil."[34] The closure of narrative through denouement is imitated as theater by the authorities when the blind Sacchetti is led away like a latter-day Dostoyevsky to be shot, only to be reprieved. The reprieve is enacted through a revelation that the prison officials are in fact transformed inmates. This bizarre twist incongruously suggests a self-empowerment of the inmates, which everything in the body of the narrative excludes. Reprieve through biological chance is more usual, as happens in *The Andromeda Strain* (1971). Here, Project Scoop, the search for new biological weapons of war, results in a bacteria being brought back to Earth from near space. Not even a top-secret facility for dealing with such a case can counter the bacteria, and human life is only saved by the mutation of the virus into a benign form.[35]

■ The experiments described so far have as notional goals the discovery of information that will help the West in the conduct of the Cold War. But results never match expectations because the human subject is more complex than the experimenters recognize, hence the increasing complexity of the narratives themselves. We have already seen this in the metafictional dimension to *Camp Concentration* where we read of the authorities reading Sacchetti's journal. The same self-consciousness informs the 1960s British television series *The Prisoner* (1967–68), which made one of the most surreal applications of a controlled environment for experimentation. Its seventeen episodes depict the experiences of a British secret service agent who has resigned his post and been taken, while drugged, to a remote coastal location known simply as "the village." The script editor George Markstein had worked for British intelligence during the war and remembered an isolated lodge near Inverness where agents were kept incommunicado.[36] He planned the series to deal with "brainwashing and social control in the post-war era."[37] The series was partly shot in the unique Welsh village of Portmeirion, which blends a medley of architectural styles and which lent itself to the evocation of a mysterious and labyrinthine environment. The eponymous Prisoner, known throughout the series as Number 6, wakes from a drugged sleep in the Village and undergoes a series of experiments designed to extract information from him. No proper names are used, either by the characters who are designated by numbers or titles, or in the village. As a result the village and the setting of the series cannot be related to any specific place. The Village's picturesque, apparently benign, surface conceals an elaborate surveillance apparatus directed from a huge control suite that includes underground medical facilities. An Orwellian network of hidden microphones and cameras constantly monitors the movements of the inmates, and it is a crucial feature of the place that all doors are automatic.

The Village is a bounded terrain from which no one can escape, except to their deaths. Bizarrely, its resemblances constantly shift from a carnival setting to holiday camp, but each episode dramatizes a new facet of its totalitar-

ian regime. Episode 12 ("A Change of Mind") brings out its Orwellian dimension most clearly through images like a Kitchener–Big Brother poster
that declares, "The Community Needs You!" In a pastiche of Communist
show trials, Number 93 is being tried for "disharmony" in his behavior. The
means of maintaining communal harmony, typical of the series, is a procedure disguised as social therapy. A lobotomy guarantees "instant social conversion" of those guilty of "unmutual" acts. The central metaphor of manipulation here is that of the chess game: "we're all pawns," one inmate remarks,
and indeed episode 9 ("Checkmate") actualizes this metaphor when the vil-
lagers dress up as human chess pieces. The metaphor entails movers as well
as a script of moves and constantly foregrounds the problem of freedom. In
one of the most satirical episodes, the Prisoner, played by Patrick McGoohan, dismisses the crowd participating in an election as "brainwashed imbe-
ciles," only to find himself strapped into a lie-detecting machine, after which
he too can participate in the political game.

The opening footage for each episode concluded with Number 6 insisting: "I am not a number. I am a free man," but his words are repeatedly being
contrasted with his circumstances. Despite his ringing declaration, we never
know his name, only his relation to an elusive power structure. His antagonist
throughout is Number 2. Number 1 is a figure of reference, only an implied
presence at the other end of a telephone. Number 2, by contrast, changes
person, sometimes within the same episode, and admits that he too (like the
interrogator in *Darkness at Noon*) is a prisoner of the system. By concealing
the identity of those in power, *The Prisoner* conflates two Cold War fears: fear
of the growing power of the intelligence services, and fear of the growing
similarity between the two blocs. The series possess an episodic, cyclical
rhythm whereby Number 6 tries to leave the Village or defeat its controllers,
only to fail. Hence the second central metaphor. Like *The Manchurian Candidate*, circles are everywhere: the giant wheel of a penny-farthing has become the Village logo; we repeatedly see revolving spools of tape, and within
the circular settings of the committee and control rooms, human agents revolve around a central axis. Imagistically, this denies narrative progression
and reinforces the status of the Village as a place of confinement.

Circles also imply the failure of the authorities in their main purpose,
which is to discover what Number 6 knows and why he resigned. Nothing
demonstrates the Cold War context of the series so clearly as the reification
of Number 6 into a source of information. To access this information, his
manipulators deploy an entire technological arsenal. Other inmates in the

Village represent alternative or parallel versions of Number 6. In the first episode he sees his own possible future in a man with a shaven head and electrodes on his temples. The second episode introduces an Estonian woman who has also resigned and who is interrogated at length by an electronic voice asking over and over again "what was in your mind?" In short, Number 6 is converted into an experimental "subject" (the term is constantly repeated) where the experiments have a specific and, needless to say, nontherapeutic aim. One new electronic device can tap into his brain energy and transform it into pictures (an anticipation of the later television series *Cold Lazarus*); another induces hypnosis; in a third, electric shocks change his reflexes from right- to left-hand; lobotomies have already been mentioned; yet another device can transfer a mind to another body; and finally regression to infancy can be technologically induced.

The Village combines the functions of holiday resort, prison, and—most important in this context—clinic. It becomes the site for a sequence of experiments on Number 6, the nonconsenting subject who may well have been the victim of a prior secret experiment.[38] The sign in front of his house announces "private," but each episode challenges cherished beliefs about the self—the integration of mind and body, "privacy" of consciousness, and so on. Memory images projected onto a screen suggest a simplified model of memory like a tape recorder. In the sixth episode ("The General") a scientist has devised a method of speed learning where a "Sublimator" can do away with the need for sight: "It is imposed directly onto the cortex of the brain and is with occasional boosts virtually indelible."[39] This was one of the first episodes to be shot, and the assistant editor describes its theme as the direct implanting on the brain of extraordinary knowledge by a computer "using subliminal perception. As the superimposed intellect seeped in, individual will power was sapped out."[40] This updated version of subliminal learning operates, like the tachistoscope described in chapter 3, at fantastic speed. More important, these devices challenge the role of the body as mediator between mind and environment. The authorities in *The Prisoner* attempt to break down the human subject into malleable parts without destroying the value of that subject in the process. At another point, a dialogue occurs between a scientist who declares smugly, "Every man has his breaking point," to which Number 2 retorts that the aim is appropriation, not destruction: "He must be won over."[41] The first quotation repeats a catchphrase that emerged in the debate over the Korean POWs and that remains an open question throughout the series: will Number 6 break?[42] In episode 8 ("Dance of the Dead") the visual echoes of the Nazi concentration camps put in its context the attitude that human beings are dispensable raw material, but, again typical of the series, another Number 2 echoes the scientist's words so that it proves impossible to stabilize a contrast between administrative and experimental purposes.

At the beginning of the series, Number 2 promises (threatens) the Prisoner: "You will be cured." Structuring every episode, the discourse of therapy is, of course, a screen for a power play that challenges the Prisoner's presumptions of individuality and social stability. Each episode confronts him with a kind of environmental intelligence test: a theater with a hidden script, a game with concealed rules. His reactive role thus involves him in resisting the machinations of Number 2 by trying to identify the operative conditions of each test.

The most extreme experiment Number 6 undergoes occurs in episode 5 ("The Schizoid Man"), where another inmate, Number 12 (number 6's double, or the sum of 6 x 2), is trained to impersonate his double. Early in the episode we see Number 6 undergoing conditioning to change his reflexes, and when the two figures confront each other the only distinguishable sign is that one is wearing a white jacket, the other a black. Of course, this is an utterly unreliable means of identification, as is borne out when Number 6 changes jackets toward the end, hoping to escape by masquerading as his double. As usual, this is another experiment that gets out of control because no reliable test of identity emerges. Fingerprints prove nothing because, as the "white" Number 6 observes, "The trouble with science is that it can be perverted." Similarly a test of rapport with cards proves to be a betrayal. A new twist is added to Number 6's captivity by this episode, which demonstrates the ease of constructing an identity. Shortly after his arrival in the village, Number 6 declares one of his most ringing refusals: "I will not be pushed, filed, stamped, indexed, briefed, debriefed, or numbered. My life is my own."[43] A repeated opening shot of a huge store of files belies this refusal in the past. The question now is, can Number 6 resist the experiments that are essentially continuing this process of bureaucratization? Given the extent of the dossier on him, can Number 6 possibly avoid predictable reactions? Each experiment is at once a test and a game whose rules the Prisoner must identify. Wise to the covert procedures of the intelligence services, Number 6 avoids drinking drugged tea; during the experiment on brain projection he changes the contents of a syringe; and he closes the speed-learning experiment by burning out the computer when he poses the question "why?" Far from being a passive subject, the Prisoner ducks and weaves to avoid the machinations of Number 2. In the last episode he appears to have achieved freedom when he returns to his London home. Tony Williams takes this event at face value, then speculates on the ambiguity of the whole series: "*The Prisoner* may represent a disguised example of ideological entrapment, highly influenced by British cultural factors of class, white male hegemony, and the futility of revolt against a pervasive establishment."[44] Number 6 actually resembles Harry Palmer, the protagonist of *The Ipcress File*, in being trapped within a government structure but ridiculing the more conservative members of that hierarchy. The first holders of Number 2's position are accordingly parodic versions of the British gentry, complete with shooting-sticks and college scarves.

Reality in *The Prisoner* is presented as a masquerade, an impression heightened by the bright colors of the buildings and costumes and made explicit at one point in a carnival. At the end of the elaborate "escape" from Lithuania in episode 2, a discrepancy reveals the whole process to have been a simulation. Experiments even suggest that it is possible to access and shape dreams. The apparent malleability of the real is reinforced in every episode when we watch the controllers watching events on a screen. The metadimension in every representation demonstrates the authorities' desire to maximize visibility through surveillance and also foregrounds aspects of the television medium: notions of script, theater, acting skill, and so on. By repeatedly breaking reality frames, so that characters might occur both within and outside dreams, the series implicates the viewer in the processes of surveillance and compels Number 6 to function as observer and agent at one and the same time. Unnervingly, apart from specific experiments, his entire environment is being used as a means of interrogation.

Of the novel tie-ins with the series, Thomas M. Disch's *The Prisoner* (1969) is one of the most sophisticated narrative adaptations. Disch was commissioned in the autumn of 1968 as the series was ending its first run on U.S. television and was not able to influence the 1968 episodes or future episodes since the series was discontinued.[45] In his novel, Disch creates a paranoid edge to his narrative prologue—a description of Number 6 and his lover having a lavish dinner in London—by presenting dialogue as a covert sparring where each participant scores points. The contextualizing description is kept down to a minimum so that each detail appears to be surcharged with potential significance (two examples: the protagonist eats at table 6 and leaves Paddington through gate 6), feeding the reader's growing suspicion of conspiracy. The Prisoner's perception of the Village as the "conception, surely, of a single, and slightly monstrous, 'mind'" extends this paranoia into his entire immediate environment.[46]

The progression of Disch's novel depends far more than the series on inferences by the Prisoner. Like Kafka's K (Number 2's green-domed control building is the obvious equivalent of the Castle), Number 6 is compelled by his lack of information to speculate on events and particularly on the vulnerable state of his own subjectivity. From an early stage he considers that he might have been "tampered with"; indeed Number 2 confirms his brainwashing but denies responsibility for it. In one of the novel's most Gothic episodes, Number 6 gains access through a sliding panel in the Village church to an underground warren of laboratories. In one, a woman is being taken through an extended word-association sequence; in another Number 6 finds a film running that turns out to be "The Schizoid Man" from the series. Was it left running deliberately for him? Number 6 fragments at this point into three guises: agent, double, and spectator.

Disch then cues in a sequence of scenes where the Prisoner's identity is further destabilized. In one he is fed a fantasy of having a new face grafted on to his body (or is it his face on to a new body?). In another, his lover Liora arrives at the Village but doesn't recognize him. Now her name is Lorna, which combined with her first name, echoes that of Poe's dream woman Lenore. Their conversation now contains inconclusive attempts to verify their respective stories, which carry the somber implication voiced by Number 6: "If neither of us is lying, it's a plot against both our sanities."[47] What is described in the novel as an attempt to recover lost time involves verifying and completing memory sequences that are ultimately unverifiable because they might have been planted. Number 6 and the reader are thus caught in a spiral of representations that is thematized by a Village production of Shakespeare's dark drama of disguises, *Measure for Measure*. The culmination of this process comes when Number 6 is experimentally regressed in a sensory deprivation tank to a quasi-fetal state. Conducting the experiment, Number 14 keeps up a hypnotic monologue that explains the process while putting it into practice. What is kept as a tenuous element of selfhood in the series is here denied, and Number 14 spells out the double-bind in brainwashing:

> Though it would take at most 48 hours to transform you, or someone of your sort, into a perfectly loyal minion, such a transformation would virtually destroy those qualities that would make your loyalty worth having: initiative, creativity. . . . The usual techniques of brainwashing

affect these virtues the way ordinary laundering affects the more perishable kinds of clothing: at worst, they are demolished.[48]

Since the goal is transformation not destruction, as in Alfred Bester's *The Demolished Man*, the process is elaborate, gradual, and unfinished. Right to the end of the novel Disch maintains a consistent view of the real as recessive. Even when Number 6 gets a chance to meet Number 1, this might simply be the "penultimate imposture." Patrick McGoohan, who played the Prisoner and took a large part in the production, explained that there was a central tension in the core situation between the managerial power exercised through Number 2 and self-asserting individuality of Number 6 that could never be resolved. Indeed, there were vociferous protests when the series ended without any clear resolution.[49] Throughout the novel the twin concepts of freedom and selfhood are constantly destabilized. One kind of captivity shades into another. One memory might be too unclear to give the self continuity; another might be so clear that it might have been implanted. Within the confined spaces of the Village, Number 6 wavers between differing unverifiable hypotheses about his identity.

■ *The Prisoner*, series and novel, describes the difficulty of stabilizing the subject, which becomes evident partly from the alternation between Number 6's rapid movements around the Village and his temporary submission to a stereotaxic frame that grips his head. Number 6's identity is constantly threatened, fractured, and destabilized, but he never undergoes the extreme transformation described in two novels that explore not mind control but mind substitution. Ralph Blum's *The Simultaneous Man* (1970) deals with a secret experiment in an American laboratory to substitute the mind of a scientist for that of a prison volunteer. Robert Silverberg's *The Second Trip* (1972) describes the state's erasure of the mind of a murderer in twenty-first century New York.

In *The Simultaneous Man* a black veteran of the Korean and Vietnam wars, now convicted of murder, is referred to as 233/4 or quite simply the "Subject." He is participating in Project Beta, a fictional version of MK-ULTRA, which Blum contextualizes as growing out of American attempts at developing "techniques which, when employed in the interrogation of a hostile subject, would facilitate information retrieval."[50] Blum himself contributed to this project in 1954 when, like Ken Kesey, he took LSD in a Boston hospital.[51] This experience is written into the biography of the scientist in his novel. Under Beta, 233 will have his memory erased to be replaced by that of the project scientist, Dr. Andrew Horne. The process is described as a symbolic death of the old self after which 233 lies for months in a metal casket (the "coffin") receiving the input of his new memory. When he regains consciousness he will be 234. Although 233 speaks briefly before his operation and right at the end of the novel, the "Subject" for the most part stays just that, the subject of discussion and experimentation. Blum gives excerpts from the "Input" tapes, which are summaries of Horne's experience. In other words, the "Subject" functions like a template onto which Horne's identity is reproduced.

Blum complicates his narrative in two ways. First, the experiment is conducted through a dialogue between Horne and his opposite number, a member of the military, who expresses a crudely mechanistic model of the mind. He speaks in characteristically short, simplistic statements: "You have a war. You want what he knows. So you extract the contents of his mind."[52] The whole point of the narrative is to show that the process is not as easy as shelling peas. Horne's dream is, by contrast, more sophisticated but more elusive. He aims at locating the brain center, where information becomes knowledge. The second factor to emerge is that Horne had been interned in Korea and subjected to a long and probing interrogation by a Chinese officer named Chon. In defense, Horne creates a "counterfeit man," a despised version of himself that he can criticize in Chon's presence. We need to bear in mind one other piece of information about Horne. He has already created a "Remake," a precursor to 233, who has failed, collapsing into a vegetative state.

The Simultaneous Man replaces linear narrative with replications and duplications. The second experimental subject is 233, who will become a shadowy double of Horne himself, a grotesque actualization of the hated self-image he created in Korea, who later defects to the Soviet Union. The "memory" input fed to 233 has been filmed from a reconstruction of the Korean prison camp. If he is abstracted into the "Subject," Horne correspondingly becomes part of the process he is directing—the "Source." In fact, throughout the novel Horne casts himself, like Ishmael in *Moby-Dick* (the subject of explicit allusion in the novel), as a would-be reader of natural signs, trying to decipher the encoded language of the brain. His dream of becoming a scientific pioneer blends easily into the world of espionage through the congruence of discourse for both fields. Unlike Silverberg, Blum posits a limit to the reconstruction of personality in the parietal lobe that protects the "original imprint" beyond which the experimenters cannot go.

The intrigue of the last section of the novel revolves around whether 233 has given all his (that is, Horne's) knowledge to the Soviets. In order to verify this Horne pursues his double, now known as "Black Bear," to Leningrad, where he imagines an endless recession of consciousness between the two: "*Horne thinking about Horne thinking about Horne . . .* "[53] When they meet, Horne is shocked to see the other aging rapidly, apparently on the verge of death. Black Bear has not lost all his original memories, but has experienced a pigment reversal of his white skin. He uses the central metaphor running through the fiction of mind control when he declares to his prototype: "I'm washing out." The intransitive verb form leaves the agency unspecified. Very briefly Black Bear verbalizes his own impending death. In the final scene Horne collapses after consuming a drugged drink and the novel hints ironically that he might himself be used in an experiment by the Soviets. Harold Berger has drawn a comparison between *The Simultaneous Man* and David Karp's *One* (see chapter 3) as being novels where "characters hold back some part of themselves from the mind invaders," but this attributes a determination to both protagonists that is missing in both novels.[54] The institutional doubling that occurs in the Russian sections is a confirmation to Horne that the Soviets have been engaged in exactly the same kind of neurological research as the Americans. The director of the Leningrad institute proves to have been a Soviet monitor in Horne's Korean prison camp. By that point the spiraling of agent and subject, experimenter and experimentee has become total.

Robert Silverberg's *The Second Trip*, through allusions to Orwell, invites reading as a single-issue dystopia, the issue being the state practice of expunging the identity of a rapist and reconstructing a new identity within the "physical container" of the body. The novel opens after this has taken place. Paul Macy has left the Rehabilitation Center and is renegotiating the experience of walking the street like a patient after an operation. By coincidence he meets a girl named Lissa who was the model for his former self, the sculptor Nat Hamlin. Not only does she recognize him—his appearance stays unchanged—but her telepathic faculty triggers traces of Hamlin, who gradually comes to jostle Macy for occupation of his consciousness. As John Flodstrom has explained, "in this case of memory annihilation and the construction of a new personality . . . the re-emergent original personality associated with the body does not identify with the constructed personality within the body. This, then, is more similar to a case of multiple personality than to one of a recovering amnesiac."[55] The treatment Hamlin has undergone takes to an extreme that in *A Clockwork Orange* and resembles the state-enforced identity change in David Karp's *One*. Like the latter, the treatment does not work, and the central consciousness of the novel turns into the site of a struggle between two wills for supremacy. Silverberg's prototype here is *Dr. Jekyll and Mr. Hyde* (the comparison is drawn explicitly) as psychodrama between good and bad selves, superego and id. The most powerful dialogues in *The Second Trip*, therefore, are internal ones, where the sexual predator Hamlin attempts to "come back to life," an event that the state psychologists regard as impossible. Macy becomes the victim of a failure of treatment and the events of the novel question the summarized theory of unraveling, attacking, or flushing out the old identity: "The web of experiences and attitudes is wiped away, leaving the body a tabula rasa, a blank sheet, without identity, without soul, without memory. So, then: feed in a new identity, any identity you like." Like Thomas Pynchon's Pointsman, whose desire for his patients is to "write on them new words of himself," the state creates what in intelligence would be called a "legend," a new name, biography, job skills, and so on.[56]

The psychological struggle for occupation of a single body contradicts the neatness of the practice quoted earlier, and Silverberg's novel revives the tradition of the psychomachia, which is expressed most startlingly as two mental voices occupying the same space of consciousness or through figures of inner battle. Like Stevenson's novel, the narrative oscillates between the third and first persons; and moments when Hamlin's malign self assaults Macy or Lissa are presented as literal seizures or possessions. The ending of the novel comes with Macy's finally purging his bad self. *The Simultaneous Man* foregrounds the conduct of secret experiments by the intelligence community. Silverberg keeps his institutions well within the background and, although the treatment seems to have misfired, it is the constructed personality that is given narrative priority and that finally succeeds. Thus, where *The Simultaneous Man* disturbs political, psychological, and experimental polarities without resolution, *The Second Trip* narrates the triumph of the socialized self.

■ One figure has haunted Western discussions of brainwashing and mind control, that of Ivan Petrovich Pavlov. He became associated with clinical methods for the physiological explanation of behavior and, during the rehabilitation of his theories in Russia after World War II, with the theories underpinning the promotion of "new Soviet Man." As the pioneer of quantitative forms of analysis, Pavlov's name became virtually synonymous with behaviorism. The latter involved a view of the individual as being "composed of certain habit systems which come into operation in response to varying situations."[57] According to Tony Tanner, from whose classic study *City of Words* this quotation comes, such a view was anathema to American novelists writing in the mid-century because of its apparent determinism and because it seemed to exclude the possibility of language to create anti-environments that questioned the conventional.

It is very unusual for a novelist to refer to Pavlov, even more to quote from his works, but this is what happens in Thomas Pynchon's 1973 novel *Gravity's Rainbow*, which includes among its characters an American intelligence agent who is being scrutinized by a Pavlovian in order to understand an unusual physical characteristic he possesses. The novel is set initially in London during the last year of World War II, and it seems that there is a direct correlation emerging between v-2 rocket drops and the erections of Lieutenant Tyrone Slothrop, a U.S. intelligence officer. Although he is an investigator pursuing data about the v-2, he is himself under observation by a psychological warfare group headed by Dr. Edward Pointsman. Slothrop pursues the retreating Nazis into the Continent and is himself pursued as far as Zurich, which is fast establishing itself as the espionage capital of Western Europe, at which point Slothrop manages to give his pursuers the slip. His triumph is short-lived, however, because he discovers papers that prove that as a small child he was sold by his parents to the German company I. G. Farben as part of an experiment. This moment of discovery brings Slothrop's fear to a peak, as if a nightmare has been realized: "Once something was done to him, in a room, while he lay helpless . . . " He figures this as a "forbidden room, at the bottom edge of his memory. He can't see it, can't make it out. Doesn't want to. It is allied with the Worst Thing."[58] Thus, like John B. Watson's Infant Albert (the comparison is drawn within the novel), Slothrop became a guinea pig without knowing anything about it, in an experiment at inducing conditioned reflexes.

The peculiar predictability of Slothrop's sexual responses fascinates Pointsman and his colleagues, who come up with different explanations ranging from a "statistical oddity" to precognition and psychokinesis. In other words, Slothrop functions like an experimental oddity in the novel, an enigma. Yet again, and it is made all the more obvious by the novel's descriptions of competing intelligence agencies, we encounter a character who is perceived by others in informational terms. Slothrop's own discovery takes place within a whole series of crises of agency where a character's assumed autonomy proves to be elusive. Allusions to behaviorism are crucial to this effect, as Thomas Schaub has explained: "The novel is thick with behavioural terminology, and that theory of behaviour is part of the book's threatening determinism, in which history is a large Skinner box and 'freedom' is an illusion of our conditioning."[59] At one point a character admits to Slothrop that he fears a total loss of autonomy to an anonymous "Them" and expresses this fear through a technological image that derives from Delgado's experiments rather than the mid-1940s, the novel's present: "I've been given the old Radio-Control-Implanted-In-The-Head-At-Birth problem to mull over."[60] Control is embodied in one of the key media of the novel—radio—but also identified as an agonizing problem of proof where the individual loses any plausible means of self-authentication.

Pointsman, who may be a parody of the devoutly Pavlovian psychologist William Sargant (see chapter 2), treats Pavlov's *Conditioned Reflexes and Psychiatry* (1941) as his scripture. It is quoted and referred to as "The Book," owned collectively by Pointsman's group of seven, who gradually die off leaving him the sole survivor. Pointsman is drawn to a specific section of Pavlov's text where he discusses the physiological basis for paranoia. He explains the stimulus-and-response sequence of behavior as an excitation of different points on the cortex (hence Pointsman's name), which can go through a number of different stages. The strangest of these he designates the "ultraparadoxical phase," where a stimulus is elided and only works in its absence. This "weakening of the idea of the opposite" demonstrates a loss of contact with reality that for him leads to pathological symptoms.[61]

Pavlov's discussion is premised on sharp distinctions between opposites and on a linear notion of cause and effect, which Thomas Schaub shows to be challenged at every point in *Gravity's Rainbow*. For him, the novel "calls the absoluteness of that idea [cause and effect] into question, and moves both characters and readers into the uncertain ground between the distinctness of successive events and the timeless complementarities of meaning."[62] Pavlov applies traditional analytical practice to man considered as a system, and it is the method of "decomposition into parts" that the novel works against.[63] Pynchon destabilizes the notion of an experimental space containing Pointsman's quarry Slothrop, who moves from one set of circumstantial stimuli to another. The laboratory is itself figured as a maze under observation where Pointsman himself becomes the subject of another's experiment. Then Pavlovian methodology is debated by other characters who question its ethics and operative assumptions. Pointsman's opposite is the statistician Roger Mexico, whose concern for the larger "body" of London actually complements the former's obsession with the individual cortex.[64] And Pointsman himself is shown to be the very opposite of a detached experimenter. Rather he is haunted by a fear that his own reality system will collapse and that Slothrop will escape. Casting the latter as a monster, he insists to himself: "*We must never lose control. The thought of him lost in the world of men, after the war, fills me with a deep dread I cannot extinguish.*"[65] Pynchon is as alert as William Burroughs to the power play, and therefore the political dimension, in the notion of control. Pointsman fears that his experimental subject will elude him and internalizes this anxiety as a crisis to his own subjectivity. The very collapse of the distinction between inside and outside that he dreads is already happening within his thoughts. And so, unconsciously, he is already demonstrating the symptoms Pavlov associated with paranoia. Finally, Pynchon undermines the discreteness of the experimental subject by building up a complex and expanding textual field of analogies and connections.

Pynchon sets his action against a backdrop of competing intelligence agencies. Sol Yurick does the same in his 1982 novel *Richard A*, which also describes a guinea pig apparently betrayed by his parents. Yurick's choice of title may derive from the "A" treatment given to unwitting subjects under the CIA Artichoke program of hypnosis or alternate injections of sodium pentothal and Benzedrine.[66] This time the year is 1962; the competition between rival agencies within the United States. The title character is Richard Aquilino, a communications expert who has discovered ways of bugging the most secret telephone conversations. His antagonist is an agent named Keats, ostensibly working for the CIA-backed Coffin Foundation. Brainwashing is introduced into the novel as a hypothesis that Keats uses to terrify a colleague who has been held captive by the Soviets in the 1950s. When the latter objects "This isn't *Darkness At Noon*," Keats retorts: "Nor is it *The Manchurian Candidate*, but what if . . . they altered your mind and part of that altering was to forget what happened?"[67] The point here is not so much the specific likelihood of the charge so much as to familiarize the reader with the technical possibilities of interfering with the "brain's circuitry." Like Slothrop, Richard poses a threatening enigma to the authorities. Although Keats states "We need to know what he knows," in such a media-centered novel it is even more important to discover how he retains and transfers information. Keats's answer is the by now familiar one of posthypnotic suggestion released by some trigger phrase or image. He stresses the Soviets' longstanding skill in this area because they have "been doing experiments in mind control all the way back to Pavlov."[68]

In order to verify this hypothesis Richard is seized and put in a clinic that does "favors" for the intelligence service. Slothrop situates his nightmares in a room; Richard is literally subjected to total physical surveillance: "The room Richard was being kept in had been turned into a monitoring box, a kind of gigantic stress-analyzer and lie detector. Its walls were embedded with instruments that could receive—and broadcast—signals." These devices and the psychologist working on him are all being used to access Richard's suppressed memory of his childhood. As if uncovering a trauma, he begins to suspect that his father—by this point his parents have been revealed as Communist agents—was implanting information disguised as fairy stories: "*From what corners of his memory did such words come from?* Had they been encrypted in his father's ancestral memory-stories?"[69] Yurick plays with the reader's memories of *The Manchurian Candidate* to diverge from this narrative template at a number of points. Our expectations of parental exploitation are denied. As Keats explains to the bemused Kennedy, Richard is turned under the MK-ULTRA scheme into a CIA pawn to warn the President of false dangers so that he will be resolute in the Cuban missile crisis.[70] Richard approaches Kennedy not to assassinate him but to pass on planted information. At a number of points in the novel Richard registers crises of subjectivity similar to Slothrop's. He fantasizes a loss of self as he is dispersed around the telephone network, one of many interlocking systems for storing and transferring information in the novel. Later he experiences a different loss of autonomy: "Everyone was trying to turn him into an instrumentality, a telephone, a conduit, trying to push his buttons, using him, using him, controlling him."[71] Yurick skillfully evokes a baroque network of agencies that might be manipulating Richard, but conservatively produces a single clear explanation at the end of the novel whose frame describes Richard's plan of revenge against Keats, the revenge of a social underdog against a manipulative member of the power elite. Similarly, the 1997 film *Conspiracy Theory* describes the tale of a New York cab driver who has been trained as an assassin under the continuation of the MK-ULTRA program. With the help of a Justice Department attorney, he takes his revenge on the scientist directing that program.[72]

■ The depiction of guinea pigs tends toward melodrama, as we have seen, because these narratives include the most severe crises of subjectivity or autonomy. There is at the same time a grotesque black humor to novels like Disch's *Camp Concentration*, when the protagonist witnesses bizarre events that the institutional authorities have a vested interest in downplaying as symptoms or experimental data. In one of the most recent treatments of this theme, Robert Steven Rhine's "Fast Acting Xilotripimene," the black humor is created by the deadpan narrative tone that mimics the solemnity of the military and medical personnel designing and executing the experiments. John Milford, a convicted murderer, has saved himself from execution by volunteering for secret army trials of a drug that prolongs experience under a program called "L.H. [Laboratory Humans] studies." The story presents a sequence of episodes labeled "scenarios" where different aspects of the drug are tested. Milford is strapped naked on a surgical table in a blindingly white, featureless room somewhere in a military base. Milford himself has been thoroughly investigated to find his favorite dishes and sexual preferences—in short he has been converted into data. Each experiment then exploits this information through tests that seem grotesquely remote from battle conditions. For instance, he is given a taste of lobster Newburg, which lingers distractingly while the following operation is conducted: "The doctor, while humming, used the scalpel to quickly slice the skin off the bottom of Milford's left foot, as quick as a sheep shearer removes a pelt, leaving raw flesh underneath. You might think Milford screamed in agony, but the lobster had its claws on his psyche."[73] The narrative contradicts the projected reader response by showing the effects of the drug, which resemble an induced reflex, distracting the subject from the expected pain responses.

The experiments quite literally strip Milford bare. A group of clowns induce a laughing fit while his skin is removed. A girl named Candy, with implicit acknowledgement to Terry Southern, induces an orgasm that cannot stop, even while his penis is being skinned. The peak of the tests comes when lemon and salt are applied to his raw flesh "to determine subject sensitivity," the result being measured in screams. At the end of the story, as happens in earlier novels of experimentation, Milford has been given a new identity and also fitted with a new skin. The narrative cuts off with Milford wondering if he made the right choice between execution and experimentation. The very brevity of the story gives the narrative its power because Rhine denies the reader the space to wonder about its implications. The obsessive interest by the Pentagon in the drug is ridiculed as is the impassive "professional" manner of the doctor who carries out these sadistic experiments. But the irony bends round to include Milford himself who—because of the drug?—responds to his plight only on the physical level.

There are clear signs in the narratives discussed in this chapter of a growing self-consciousness about the theme of mind control, demonstrated in the allusions within the text to earlier works. Such self-consciousness does not dismiss the subject but instead distances the reader from the narratives in order to consider its implications for how the mind relates to the individual's immediate environment and for the relation between the individual and the state. The fiction that has pursued these issues further, particularly since the 1980s, produces in even more intricate narratives the interfacing between humans and computers.

ten

Cyberpunk and Other Revisions

As we have seen, the notion of brainwashing was constantly changing as it was applied to different political, medical, and social contexts. New technological possibilities, the waning of Cold War anxieties, and a perception that certain themes had become outmoded, all played their part in these changes. This chapter will consider different forms of revision: revision of the notion of exploitive enemy, of the relation between human and machine, and of the surge of interest in virtual reality, all factors that ultimately disperse the issue of brainwashing or mind control into the varied facets of what Sherry Turkle in *Life on the Screen* (1995) has described as a "culture of simulation."

The majority of narratives considered so far have portrayed the political dangers of mind control. From the 1970s onward, however, commerce has been increasingly shown to be a manipulative agency. In *The Terminal Man* a medical experiment with far-reaching implications for social control goes dramatically wrong. In *Drug of Choice* (1970), also by Michael Crichton but published under the pseudonym John Lange, a recreational drug is promoted that induces extreme suggestibility in the subject. The novel follows the pattern of an investigative thriller, as Roger Clark, a Los Angeles intern, tries to uncover the mystery of a drug that produces extended coma. As in *The Terminal Man*, a paranoid theme is introduced by a film star who is con-

vinced that an enormous corporation is controlling her life. Clark joins her
for a holiday on a paradisal Caribbean island, but when he awakes on the
second day he finds it a place of squalor. One of the resident doctors explains
the island as a "kind of extreme experiment." "We assume," he continues,
"that mental state colors our experience irrespective of objective reality. . . .
But suppose that the mental state could be controlled independent of experience?"[1] The drug is never named, except ironically as the "drug of choice,"
ironically because it is designed to remove a user's capacity to choose and to
transform him or her into a totally passive consumer. It is appropriate for the
drug not to be named because it acts like an invisible force, only perceptible
through the changes in consumers' behavior. The familiar paraphernalia of
brainwashing is now brought in to persuade Clark to work for a company
called Advance Inc. Sensory deprivation is followed by a series of electrical
shocks. Crichton manages local effects well, like the total disparity between
the supposed holiday-makers' self-perceptions and their actual circumstances, but his reliance on the thriller paradigm that leads up to a climax where
Clark plants a bomb in the Advance offices deflects the reader from the more
sinister implications of his narrative. Prior to the bombing, the company notes
are removed, and nothing has been concluded by destroying their premises.

Robin Cook's *Mindbend* (1985) displays similar problems with its ending.
Once again the pharmaceutical industry is presented as a malign and exploitive force within medicine. This narrative approaches the issues from opposite
ends of the medical service: on the one hand, Adam Schonberg, a medical
student, joins a pharmaceutical company and almost falls victim to their brainwashing methods; on the other hand, his pregnant wife almost loses her baby
after a spurious diagnosis that it is diseased. Prior to Adam's job change a number of unrelated narrative fragments tantalize the reader with their hidden connections. Thus an aborted fetus is shipped to the Caribbean, and a doctor attacks his wife in the grip of a manic seizure: "The pupils were large, and he
seemed to be looking right through her,"[2] The connecting link in all such
details is a mysterious private clinic in New York, and the recurring facial features are yet again the traditional signs of robotization: fixed stare, toneless voice,
and so on. Once Adam joins the Arolen company he hears more and more
about their conference cruises, where doctors are persuaded to abandon their
practices, promote Arolen products, and join the staff of the Julian Clinic.

On one of these cruises Adam discovers that the boat is functioning like
a floating clinic. Casually expecting brainwashing through the lectures, he

actually finds that the movie theater doubles as a laboratory: "the seats were very different from those in a regular movie house. Each one looked like a miniature electric chair with a myriad of electrodes and straps . . . the doctors were stark naked and were restrained by leather straps. They all wore helmets fitted with earphones and surface electrodes for stimulation. They all seemed to be heavily drugged. . . . More wires snaked around their bodies and were attached with needle electrodes to various nerve sites."[3] This is the climactic image of the novel where the doctor–patient relation has become reversed and where the inmates are being conditioned to recommend Aroler products. Cook conflates the 1950s notion of "hidden persuaders" with mind-control techniques that can get out of control, as happens in *The Terminal Man*. This is the emerging context of the aggressive doctor who kills his wife and himself, and of an inmate who Adam improbably manages to smuggle out of the company complex in Puerto Rico. The latter figure has only just begun the conditioning process and so has had electrodes implanted in his brain, but the indoctrination has not begun. When he escapes, the company "technician" attempts to make him self-destruct. A transmission induces a burst of mania similar to Benson's in *The Terminal Man*: "Alan grabbed his head. . . . His eyes snapped open and his lips rolled back to expose his teeth."[4] The result, to one of his victims, is the "materialization of a monster," who bites off an ear and beats a man to death with his bare hands. More important than being a monster, Alan becomes evidence in Adam's case against the company, and he introduces him to his father (conveniently a key member of the Food and Drug Administration). The novel concludes with a symbolic reunion between Adam, his estranged husband, and his wife, who has now given birth.

This closure evades the implications of the narrative, however. Cook's application of the imagery of brainwashing as a means of achieving loyalty to the company suggests that Arolen functions like a miniature state. The company possesses elaborate Orwellian dossiers on all doctors, and the analogy with *Nineteen Eighty-Four* extends to the key Arolen product, "conformin," which "changes the most disturbed individual into an exemplary citizen." The cruise boat thus produces the personnel for the dystopian Julian Clinic, which nevertheless has had notable successes from its use of fetal tissue implants. These impress Adam, "though he knew the ends could never justify the means."[5] The brainwashing converts the doctors into victims, not the patients, and company practices pursue morally dubious means but not toward malign ends. And above all, the overriding commercial interests of the company (that dictate their policy of secrecy and induced "conversion") are so integrated into the financial structure of the country that the exposure of one notorious case is insignificant since the commercial imperative remains unchanged.

Spider Robinson's *Mindkiller* (1982) explicitly continues the theme of Larry Niven's story "Death by Ecstasy" (see chapter 8) and the discovery by James Olds in the 1950s of the pleasure centers in the brain. Stimulation of the brain's pleasure centers with electronic brain implants has produced "wireheading," a recreational electronic pursuit of pleasure similar to "plugging into" virtual reality. The novel pursues two narrative strands: a demonstration of the human cost of wireheading to a girl who almost dies and the investigation of what happened to the protagonist's wife after she became involved in a mysterious Swiss-based company conducting neurological research. Like the two novels discussed earlier, *Mindkiller* draws on the thriller paradigm of search and exposure. Norman Kent finally confronts the arch-conspirator Jacques LeBlanc who resembles no one more closely than James Bond's opponents. Although he notionally represents a company, he personifies the drive for power (specifically to corner the world market in wireheading): "As long as he can snip sections out of memory-tape, and keep a monopoly of the secret, he's God."[6] Again as in the Bond narratives, Kent has to experience the new technology when he is strapped into the fiendish LeBlanc's "pleasure machine." The drama is awkwardly motivated here because the episode attempts to combine wireheading, interrogation, and the psychological death of Kent. However, Kent does not suffer psychological death, because his faculties are needed in the following scene when LeBlanc explains the history of his experiments. Throughout the novel mental processes are expressed through the same imagery of tape recording, a trope that was frequently used in 1950s science fiction, and LeBlanc claims to have mastered the technique of memory transfer from one individual to another. The erasure phase, "mindwipe," resembles the beginning of brainwashing; the second, "mindfill," involves the implanting of false memories. Unfortunately, this unfolds so late in the novel that its dramatic potential cannot be realized.

■ We saw in chapter 6 how William Burroughs conceived of a deep-level biological program that combined aspects of the genetic code and of a virus. Again and again in his sketches he imagined such a virus running out of control, especially if created through secret experiments under agencies like the CIA. This subject was picked up in the 1980s by Greg Bear whose novel

Blood Music (1985) describes the worldwide catastrophe that follows experimentation on DNA. Vergil Ulam, a brilliant but socially withdrawn researcher on biotechnology for the Genetron company, juggles work on biochips with a private project to produce blood cells that think—"noocytes."[7] In Bear's original short story of the same title the narrator is his friend Bernard, an important intermediary between the scientific technicalities and the reader. He hears of Vergil's success at creating huge molecules with ribosome "encoders" or "readers" supporting the basic RNA "tape." Bear's choice of metaphors here moves his subject well away from mechanistic versions of personality patterns found in science fiction narratives of the 1950s and 1960s by suggesting that the molecules shape themselves in response to shifting biological circumstances. Bernard the narrator realizes with horror that Vergil is not just a bio-designer, but also the carrier of these molecules that are reshaping his body; he even imagines himself as a "super-mother." Glimpsing the possibility of an epidemic, he electrocutes his friend as an act of mercy and in the hope of containing the experiment. But it is too late. Bernard and his wife have become infected. Apart from their physical suffering, Bernard experiences the loss of autonomy: "I was already receiving messages; it was becoming clear that any sensation of freedom we experienced was illusory." The story ends with this loss of self expressed as the struggle of the very minds that the human subjects are losing: "Our intelligence fluctuates daily as we are absorbed into the minds within."[8] The short story form creates a claustrophobic narrative that focuses on the fate of three specific characters, with implications for the rest of the world, which the novel develops in more depth.

Both short story and novel draw analogies between their narratives and *Frankenstein* as different versions of the experiment-gone-wrong. However, only the novel considers the spread of an epidemic. As North America becomes infected, Bernard is taken to an isolation laboratory in Germany where he engages in an internal dialogue with his own blood cells and at a crucial point appears to be liberated from the confines of his body ("I am cut loose"). In Pat Cadigan's *Synners* the dream of separation from the confines of the body leads to death. Here the transition is expressed as an informational rite of passage: Bernard becomes "encoded" and his consciousness is relocated within his blood stream. A total separation from external reality has taken place. Bear also introduces a new character who seems to be immune to the virus, a young New Yorker called Suzy. Through her the action in effect shifts genre into a replay of *Invasion of the Body Snatchers*. She engages in a number of dialogues with members of her family she thought were dead. In one of these exchanges Suzy is told by her mother of the new molecules: "They love us." Her reply displaces the reader from 1980s biotechnology to 1950s fear of mass anonymity: "You're brainwashed," she retorts. "I want to live." Her mother insists that the change has increased their vitality: "Honey, we're not brainwashed, we're convinced."⁹ Although Bear retains the vocabulary of biology, these sections of the novel turn into a debate between individual identity and a newly emerging group mind. What makes it difficult for Suzy to resist is the gradual removal by her mother and others of the virus's demonization. The cells originate in humans, so are not alien. They are like a virus in needing a host, but no longer destroying humans. Indeed, humans can achieve a kind of immortality through duplication. Her mother tells the horrified Suzy that the process is "like being Xeroxed": "if I die here, now, there's hundreds of others tuned in to me, ready to *become* me, and I don't die at all. I just lose this particular me."¹⁰ If the single self ceases to exist, either the new beings will look identical due to a form of cloning, or the body becomes a shell containing internally identical entities. The acceptance of change by Bear's transformed characters gives an evolutionary inevitability to the action. Although a radical change to humanity has taken place, this change is not presented as a catastrophe.

Patricia Anthony's *Brother Termite* (1993) also undertakes a revision of the notion of alien-ness by combining the genres of political thriller and extraterrestrial invasion, but, unlike *Blood Music*, scarcely refers to technology at all. At a point during the Eisenhower presidency, creatures from another planet land on Earth. They establish themselves so successfully in America that they even find positions in the White House. Anthony's title suggests that these creatures are embodiments of one of the standard sources of science fiction horror in the 1950s—the hive mind. However, their otherness is minimized by suppressing their appearance and stressing instead their communal consciousness. The Cousins, as they are called, speak with an idiomatic American register that makes them in effect a collective alternative to the divided realist characters who play political roles in the novel. Most striking of all, the focalizer is a Cousin called Reen-Ja, which means that the implicit norm in the narrative perspective is that of the supposed aliens. Reen-Ja even throws out allusions to Godzilla and *The War of the Worlds* in such a way that the conventional representation of the alien itself becomes defamiliarized. *Brother Termite* is rich in reference to the American presidency, especially to Kennedy's assassination, and the novel repeats ironically the conspiracy theory that Kennedy and his brother were killed by aliens.

Contemporary commentators like Lincoln Lawrence argued that the assassins were brainwashed automata, whereas Anthony turns the notion of mind control in a benign direction. The main narrative impetus to *Brother Termite* lies in Reen-Ja's investigation of a political conspiracy at the heart of the Washington establishment that causes the President's apparent suicide and the deaths of Cousins. During this investigation he confronts an FBI agent. Grasping his hand, Reen-Ja induces a helpless openness in the other: "Hopkins could see as a Cousin saw. He could look past the unremarkable face straight into Reen where the soul itself murmured identity."[11] Technology is totally absent in this exercise of control through touch. The next stage in the man's response is terror, but specifically terror at not being able to hide the fact that he has committed murder. He admits his guilt and then, on Reen's instructions, shoots himself. In other words, mind control is used here to counter conspiracy not foment it. The contact described in the quotation above has a spiritual dimension that transcends language, hence the emphasis on special vision. The ultimate revelation comes when Reen learns that the CIA has been pursuing secret experiments on animals and then Cousins to design a toxic virus. The episode resembles an interrogation under scopolamine with the difference that the subject is fully aware of his inability to do anything but tell the truth. Unlike *The Manchurian Candidate*, where Raymond Shaw's mother embodies conspiratorial connections, *Brother Termite* describes an institutional betrayal of the United States by the CIA.

■ The most radical revision to the notion of mind control occurs in those works that depict the brain as an "extremely complex biological machine."[12] The dream of controlling the mind has been imagined as a separation, often a liberation, of the brain from the confines of the body. *Donovan's Brain* dramatizes the seepage of an ego from an artificially preserved brain into the consciousness of its preserver, reversing the relation between the experimenter and his subject. The scientist here becomes subjected to the surviving will of the "dead" tycoon. In Raymond F. Jones's *The Cybernetic Brains* (1962) the brains of the dead have become reified by a controlling organization, the Cybernetics Institute, into sources of information transfer, neither extinct nor truly alive since Jones associates vitality strongly with individual autonomy. And William Hjortsberg's *Gray Matters* (1971) punningly explores the limbo state of thousands of brains stored indefinitely until they can be "decanted" into bodies. Center Control monitors these brains through electronic auditors that check that each consciousness is functioning within the system. The

novel depicts a brave new world of technological order—"hatcheries" produce the necessary fetuses—and any diversion from the technologically maintained norm is presented as social irresponsibility or worse. Hjortsberg pro-
nounces a parodic epitaph on the "illusions of identity" that include a
presumption of the inseparability of mind from body and a singularity distinct from the collective. Of one character we are told: "His every thought
and experience, even the unknown depths of his subconscious, is recorded
on micro-encephalograph tape. His dreams are preserved on old auditing
tapes." A rebellious consciousness is warned by Center Control: *"There is no
such thing as individual mind . . . there is only the One Mind . . . All of your
thoughts, both conscious and unconscious, will be erased and the tapes of the
other resident substituted."*[13]

The concept of transferring the self on to a tape has been discussed by Ed
Regis who traces its history back to the 1950s. In Arthur C. Clarke's *The City
and the Stars* (1956), for instance, humans are defined as a structure or pattern
that has been analyzed and stored as information. Regis quotes the cybernetic
theorist Bob Truax as asking "why not take a human mind, transfer it to a
computer, and let that person's memories come alive inside it?"[14] But how do
you transfer a mind? The speculations on how the mind can be converted
into a data bank with backups in case anything goes wrong is based on the
premise that "the human mind in all its aspects can be fully and accurately
described by the information processing model."[15] Partly this results in an exaggerated sense of the potential of computers; partly it stems from a desire to
escape from the body expressed in the writings of figures like Hans Moravec.[16]

If the mind is conceived in informational terms, then the phrase the "code
of the brain" takes on a particular resonance as lending itself to reproduction,
transmission, and manipulation. We saw examples of how this might work in
chapter 6, and Robert A. Smith's 1975 novel, *The Kramer Project*, explores
possible applications of cerebral frequencies within the Cold War context. A
preamble to this novel describes an experiment in California where a woman
is linked to a computer through an electrode helmet. Once she concentrates
on a particular thought, the computer scans the electric charge and transmits
it onto a TV monitor. The inference is put crudely but dramatically: "a computer can read the human mind. It can identify brainwaves associated with
specific thoughts and translate them into instructions."[17] This process of
thought control was being explored in the 1970s by the Advanced Projects
Research Agency in Washington, which was examining the possibility of designing a fighter plane guided directly from the pilot's brain.[18]

Such a direct linkage has been realized in Craig Thomas's techno-thriller *Firefox* (1977), where the Soviet Union has designed a brain-directed plane, which is stolen by an American pilot. Here the action plot is based on an anxiety by the Americans that the Soviets have leaped ahead of them in technological research. Exactly the same anxiety emerges in *The Kramer Project*, where the Soviet Union has designed a link-up between human and computer such that the subject's brainwaves are accelerated by the computer and transmitted into the Strategic Air Command computer in such a way that missile launches can be sabotaged or preempted. Meanwhile, back in the United States a neurologist is pursuing similar research, but on chimps. *The Kramer Project* is a nuclear brink narrative, timing each section within a sequence where the overriding question is whether the Americans will be able to catch up with the Soviets technologically in time to thwart their plans to trigger a U.S. missile launch that would justify their own nuclear attack. When an American is wired up to the SAC computer, it is striking that he can no longer distinguish between mind and machine. He states, "The computer hardware is simply an extension of my own neural structure. It's impossible to differentiate on that basis."[19] He continues that he has "turned over" a number of faculties to the computer including monitoring heartbeat. Both superpowers have used their respective guinea pigs as extensions of their defense computers and therefore of their foreign policy. But, as happens in David Feltham Jones's *Colossus* (1966), where supercomputers start communicating directly with each other, the two men circumvent their military controllers and start acting together to prevent a nuclear war. This they do, but at the cost of their lives. Each man dies in agony from the serum they had taken to speed up their brains. Each has been converted into an instrumentality and destroyed by the unexpected consequences of this transformation.

The possibility of recording the self results in a new significance being attached to the computer chip. At the opening of Michael Berlyn's *The Integrated Man* (1980) a man treads on a chip containing "what had once been the personality of Donald Sherman."[20] In this scene, old and new images of the self—body and tiny chip—contrast grotesquely in scale. Here an industrial cartel maintains its hold on its labor force through a system of brain implants. Miniature plastic sheets or chips can be inserted in the base of the skull, which resituate a personality in a new body. Through this device miners can be converted into guards for the company, thereby ensuring control by the managing elite. In George Alec Effinger's futuristic detective novels, a similar device circulates. "Plug-in personality modules," originally designed for subjects with neurological disturbance, have now become commercialized and circulate freely as attractive personae, sometimes even modeled on fictional characters. Thus the protagonist can take on the persona of Nero Wolfe, the serial hero of Rex Stout's detective novels. In Berlyn, the chip recording gives a concrete form to fears of industrial control. In Effinger, by contrast, the modules actualize the social behavior of their wearers, representing the latter as a kind of performance. Gregory Benford draws on the same technology in his Galactic Centre novels where his saving remnant of human voyagers carry with them "aspects" or "recorded personalities" from the past that are stored in chips. His narratives set up dialogues between human and nonhuman intelligences that debate, among other subjects, the nature of what is stored on these chips. An "aspect" might assert its own existence independently of human control, as if embodying an unruly memory that might come to the surface unpredictably. Even here, though, there is a problem of representation. In *Furious Gulf* (1994) a character explains that such chips are Personalities: "A Personality was a full embodiment of the neural beds. It carried features of the original person that went far beyond his or her skills and knowledge."[21] Although these objects are described as interactive information sources it is not made clear how they possess the generative potential of a mind rather than simply being a record of past instances.

The implant has replaced psychological programming as a demonized form of mind control. The protagonist of Lewis Shiner's *Frontera* (1984), Kane (probably named as carrying a secret stigma), discovers that his uncle has subjected him to "some kind of implant wetware" that is, a character explains, much more serious than brainwashing. In the wake of the collapses of the United States and the Soviet Union, Kane flies to Mars to revive a colony there. Only late in the novel does he come to realize that he has been programmed to destroy the domed settlement by firing a pistol. Like Pynchon's Tyrone Slothrop, he is a figure betrayed by his family, except that in this case his family is inseparable from the commercial combine employing him. Kane experiences a Grail-like revelation of internal patterned information forming a congruence with his external situation: "From somewhere behind his eyes a ghostly schematic of a circuit card formed and began to spin into his field of vision, slowly turning through all its axes and dropping away from him, towards its physical counterpart below."[22] Although this moment brings him a peak of pleasure it has its darker side because the internalized image of circuitry depresses Kane's heroic potential and implies that he has become a function within a technological complex. Indeed, the triggering of his program by a rhyme and his subsequent alienation from his own actions recall the older pattern of the Manchurian Candidate.

Shiner does not address the metaphysics of his novel's action, whereas Rudy Rucker's *Software* (1982) and *Wetware* (1988) contain a running debate over the relation of humans to machines. In the first of these, robot intelligences on the moon are killing humans for their "brain-tapes;" that is, they are extracting the defining information each individual carries within. Soul and individuality become aspects of this organic "software" that is required for the organ tanks on the moon. Opposition to this program is voiced through echoes of older science fiction: "Soul-snatchers! Puppet-masters!" exclaims one human character. The allusions to Heinlein's 1951 novel and to *Invasion of the Body Snatchers* (in *Wetware* split-open bodies are compared to seed pods) point to alien attempts to control human subjects, a notion that is difficult to sustain in this new narrative context, and all the more so in *Wetware*. Still set on the moon, the later novel describes a drug that softens the human body into surreal forms. Shapes and entities, robot intelligences and humans alike, blur together so radically that traditional distinctions cannot be maintained.

In science fiction from the 1980s onward, we increasingly see characters enmeshed in technological systems that are liable to manipulation, like the chips in *The Integrated Man*, and that leave no area of the self immune from violation. Scott Bukatman has identified in this fiction a "new uncertainty of bodily definition and subject knowledge" as the former is deconstructed. Among other works he cites *Blood Music* as attempting to describe a "passage beyond the body, beyond the flesh, in hyper-bodily terms," quoting the scene where Bernard responds to a "cell voice" and gradually shakes off all familiar sensations as he feels to be entering an indefinable inner space.[23]

The uncertainty Bukatman identifies informs Rebecca Ore's powerful eco-thriller *Gaia's Toys* (1995), which destabilizes both the mind and body of its protagonist. Ore counterpoints the actions of three characters whose lives intersect at different points. First there is Willie, a Tibetan war veteran (a transposed version of Vietnam) who has been infected with a virus while on service. Returned to America, he works at Roanoke Central, a huge industrial combine that he suspects of supplying war materials for the government. He can never prove this since the company carries out "retro-wipes," or memory erasures of what goes on inside the factory. Willie thus acts as a witness to the new form of the military-industrial complex operating in the United States. The third main character is Dorcas, an expert on gene modification whose parents are staving off old age by elaborate cosmetic surgery: "The Raes were rich enough to buy youth until their brains went."[24] Dorcas practices the technology of body modification, specializing in insects, but the novel clearly implies that this technology could be applied to humans.

The second main character in *Gaia's Toys* is in many ways the most complex. Allison (Allie), a middle-aged member of a terrorist group, is planting a bomb in a refinery when she is caught by the federal authorities. Virtually every item of information we are given about her is unreliable or ambiguous. She might have been abandoned by her parents, maybe even literally thrown from their car. She then performed under a masturbation machine in a sex club, another example of interfacing with technology. Then she has operated within the terrorist group under an alias. Since Allie narrates her own sections the reader's certainty is further limited to her own perceptions and experiences. Once captured, she learns first that her bomb is a nuclear device and also that she has an electronic implant in her spine. So not only has she been deceived by her own group, she is also "bugged," a concept that takes on a range of meanings as the novel progresses. In the society of *Gaia's Toys* welfare cases spend time on the Web through direct brain interfacing, a practice that induces fugue and so can never build up their memories, another traditional source of identity. Allie is subjected to a similar technological device but for purposes of examination. An electronic cone is fitted over her head that can scan her brain and project her memories onto a monitor and, once the authorities are sure that she is not lying, Allie is offered a new appearance. A "cover" in the traditional sense for crime fiction is here given a literal biotechnological meaning as Allie's body is made over. Her head too is "wired," either to monitor her perceptions like a microphone or to monitor her own thoughts. Again and again Allie suspects that her feelings and reactions have been programmed into her. At one point she reflects "I'd never have control of my life again," but this is a false fear since she has no authentic point of autonomy to measure her experiences against.[25] Allie—even her designation is rather unsure—finds that her experiences after arrest destabilize her past, bringing into question her memories and the figures contained in them. For instance, after her own transformation she is taken to meet Jurgen, a former member of her group who has turned himself over to the federal police and become transformed to such an extent that only a certain rhythm in his movements enables Allie to recognize him. At the end of the novel Allie has rejoined her eco group and is preparing for yet another transformation: "After today," she reflects, "I won't be Allison anymore."[26] There is no closure to the novel, merely a prelude to fresh transformations. This theme is given a grotesque coda when Dorcas's parents feed her a gene degrader that kills her at the point where she is producing a clone of herself.

One factor in *Gaia's Toys* that fragments Allie's character is the way in which the novel elaborates a traditional concern of the thriller genre, namely the search for information. Ore depicts a society where the technological means of monitoring, scanning, and modifying the mind have become so sophisticated that there remains scarcely any method of verifying identity. Measuring brain waves apparently gives a relatively reliable "signature" for the self. Allie is apprehended (pun intended) as a series of overlapping guises—terrorist, orphan, fugitive, "drode head" (a police-inspired masquerade), and so on. Just as in the thriller or detective novel, the search for information is constantly foregrounded, in this novel the police repeatedly attempt to authenticate Allie's subject positions. Has she really had a change of heart from terrorism? The answer is not clear-cut. In a traditional first-person narrative a gap might be revealed between public and private selves. Here, however, Allie has no means of authenticating her own thoughts. Like Willie, she can only think in hypotheses, unverified possibilities. Her consciousness thus becomes an inner mirror of the problem faced by the police. They wonder whether she is tricking them; she repeatedly figures her self as a puppet manipulated by them. As a further twist to the novel's mirroring, Allie is used by the eco-terrorists as well as the police to get access to Dorcas. The quick-fire dialogues between Allie and the police keep returning not only to information but to Allie's self-images. They make up an intermittent interrogation of her identity and at the same time have an external purpose in trying to locate Dorcas who has been manufacturing psychotronic mantises. These "bugs" add an ecological dimension to the meanings of the term, which range from virus (electronic or organic) to miniature monitoring device. The punning on different senses to "bug" dates back to *Nineteen Eighty-Four*, but here the references range from species issues through the body's vulnerability as organism to the surveillance of the self.

Gaia's Toys impressively weaves uncertainty about identity into its central narrative that concerns the search for information to an important extent. It no longer makes sense to talk of character here since names and other defining aspects prove to be too unstable. Instead of a single stable self, we have series of personae behind which it is no longer possible to locate a core identity. In that sense the novel exemplifies Fredric Jameson's postmodernist aesthetic of depthlessness.

■ The fiction of Pat Cadigan does not quite erase the notion of a core self, but engages in a dialogue with earlier images of mind control while exploring different aspects of virtual reality. Her first novel, *Mindplayers* (1987), uses the central metaphor embedded within brainwashing to articulate different forms of mind modification that become evident when the narrator-protagonist falls foul of the law at the beginning of the novel. In this society personality itself has become commodified into behavior styles that can be put on and dropped rather like clothes. There is even a consumerist pride in "wearing" the "mental equivalent of a mask" with the sign of its designer. These versions of the self are sold under license, and *Mindplayers* opens with Alexander Haas ("Deadpan Allie") unwisely accepting a stolen "madcap" from a friend. This device is a sophisticated helmet for inducing psychosis, which is here not a threat to the self so much as a temporary style it can inhabit. Allie's particular psychosis involves a paranoid conviction that thoughts are being beamed into her mind. Cadigan ironically deflects this conviction, shared by a number of Philip K. Dick's protagonists, into a form of electronic surveillance by the authorities, who trace the stolen helmet and arrest Allie. A number of important themes have been established in this opening chapter: the disparity between a core self and electronically simulated social selves, the monitoring of consciousness, and the practice of the Brain Police. Allie describes the latter's procedure as follows: "You lose consciousness when you're dry-cleaned; afterward, you dream or you drift. When the fog cleared, I was lying naked on a slab in a boxy gray room while the Brain Police photographed everything inside and out. I could see the mug-holo taking shape in the tank on the ceiling. . . . [M]aybe I was still at the dry-cleaner's waiting for treatment and this was a psychotic dream."[27] Cadigan is exceptionally skilful at building up the plausibility of her images by juxtaposing them with specifics familiar to the reader. So Allie is having a mug shot taken but the "holo" affix suggests a total copying of the self, mind and body. Indeed, as the novel progresses, the distinction between inside and outside collapses. Allie demonstrates awareness of procedures but is so enmeshed within them that, here as throughout the novel, she is struggling to understand the nature of her experiences. One obvious sign of difficulty in this scene is her uncertainty: is she under arrest or just dreaming? If the procedure she describes in the first sentence just quoted is true, then her capacity to verify her experience is seriously compromised.

The Orwellian label Brain Police is brought into a non-Orwellian context of theft not political dissidence. As Cadigan has explained in interview, "if you have commerce in mental states then you have crime and if you have crime you have law enforcement to deal with it. . . . [W]ouldn't it be interesting if the brain police weren't thought police but people who were actually trying to protect your brain."[28] In other words, the immediate rationale for the police is commercial rather than political. When members of the police appear in the novel, they do not wear threatening uniforms, which reflects their quasi-therapeutic role. Nevertheless, the verbal traces of hard-boiled detective fiction in Cadigan's vocabulary cannot completely smother the echo of thought-crime and the capacity the Thought Police possess in *Nineteen Eighty-Four* to monitor the subject's inner thoughts. This is where the tropes of washing the self take on a sinister force that is debated vigorously by Allie with her lawyer. There is a stage worse than "dry-cleaning," and that is the "full wash" that has been banned "to prevent the government from correcting people into obedient robots. Mindplay was never intended to be mind control." To this Allie retorts: "Choosing between having every detail of your mind exposed or being *corrected* isn't much of a choice. The Mental Strip Search is just one step removed from brainwashing."[29] In the original understanding of brainwashing, heterodoxy was represented as a pollution of the self that had to be cleaned by reeducation, but, as techniques of mind alteration developed a sophistication that did not need the subject's consent, the metaphor veered toward an erasure of the self. In Cadigan's novel such alteration is referred to in terms that seem incongruously physical. But a key set of apparently hybrid terms, starting with the novel's title, force together mind and body or mind and physical environment. "Mindplaying" is a kind of psychotherapy; "mindsuck" a form of murder where the mind is extracted from the body, leaving it an empty shell; and "mindrape" a similar act of violation that recalls Joost Merloo's study of brainwashing discussed in chapter 2.

Reality in *Mindplayers* is not a given physical environment so much as an opening presumption in Allie that becomes less and less stable as the narrative progresses. Her treatment after wearing the madcap resembles a kind of punishment and therapy, a combination we have considered in earlier chapters. The Brain Police assemble a profile of her personality by examining the traces of her actions in her brain chemistry (an organic form of monitoring the "hits" of her personal computer). After "dry-cleaning" she has to have her "reality affixed," a re-adjustment that is helped by periods "under the belljar" if she goes into shock. The last treatment that induces amnesia impresses Allie as a kind of death: "it . . . felt too much like being buried alive."[30] Once again the echo of an earlier writer, here Sylvia Plath, is strategic in raising questions about the nature of Allie's experience. Every act performed on her mind carries with it a lingering fear that it has been altered without her consent, and her inability to resolve this suspicion gives *Mindplayers* a paranoid subtext.

In the course of the novel Allie experiences an ideological repositioning from criminal subject to licensed investigator. She undergoes mindplayer training at a corporation and gains her credentials as a "pathosfinder," a kind of psychotherapist. From the object of investigation she becomes an investigator in her own right. At the beginning her mind is analyzed; later she enters the consciousnesses of her subjects and becomes something of an expert in personality scrutiny. During her training at J. Walter Tech, Allie has to spend periods hooked up to the "pool," a collective "consensual reality" that she is relieved to exit from. The location and technology of this process gives us yet another echo of an earlier narrative of mind alteration. The devices for entering the pool are "pods" that are housed in the basement of the company building. In *Invasion of the Body Snatchers*, of course, the pods carry the possibility of a transformation into a new form of life and, in a case like Becky Driscoll's, are hidden in the basement. Cadigan has confirmed that the most powerful images of brainwashing were lodged in her memory during the Cold War, particularly by *The Manchurian Candidate*, which raised the "possibility that people could be brainwashed so thoroughly and extremely that they would believe they were sitting through a ladies' garden club meeting, and find nothing odd about one man being ordered to kill another one."[31] In her later novel, *Dervish Is Digital*, a series of "bodysnatching" cases leads the protagonist to reflect that the situation sounds like "one of those mass hysteria things," unconsciously echoing the claim made early in *Invasion of the Body Snatchers* that the community is falling victim to a contagious delusion.[32] Note here the nonrecognition of incongruity that she remembered from the famous prison camp sequence, where the slow circular tracking of the camera implies a continuity and homogeneity of scene totally contradicted by the transformations of the characters. In *Mindplayers* Cadigan gives relatively little description of setting, concentrating instead on dialogue and virtual reality. This method foregrounds perceptions of the real and in effect pluralizes reality into sequences of personal symbolism that recall dream, with the difference that all boundaries are permeable: across consciousnesses, between dreaming and waking, and so on. At the end of the novel we find Allie in a crisis of subjectivity; she fears her self might break apart: "Choose: A whole self, or just an accumulation of elements that soon wouldn't be more than the sum of their parts. Madness. Fragmentation."[33]

Such fragmentation approaches the notion of decentering explained by Sherry Turkle: "Today's computational models of the mind often embrace a postmodern aesthetic of complexity and decentering. Mainstream computer researchers no longer aspire to program intelligence into computers but expect intelligence to emerge from the interaction of small subprograms."[34] Her study of the cultural impact of the Internet, *Life on the Screen* (1995), for the most part discusses forms of self-empowering, where roles and aspects of the self can be acted out electronically. However, she does pause to question the utopian liberation from ownership and social control that is sometimes claimed for the Web. Extrapolating from Jeremy Bentham's notorious "ideal" prison, the Panopticon, where inmates can be watched constantly, she writes: "in our day, increasingly centralized data bases provide a material basis for a vastly extended Panopticon that could include the Internet. Even now there is talk of network censorship, in part through (artificially) intelligent agents capable of surveillance."[35] Such agents are described in Neal Stephenson's *Snow Crash* (1992) as "gargoyles," humans with different electronic devices attached to themselves who monitor the VR "Metaverse," collecting information for the Central Intelligence Corporation. Technological processes are shown to be reversible, however. At one point in *Snow Crash* human figures are seen with antennas attached to their heads, glassy-eyed "like they've been brainwashed," who appear to be the recipients of electronic transmission not simply gatherers of information. Such surveillance is of concern to Cadigan both within her fiction and in American society. In 1996 she attended a Computers Freedom and Privacy meeting at MIT, where she indignantly rejected a plan being promoted by the White House that universal electronic monitoring was essential to protect citizens from terrorism.

Sherry Turkle identifies local continuities of behavior that bear on science fiction in the following way. Among other topics, she demonstrates how computer games can offer temporary performative selves that the subject can adopt, and similarly in Pat Cadigan's fiction selfhood becomes segmented into different personas that emerge and disappear in her narratives. Discussing cyberpunk culture, Mark Dery sees a mechanization of the body taking place through its "redefinition as a commodity," and his point could stand all the more powerfully as a comment on Cadigan's fiction in its commodification, not only of the body, but of aspects of the mind we tend to assume as "belonging" to a core self.[36] In *Mindplayers* memories can be traded. In this novel and in *Synners* (1991), Cadigan's portrayal of a futuristic entertainments industry in Los Angeles, desired social personas can be acquired electronically. But at the same time, Cadigan shows characters contesting the new technology. In *Synners*, for example, one character warns the promoters of brain implants for entertainment that they have a major presentational problem on their hands since the technology "looks like a faster, easier way of mind control and brainwashing, all that shit."[37]

Cadigan revives the notion that was emerging during the 1950s in the United States that commerce and the media were engaged in processes of brainwashing every bit as dangerous as the demonized practices of the Communists. In *Synners* or *Tea from an Empty Cup* (1998) she shows the addictive nature of VR technology that can actually bring about death. In this respect, Cadigan demonstrates a more critical version of a perceived continuity between the drug culture of the 1960s and computing that was shared by Timothy Leary in his later years. Robert Anton Wilson has also re-expressed the social dimension to brainwashing in works like *Prometheus Rising* (1983), where he draws on John Lilly's research into sensory deprivation to show how initiation into institutions like the army follows a pattern of breaking old bonds as a prelude to installing new ones.[38] Wilson's conception of the human "biocomputer" gives us one of many links between his writings and cyberpunk fiction, and he has several times expressed interest in different brain machines, which use magnetic pulses and other techniques.

Cadigan's most demanding novel to date, *Fools* (1992), combines her interest in VR, her portrayal of behavior as drama, and research she did into Multiple Personality Disorder. She has described this novel as showing the idea of different social selves taken to an extreme.[39] *Fools* institutionalizes such concerns by attempting to answer the question: "What would happen if you were someone deep undercover and didn't know it?"[40] This deeply paranoid possibility recalls many such moments in Philip K. Dick's novels—in *Liars, Inc.* for instance—where the protagonist suspects that thoughts have somehow been planted in his consciousness. *Fools* continues the society of *Mindplayers* but fractures the narrating voice into a number of different personas, shifts from one to the other being signaled by changes in the novel's typeface. Whereas in the first novel the Brain Police was an institution distinct from the narrating self, now the Brain Police has become internalized into one guise of the self. Three main personas are named: Marya the undercover police agent, Marva an actress, and Marceline an Escort or specialist in memory adjustment. The common initial warns the reader against distinguishing sharply between these personas, whose names are suppressed in a narrative where each persona tries to understand her respective situation. *Fools* is an intensely claustrophobic novel because description is virtually nonexistent and the reader as a result is situated within sequences of consciousness. The primacy (and vulnerability) of subjective perception is articulated through the figure of the distorting funhouse mirror. Everything seems to be a reflection, representation, or simulacrum of something else. Uncertainty has become a condition of being. Each speaker constantly asks herself: *whose* memory do I have? *whose* reflection? even "whose body am I wearing?"[41] If one persona is an unconscious deep-level agent for the Brain Police, she resembles the "sleepers" of Cold War thrillers like *Telefon* who wait for external triggers, and here we can locate the paranoid dimension to Cadigan's narration. Since every traditional determinant of the self (body, memory, and so forth) is liable to manipulation or alteration, the fear recurs throughout *Fools* that "we've *all* been tampered with." No original pristine self is accessible, so anonymous external sources of agency are imagined, as fantasy ("aliens, I thought, bombarding my head with thought-control rays") or as a condition of the discourse: "They'd given her my personality in an overlay and given her my appearance as well."[42] One of the most drastic of these operations on the self is to be "bodysnatched" where the whole body is substituted.

Fools denies its characters any phase prior to such interference or alteration by "them," a catch-all pronoun indicating manipulative agencies. The reporter-narrator of John Varley's *Steel Beach* learns that it has become the norm for brains to be "augmented." The invention and insertion of false memory is very similar to the creation of a persona in Cadigan's fiction, with the difference that Varley shows how close this process is to the invention of a fictional character by an author. Story, background, and physical gesture all have to be composed in harmony with each other. The narrator then reflects how he has become a recipient at the hands of a figure who combines the functions of author, neurologist, and computer expert: "He had written the entire story, dumped it into the cyber-augmented parts of my brain where, at the speed of light, it was transferred to the files of my organic brain, shuffled cunningly in with the rest of my memories, the legitimate ones."[43] The oscillation in this vocabulary between organic and inorganic reflects the interpenetration of the one by the other. Characters in such contexts have become hybrid entities, cyborgs in effect.

Bodysnatching recurs in *Dervish Is Digital* (2000) where yet another shift has occurred in the positioning of the protagonist. Now she is a fully fledged police officer dealing with Techno Crime. This novel draws on Chandler to set up a *noir* crime investigation where the protagonist keeps losing her bearings from spells in VR and drug doses. There is a far clearer narrative flow than in *Fools*, but we are presented with yet another totally monitored environment. The rapid electronic circulation of information means that surveillance is easy, a state of affairs Cadigan sums up in a cityscape image: "It was a profile that, outwardly, had changed very little in the last seventy years. The changes took place on the inside now, the space rearranged, refitted, revised, having little if any effect on the exteriors. As if . . . there was some hostile, omniscient observer that humans were trying to fool into believing that absolutely nothing was happening, nothing at all, nothing going on here but the status quo, boss. Maybe this was the standard learned behavior of a society that had put itself under permanent surveillance."[44] The eye of the all-seeing God is secularized, as in Philip K. Dick's *Eye in the Sky* (1957), into a malevolent Big Brother scrutinizing the city. Ironically, despite the reference to an external observer, this is a self-imposed system of surveillance, but then, as Michel Foucault has shown, such internalization of surveillance is the true sign of a power process at work. Cadigan has remained fascinated by the practices of cults and accusations of sexual abuse because they tend toward the "ultimate in brainwashing": the capacity of subjects to convince themselves of it.[45] Exactly this subject arises in *Dervish Is Digital* when the protagonist Konstantin finds herself stopped in a Hong Kong casino because her behavior does not match the norm for playing the tables. She has already expressed her incredulity over people living voluntarily in a dictatorship that brainwashes its citizens. In the casino a cyborg monitor explains to her that she can be "regularized" through a "complete program of conditioning and behavior phasing." But that's brainwashing, objects Konstantin, whereupon the cyborg rejoins: "brainwashing is too inexact a term, leading to misunderstanding and misrepresentation."[46] Too inexact because it carries Cold War traces of a stark opposition between regime and individual will that has blurred in this society.

■ The possibility raised in Kennaway's *The Mind Benders* was that the self might lose its consciousness of the difference between body and surroundings, although, as we saw in the previous chapter, his narrative keeps the potential for horror in the subject firmly buttoned up within social realism. The most dramatic moments in this narrative were those where the experimental subject felt himself to be dissolving as the temperature between body and physical context evened up. One of the most original and innovative novels to address the possibility of the brain's continued life apart from the body by exploring how it makes contact with its environment is Joseph McElroy's *Plus* (1976). McElroy has recorded his admiration for William Hjortsberg's *Gray Matters*, which he praises because it "brilliantly contrives not comic deflation that may come from real experience but instead, sensational humor released by an unwillingness to give further attention to a complicated subject."[47] McElroy develops at least two themes explored in Hjortsberg's novel: the power relation between Center Control and the "residents," as the stored brains are called, demonstrated by the rebellion of one brain; and the ways in which a disembodied brain makes contact with its surroundings. *Plus* describes the brain of an engineer, who had died in a nuclear war, which is used in an experiment by being housed in a capsule orbiting the Earth and controlled from Christmas Island in the Pacific. In *Gray Matters* the character Philip Quarrels was an astronaut and, as such, a participant in a new system of "cerebromorphs" ("brain-shapes") using neurotransmitters that could make long space voyages. McElroy makes this into his central subject, specifically exploring how the brain forms contact and even maps its physical surroundings.

In McElroy's novel, this process is enacted partly through a dialogue between Imp Plus (an anagram of "Impulse," an entity to which something will be added), the central consciousness of the novel, and Cap Com, otherwise known as Ground. Here is where the power theme of the novel focuses. One critic has argued that the desire of Imp Plus to return to past memories constitutes his "resistance to the process of subjugation."[48] If we conceive of Imp Plus as a guinea pig within the American space program, we would assume that it was rendered passive by the technology of brain housing, nourishment, and electronic monitoring. The space capsule in that respect could be imagined as an experimental space containing the consciousness of Imp Plus, a kind of laboratory in space. As the novel progresses, however, we develop a split sense of the brain as passive organism and as generative force. For David Porush the latter signs reflect a "human brain rejecting the tyranny of the mechanical role assigned it."[49] The operative contrast, however, is not between mechanism and organism but between expected and actual replies to Cap Com's messages, between directed and "bodied" responder. In the early sections of the novel the narrative foregrounds the pathos of what Imp Plus has lost: fragmentary memories of limbs and organs, of words, and of romantic encounters with a girl in California. Through an extraordinarily disciplined narrative discourse McElroy describes the active self-consciousness of this brain that attempts to map itself within the space capsule. Drawing on the intricacies and terminology of neurobiology, McElroy exploits the function of the limbic system as processor of light and other impulses, briefly establishing metaphorical relationships between Ground as parent, Imp Plus as child, and the space capsule as a body containing the central consciousness.[50]

As Imp Plus develops, it grows a kind of body that gives concrete form to its location. From being measured through devices like a "dilatometer," Imp Plus engages in self-mapping where the linguistic traces of its bodily existence gradually shift round from memory to present physical exploration. The novel's discourse thus oscillates between compulsion and deliberate choice. On the one hand "he had no choice but to go on and understand what was going on," a typically Beckett-like formulation that puns on progression and happening; on the other hand we are told: "He was free, if not of Ground's transmissions. . . . He saw more than he used."[51] Two key processes are taking place here. First, although messages from earth cannot be blocked, Imp Plus can withhold replies, which "he" does; and we should note here the insistent humanizing effect of McElroy's language in this novel that constantly evokes an adult male. Second, Imp Plus is attributed with a dynamic perception. Verbs of seeing, feeling, moving, and so on reflect an active effort by Imp Plus to discover his physicality, location, and relation to Earth. Late in the novel, his reaction to one of Cap Com's messages runs as follows: "Oh here was a test, a test like asking to identify what was located next to the gauge registering nitrogen reaction in the beds." By this point the language has closely approached the silent speech of thought. We are positioned so that we can distinguish between reaction (automatic physical change), response (a sophisticated classification of the message), and the reply that follows, namely, "NEGATIVE, NEGATIVE, NEGATIVE, Imp Plus heard himself say."[52] As Imp Plus develops a silent "voice," the issue of power is dramatized more and more through a series of wordplays, on electricity, for example, as if Imp Plus is dependent on an external source for his existence; or on the term "bonds" that initially signifies entrapment and then the physical state of his being. Cap Com treats Imp Plus "like some alien monitor" but his responses to the sensory environment resemble the growth in consciousness of a child and thereby naturalize Imp Plus as a human being. His shifts in self-perception come to bear on the figure of the lattice. At first suggesting captivity, the lattice then, like the metaphor of the neural net, expresses texture and thus physical being. The ironic conclusion to the novel comes when Imp Plus achieves independence from Cap Com, but at the expense of his very existence as the capsule burns up on reentry into the Earth's atmosphere.

■ The fiction discussed in this chapter builds its narratives on an interpenetration of mind and technology that disperses the issue of mind control into other aspects of this interfacing. Boundaries between the organic and the technological increasingly blur, as do those between objective reality and virtual reality in the works of Pat Cadigan, Neal Stephenson, and others. In the latter's *Snow Crash* (1992) the reader follows characters' moves to and fro between conventional reality and the "Metaverse," which is explained as a "fictional structure made out of code."⁵³ John Varley's 1984 story "PRESS ENTER" dramatizes such a blurring of boundaries by describing the invasion of domestic and emotional space by computer technology. Victor Apfel is an ex–Korean War POW whose skull was fractured and who was brainwashed. One day he receives repeated computer-generated telephone messages to go to his neighbor's apartment, where he discovers that apparently this neighbor has committed suicide. Then he meets Lisa, a young Vietnamese woman and expert hacker, who has also been invited to the same apartment. The first mystery then is the identity of Kluge the neighbor. He exists on no database, has been living under an alias, has perpetrated major computer frauds, and was investigating possible neurological links with computers. It is Lisa who uncovers this information but, as her search progresses, she also uncovers Apfel's suppressed traumas. Their sexual relationship thus reflects a telescoping of spaces and themes in the story. They spend some time in Kluge's apartment, some in Apfel's. For N. Katherine Hayles, Lisa "goes too far when she usurps the masculine role of penetration . . . into the masculine realm of computer sentience."⁵⁴ The malfunction of Kluge's computer screen triggers seizures in Apfel, which he barely survives, and once he has recovered Lisa takes her own life (using a microwave oven). Technology penetrates every area of feeling in this story, which ends on a note of paranoid trauma with Apfel isolated in a house from which all wiring has been stripped. He has found some respite from the network of telephones and electrical wiring, but at the expense of all social contact. At the beginning of the postwar period mind control was imagined as an invasion of mental space by an alien force. By the 1980s and 1990s, however, it has become impossible to separate the human from the technological. This intermeshing is reflected in the ambivalent perceptions of technology, which proves to be desired but destructive.

Appendix

Fiction Cited in the December 1960 Report of the
Society for the Investigation of Human Ecology

■ The Society for the Investigation of Human Ecology was incorporated in 1955 with Harold Wolff as President. It was a CIA-backed organization that channeled funds into psychological research projects with intelligence potential. In 1961 it was renamed the Human Ecology Fund. The 1960 report contains extensive lists of scientific reports and journalistic accounts, and acknowledges significant input from, among others, Albert D. Biderman, Raymond A. Bauer, Lawrence E. Hinkle Jr., Edward Hunter, Robert J. Lifton, and Joost A. M. Meerloo. The comments on different works appear in the report. In this listing authors' first names have been given and additional explanation is in parentheses.

1. Philip Crosbie, *Three Winters Cold.* Dublin: Browne and Nolan, 1955 (memoir of Korean War).
2. Czeslaw Milosz, *The Captive Mind.* New York: Vintage Books, 1955. A novel depicting the psychological adjustment of various kinds of intellectuals to the Communist system.
3. David Karp, *One.* New York: Vanguard Press, 1953. A novel based on brainwashing in a totalitarian state.
4. Arthur Koestler, *Arrival and Departure.* New York: Macmillan, 1943 (accounting of a displaced person in Neutralia).

5. Arthur Koestler, *Darkness at Noon*. New York: Macmillan, 1941. Classic fictional portrayal of Soviet techniques of confession extraction, highlighting the particular problem of the Communist (or ex-Communist) prisoner. Illustrates relationship between interrogators and prisoner.

6. Arthur Koestler, *Dialogue with Death*. Trans. by T. and P. Blewitt. New York: Macmillan, 1942 (memoir of Spanish Civil War, originally called *Spanish Testament* [1937]).

7. George Orwell, *Nineteen Eighty-Four*. New York: Harcourt Brace, 1949. Popular prophetic novel which selects only the evils of modern society and caricatures them to their logical extremes. He satirizes, for instance, the evil potential of modern communication techniques.

8. Ayn Rand, *Anthem*. Caxton, 1946.

9. Duane Thorin, *Ride to Panmunjon*. Chicago: Regnery, 1956. A novel by a decorated former POW in North Korea describing treatment and indoctrination, with philosophical speculations concerning characterological [*sic*] factors in resistance and collaboration.

10. Manuel Van Loggem, *Insecten in Plastic*. Amsterdam, 1952. 73 pp. A Dutch novelist gives an introspective description of the brainwashing procedure. The artists in a totalitarian state are reformed into insects in plastic. (This book was the *Boekenweekgeschenk* for 1952, given free to anyone buying a book during the National Book Week.)

Notes

■ Introduction

1. The best guide to nuclear war fiction remains Paul Brians, *Nuclear Holocausts: Atomic War in Fiction, 1895–1984* (Kent, Ohio: Kent State Univ. Press, 1987).

2. Bowart, *Operation Mind Control*, 54–55.

3. Dulles, *The Craft of Intelligence*, 209.

4. Foucault, *Discipline and Punish*, 202–3.

5. Laing, *The Divided Self*, 12. More recently, Robert D. Hinshelwood argued in *Therapy or Coercion*, 129–45, that psychoanalysis aims at the integration of the subject, while brainwashing and torture are directed at disintegration

6. Melley, *Empire of Conspiracy*, 36.

7. O'Donnell, *Latent Destinies*, 9.

8. Scheflin and Opton, *The Mind Manipulators*, 23, 469. Another valuable source of information has been the transcripts of the Toronto radio station CKLN-FM Mind Control Series. To read the transcripts from this series cited in this book, as well as other transcripts in the series, please see "CKLN-FM Mind Control Series Table of Contents (updated July 1998)," http://heart7.net/mcf/ckln-hm.htm (accessed December 5, 2003).

9. The phrase "battle for men's minds" was used by William Donovan, one of the founders of the CIA, and picked up by President Eisenhower, Allen Dulles, and others (see, for example, Anisimov, *The Ultimate Weapon*, v). For commentary on CIA medical abuse, see Thomas, *Journey into Madness*, and Herman, "The Career of Cold War Psychology," 52–85.

10. Bloch and Reddaway, *Russia's Political Hospitals*, 27.

11. Berger, *Science Fiction and the New Dark Age*, 110. Heinlein's "They" is collected in *6 X H*.

12. Hebb, "The Motivating Effects of Exteroceptive Stimulation," 110; Delgado, *Physical Control of the Mind*, 59, 65.

13. Szasz, "Some Call It Brainwashing," 11. Boulton, *The Making of Tania*, has argued that a San Francisco "expert in the politics of revolutionary warfare and thought reform" was brought in to confirm that Patty Hearst went through a process similar to that administered by the Chinese Communists because the Hearst family was unable to accept that she had rejected them.

14. Biderman, "The Image of 'Brainwashing,'" 547, 551, 553.

15. Somit, "Brainwashing," 138–43.

16. Althusser, *Lenin and Philosophy and Other Essays*, 161–62.

17. Tanner, *City of Words*, 15.

18. Packard, *The Hidden Persuaders*, 266.

19. Ginsberg, *Deliberate Prose*, 4, 112.

20. Friedan, *The Feminine Mystique*, 285–88.

21. Shea and Wilson, *Illuminatus! Part II*, 208.

22. Wilson, *Prometheus Rising*, 130.

23. Wilson with Hill, *Everything Is under Control*, 90–92. The first phase infantilizes the subject, which induces him or her to "imprint the person who feeds them as a mothering or nurturing object." Then follows the instilling of guilt feelings until in the final phase where the "subject is taught to parrot the words and ideas of the group into which they are being initiated" (91).

24. Twain, *A Connecticut Yankee in King Arthur's Court*, 126. One of Twain's narrators declares: "training is all that there is *to* a person. We speak of nature; it is folly; there is no such thing as nature; what we call by that misleading name is merely heredity and training."

25. Toole, *A Confederacy of Dunces*, 263.

26. Buchan, *The Three Hostages*, 71.

27. Storr, "Introduction," *Land under England* by Joseph O'Neill, 1–3.

28. O'Neill, *Land under England*, 160. Stanton A. Coblentz's *Hidden World* (1935) uses a similar convention of access to another world through a mine. Here an "anti-thought serum" is used on soldiers and business employees.

29. Wells, *Men Like Gods*, 225–26.

30. Hammond, ed., *The Complete Short Stories of H. G. Wells*, by H. G. Wells, 337.

31. Huxley, foreword to *Brave New World*, xxiii.

32. Gernsback, *Ralph 124C41+*, 49.

33. Kumar, *Utopia and Anti-Utopia in Modern Times*, 257.

34. Wyndham, *Exiles on Asperus*, 61.

35. Kelley, "Famine on Mars," 77. Probably by coincidence, Kelley's Combine anticipates the nationwide organization of the same name imagined by Chief Bromden in Ken Kesey's *One Flew Over the Cuckoo's Nest*.

36. Campbell, "The Brain Stealers of Mars," 770.

37. Rand, *Anthem*, 14, 108. See also Branden, *The Passion of Ayn Rand*, 142. The Society for the Investigation of Human Ecology, which listed Rand's *Anthem* as an

example of the fiction of brainwashing in *Brainwashing: A Guide to the Literature*, 51 (see appendix), was a CIA front organization and one of the main funding sources for the MK-ULTRA project. The society's head was Cornell neurologist Harold Wolff, who directed the secret report to the CIA on brainwashing in 1953.

38. Wilder Penfield was to pioneer experiments in the 1930s to localize brain functions, which made possible electronic brain stimulation after World War II by José Delgado and others.

39. Jameson, *Then We Shall Hear Singing*, 17, 19.

40. Crossley, *Olaf Stapledon*, 276.

41. Stapledon, *Darkness and the Light*, 67–69.

42. Boon, "Temple Defiled," 48.

■ 1. Precursors: *Nineteen Eighty-Four* in Context

1. Althusser, *Lenin and Philosophy, and Other Essays*, 158, 162, 168.

2. Saunders, *Who Paid the Piper?* 295–98.

3. Zamyatin, *We*, 206, 224.

4. Orwell, *Complete Works*, vol. 18, 14.

5. Csicsery-Ronay Jr., "Zamyatin and the Strugatskys," 244.

6. Huxley, *Letters*, 351.

7. Huxley, *Brave New World*, 17.

8. Huxley discusses the reinforcing function of key expressions in his 1936 essay "Words and Behaviour" in volume 4 of his *Complete Essays*, 48–58.

9. Posner, "Orwell Versus Huxley," 10–11.

10. Koestler, *The Yogi and the Commissar*, 133.

11. Weissberg, *Conspiracy of Silence*, viii; Cesarani, *Arthur Koestler*, 151; Koestler, *The Invisible Writing*, 479. Victor Serge's novel *The Case of Comrade Tulayev* (written 1941–42, published 1951) deals with the same subject where a security commissar is arrested, interrogated at length, and forced to confess to crimes on the principle that "to obey is still to exist."

12. Harris, *Astride the Two Cultures*, 115; Koestler, *Darkness at Noon*, 20.

13. Koestler, *Darkness at Noon*, 109, 480; *The Invisible Writing*, 480.

14. Koestler, *Darkness at Noon*, 116, 69, 246.

15. Crossman, *The God That Failed*, 69. In his contribution to this postwar collection of statements by former Communists, Koestler writes, "The necessary lie, the necessary slander; the necessary intimidation of the masses to preserve them from short sighted errors; the necessary liquidation of oppositional groups and hostile classes; the necessary sacrifice of a whole generation in the interest of the next."

16. O'Neill and Demos, "The Yeshov Method," 423, 428.

17. Koestler, *Darkness at Noon*, 101.

18. Koestler, *The Invisible Writing*, 479.

19. Koestler, *Darkness at Noon*, 56, 101, 234.

20. Ibid., 228; Berger and Luckman, *The Social Construction of Reality*, 132.

21. Cesarani, *Arthur Koestler*, 384.

22. Orwell, *Complete Works*, vol. 12, 359. In 1946 Orwell campaigned to rescue

Trotsky's name from the allegation made in the Moscow trials that he had advocated links with the Nazis.

23. Orwell's attitude to Koestler's writing is discussed in T. R. Fyvel's, "Arthur Koestler and George Orwell," in *Astride Two Cultures*, ed. Harris, 149–61.

24. Meyers, *George Orwell*, 249; Crick, *George Orwell*, 395.

25. Orwell, *Complete Works*, vol. 20, 319. Orwell's list of alleged Communists is published in appendix 9 ("Orwell's List of Crypto-Communists and Fellow-Travellers") and discussed in Murray, "Orwell Was Recruited to Fight Soviet Propaganda."

26. Orwell, *Nineteen Eighty-Four*, 248.

27. Rogge, *Why Men Confess*, 246.

28. Orwell, *Complete Works*, vol. 9, 4, 83.

29. Posner, "Orwell Versus Huxley," 15.

30. Orwell, *Nineteen Eighty-Four*, 174. In his review of *Darkness at Noon*, Orwell glossed Gletkin's logic as implying that "anyone capable of thinking a disrespectful thought about Stalin would, as a matter of course, attempt to assassinate him" (*Complete Works*, vol. 12, 358).

31. Whyte, *The Organization Man*, 31.

32. London, *Behavior Control*, 86, 92.

33. Kies, "Fourteen Types of Passivity," in *The Revised Orwell*, ed. Rose, 47–60.

34. Orwell, *Nineteen Eighty-Four*, 21.

35. Kumar, *Utopia and Anti-Utopia in Modern Times*, 318.

36. Hunter, *George Orwell*, 93; Pêcheux, *Language, Semantics, and Ideology*, 107; Orwell, *Nineteen Eighty-Four*, 166; Meyers, *George Orwell*, 265.

37. Orwell, *Nineteen Eighty-Four*, 71.

38. Ibid., 269, 255.

39. Trunnell, "George Orwell's 1984," 263, 268; Milosz, *The Captive Mind*, 75–76.

40. Althusser, *Lenin and Philosophy, and Other Essays*, 168; Orwell, *Nineteen Eighty-Four*, 276, 257, 255, 261, 284, 299.

41. Orwell, *Nineteen Eighty-Four*, 254.

42. Ibid., 276–77.

43. Hunter, *George Orwell*, 216; Orwell, *Nineteen Eighty-Four*, 267, 268, 266, 267.

44. Walsh, *From Utopia to Nightmare*, 108; Orwell, *Nineteen Eighty-Four*, 269.

45. Norris, "Language, Truth, and Ideology," 245.

46. Meyers, *George Orwell*, 271, 293.

47. Deutscher, *Heretics and Renegades and Other Essays*, 36, 35.

48. Details from BBC2 documentary on Rudolph Cartier, 1994.

49. Boer, *Cardinal Mindszenty*, 10; Seldes, *The People Don't Know*, 210, 189.

50. Scheflin and Opton, *The Mind Manipulators*, 113.

51. Vogeler, *I Was Stalin's Prisoner*, 199. Some editions list Leigh White as coauthor.

52. Ibid., 139. Based on an interview with Vogeler, the psychoanalyst Dr. J. C. Moloney argued that "mind washing," as he called it, had succeeded in his case because it replaced his stern German father: "By obeying the communists'" orders to memorize, recite, and sign the confession, Vogeler was merely acceding to the only authority which any longer seemed real to him" ("Analyse 'Mind Washing,'" 311).

53. Dos Passos, *The Major Nonfictional Prose*, 214–15. In a 1952 review of Whittaker

Chambers' *Witness*, Dos Passos expressed his conviction that the rumors circulating about Chambers and Vogeler were a Communist-inspired smear campaign.

54. Gallico, *Trial by Terror*, 3. The novel was adapted as a film in 1952 with the title *Assignment: Paris.*

55. Ibid., 71.

56. Ibid., 155.

57. Ibid., 174.

58. Ibid., 36.

59. Ibid., 179–80.

60. Ruff, *The Brain-Washing Machine*, 71.

61. Scheflin and Opton, *The Mind Manipulators*, 149, write that in 1956 the CIA was considering building a laboratory that would include a "special chamber, in which all psychologically significant aspects of the environment [could] be controlled."

62. Ruff, *The Brain-Washing Machine*, 80, 78.

■ 2. Brainwashing Defined and Applied

1. Adams, "Thinking to Order," review of *Brainwashing* by Edward Hunter.

2. Schein, Schneier, and Barker, *Coercive Persuasion*, 16.

3. Scheflin and Opton, *The Mind Manipulators*, 229–30, 231.

4. Hunter, *Brain-Washing in Red China*, 10.

5. Hunter, "'Brain-Washing' Tactics Force Chinese into Ranks of Communist Party." This article also appeared in *New Leader* for October 7, 1950, under the title "Brain-Washing in 'New' China." The hyphen in "brain-washing" was soon dropped.

6. Hunter, *Brain-Washing in Red China*, 329.

7. Hunter, *Brainwashing*, 186.

8. Ibid., 184; *Brainwashing from Pavlov to Powers*, 309. In the latter expanded edition Hunter included Gary Powers, the U-2 pilot shot down over Soviet Russia. This was in line with CIA policy, since on May 31, 1960, the director, Allen Dulles, warned against putting credence on what Powers might say if brought to trial because "by that time they [the Soviets] will have had a more thorough opportunity for a complete brainwashing operation." (Statement to U.S. Congress. Senate Foreign Relations Committee, CIA declassified TS # 172676, 15.)

9. Meerloo, *The Rape of the Mind*, 20, 51.

10. Hunter, *Brainwashing*, 30.

11. Sargant, *Battle for the Mind*, 148.

12. Hunter, *The Black Book on Red China*, 132, 134. The British publishers of Hunter's *The Story of Mary Liu* promoted it on even more antinomian lines than Hunter as a version of the "ages-old conflict between darkness and light" with "communism the devil for our age" (Edward Hunter to Paul Linebarger, September 13, 1956, Linebarger Papers).

13. Hunter, *Communist Psychological Warfare (Brainwashing)*, 15, 14. Later in the consultation Hunter draws an analogy between the Communist state and a nest of ants, another tactic in demonizing Cold War enemies as an alien species.

14. Hunter, *Communist Psychological Warfare*, 1–2.

15. Dulles, "Brain Warfare—Russia's Secret Weapon," 54, 56. These passages were

taken from an address to Princeton alumni delivered by Dulles the previous month. Dulles later read William Sargant's *Battle for the Mind.*

16. Van Coillie, *I Was Brainwashed in Peking*, 40. This translation does not give the date of the original publication.

17. Ibid., 274.

18. Winance, *The Communist Persuasion*, 23.

19. Ibid., 186, 196.

20. Central Intelligence Agency, "A Report on Communist Brainwashing" http://www.totse.com/en/conspiracy/mind_control/165615.htm (accessed April 2, 2004).

21. Meerloo, "The Crime of Menticide," 595; *Rape of the Mind*, 28, 35.

22. Meerloo, "Pavlovian Strategy as a Weapon of Menticide," 810; "Pavlov's Dogs and Communist Brainwashers."

23. Dollard, "Men Who Are Tortured by the Awful Fear of Torture."

24. Schein, Schneier, and Barker, *Coercive Persuasion*, 18; Brown, *Techniques of Persuasion*, 253.

25. Meerloo, *Rape of the Mind*, 40–41.

26. Ibid., 47.

27. Ibid., 117, 132.

28. Victorian, *Mind Controllers*, 70.

29. Sargant, *Battle for the Mind*, 215; similarly Edward Hunter was reportedly "fond of saying that the Soviets brainwashed people the way Pavlov had conditioned dogs" (Marks, *The Search for the "Manchurian Candidate,"* 128).

30. Brown, *Techniques of Persuasion*, 291.

31. Shalizi, review of *Battle for the Mind* by William Sargant.

32. Rogge, *Why Men Confess*, 241.

33. Huxley, *Letters*, 823.

34. Huxley, *Complete Essays*, vol. 4, 20.

35. Huxley, *Letters*, 605; Aldous Huxley to Philip Wylie May 22, 1949, Wylie Papers. Huxley repeated the same point in 1950 when he noted that hypnopaedic techniques were being used by the U.S. Army and concluded that the "systematic brutality" described by Orwell would soon become a thing of the past (Huxley, "A Footnote about 1984").

36. Huxley, *Moksha*, 168, 171.

37. Ibid., 167, 170.

38. Leiber, "Snaring the Human Mind," 57, 56, 60.

39. Ibid., 130.

40. Huxley, *The Human Situation*, 212.

41. Ibid., 31, 207.

42. Huxley, *Complete Essays*, vol. 5, 298.

43. Huxley, *The Human Situation*, 146–47.

44. Huxley, *Letters*, 847.

45. Ibid., 822; Huxley, *Complete Essays*, vol. 6, 259.

46. Huxley, *Complete Essays*, vol. 6, 270.

47. "Huxley Fears New Persuasion Methods Could Subvert Democratic Procedures," *New York Times*, May 19, 1958.

48. Huxley, *Complete Essays*, vol. 6, 261–62.

49. Huxley, *Letters*, 823.

50. Koestler, *Drinkers of Infinity*, 150.

51. Black, *Acid*, 48. According to David Black, this conference was covertly funded by the CIA under its MK-ULTRA program.

52. Koestler, *Drinkers of Infinity*, 214.

53. Ibid., 221.

54. This booklet is available at http://www.geocities.com/Heartland/7006/psychopolitics.html (accessed April 2, 2004). The authorship of this booklet is discussed by Stephen A. Kent in "Brainwashing in Scientology's Rehabilitation Project Force (RPF)," http://www.skeptictank.org/hs/brainwas.htm (accessed April 7, 2004). Kenneth Goff was a member of the Communist Party from 1936 to 1939 and testified to HUAC about this booklet. See also Watson, *War on the Mind*, 340.

55. Foundation of Human Understanding, *Brain-Washing*, ed. Goff, 8. The 1991 reprint by the Foundation of Human Understanding (Grants Pass, Oregon) contains differences from the original text.

56. Foundation of Human Understanding, *Brain-Washing*, 9, 19, 29, 21, 30.

57. Ibid., 42, 53.

58. Biderman, "The Image of 'Brainwashing,'" 560; Foundation of Human Understanding, *Brain-Washing*, 52, 55.

59. National Security Council Papers, "Evaluation of Booklet *Brain-Washing: A Synthesis of the Russian Textbook on Psychopolitics*," March 20, 1956. NSC Papers, OCB File 702.5, Dwight D. Eisenhower Library, Abilene, Texas.

60. Letter from J. Edgar Hoover to special agent in charge, Los Angeles, April 17, 1956. From "The H-Files: FBI Files on L. Ron Hubbard."

61. "Brain-Washing: A Synthesis of the Romantic Dystopia on Psychopolitics" (September 1996), http://home.tiscali.de/alex.sk/A_Stickley2.html (accessed April 2, 2004).

62. Campbell, "Brain-Washing," 162, 161.

63. "Brainwashing: The Communist Experiment with Mankind," April 19, 1955. NSC Papers, OCB File 702.5. Dwight D. Eisenhower Library. Hubbard's biographer, Russell Miller, states that Hubbard merely distributed the booklet. On Campbell's connections with Dianetics, see Berger, *The Magic That Works*, 100–104. Campbell's editorial, "Evaluation of Dianetics," appeared in *Astounding Science Fiction* in October 1951. Here he defined the new science as a "technique by which the mechanical problems of the physical organism can be faced and resolved" (8).

64. Central Intelligence Agency, "A Report on Communist Brainwashing."

65. Budiansky, Goode, and Gest, "The Cold War Experiments," 36.

66. Hinkle and Wolff, "Communist Interrogation and Indoctrination of 'Enemies of the State,'" 164, 169. Wolff was approached in 1953 by Allen Dulles to mount an investigation into brainwashing. The declassified material is cited here. Biderman, "Communist Attempts to Elicit False Confessions from Air Force Prisoners of War," 617. Biderman's group was funded by the Air Force as was the Study Group on Survival Training, which concluded that Communist methods were "neither mysterious nor indicative of any unusual amount of psychiatric sophistication" (Farber, Harlow, and West, "Brainwashing, Conditioning, and *DDD* (Debility, Dependency, and Dread)," 271.

67. National Security Council Papers, "Brainwashing: The Communist Experiment with Mankind: Conclusion," April 20, 1955. NSC Papers, OCB File 702.5, Dwight D. Eisenhower Library.

68. Kinkead, *In Every War but One*, 32, 9.

69. Ibid., 125.

70. Letter from Paul Linebarger June 24, 1962, Linebarger Papers, Hoover Institution, Stanford California. Linebarger inclined "slightly" to the realists. I am grateful to Alan C. Elms for bringing this letter to my attention.

71. Bauer, "Brainwashing," 42–43; Miller, "Brainwashing," 51.

72. Schein and Schneier, *Coercive Persuasion*, 18.

73. Lifton, *Thought Reform and the Psychology of Totalism*, 15, 16; Biderman, "Image of 'Brainwashing,'" 553.

74. Biderman, *March to Calumny*, 141.

75. Bauer, "Brainwashing," 47.

■ 3. Dystopias, Invasions, and Takeovers

1. Matheson, "The Waker Dreams," 104.

2. Miller, "Izzard and the Membrane," 73.

3. Ibid., 92.

4. Frank, *Forbidden Area*, 7.

5. Ibid., 19.

6. Frank, *An Affair of State*, 201.

7. Heinlein, *Double Star*, 103. Though Capek is a benign figure within the novel, the name of the Czech novelist cannot help but trigger suggestions of robots and trained creatures.

8. Linebarger, "Psychological Warfare," 26, 30. Linebarger Papers.

9. Linebarger, "The Communist Psychological Attack." Undated typescript. Linebarger Papers.

10. Linebarger, *Psychological Warfare*, 295.

11. Linebarger [Cordwainer Smith, pseud.], *The Rediscovery of Man*, 9.

12. Linebarger, *The Rediscovery of Man*, 411.

13. Linebarger [Cordwainer Smith, pseud.], *Norstrilia*, 130. This dystopia shows clear Orwellian influence in the state Hate Hall and the appearance of an official named Syme (Orwell's Newspeak specialist).

14. Linebarger, *The Rediscovery of Man*, 421, 424.

15. Pohl, *Turn Left at Thursday*, 28.

16. Roeburt, *The Long Nightmare*, 81.

17. Linebarger, *The Rediscovery of Man*, 162.

18. Skinner, *Beyond Freedom and Dignity*, 67–68. Marks, *The Search for the "Manchurian Candidate,"* 160, notes that this study was partly funded by a grant from a CIA front organization.

19. Bester, "Writing and *The Demolished Man*," in *Redemolished*, ed. Bester, 509. This collection also reprints the original 1952 preface, which did not appear in any editions of the novel.

20. Bester, *The Demolished Man*, i. This epigraph shifts tense in the final paragraph: "what has appeared exceptional to the minute mind of man has been inevitable to the infinite Eye of God." (185).

21. Scheflin, "The History of Mind Control."

22. Bester, *The Demolished Man*, 15, 158.

23. Godshalk, "Alfred Bester," 331–32.

24. Bester, *The Demolished Man*, 183.

25. Turner, "The Double Standard," 19.

26. Karp, *One*, 131. The 1955 Lion Library edition of this novel gives as its title *Escape to Nowhere (One)*.

27. Karp, qtd. in author profile, *Saturday Review*, October 26, 1957.

28. Karp, *The Last Believers*, 79. In a biographical questionnaire Karp explained that he had written the novel because the "persistence of the communist myth of a rational world in my contemporaries infuriated and saddened me" (book file on *The Last Believers*, Jonathan Cape, Publishers Association archives, Reading University, Reading, Berkshire, U.K.).

29. Karp, *One*, 13, 94.

30. Ibid., 142.

31. Corke, "The Banyan Tree," 78.

32. In McGrath's *The Gates of Ivory, The Gates of Horn*, the McCarthyist investigator–protagonist discovers to his horror that he is investigating himself.

33. Central Intelligence Agency, "A Report on Communist Brainwashing."

34. Letter from David Karp to David Seed, June 5, 1991.

35. Sullivan, *The Psychiatric Interview*, 109. It is not surprising that Sullivan's manual was recommended to CIA operatives.

36. Karp, *One*, 90.

37. Promotional statement for *One* by Clifton Fadiman, David Karp Papers, Mugar Memorial Library, Boston University.

38. Karp, *One*, 102, 180.

39. Ibid., 225, 230

40. Smith, "Rival to Orwell."

41. Bunting, "An Interview in New York with Anthony Burgess," 521.

42. Pawel, *From the Dark Tower*, 245; Karp, "Organization Men in Revolt," *Saturday Review*, June 15, 1957.

43. Taken from a review for the *Sunday Times* qtd. on the dustcover of the 1967 Victor Gollancz reprint.

44. Qtd. in Scheflin and Opton, *The Mind Manipulators*, 459; Packard, *The Hidden Persuaders*, 266.

45. Heinlein, *The Puppet Masters*, 207.

46. Bull, *Bone Dance*, 152.

47. "The Puppet Masters," *Galaxy* (Nov. 1951): 101.

48. Heinlein, *The Puppet Masters*, 50.

49. Ibid., 53.

50. Ibid., 219.

51. Sobchack, *The Limits of Infinity*, 128.

52. See also Warren, *Keep Watching the Skies!* vol. 1, 116.

53. Hoberman, "Paranoia and the Pods," 31.

54. LaValley, *Invasion of the Body Snatchers*, 88.

55. Finney, "The Body Snatchers," part 1, 65.

56. On these different versions, see Johnson, "'We'd Fight . . . We Had To,'" 5–14.

57. Finney, *Invasion of the Body Snatchers*, 7.

58. LaValley, *Invasion of the Body Snatchers*, 135.

59. Ibid., 48.

60. Rogin, "*Ronald Reagan*," 266.

61. Finney, *Invasion of the Body Snatchers*, 59.

62. Sobchack, *The Limits of Infinity*, 124.

63. The many echoes of the 1956 film in the remake tend to lack meaning because the small town context has been lost. Finney was well aware of this crucial factor. For example, when Bennell and Becky walk through the streets of the deserted Mill Valley in a paranoid reversal of the gaze, Bennell imagines the house windows as "heavy-lidded, watchful eyes, quietly and terribly aware of us" (Finney, *Invasion of the Body Snatchers*, 121). In the 1978 film, paranoia is established as an aspect of urban life. The opening sequences show passers-by looking suspiciously into the camera.

64. LaValley, *Invasion of the Body Snatchers*, 154, 155.

65. Finney, letter from 1975, qtd. in Le Gacy, "*Invasion of the Body Snatchers:* A Metaphor for the Fifties," 287.

66. LaValley, *Invasion of the Body Snatchers*, 163; McCarthy and Gorman, eds., "*They're Here . . .*" *Invasion of the Body Snatchers*, 172.

67. Biskind, *Seeing Is Believing*, 140. Biskind's discussion of the film remains one of the best explanations of how it relates to the context of the fifties. Further critical commentary on this film and the later adaptations can be found in McCarthy and Gorman.

68. Finney, *Invasion*, 176.

69. Miller, *The Crucible*, 16.

70. LaValley, *Invasion of the Body Snatchers*, 32.

71. Ibid., 38, 53.

72. Ibid., 38, 53.

73. Ibid., 88.

74. Packard, *The Hidden Persuaders*, 5. In 1984 the U.S. House Committee on Science and Technology deliberately exploited the Orwellian date to mount an investigation into subliminal communications.

75. Huxley, *Complete Essays*, vol. 6, 268–69.

76. Elliston, "Subliminal CIA." The CIA report by Richard Gafford was called "The Operational Potential of Subliminal Perception" and appeared in the Spring 1958 issue of *Studies in Intelligence*. Key's *Subliminal Seduction* (1974) warned against the use of "embeds" (key words, slogans, or symbols) in the media.

77. Pohl, *Alternating Currents*, 133.

78. Pohl, *The Man Who Ate the World*, 54.

79. Ibid., 55.

80. Ballard, *The Best Short Stories of J. G. Ballard*, 181.

81. Ibid., 186, 184.

82. Franklin, "Foreword to J. G. Ballard's 'The Subliminal Man,'" in *SF: The Other Side of Realism*, ed. Clareson, 201.

83. Marks, *The Search for the "Manchurian Candidate,"* 136, 141.

84. Huxley, *Complete Essays*, 6:270.

85. Allen, *Conversations with Kurt Vonnegut*, 93, 66–67.

86. Vonnegut, *The Sirens of Titan*, 76.

87. Ibid., 72.

88. Sigman, "Science and Parody in Kurt Vonnegut's *The Sirens of Titan*," in *The Critical Response to Kurt Vonnegut*, ed. Mustazza, 25–41.

89. Vonnegut, *The Sirens of Titan*, 90–91.

90. Within the novel Deighton documents such experiments by citing Liddell's *Experimental Induction of Psychoneuroses* and Shorvon's *Abreactions*. While these references appear to be fictitious, induction techniques were researched at Stanford University in the 1950s.

91. Deighton, *The Ipcress File*, 195.

92. Lines transcribed from film; Estabrooks, *Hypnotism*, 37.

■ 4. The Impact of Korea

1. Axelsson, *Restrained Response*, and Edwards, *A Guide to Films on the Korean War*.

2. For comment on the nonrepatriated POWs, see Zweiback, "The 21 'Turncoat GIs': Nonrepatriations and the Political Culture of the Korean War."

3. Leviero, "For the Brainwashed: Pity or Punishment?"

4. Qtd. in Engelhardt, *The End of Victory Culture*, 65.

5. Kinkead, *In Every War but One*, 9; Hastings, *The Korean War*, 330.

6. Scheflin, "The History of Mind Control."

7. Pease, *Psywar*, 152. This view has now been challenged by Endicott and Hagerman's *The United States and Biological Warfare*.

8. Engelhardt, *The End of Victory Culture*, 65.

9. Rear Admiral Daniel V. Gallery, "We Can Baffle the Brainwashers!"

10. Biderman, *March to Calumny*, 115, 82, 141, 144. In a similar vein, Lewis H. Carlson has argued that the accusations against POWs "reflected exaggeration, distortion, and Cold War paranoia, rather than reality." Bassett and Carlson, *And the Wind Blew Cold*, ix.

11. Gallery, "We Can Baffle the Brainwashers!"

12. Small, "The Brainwashed Pilot."

13. See chapter 5. Ehrhart and Jason, *Retrieving Bones*, 148, explains that James Drought's *The Secret* (1963) ironically describes the U.S. Army basic training as a kind of deconditioning, aimed at inducing unthinking obedience, a "simple school, devised to tear down any moral instruction or inclination."

14. Frank, *Hold Back the Night*, 87, 91, 167. A similar transposition occurs in Kenneth Lamott's "Memoirs of a Brainwasher," which naturalizes brainwashing as a process of psychological interrogation already practiced by the U.S. in the war against Japan.

15. Central Intelligence Agency, "A Report on Communist Brainwashing"; Bowart, *Operation Mind Control*, 57.

16. All quotations transcribed from the film.

17. Slaughter, *Sword and Scalpel*, 224.

18. Ibid., 96.

19. Transcribed from *The Rack* (MGM 1956). The script was based on a teleplay by Rod Serling who was to achieve fame through his *Twilight Zone* series.

20. Carruthers, "Redeeming the Captives," 276.

21. Young, "Missing in Action," 50.

22. Thorin, *A Ride to Panmunjon*, 106.

23. Ibid., 209, 211.

24. Kinkead, *In Every War but One*, 108–9.

25. Pollini, *Night*, statement on back of dustcover of the John Calder edition.

26. Ibid., statement on cover; Kinkead, *In Every War but One*, 48, 86, 100.

27. Kinkead, *In Every War but One*, 112.

28. "KUBARK Counterintelligence Interrogation." Although the goal is different, regression plays a part in Harry Stack Sullivan's *The Psychiatric Interview*, briefly discussed in chapter 3 in relation to David Karp's *One*.

29. Johnson, review of *Night* by Francis Pollini, *San Francisco Chronicle*, September 10, 1961.

30. Kinkead, *In Every War but One*, 131; Axelsson, *Restrained Response*, 74.

31. Hunter, *Brainwashing*, 28; Pollini, *Night*, 47, 49; Kinkead, *In Every War but One*, 108. Such rituals of submission were no mere formality. Anthony Farrar-Hockley recounts how a U.S. Air Force corporal was subjected to beatings and sleep deprivation to force a confession that the U.S. was using biological weapons in Korea (Farrar-Hockley, *The Edge of the Sword*).

32. Davies, *In Spite of Dungeons*, 60, 61, 69, describes the sheer length of indoctrination sessions, a daily diet of four hours of lectures followed by two to three hours of "group study." When Davies was caught not paying attention he was forced to state, "I confess my crime." From Davies, Pollini borrowed the term "cognition" and its use by the Communist authorities to signify a special kind of self-knowledge.

33. Pollini, *Night*, 22, 23.

34. Bartlett, *Remembering*, 199, 201.

35. Pollini, *Night*, 52; Deane, *Captive in Korea*, 154.

36. Kinkead, *In Every War but One*, 136; Lauter, review of *Night* by Francis Pollini, *New Republic*, September 11, 1961.

37. Pollini, *Night*, 123.

38. Ibid., 185.

39. Ibid., 195–96. The term "Admass" was coined by J. B. Priestley who explained it as follows: "This is my name for the whole system of an increasing productivity, plus inflation, plus a rising standard of material living, plus high-pressure advertising and salesmanship, plus mass communications, plus cultural democracy and the creation of the mass mind, the mass man" (Priestley and Hawkes, *Journey Down a Rainbow*, 51); Pollini, *Three Plays*, 86.

40. Pollini, *Night*, 86–87.

41. Van Vogt, "Van Vogt on Dianetics," 45. Van Vogt also discusses Dianetics in Platt, *Dream Makers*, 138–40.

42. Van Vogt, *The Mind Cage*, 77.

43. Ibid., 192.

44. Van Vogt, *Reflections of A. E. Van Vogt*, 110. In interviews Van Vogt has given different dates for the composition of *The Violent Man*. The earliest is 1954 when he probably began research on the subject, while the writing took place between 1958 and 1961. Van Vogt describes Lenin's pamphlet as the "prize book on the subject."

45. Van Vogt, *Reflections*, 111.

46. Van Vogt, "Van Vogt on Dianetics," 51; Van Vogt, *The Violent Man*, 334.

47. Van Vogt, *The Violent Man*, 227.

48. Ibid., 254, 255. Walker, *China under Communism*, qtd. extensively in Sargant's *Battle for the Mind*.

49. Sargant, *Battle for the Mind*, 150–51; Van Vogt, *The Violent Man*, 252.

50. Braddon, *When the Enemy Is Tired*, 15, 89. The cover on the novel declared that it was a "chilling reminder of the *Pueblo* incident."

51. Schumacher, "uss Pueblo (Ager-2)." For example, one letter concluded: "In summation, we who have been rotating upon the fickle finger of fate for such long languid months give our word to the Great Speckled Bird that we will heretofor [*sic*] in all sincerity cleanse ourselves of rottenness and vituperations."

52. Levin, "When the Enemy's Tired."

53. Braddon, *When the Enemy Is Tired*, 112.

54. Lynn, *The Turncoat*, 26, 318. Lynn served as director of production and distribution of Robert Kennedy's tv programs.

55. Ibid., 349.

56. Busch, *War Babies*, 103.

■ 5. *The Manchurian Candidate*

1. Marks, *The Search for the "Manchurian Candidate,"* 9.

2. Scheflin, "The History of Mind Control." In this same lecture Scheflin points out that such an assassin had not only been theorized but also designed by a cia subgroup led by Morse Allen that prepared a film called *The Black Art* (1954), showing an "Oriental Character" being drugged and hypnotized. For further comment on this group, see Marks, *The Search for the "Manchurian Candidate,"* 182–92.

3. Kinkead, *In Every War but One*, 77–79.

4. Mind Control Glossary, "Eleanor White's 'Freedom Isn't Free!'" www.raven1. net/glossary.htm (accessed Jan. 19, 2004).

5. Estabrooks, "Hypnotism Comes of Age."

6. Marks, *The Search for the "Manchurian Candidate,"* 20.

7. Lockridge and Estabrooks, *Death in the Mind*, 39.

8. Ibid., 117–18, 119, 129.

9. Estabrooks, *Hypnotism*, 202, 204. For a discussion of Estabrooks's "Super Spy," see Scheflin and Opton, *The Mind Manipulators*, 460–65.

10. Ross, "The cia and Military Mind Control Research." Further discussion of this subject can be found in Bross, "A Primer on Hypnosis and Mind Control" *MindNet Journal* 1, no. 58, http://visitations.com/mindnet/MN158.htm (accessed January 7, 2004).

11. Bowart, "The Secret History of Mind Control"; *Operation Mind Control*, 128, 47. Bowart alleges that Bryan was close to the CIA. The work that Condon probably consulted by Andrew Salter was *Conditioned Reflex Therapy* (1949).

12. Lawrence and Thomas, *Mind Control, Oswald and JFK*, 55–56.

13. John Marks concluded his investigation by admitting the creation of a Manchurian Candidate was theoretically possible but not proven; Scheflin and Opton conclude that it was impossible to create such an agent.

14. Sanders, "The Fantastic Non-Fantastic," 130. A valuable overview of Condon's fiction can be found in Cochran, *America Noir*, 175–93.

15. Condon, *The Manchurian Candidate*, 40.

16. Letter from Richard Condon to Henry Morgan, May 16, 1959, Condon archive, Mugar Library, Box 37.

17. Bowart, *Operation Mind Control*, 20.

18. Letter from Richard Condon to Henry Morgan, May 16, 1959.

19. Condon, *The Manchurian Candidate*, 202, 130.

20. Levine, *The Mind of an Assassin*, 214.

21. Frank's review appeared in the *Washington Post* on April 26, 1959, and Sherman's notice in the *St. Louis Post Dispatch* the same month (cuttings in Condon archive, Box 36).

22. This was noted by Frederic Morton in his *New York Times* review, where he declared that Condon "compresses (a) a breathlessly up-to-date thriller, gimmicked to the gills, from judo to narcohypnosis; (b) a psychoanalytic horror tale about (what else?) a mother and a son; and (c) an irate sociopolitical satire that tries to flay our shibboleths alive."

23. Condon, *The Manchurian Candidate*, 325.

24. Because of its malleability, the whole notion of memory becomes unusually complex in this novel. Shaw's "recall" of the supposed action in Korea for which he is decorated is always phrased by him in the future tense as a series of scripted predictions of events that never actually happened, which suggests that his "memory" might have been implanted.

25. In the film adaptation, Marco's reading helps to contextualize the action. Among his books is Francis X. Busch's *Enemies of the State* (1954), which discusses four famous American trials, the last being that of the Rosenbergs.

26. Sanders, "The Fantastic Non-Fantastic," 129.

27. Condon, *The Manchurian Candidate*, 206, 260.

28. Ibid., 339–40.

29. Condon, "A Candidate from Manchuria?" Condon archive, Mugar Library, Box 36.

30. Letter from Richard Condon to Henry Morgan, May 16, 1959.

31. Friedman, "Condon's *The Manchurian Candidate*," 511.

32. Wylie, *Generation of Vipers*, 184–204. For a valuable discussion of the domestic ideology in Cold War films, see Rogin, "Ronald Reagan," 236–71.

33. A discussion of gender roles in the film, which would apply equally well to the novel, is given in Jackson, "*The Manchurian Candidate* and the Gender of the Cold War," 34–40.

34. Bowart, *Operation Mind Control*, 13.

35. Letter from Richard Condon to Robert Landry, April 22, 1959, Condon archive, Mugar Library, Box 36.

36. Letter from Richard Condon to Henry Morgan, May 16, 1959.

37. Letter from Richard Condon to John McManus of the *Detroit News*, May 20, 1959, Condon archive, Mugar Library, Box 36. In his review of *The Manchurian Candidate*, McManus claimed that Condon "did not heed the lesson America gave demagogues through its final treatment of McCarthy" but Condon hotly denied that the threat of demagoguery had lapsed with the fall of the senator.

38. Letter from Richard Condon to Patricia P. de Fuentes, June 4, 1959, Condon archive, Mugar Library, Box 36.

39. For further details on the Iselin–McCarthy parallels, see Seed, "Brainwashing and Cold War Demonology," 546–50. Just before publication, Condon was asked by his editor to make the McCarthy parallels a little less obvious.

40. Condon, *The Manchurian Candidate*, 146, 79.

41. Qtd. in *The Progressive* (April 1954): 47.

42. Welch, *The Politican*, 5. Hoberman, "When Dr. No Met Dr. Strangelove," 18, argues that *The Manchurian Candidate* represents a comic version of this work—the John Birch Society's *Black Book* circulating since 1958—that claimed that Eisenhower was the "dedicated agent of a vast Communist conspiracy, who had been painstakingly manoeuvred by his Kremlin handlers into the White House."

43. Condon, *The Manchurian Candidate*, 115.

44. Ibid., 161.

45. In an article entitled "Who's Brainwashed Now?" Condon attacks the paranoia of the "Radical Right" in the United States for, among other reasons, promoting a story that the World Health Organization was brainwashing the world. Condon archive, Mugar Library. This article implies that the melodrama of *The Manchurian Candidate* is partly a burlesque of right-wing thinking.

46. Ivie, "Diffusing Cold War Demagoguery," 74–75.

47. Condon, "Who's Brainwashed Now?" manuscript essay, 1962, Condon archive, Mugar Library.

48. "Richard Condon," in *Contemporary Authors Autobiography Series*, 196; Scheinfeld, review of *The Manchurian Candidate* by Richard Condon, *Films in Review* 39, no. 11 (Nov. 1988): 540. The film was released in 1962 and directed by John Frankenheimer. It starred Frank Sinatra as Ben Marco, Laurence Harvey as Shaw, and Angela Lansbury as Shaw's mother. A 2004 remake was directed by Jonathan Demme, starring Denzel Washington as Marco, Liev Schreiber as Shaw, and Meryl Streep as Shaw's mother, who is now a U.S. senator.

49. Doherty, "A Second Look," 31, has argued of the brainwashing theme that "the invasion from without seems more personal than political, more about an assault on selfhood than nationhood"; but this is to ignore the other casualties of brainwashing, and the external symbolism of the film generally.

50. Axelrod, "The Manchurian Candidate. Screenplay: Final Shooting Script" (January 10, 1962), Condon archive, Mugar Library.

51. Marcus, *The Manchurian Candidate*, 25.

52. From Frankenheimer's commentary on the DVD recording of *The Manchurian Candidate*.

53. Editorial page in United Artists' press book on *The Manchurian Candidate*, British Film Institute Library, London.

54. Hunter, *Brainwashing*, 156–57. Kinkead, *In Every War but One*, 205–7, also comments on the obtrusive use of a clock face in an interrogation film.

55. Condon, "Tomorrow Will Be Today, Philosophers Now Report," manuscript essay, 1962, Condon archive, Mugar Library.

56. Ibid.

57. Condon, *Emperor of America*, 112; Karp, "A Look Back into the Tube," 97; Scheinfeld, review of *The Manchurian Candidate*, 545.

58. Axelrod, "The Manchurian Candidate. Screenplay: Final Shooting Script" (January 10, 1962), Condon archive, Mugar Library.

59. Marcus, *The Manchurian Candidate*, 48.

60. Hoberman, "When Dr. No Met Dr. Strangelove," 19.

61. Scheinfeld, review of *The Manchurian Candidate*, 542.

62. Ibid., which glosses representations of Lincoln as signifying "duplicity and hypocrisy," and the American eagle as being "correlated with death and the military."

63. These resemblances are partly verbal, as when Marco compares Shaw to Humpty Dumpty, and partly visual, as in Jocie's card costume that recalls the Red Queen's croquet ground.

64. Transcribed from the film. Axelrod, "The Manchurian Candidate. Screenplay: Final Shooting Script" (January 10, 1962), Condon archive, Mugar Library. The third sentence reads as follows in the shooting script: "I told them to build me an assassin. I wanted a killer . . . a killer whose brain has been conditioned to kill, and to then forget he has ever killed. . . . I wanted a killer from a world filled with killers."

65. Marcus, "The Last American Dream," 5.

66. Carruthers, "*The Manchurian Candidate* (1962) and the Cold War Brainwashing Scare," 84. Rogin, "*Ronald Reagan*," 252, asserts that the film's aim was to "reawaken a lethargic nation to the Communist menace."

67. Dick, "Drugs, Hallucinations, and the Quest for Reality," 169.

68. Richard Condon letter to *London American*, September 5, 1960, Condon archive, Mugar Library, Box 37.

69. Condon, "'Manchurian Candidate' in Dallas," *The Nation*, December 28, 1963.

70. Bowart, *Operation Mind Control*, 15. All copies of the U.S. edition of Bowart's *Operation Mind Control* were bought up as soon as it appeared, but the text is available through the Freedom of Thought Foundation. In the 1980s he planned a sequel collaboration to be called *The Invisible Third World War* but abandoned the project after he failed to place it with a publisher. Bowart subsequently acted as consultant for the 1997 film *Conspiracy Theory*. His Freedom of Thought Foundation has an online "Mind Control Bibliography" at http://www.azstarnet.com/~freethtbibliogr.htm (accessed January 8, 2004).

71. Condon, *The Whisper of the Axe*, 31.

72. Ibid., 136.

73. Ibid., 138.

74. Ibid., 156, 178–79.

75. This is also an intended plan in the 1974 film of Algis Budrys' *Who?* (1958), where a Western scientist is returned from East Germany after his life is saved after a car crash. Because he has been given a simulated metal face, there is ultimately no way to prove his identity. The FBI investigator suspects that he might have been "completely brainwashed" to sabotage the secret project he was working on. Conversely, his Soviet handler asks the surgeon, "Is it possible to brainwash him, make him one of ours?" The answer is no because there is too little undamaged body surface to monitor the signs of fear, etc., that would make such a transformation possible.

76. Fox, review of *Telefon*, dir. Siegel, *Films and Filming* 24, no. 9 (June 1978): 38.

77. Wager, *Telefon*, 63.

78. Ibid., 167–68.

■ 6. William Burroughs

1. Burroughs, *The Letters of William S. Burroughs, 1945–1959*, 331.

2. Ginsberg, *Deliberate Prose*, 49.

3. Burroughs, *Last Words*, 207.

4. Burroughs, *Ah Pook Is Here and Other Texts*, 21.

5. Burroughs, *Queer*, 91.

6. Ballard, "J. G. Ballard on William S. Burroughs' Naked Truth."

7. Scheflin and Opton, *The Mind Manipulators*, 447–48, present the Assassins as the prototype of the Manchurian Candidate, and Condon uses an encyclopedia entry on the Assassins as an epigraph in his novel.

8. Burroughs, "The Hallucinatory Operators Are Real," 6.

9. Burroughs, *Blade Runner, A Movie*, 10. Burroughs took his title for this screen outline from Alan Nourse's 1974 medical dystopia, *The Bladerunner*. The title was then taken for the 1982 movie adaptation of Philip K. Dick's novel *Do Androids Dream of Electric Sheep?* itself retitled for the movie tie-in.

10. Burroughs, *The Letters of William S. Burroughs, 1945–1959*, 269.

11. Burroughs, *The Wild Boys*, 97.

12. Burroughs, *Naked Lunch*, 21.

13. Ibid.

14. Mottram, *William Burroughs*, 46.

15. Burroughs, *Naked Lunch*, 25.

16. Pounds, "The Postmodern Anus," 219; Murphy, *Wising Up the Marks*, 80–84.

17. Burroughs, *Naked Lunch*, 215.

18. Hibbard, *Conversations with William S. Burroughs*, 89.

19. Ibid., 98.

20. In 1980 Burroughs addressed a conference on psychiatry in Milan where he flatly denied the existence of the Freudian unconscious. See Bockris, *With William Burroughs*, 138.

21. Burroughs, *The Adding Machine*, 116.

22. Loydell, *My Kind Of Angel*, 17; Burroughs, *The Adding Machine*, 153, 154.

23. Burroughs, *Ah Pook Is Here*, 132.

24. Kostelanetz, "William Burroughs on Writing," 336.

25. Burroughs with Odier, *The Job*, 138.

26. Burroughs, *Interzone*, 79. Burroughs here inverts the demonization of Communist totalitarianism, arguing that the subject finds a paradoxical freedom and pride since "the forces that were intended to crush his dignity and existence as an individual delineated him so that he had never felt surer of his own worth and dignity."

27. Lilly's experiments were described in James Kennaway's 1963 novel *The Mind Benders* and the film of the same title starring Dirk Bogarde (see chapter 9).

28. Delgado, *Physical Control of the Mind*, 191. Delgado's research was funded by the Office of Naval Research. Throughout his study he insisted that the individual was inseparable from the environment, was a "transitory composite of materials borrowed from the environment" (65). Here the environment is given materiality, but not the body housing the brain that processes this external data.

29. Burroughs speculates on the possible military applications of Professor Vladimir Gavreau's experiments on infrasound in *The Job*, 62–64. For reflections on the Soviet use of radio transmissions in psychological warfare, see Possony, "Psyops" and "The Brain Wave Machine," both in *There Will Be War IV*, ed. Pournelle and Carr, 255–63, 263–64.

30. Bockris, *With William Burroughs*, 37–38.

31. Kazin, *Writers At Work*, 172.

32. Hibbard, *Conversations with William S. Burroughs*, 39–40, 93.

33. Burroughs, *Exterminator!* 104.

34. Lawrence and Thomas, *Mind Control, Oswald and JFK*, 84. RHIC stands for "Radio Hypnotic Intercerebral Control."

35. Kesey, *The Further Inquiry*, 117, 126.

36. Acker, *Hannibal Lecter, My Father*, 17. Acker has several times expressed her respect for Burroughs's alertness to the connections between language and power, including her obituary "William Burroughs," http://acker.thehub.com.au/ackademy/burroughs.htm (accessed January 10, 2004).

37. Acker, *Empire of the Senseless*, 142; *Bodies of Work*, 13.

38. For details on "Midnight Climax," see Marks, *The Search for the "Manchurian Candidate*," 89–101.

39. Acker, *Empire of the Senseless*, 146.

40. O'Donnell, *Latent Destinies*, 99–101.

41. Burroughs, *Interzone*, 123.

42. Smith, *Mechanisms of Virus Infection*, 12.

43. Burroughs, *The Western Lands*, 60; Burroughs and Odier, *The Job*, 12.

44. Burroughs, *Ah Pook Is Here*, 141.

45. Burroughs, *The Soft Machine*, 108. This edition reprints the final version of this novel published in 1968 by Calder and Boyars, the first being the Olympia Press edition of 1961 and the second the Grove Press edition of 1966.

46. Burroughs, *The Soft Machine*, 130. Burroughs gives a metafictional title to this page as the "Appendix to the Soft Machine," implying the vulnerability of the body of the text itself to parasitic misreadings.

47. Russell, *Three To Conquer*, 186. Burroughs has also mentioned Barrington J.

Bayley's *The Star Virus* (1970) as a novel that helped shape his thinking on the concept of virus. Russell's 1964 novel, *With a Strange Device*, describes the use by Communist agents of a stereoscopic projector (a "fully automated brainwashing" device) synchronized to the rhythms of the viewer's optic nerve, which induces hypnosis. The subjects, workers in an American weapons plant, can then be given a false memory, which makes them leave their posts.

48. Kazin, *Writers at Work*, 172.

49. Burroughs, *The Western Lands*, 193.

50. Burroughs and Odier, *The Job*, 187.

51. LaValley, *Invasion of the Body Snatchers*, 103.

52. Ross, *No Respect*, 45, 47; Rogin, "Ronald Reagan," 263–64.

53. Rose, "Cultural Paranoia, Conspiracy Plots, and the American Ideology," 104.

54. Kazin, *Writers at Work*, 172.

55. Olson was working for the Army Chemical Corps' Special Operations Division that specialized in refined toxins, including LSD, which the CIA secretly admitted to be the trigger to his suicide (see Marks, *The Search for the "Manchurian Candidate*," chapter 5).

56. Burroughs, *The Adding Machine*, 25.

57. Burroughs, *The Burroughs File*, 45.

58. Wood, "William S. Burroughs and the Language of Cyberpunk," 14.

59. Burroughs, *Nova Express*, 129.

60. For a useful discussion of verbal parasitism that links Burroughs with theorists like Roland Barthes and J. Hillis Miller, see Lydenberg, *Word Cultures*, 131–34.

61. Burroughs and Gysin, *The Third Mind*, 101.

62. Clark, *The Genetic Code*, 22.

63. Burroughs, *Cities of the Red Night*, 277.

64. Shaviro, *Doom Patrols*, 103. Chapter 10 of this work, "William Burroughs," is in effect an extended meditation on the virus trope.

65. Burroughs, *Ah Pook Is Here*, 115.

66. Burroughs, *Interzone*, 110, 111.

67. Burroughs and Odier, *The Job*, 61–62.

68. Burroughs, *Exterminator!* 68.

69. Faroohar, "William Burroughs," 35.

70. Burroughs, *The Letters of William S. Burroughs, 1945–1959*, 432; Burroughs, *Last Words*, 64.

71. Morgan, *Literary Outlaw*, 440–42.

72. Hibbard, *Conversations with William S. Burroughs*, 57.

73. "Burroughs on Scientology," *Ali's Smile*, 70–72. Burroughs's attitude to Scientology is discussed in Miles, *William Burroughs*, 184–86.

74. Burroughs was familiar with the CIA experiments on distance viewing (see Hibbard, *Conversations with William S. Burroughs*, 182).

75. Burroughs, *The Adding Machine*, 150.

76. Ibid., 150–52.

77. Coincidentally, 1974 was also the year when Philip K. Dick became convinced that he was being subjected to psychotronic transmissions by the Soviets. See

Gorightly, "PKD, the Unicorn, and Soviet Psychotronics," http://www.alphane.com/moon/PalmTree/unicorn.htm (accessed April 8, 2004).

78. For information on this subject, see Kress, "Parapsychology in Intelligence"; Marrs, *The Enigma Files*; and the Star Gate Collection (declassified CIA documents) http://stargate.collection.free.fr/Elements/news.php3 (accessed January 12, 2004).

79. Rossmann, *The Mind Masters*, 17.

80. Burroughs, *My Education*, 121.

81. Strieber, *Black Magic*, 94, 96.

82. Ibid., 58.

83. Strieber, *Majestic*, 40; Loydell, *My Kind of Angel*, 31.

84. Strieber, *Majestic*, 168, 205.

85. Strieber, *The Secret School* and *Confirmation*. For comments on the latter, see Nickell, "Alien Implants."

86. Mills, *The Power*, 235.

87. Collins, *Maze*, 58, 148–49.

88. Ibid., 120.

■ 7. Psychotherapy and Social Enforcement

1. Szasz, *The Age of Madness*, xv, xx.

2. Tarsis, *Ward 7*, 120.

3. Warren, *All the King's Men*, 337–38.

4. It is a measure of how the lobotomy became politicized that a 1952 report of the U.S. government's Psychological Strategy Board should discuss the benefits of lobotomizing the members of the Soviet politburo (Budiansky et al., "The Cold War Experiments").

5. Wiener, *Cybernetics*, 148.

6. Del Torto, "The Human Machine," *Neurotica* 8 (Spring 1951): 34. The run of this magazine was reprinted as *Neurotica, 1948–1951* (London: Jay Landesman, 1981).

7. Wolfe, *Limbo*, 435, 47, 49–50.

8. Ibid., 7, 47.

9. I have discussed these and other ironies in "Deconstructing the Body Politic in Bernard Wolfe's *Limbo*."

10. Ellison, *Shadow and Act*, 28.

11. Bloom, *Ralph Ellison: Modern Critical Views*, 41; Ellison, *Invisible Man*, 189.

12. Ellison, *Invisible Man*, 192–93.

13. Bowart, *Operation Mind Control*, 158.

14. Ellison, *Invisible Man*, 203.

15. Lee and Shlain, *Acid Dreams*, 48, 64. Huxley reportedly suggested to Jolly West the use of hypnosis as a prelude to acid trips.

16. Black, *Acid*, 61, 62. Leary and his organization were under CIA observation from at least 1963. Bizarrely, it has been suggested that Leary himself was working for the CIA. See Riebling, "Tinker, Tailor, Stoner, Spy."

17. Lee and Shlain, *Acid Dreams*, 59. For further commentary on this subject, see

Buckman, "Brainwashing, LSD and CIA," 8–19. Chapter 7 of Marks, *The Search for the "Manchurian Candidate,"* also gives valuable background.

18. Perry and Babbs, *On the Bus*, 11–12; Kesey, *Kesey's Garage Sale*, 7. Kesey was to return to psychiatric themes in his 1986 collection *Demon Box*, where his surrogate character hears of group therapy in a large tub, managed by a local guru, called "Woofner's Brainwash," sensory deprivation experiments, and the different drugs being used on those in mental care. The psychiatrist in *Demon Box* was modeled on Fritz Perls of the Esalen Institute of Big Sur. I am grateful to Bennett Huffman for the latter information.

19. Rosenwein, "A Place Apart," 43.

20. Goffman, *Asylums*, 24.

21. Wolfe, *The Electric Kool-Aid Acid Test*, 47–48.

22. Kesey, *One Flew Over the Cuckoo's Nest*, 27, 29.

23. Kesey, *Kesey's Garage Sale*, 7.

24. Manning, *The Therapeutic Community Movement*, 185.

25. Kesey, *One Flew Over the Cuckoo's Nest*, 47.

26. Manning, *The Therapeutic Community Movement*, 36.

27. Sedgewick, *Psycho Politics*, 180.

28. Solomon, *Mishaps, Perhaps*, 37. This article and its companion piece, "Further Afterthoughts of a Shock Treatment," were first published in *Neurotica* in 1950 and 1951. The African American poet Etheridge Knight deals with this same subject in his 1969 poem, "Hard Rock Returns to Prison from the Hospital for the Criminally Insane," where lobotomy and electroshock treatment are described as a form of castration.

29. Edward Loomis, qtd. in Collins, "Carl Solomon," 508.

30. Solomon, *Mishaps, Perhaps*, 9, 50. The manual that Solomon quotes is L. B. Kalinowsky and P. H. Hoch, *Shock Treatments and Other Somatic Treatments in Psychiatry* (1946).

31. Ginsberg, "Howl," part 1.

32. From *Views of a Nearsighted Cannoneer* (1961), excerpted in Szasz, *The Age of Madness*, 285.

33. Wolfe, *The Electric Kool-Aid Acid Test*, 44.

34. Kesey, *One Flew Over the Cuckoo's Nest*, 339.

35. Ibid., 8.

36. Ibid., 26–27.

37. Melley, *Empire of Conspiracy*, 36.

38. Kesey, "The Art of Fiction CXXVI," 79.

39. Kesey, *One Flew Over the Cuckoo's Nest*, 346.

40. An undated draft of *One Flew Over the Cuckoo's Nest* ("I think it way time") in the Kesey papers, University of Oregon (Box 3, Folder 4), describes Bromden's shock treatment as a kind of interrogation by "one of the murder combines"; Kesey, *One Flew Over the Cuckoo's Nest*, 227.

41. Manuscript draft of *One Flew Over the Cuckoo's Nest*, Kesey papers, University of Oregon.

42. Kunz, "Mechanistic and Totemistic Symbolization in Kesey's *One Flew Over the Cuckoo's Nest*," 82.

43. Leary, *The Politics of Ecstasy*, 33.

44. Kesey, *One Flew Over the Cuckoo's Nest*, 266.

45. Ishmael Reed's parodic version of the United States in *The Free-Lance Pallbearers* (1967) contains a "shock shop," where ECT ensures the standardization of social behavior. Walter Freeman, the most notorious promoter of lobotomies, admitted that they caused a "death" of the psyche or radical damage to self-recognition (Scheflin and Opton, *The Mind Manipulators*, 256).

46. Kesey, *One Flew Over the Cuckoo's Nest*, 270.

47. Safer, "'It's the Truth Even If It Didn't Happen,'" 138.

48. Forman, qtd. in Peary and Shatzkin, *The Modern American Novel and the Movies*, 271.

49. MacDonald, "Control by Camera," in Searles, *A Casebook on Ken Kesey's* One Flew Over the Cuckoo's Nest, 166.

50. Zubizarreta, "The Disparity of Point of View in *One Flew Over the Cuckoo's Nest*," 63.

51. Safer, "'It's the Truth Even If It Didn't Happen,'" 137.

52. Forman, qtd. in Zubizarreta, "The Disparity of Point of View in *One Flew Over the Cuckoo's Nest*," 68.

53. Kesey, *One Flew Over the Cuckoo's Nest*, 14, 15.

54. Ibid., 309.

55. Zubizarreta, "The Disparity of Point of View in *One Flew Over the Cuckoo's Nest*," 64.

56. Scheflin and Opton, *The Mind Manipulators*, 390, 385. A 1949 Rand Corporation report included reference to ECT as helping mind control (Bowart, *Operation Mind Control*, 251).

57. Marks, *The Search for the "Manchurian Candidate*," 133, 134.

58. In Thomas, *Journey into Madness*, 105–13, Ewen Cameron summarizes a case strikingly like that of Plath's narrator. The subject of this case also endures repeated ECT sessions and is fascinated by the Rosenbergs' execution.

59. Radosh and Milton, *The Rosenberg File*, 283, 419. The CIA conceived a plan to convert the Rosenbergs to anticommunism for its propaganda value (359).

60. Frame, *Faces in the Water*, 26.

61. Willeford, *The Machine in Ward Eleven*, 33. Unlike Kesey's McMurphy, the narrator does not receive a lobotomy but is transferred to the state mental hospital after his act.

62. Doctorow, *The Book of Daniel*, 212.

63. Plath, *The Journals of Sylvia Plath*, 80.

64. Unpublished journal entry, qtd. in Rose, *The Haunting of Sylvia Plath*, 195, 197.

65. De Lauretis, "Rebirth in *The Bell Jar*," 125.

66. Bronfen, *Sylvia Plath*, 106.

67. Plath, *Johnny Panic and the Bible of Dreams*, 33

68. Macpherson, *Reflecting on* The Bell Jar, 23; Plath, *Letters Home*, 163; Plath, *Johnny Panic and the Bible of Dreams*, 93.

69. Nelson, "Penetrating Privacy," 90.

70. Plath, *The Bell Jar*, 69.

71. Ibid., 79.

72. Macpherson, *Reflecting on* The Bell Jar, 70; Plath, *The Bell Jar*, 117–18.

73. Plath, *The Bell Jar*, 175.

74. Fromm, *The Sane Society*, 13.

75. Macpherson, *Reflecting on* The Bell Jar, 96.

76. Ingersoll, *Putting the Questions Differently*, 35. Lessing admired Laing's challenges to the British medical establishment but rejected Thomas Szasz's insistence that mental illness did not exist.

77. Lessing, *Briefing for a Descent into Hell*, 17, 125.

■ 8. The Control of Violence

1. Siodmak, *Donovan's Brain*, 8, 33, 51.

2. Siodmak, *Hauser's Memory*, 13.

3. Niven, "Death by Ecstasy," 69.

4. Crawford, "Medico-Political Considerations of Psychosurgery," 112; Valenstein, "Science-Fiction Fantasy and the Brain," 29.

5. Qtd. in Valenstein, *The Psychosurgery Debate*, 42.

6. Kubrick interview in Ciment, *Kubrick*, 149.

7. Burgess, 1985, 92.

8. Burgess, "Clockwork Marmalade," 198.

9. Burgess, *Enderby*, 443. Enderby makes his statement during an interview on an American television talk show where the interviewer considers that brainwashing could be used to eradicate violence but is "fundamentally inhuman." He continues by proposing a form of applied behaviorism: "We must so condition human mind [*sic*] that reward is expected for doing good not the other way round."

10. Burgess, *A Clockwork Orange*, ix.

11. D'haen, "Language and Power in Orwell and Burgess," 46.

12. Burgess, *A Clockwork Orange*, 23. The writer is working on a book to be called *A Clockwork Orange*, designed to protest against the imposition of mechanistic processes on humans. Alex displays his "humanity" by tearing the manuscript to shreds, beating the author, and raping his wife.

13. The theme of control connects these two works: in the first the control of random violence, in the second the control of the birth rate and food supply. The War Department in *The Wanting Seed*, set against an Orwellian background of polarized power blocs, is used as an agency for population control by simulating battles where one side is wiped out. The latter novel describes the failure of humanity's control of the environment, a concept that is addressed as primarily a social issue in *A Clockwork Orange*.

14. Burgess, "Clockwork Marmalade," 198. The Greater London Council was considering banning the film, and the then-British Home Secretary Reginald Maudling saw the film in a private viewing with a member of the British Board of Film Censors. The MP Maurice Edelman is credited with coining the phrase "pornography of violence" and arranged a special viewing of the film for MPs on January 26, 1972.

15. Gehrke, "Deviant Subjects in Foucault and *A Clockwork Orange*," 278. Since Alex is the narrator, Gehrke argues, it is less important where he is than to note the four subject-positions he goes through as criminal, convict, patient, and citizen.

16. Burgess, 1985, 178. Burgess mentions *Facial Justice* in relation to dystopias in this same volume (62).

17. Burgess, *A Clockwork Orange*, 108.

18. Ibid., 100.

19. Ibid., 104.

20. Ibid., 126–27.

21. Ibid., 21–22.

22. Ibid., 123. Alex would agree with Brodsky on the benefits of avoiding drugs. Early in the novel, he comments ironically on the popularity of "synthemesc" (i.e. synthetic mescaline) under which "you lost your name and your body and your self and you just didn't care" (3).

23. Ibid., 174.

24. Burgess, "Clockwork Marmalade," 198.

25. Burgess, prefatory note to *A Clockwork Orange: A Play with Music*, vii.

26. Burgess, *A Clockwork Orange*, 114.

27. Burgess, "Clockwork Marmalade," 199.

28. Bunting, "An Interview in New York with Anthony Burgess," 525.

29. Burgess discusses this chapter in his 1986 introduction to *A Clockwork Orange*, vii–ix.

30. Burgess, *A Clockwork Orange: A Play with Music*, vi.

31. Ciment, *Kubrick*, 157.

32. Burgess, "Clockwork Marmalade," 198.

33. Burgess, 1985, 92.

34. Burgess, *A Clockwork Orange*, 83.

35. Skinner, *Science and Human Behavior*, 7.

36. Schuster, "Skinner and the Morality of Melioration," 103.

37. Skinner, *Science and Human Behavior*, 111; Skinner, *Beyond Freedom and Dignity*, 200.

38. Skinner, *About Behaviorism*, 189.

39. Burgess, 1985, 87, makes a similar point about Pavlov whose materialism he sees as reflecting a kind of literal belief in the perfectibility of man.

40. Skinner, *Beyond Freedom*, 5, 182.

41. Skinner, *Walden Two*, 172. In his 1976 essay on the novel, "Walden Two Revisited," Skinner comments on exactly the problem discussed throughout this chapter: "We could solve many of the problems of delinquency and crime if we could change the early environment of offenders" (xi).

42. Skinner, *Beyond Freedom*, 39.

43. Skinner, "Utopia as an Experimental Culture," 37.

44. Skinner, *Beyond Freedom*, 202, 203.

45. Qtd. in Bowart, *Operation Mind Control*, 159.

46. Burgess, 1985, 89.

47. Bunting, "An Interview in New York with Anthony Burgess," 521.

48. Burgess, "Clockwork Marmalade," 198.

49. Burgess, "A Fable for Social Scientists," 14.

50. Bailey, "A Clockwork Utopia."

51. Sobchack, "Décor as Theme," 98.

52. Huston, "Tolchoked by Kubrick."

53. Bailey, "A Clockwork Utopia."

54. Kubrick, *Stanley Kubrick's Clockwork Orange*, reel 2.

55. Phillips, *Stanley Kubrick*, 111.

56. Kubrick, *Stanley Kubrick's Clockwork Orange*, reel 15. The change to Alex's surname happens so quickly that few viewers spot it.

57. Alex's description of his experiences in the film is more explicit than in the novel. He notes that he is bound in a "straitjacket" in the "chair of torture."

58. Kubrick, *Stanley Kubrick's Clockwork Orange*, reel 9.

59. Bailey, "A Clockwork Utopia," 22.

60. For a discussion of how Alex's violence relates to the commodities of modernism, see Cohen, "Clockwork Orange and the Aestheticization of Violence."

61. Elsaesser, "Screen Violence," 187. Elsaesser denies a political coherence to the film and novel alike, and makes no attempt to distinguish between Alex's victims by gender, age, etc.

62. Burgess, *Clockwork Orange*, 179, 181.

63. Valenstein, "Science-Fiction Fantasy and the Brain," 30, argues that the experiment simply showed that the stimulus produced a repetitive circling movement in the bull.

64. Delgado, *Physical Control of the Mind*, 59, 179, 191. From 1952 onward the CIA was experimenting with the control possibilities of surgically placed electronic brain implants in their Project Moonstruck.

65. Clarke, *Profiles of the Future*, 191.

66. Ibid., 196.

67. Rorvik, "Someone To Watch Over You (For Less Than 2¢ a Day)."

68. Rorvik, *As Man Becomes Machine*, 151. The first U.S. and U.K. editions were subtitled, *The Next Step in Evolution*. Skinner's discussion of Huxley's satirical use of the conditioned reflex in *Brave New World* can be found in his "Utopia as an Experimental Culture," 32–34.

69. Bryant, "You Are in My Power, You Will Do What I Tell You!" 51, 52.

70. Scheflin and Opton, *The Mind Manipulators*, 345, 346.

71. Anthony and Margroff, *The Ring*, 62.

72. Mason, "New Threat to Blacks," 66.

73. Valenstein, *Psychosurgery Debate*, 40.

74. Pines, *The Brain-Changers*, 205; Mark and Irwin, *Violence and the Brain*, 93–96. Pines (a journalist, not a medical specialist) gives a useful history of the experiments by Wilder Penfield, James Olds, John Lilly, and others on different forms of ESB.

75. Hibbard, *Conversation with William S. Burroughs*, 189. Burroughs was also deeply impressed with *A Clockwork Orange* and wrote a promotional statement for the novel. Bockris, *With William Burroughs*, 74.

76. Crichton, *The Terminal Man*, i–ii.

77. Ellison, "The Terminal Man," 77.

78. For a discussion of the parallels between Crichton's character and Mark and Irwin's patients, see Valenstein, *Brain Control*, 250–53.

79. Included in the 1973 Bantam edition of *The Terminal Man*.

80. Crichton, *The Terminal Man*, 117.

81. Ibid., 176.

82. As Crichton recognizes in his 1994 author's note to *Five Patients*, his 1970 study of Massachusetts General Hospital, the sheer size of computers at the time of writing *The Terminal Man* dated the novel and, by implication, made it possible for him to use it as a large discrete power source. The subsequent development of miniature computers removed this symbolic linkage between size and threat.

83. Lilly, *The Scientist*, 91, 147–53.

84. Crichton, *The Terminal Man*, 208.

85. Burgess, *A Clockwork Orange*, 128.

86. Crichton, *The Terminal Man*, 78.

87. Edwards, "People in Trouble," *New York Review of Books*, July 20, 1972.

88. Sturgeon, "The Terminal Man," 32–33.

89. Trembley, *Michael Crichton*, 48; Ellison, "The Terminal Man," 76.

90. Qtd. in Valenstein, *Brain Control*, 5.

91. When Benson goes to Doctor Ross's apartment to attack her while she is taking a shower, the sexual pathology to the attack is underlined by the obvious echoes of *Psycho*.

92. Ellison, "The Terminal Man," 77, felt that the novel's disturbing subtext focused on the connotations of the key word "terminal."

93. Rorvik, *As Man Becomes Machine*, 154.

94. Valenstein, *Brain Control*, 88.

95. Jones, "Feminist Science Fiction and Medical Ethics," 175.

96. Piercy, *Woman on the Edge of Time*, 193, 204.

97. Moylan, *Demand the Impossible*, 123–24.

98. Piercy, *Woman on the Edge of Time*, 279. For commentary on the motif of the monstrous, see Seabury, "The Monsters We Create," 131–43.

99. Piercy, *Woman on the Edge of Time*, 281, 282.

100. Kessler, "*Woman on the Edge of Time*: A Novel 'To Be of Use,'" 315.

101. Moylan, *Demand the Impossible*, 143.

■ 9. The Guinea Pigs

1. Collins, *In the Sleep Room*, 58, 135. For further commentary, see Gillmor, *I Swear by Apollo*.

2. Marks, *The Search for the "Manchurian Candidate*," 143.

3. Hebb, "The Motivating Effects of Exteroceptive Stimulation," 111.

4. A restatement of the Communist allegation that the U.S. was using biological weapons in Korea.

5. Pohl and Kornbluth, *The Wonder Effect*, 154.

6. The publisher's note to *The Mind Benders* states: "This story was suggested by experiments on the Reduction of Sensation recently carried out at MacGill [*sic*] University in Canada, at the University of Indiana, and other Universities in the United States."

7. Kennaway, *The Mind Benders*, 37, 40.

8. Vernon, *Inside the Black Room*, 15–16, an experimenter in sensory deprivation at Princeton, mentions these two popular perceptions of how these experiments could be applied but denies that the scientists were trying to achieve such purposes. Although he unsuccessfully wove political propaganda into some experiments, Vernon distinguishes his research from brainwashing with the following proviso: "Although America has never used such a technique and presumably never will, there can be no doubt that we could build a very effective brainwashing technique" (41). Vernon also draws a comparison between a subject's terrified experience of SD and Room 101 in *Nineteen Eighty-Four* (153).

9. Kennaway, *The Mind Benders*, 91, 92.

10. Ibid., 87, 95, 91.

11. Hebb, "The Motivating Effects of Exteroceptive Stimulation," 110. For Hebb, this was the lesson of Chinese Communist brainwashing.

12. Transcribed from the film. The most powerful image of the entrapped experimental subject here is of Longman (played by Dirk Bogarde) dressed as a frogman, held by ropes in suspension in the tank.

13. Kennaway, *The Mind Benders*, 136, 159.

14. French, *Circle of Revenge*, 96, 111.

15. Fleming, *On Her Majesty's Secret Service*, 130.

16. Disch, *Under Compulsion*, 148, 142.

17. Disch, *On Wings of Song*, 46.

18. Disch, *Bad Moon Rising*, viii.

19. Ibid., 297.

20. Disch, "Camp Concentration," Disch papers, Beinecke Library, Yale University, Princeton, New Jersey.

21. Disch's phrase in "Camp Concentration."

22. This story was rejected by U.S. publishers as "unsaleable" and finally appeared, like *Camp Concentration*, in the British journal *New Worlds*.

23. Disch, *Under Compulsion*, 96.

24. Disch, "Camp Concentration."

25. Disch, *Camp Concentration*, 32.

26. Ibid., 149.

27. Swirski, "Dystopia or Dischtopia?" 164.

28. Bain, *The Control of Candy Jones*, 60–61. For another memoir by a subject of CIA mind control, see O'Brien with Phillips, *Trance Formation of America*.

29. Scheflin and Opton, *The Mind Manipulators*, 470.

30. In chapter 46 of his novel Mann describes the national shame of the "torture-chamber" (the concentration camps) being thrown open to public view. Yet revelation remains a complex issue for all the narratives considered in this chapter, because so often processes are concealed beneath layers of secrecy.

31. O'Neill, "The Future in Books," 129.

32. Disch, *Camp Concentration*, 167.

33. Delany, *The Jewel-Hinged Jaw*, 187. Miller, "The Reference Library," 171, more bluntly describes the ending of the novel as a "stereotyped science fictional cop-out."

34. Francavilla, "Disching It Out," 247.

35. Crichton's novel gives his reader a fantasy of vicarious access to top-secret projects by simulating government documents in its preamble.

36. Rogers, *The Prisoner and the Danger Man*, 131.

37. Rakoff, *Inside the Prisoner*, 55.

38. The tests include drug-induced visualizations (3), lie-detection (4), psyche-delic duplication (5), subliminal suggestion (6), spatial replication (7), lobotomy (12), mind transfer (13), and induced regression to childhood (16).

39. Carrazé and Oswald, *The Prisoner*, 92.

40. Rakoff, *Inside the Prisoner*, 24.

41. Carrazé and Oswald, *The Prisoner*, 107.

42. Specifically the phrase was applied to the conduct of prisoners of war. *The Prisoner* resituates the notion of captivity within Number 6's own culture, thereby confirming an early statement by Number 2 that "both sides are becoming identi-cal" (Carrazé and Oswald, *The Prisoner*, 47).

43. Carrazé and Oswald, *The Prisoner*, 36.

44. Williams, "College Course File: Television Studies / Television Theories— Series and Mini-Series," 49. In Rogers, *The Prisoner and the Danger Man*, 139, Mc-Goohan, who wrote the script for the final episode, stated in a 1984 interview that when Number 6 enters his London house, "you *know* it's going to start all over again . . . when the door opens on its own—and there is no one behind it—exactly as the doors in the Village open, you *know* that someone's waiting in there, to start it all over again. He has no freedom."

45. Disch was sent dialogue-only scripts to work from (letter from Thomas M. Disch to David Seed, November 1, 1998). Other novels based on the series are David McDaniel's *The Prisoner: Who Is Number Two?* (New York: New English Library, 1982) and Hank Stine's *The Prisoner 2: A Day in the Life* (London: Dennis Dobson, 1979). Rakoff's *Inside the Prisoner* also gives valuable commentary on the series.

46. Disch, *The Prisoner*, 19.

47. Ibid., 113.

48. Ibid., 151.

49. Carrazé and Oswald, *The Prisoner*, 6, 226.

50. Blum, *The Simultaneous Man*, 22. The symbolism of beta in this novel cov-ers the second of a series, the higher frequency brain waves associated with agitation or concentration, and the goal of a project.

51. Marks, *The Search for the "Manchurian Candidate,"* 118–19.

52. Blum, *The Simultaneous Man*, 24.

53. Ibid., 137.

54. Berger, *Science Fiction*, 105.

55. Flodstrom, "Personal Identity in the Majipoor Trilogy, *To Live Again*, and *Downward to the Earth*," 76.

56. Silverberg, *The Second Trip*, 58; Pynchon, *Gravity's Rainbow*, 51. Silverberg also deals with surgical mind alteration in his 1974 story, "In the House of Double Minds" (collected in *The Feast of St. Dionysus*, 1975) where children routinely undergo operations to sever their two hemispheres.

57. Tanner, *City of Words*, 424.

58. Pynchon, *Gravity's Rainbow*, 290, 291.

59. Schaub, *Pynchon*, 90.

60. Pynchon, *Gravity's Rainbow*, 541–42.

61. Pavlov, *Conditioned Reflexes and Psychiatry*, 148.

62. Schaub, *Pynchon*, 92.

63. Pavlov, *Conditioned Reflexes and Psychiatry*, 144. Pavlov says relatively little about the applicability of his ideas to humans, but the conclusion to *Conditioned Reflexes* (1927) includes a discussion of hypnosis potentially relevant to mind control.

64. Melley, *Empire of Conspiracy*, 92.

65. Pynchon, *Gravity's Rainbow*, 147.

66. Marks, *The Search for the "Manchurian Candidate,"* 40–41, 186. Yurick had read Marks's book and was re-creating his own version of the Manchurian Candidate, so this source is very likely.

67. Yurick, *Richard A*, 42–43.

68. Ibid., 76, 80.

69. Ibid., 202, 235.

70. The novel feeds a retrospective awareness of covert activities back into the 1960s. Yurick has recorded his impressions of that decade as a time of unrestrained rival agencies in his essay "The Other Side," where he cites Marks's *The Search for the "Manchurian Candidate,"* among other works (Sayres et al, *The 60s without Apology*, 304–8).

71. Yurick, *Richard A*, 401.

72. The scientist explains to the attorney that his program was "Manchurian Candidate kind of stuff." Marks, *Conspiracy Theory*, 172.

73. Rhine, *My Brain Escapes Me*, 26.

■ 10. Cyberpunk and Other Revisions

1. Lange [Michael Crichton], *Drug of Choice*, 84–85.

2. Cook, *Mindbend*, 35.

3. Ibid., 176.

4. Ibid., 243.

5. Ibid., 210, 216.

6. Robinson, *Mindkiller*, 196. In his acknowledgements Robinson describes Niven's "Death by Ecstasy" as the "definitive story on the subject."

7. Bear's "noocytes" have been compared to microrobots doing comparable acts within the body.

8. Bear, *Tangents*, 39, 40.

9. Bear, *Blood Music*, 207. Suzy's own comparison here is between the changed humans and the Moonies, but the opposition between mass and individual dates back to the 1950s.

10. Bear, *Blood Music*, 208.

11. Anthony, *Brother Termite*, 157.

12. Regis, *Great Mambo Chicken and the Transhuman Condition*, 5.

13. Hjortsberg, *Gray Matters*, 88, 157.

14. Regis, *Great Mambo Chicken and the Transhuman Condition*, 154.

15. Roszak, *The Cult of Information*, 180.

16. Regis, *Great Mambo Chicken and the Transhuman Condition*, 205. Moravec exchanged letters with the science fiction novelist Frederik Pohl about collaborating on a story about a computer virus that wants to assemble a physical body.

17. Smith, *The Kramer Project*, i.

18. Watson, *War on the Mind*, 104.

19. Smith, *Kramer Project*, 184.

20. Berlyn, *The Integrated Man*, 2.

21. Benford, *Furious Gulf*, 36.

22. Shiner, *Frontera*, 201, 243–44. The novel was originally composed as the story "Soldier, Sailor." In the narrative, tension is set up between Kane's template of the hero (taken from Joseph Campbell) and the sequence fed into his programming.

23. Bukatman, *Terminal Identity*, 267, 270.

24. Ore, *Gaia's Toys*, 56.

25. Ibid., 185.

26. Ibid., 242.

27. Cadigan, *Mindplayers*, 6.

28. Kenny and Neilson, "The Cyberpunk Techofeminist," 27. The name Brain Police was taken from a Frank Zappa song but still carries Orwellian echoes.

29. Cadigan, *Mindplayers*, 41.

30. Ibid., 120.

31. E-mail message from Pat Cadigan to David Seed, June 10, 1999. In *Synners* VR addicts are called "pod-people."

32. Cadigan, *Dervish Is Digital*, 53.

33. Cadigan, *Mindplayers*, 272.

34. Turkle, "Who Am We?"

35. Turkle, *Life on the Screen: Identity in the Age of the Internet*, 248.

36. Dery, *Escape Velocity*, 232. Dery's discussion gives an excellent context for approaching writers like Pat Cadigan and, among his many insights, he derives a new confusion over the self from cybertechnology: "We don't know what to make of ourselves precisely because we are, more than ever before, able to *remake* ourselves" (223).

37. Cadigan, *Synners*, 69.

38. Wilson, *Prometheus Rising*, 129–31.

39. Another work that made an impact on Cadigan was Flo Conway and Jim Siegelman's 1978 study of cult brainwashing, *Snapping: America's Epidemic of Sudden Personality Change* (Philadelphia, Pa.: Lippincott, 1978).

40. Kenny and Neilson, "The Cyberpunk Techofeminists," 26–27; e-mail message, Pat Cadigan to David Seed, June 10, 1999.

41. Cadigan, *Fools*, 152.

42. Ibid., 72, 71, 97.

43. Varley, *Steel Beach*, 96.

44. Cadigan, *Dervish Is Digital*, 46.

45. E-mail message, Pat Cadigan to David Seed, June 11, 1999.

46. Cadigan, *Dervish Is Digital*, 21, 22.

47. McElroy, "Neural Neighborhoods and Other Concrete Abstracts," 210.

48. Miller, "Power and Perception in *Plus*," 174.

49. Porush, *The Soft Machine*, 178.

50. Hadas, "Green Thoughts on Being in Charge," 146, 144.

51. McElroy, *Plus*, 118, 121.

52. Ibid., 187.

53. Stephenson, *Snow Crash*, 197.

54. Hayles, "The Life Cycle of Cyborgs," 168. Hayles sees Lisa's death as the result of a kind of gender trespass, but both main characters are sexual casualties of war where the mutual implications of "entering" are traumatizing and fatal.

Bibliography

■ Archives

Richard Condon Archive. Mugar Memorial Library. Boston University. Boston, Massachusetts.

Thomas M. Disch Papers. Beinecke Library. Yale University. Princeton, New Jersey.

David Karp Papers. Mugar Memorial Library. Boston University. Boston, Massachusetts.

Ken Kesey Papers. University Library. University of Oregon. Eugene, Oregon.

P. M. A. Linebarger Papers. Hoover Institution. Stanford University. Stanford, California.

Publishers Association Archives. Reading University. Reading, Berkshire, United Kingdom.

National Security Council Papers. Dwight D. Eisenhower Library. Abilene, Texas.

Philip Wylie Papers. University Library. Princeton University. Princeton, New Jersey.

■ Books and Articles

Acker, Kathy. *Bodies of Work: Essays.* London: Serpent's Tail, 1997.

———. *Empire of the Senseless.* London: Picador, 1988.

———. *Hannibal Lecter, My Father.* New York: Semiotext(e), 1991.

———. "William Burroughs." http://acker.the hub.com.au/ackademy/burroughs. htm. Accessed January 10, 2004.

Adams, Donald James. "Thinking to Order." Review of *Brainwashing* by Edward Hunter. *New York Times Book Review*, May 20, 1956.

Allen, William Rodney, ed. *Conversations with Kurt Vonnegut.* Jackson: Univ. Press of Mississippi, 1988.

Althusser, Louis. *Lenin and Philosophy, and Other Essays.* Trans. Ben Brewster. London: NLB, 1971.

Amis, Kingsley. *The Anti-Death League.* Harmondsworth: Penguin, 1968.

Anisimov, Olga. *The Ultimate Weapon.* Chicago: Henry Regnery, 1953.

Anthony, Patricia. *Brother Termite.* London: Hodder and Stoughton, 1995.

Anthony, Piers, and Robert E. Margroff. *The Ring.* New York: Ace, 1968.

Axelrod, George. "The Manchurian Candidate. Screenplay: Final Shooting Script." January 10, 1962. Condon archive. Mugar Library.

Axelsson, Arne. *Restrained Response: American Novels of the Cold War and Korea, 1945–1962.* Westport, Conn.: Greenwood, 1990.

Bailey, Andrew. "A Clockwork Utopia: Semi-scrutable Stanley Kubrick Discusses his New Film." *Rolling Stone,* January 20, 1972.

Bain, David. *The Control of Candy Jones.* London: Futura, 1979.

Ballard, James Graham. *The Best Short Stories of J. G. Ballard.* New York: Holt Rinehart, 1978.

———. "J. G. Ballard on William S. Burroughs' Naked Truth." *Salon.com,* September 2, 1997. http://archive.salon.com/sept97/wsb970902.html. Accessed January 10, 2004.

Bartlett, Frederic Charles. *Remembering.* Cambridge: Cambridge Univ. Press, 1964.

Bassett, Richard, and Lewis H. Carlson. *And the Wind Blew Cold: The Story of an American POW in North Korea.* Kent, Ohio: Kent State Univ. Press, 2002.

Bauer, R. A. "Brainwashing: Psychology or Demonology?" *Journal of Social Issues* 13, no. 3 (1957): 41–47.

Bayley, Barrington J. *The Star Virus.* New York: Ace, 1970.

Bear, Greg. *Blood Music.* London: Arrow, 1988.

———. *Tangents.* London: Gollancz, 1990.

Becker, Stephen. *Dog Tags.* London: Barrie and Jenkins, 1974.

Bell-Metereau, Rebecca. "*Altered States* and the Popular Myth of Self-Discovery." *Journal of Popular Film and Television* 9, no. 4 (1982): 171–79.

Benford, Gregory. *Furious Gulf.* London: Gollancz, 1994.

Berger, Albert I. *The Magic That Works: John W. Campbell and the American Response to Technology.* San Bernardino, Calif.: Borgo, 1993.

———. "Towards a Science of the Nuclear Mind: Science-Fiction Origins of Dianetics." *Science-Fiction Studies* 16, no. 3 (1989): 123–44.

Berger, Harold L. *Science Fiction and the New Dark Age.* Bowling Green, Ohio: Bowling Green Univ. Popular Press, 1976.

Berger, Peter L., and Thomas Luckman. *The Social Construction of Reality.* Harmondsworth, U.K.: Penguin, 1976.

Berlyn, Michael. *The Integrated Man.* New York: Bantam, 1980.

Bester, Alfred. *The Demolished Man.* Chicago: Shasta, 1953.

———. *Redemolished.* New York: ibooks, 2000.

Biderman, Albert D. "Communist Attempts to Elicit False Confessions from Air Force Prisoners of War." *Bulletin of the New York Academy of Medicine* 33, no. 9 (1957): 616–25.

———. "The Image of 'Brainwashing.'" *Public Opinion Quarterly* 26 (1962): 547–63.

———. *March to Calumny: The Story of the American POWs in the Korean War.* New York: Arno, 1979.

Biderman, Albert D., and Herbert Zimmer, eds. *The Manipulation of Human Behaviour.* New York: John Wiley, 1961.

Bigsby, Christopher W. E., ed. *Approaches to Popular Culture.* London: Arnold, 1976.

Biskind, Peter. *Seeing Is Believing: How Hollywood Taught Us to Stop Worrying and Love the Fifties.* New York: Pantheon, 1983.

Black, David. *Acid: The Secret History of* LSD. London: Vision, 1998.

Bloch, Sidney, and Peter Reddaway. *Russia's Political Hospitals.* London: Futura, 1978.

Bloom, Harold, ed. *Ralph Ellison: Modern Critical Views.* New York: Chelsea House, 1986.

Blum, Ralph. *The Simultaneous Man.* New York: Bantam, 1971.

Bockris, Victor. *With William Burroughs: A Report from the Bunker.* Rev. ed. New York: St. Martin's Griffin, 1996.

Boer, Nicholas. *Cardinal Minszenty.* London: B.U.E., 1949.

Boon, Kevin A. "Temple Defiled: The Brainwashing of Temple Drake in Faulkner's *Sanctuary.*" *Faulkner Journal* 6, no. 3 (Spring 1991): 33–50.

Boulton, David. *The Making of Tania: The Patty Hearst Story.* London: New English Library, 1975.

Bowart, Walter. *Operation Mind Control.* London: Fontana Collins, 1978.

———. "The Secret History of Mind Control." CKLN-FM (Toronto) Mind Control Series. http://heart7.net/mcf/radio/ckln20.htm. Accessed January 5, 2004.

Braddon, Russell. *When the Enemy Is Tired.* New York: Viking, 1969.

"Brain-Washing: A Synthesis of the Romantic Dystopia on Psychopolitics." September 1996. http://home.tiscali.de/alex.sk/A_Stickley2.html. Accessed April 2, 2004.

Branden, Barbara. *The Passion of Ayn Rand.* London: W. H. Allen, 1987.

Brody, Benjamin. "Brainwashing and Oliver Twist." *University of Hartford Studies in Literature* 14, no. 2 (1982): 62–66.

Bronfen, Elisabeth. *Sylvia Plath.* Plymouth, U.K.: Northcote House, 1998.

Bross, Darrell. "A Primer on Hypnosis and Mind Control." *David Icke E-Magazine Mind Control Archives.* http://visitations.com/mindnet/MN158.HTM. Accessed January 7, 2004.

Brown, James A. C. *Techniques of Persuasion: From Propaganda to Brainwashing.* Harmondsworth, U.K.: Penguin, 1963.

Brune, Lester H., and Robert Higham, eds. *The Korean War: Handbook of Literature and Research.* Westport, Conn.: Greenwood, 1997.

Bryant, Ed. "You Are In My Power, You Will Do What I Tell You!" *Vertex* 1, no. 1 (April 1973): 50–52, 54.

Buchan, John. *The Three Hostages.* Oxford: Oxford Univ. Press, 1995.

Bucher, Commander Lloyd M., with Mark Rascovich. *Bucher: My Story.* Garden City, N.Y.: Doubleday, 1970.

Buckman, John. "Brainwashing, LSD, and CIA: Historical and Ethical Perspective." *Journal of Social Psychiatry* 23, no. 1 (Spring 1977): 8–19.

Budiansky, Stephen, Erica E. Goode, and Ted Gest. "The Cold War Experiments." *U.S. News and World Report,* January 24, 1994.

Budrys, Algis. *Who?* London: Gollancz, 1962.

Bukatman, Scott. *Terminal Identity: The Virtual Subject in Postmodern Science Fiction.* Durham, N.C.: Duke Univ. Press, 1993.

Bull, Emma. *Bone Dance: A Fantasy for Technophiles.* New York: Ace, 1991.

Bunting, Charles T. "An Interview in New York with Anthony Burgess." *Studies in the Novel* 5 (1973): 504–29.

Burgess, Anthony. "Clockwork Marmalade." *The Listener,* February 17, 1972.

——. *A Clockwork Orange.* New York: Norton, 1986.

——. *A Clockwork Orange: A Play with Music.* London: Century Hutchinson, 1987.

——. "A Fable for Social Scientists." *Horizon* 15 (Winter 1973): 12–15.

——. *One Man's Chorus: The Uncollected Writings.* New York: Carroll and Graf, 1998.

——. *1985.* London: Hutchinson, 1978.

Burroughs, William S. *The Adding Machine: Collected Essays.* London: John Calder, 1985.

——. *Ah Pook Is Here and Other Texts.* New York: Riverrun, 1979.

——. *Ali's Smile: Naked Scientology.* Bonn, Ger.: Expanded Media, 1995. Originally appeared in the *Los Angeles Free Press,* March 6, 1970.

——. *Blade Runner, A Movie.* Berkeley, Calif: Blue Wind , 1994.

——. *The Burroughs File.* San Francisco: City Lights, 1984.

——. *Exterminator!* London: Calder and Boyars, 1974.

——. "The Hallucinatory Operators Are Real." *SF Horizons* 2 (Winter 1965): 3–12.

——. *Interzone.* Ed. James Grauerholz. New York: Viking, 1989.

——. *Last Words: The Final Journals of William S. Burroughs.* Ed. James Grauerholz. New York: Grove, 2000.

——. *The Letters of William S. Burroughs, 1945–1959.* Ed. Oliver Harris. London: Picador, 1993.

——. *My Education: A Book of Dreams.* London: Picador, 1995.

——. *Naked Lunch.* New York: Grove, 1966.

——. *Nova Express.* New York: Grove, 1965.

——. *Queer.* New York: Viking, 1985.

——. *The Soft Machine.* London: Paladin, 1986.

——. *The Western Lands.* London: Picador, 1988.

——. *The Wild Boys.* London: Corgi, 1974.

——, and Brion Gysin. *The Third Mind.* London: John Calder, 1979.

——, with Daniel Odier. *The Job.* Rev. ed. New York: Grove, 1974.

Busch, Francis X. *Enemies of the State.* Indianapolis, Ind.: Bobbs Merrill, 1954.

Busch, Frederick. *War Babies.* New York: New Directions, 1989.

Cadigan, Pat. *Dervish Is Digital.* London: Macmillan, 2000.

——. *Mindplayers.* London: Gollancz, 1988.

——. *Synners.* London: HarperCollins, 1991.

——. "An Interview with Pat Cadigan." "No Browsing" Web site. www.to.or.at/ pcadigan/intervw.htm. Accessed January 21, 2004.

Campbell, John W. "The Brain Stealers of Mars." In *Before the Golden Age Trilogy: A Science Fiction Anthology,* ed. Isaac Asimov, 764–81. London: Macdonald, 1988.

——. "Brain-Washing." *Astounding Science Fiction* 54, no. 2 (Oct. 1954): 6–7, 160–62.

——. "Evaluation of Dianetics." *Astounding Science Fiction* 48, no. 2 (Oct. 1951): 6–9, 160–69.

Camper, Frank. *The MK/Ultra Secret: An Account of CIA Deception.* Savannah, Ga.: Christopher Scott, 1996.

Cannon, Martin. *The Controllers: A New Hypothesis of Alien Abduction.* http://www.consitution.org/abus/controll.htm. Accessed April 7, 2004.

Carrazé, Alain, and Hélène Oswald. *The Prisoner: A Televisionary Masterpiece.* Trans. Christine Donougher. London: Virgin, 1995.

Carruthers, Susan L. "*The Manchurian Candidate* (1962) and the Cold War Brainwashing Scare." *Historical Journal of Film, Radio and Television* 18, no. 1 (1998): 75–94.

——. "Redeeming the Captives: Hollywood and the Brainwashing of America's Prisoners of War in Korea." *Film History* 8, no. 1 (1998): 275–94.

Central Intelligence Agency. "A Report on Communist Brainwashing." November 2, 1956. Declassified CIA document Mori ID 26927. http://www.totse.com/en/conspiracy/mind_control/165615.htm. Accessed April 2, 2004.

Cesarani, David. *Arthur Koestler: The Homeless Mind.* London: Heinemann, 1998.

Charters, Ann, ed. *The Beats: Literary Bohemians in Postwar America.* Detroit, Mich.: Gale Research, 1983.

Ciment, Michel. *Kubrick.* Trans. by Gilbert Adair. London: Collins, 1980.

Clark, Brian F. C. *The Genetic Code.* London: Edward Arnold, 1977.

Clarke, Arthur C. *The City and the Stars.* London: Orion, 2001.

——. *Profiles of the Future.* London: Scientific Book Club, 1962.

Coblentz, Stanton A. *Hidden World.* New York: Avalon, 1957.

Cochran, David. *America Noir: Underground Writers and Filmmakers of the Postwar Era.* Washington, D.C.: Smithsonian Institution, 2000.

Cohen, Alexander J. "Clockwork Orange and the Aestheticization of Violence." *CinemaSpace.* http://cinemaspace.berkeley.edu/AlexCohen/ClockworkOrange/aestheticviolence.html. Accessed January 11, 2004.

Collins, Anne. *In the Sleep Room: The Story of the CIA Brainwashing Experiments in Canada.* Toronto: Lester and Orpen Dennys, 1988.

Collins, Larry. *Maze.* New York: Simon and Schuster, 1989.

Collins, Tom. "Carl Solomon." In *The Beats: Literary Bohemians in Postwar America*, part 2: M-Z, ed. Ann Charters. Detroit, Mich.: Gale Research, 1983.

Condon, Richard. *Emperor of America.* London: Sphere, 1991.

——. *The Manchurian Candidate.* New York: Signet, 1960.

——. "'Manchurian Candidate' in Dallas." *The Nation*, December 28, 1963.

——. "Richard Condon." In *Contemporary Authors Autobiography Series*, vol. 1, ed. Dedria Bryfonski, 185–99. Detroit, Mich.: Gale Research, 1984.

——. *The Whisper of the Axe.* New York: Dial, 1976.

Constantine, Alex. *Psychic Dictatorship in the USA.* Portland, Ore.: Feral House, 1995.

——. *Virtual Government: CIA Mind Control Operations in America.* Portland, Ore.: Feral House, 1997.

Cook, Robin. *Mindbend.* London: Pan, 1986.

Corke, Hilary. "The Banyan Tree." *Encounter* 3, no. 2 (Aug. 1954): 76–79.

Counts, George S., and Nucia Lodge. *The Country of the Blind: The Soviet System of Mind Control.* Boston, Mass.: Houghton Mifflin, 1949.

Crawford, A. "Medico-Political Considerations of Psychosurgery." In *Psychosurgery and Society*, ed. J. S. Smith and L. G. Kiloh, 109–13. Oxford: Pergamom, 1977.

Crichton, Michael. *The Terminal Man.* New York: Knopf, 1972.

—— [John Lange, pseud.]. *Drug of Choice.* New York: Signet, 1970.

Crick, Bernard. *George Orwell: A Life.* London: Secker and Warburg, 1980.

Crossley, Robert. *Olaf Stapledon: Speaking for the Future.* Liverpool, U.K.: Liverpool Univ. Press, 1994.

Crossman, Richard, ed. *The God That Failed: Six Studies in Communism.* London: Right Book Club, 1950.

Csicsery-Ronay, Istvan, Jr. "Zamyatin and the Strugatskys: The Representation of Freedom in We and *The Snail on the Slope.*" In *Zamyatin's "We": A Collection of Critical Essays*, ed. Gary Kern, 236–59. Ann Arbor, Mich.: Ardis, 1988.

Cullinan, John. "Anthony Burgess's A *Clockwork Orange*: Two Versions." *ELN* 9 (1972): 287–92.

Danziger, Marie. "*Basic Instinct*: Grappling for Post-Modern Mind Control." *Literature/Film Quarterly* 22, no. 1 (1994): 7–10.

"David Karp." Author profile. *Saturday Review*, October 26, 1957.

Davies, S. J. *In Spite of Dungeons.* London: Hodder and Stoughton, 1954.

Deane, Philip. *Captive in Korea.* London: Hamish Hamilton, 1953.

Deighton, Len. *The Billion Dollar Brain.* London: Triad Granada, 1981.

——. *The Ipcress File.* St. Albans, U.K.: Panther, 1975.

Delany, Samuel R. *The Jewel-Hinged Jaw: Notes of the Language of Science Fiction.* New York: Berkley, 1978.

De Lauretis, Teresa. "Rebirth in *The Bell Jar.*" In *Sylvia Plath: The Critical Heritage*, ed. Linda Wagner-Martin, 124–34. London: Routledge, 1988.

Delgado, José M. R. *Physical Control of the Mind: Toward a Psychocivilized Society.* New York: Harper and Row, 1969.

Del Torto, John. "The Human Machine," *Neurotica* 8 (Spring 1951): 34.

Dery, Mark. *Escape Velocity: Cyberculture at the End of the Century.* London: Hodder and Stoughton, 1996.

Deutscher, Isaac. *Heretics and Renegades and Other Essays.* London: Jonathan Cape, 1969.

D'haen, Theo. "Language and Power in Orwell and Burgess." In *Essays from Oceania and Eurasia: Orwell in 1984*, ed. B. J., Suykerbuyk, 43–55. Antwerp, Belgium: Antwerp Univ. Press, 1984.

Dick, Philip K. "Drugs, Hallucinations, and the Quest for Reality." In *The Shifting Realities of Philip K. Dick: Selected Literary and Philosophical Writings*, ed. Lawrence Sutin, 167–74. New York: Pantheon, 1995.

Di Filippo, Paul. "Eye to Eye with Thomas M. Disch." *Science Fiction Eye* 11 (1992): 39–48.

Disch, Thomas M. *Camp Concentration.* New York: Carroll and Graf, 1988.

——. *Getting Into Death and Other Stories.* New York: Knopf, 1976.

——. *On Wings of Song.* New York: St. Martin's, 1979.

————. *The Prisoner.* London: New English Library, 1980.

————. *Under Compulsion.* London: Hart Davis, 1968. U.S. title *Fun with Your New Head* (1971).

Disch, Thomas M., ed. *Bad Moon Rising.* New York: Harper and Row, 1973.

Doctorow, Edgar Lawrence. *The Book of Daniel.* London: Pan, 1982.

Doherty, Thomas. "A Second Look." *Cineaste* 16, no. 4 (1988): 30–31.

Dollard, John. "Men Who Are Tortured by the Awful Fear of Torture." *New York Times Book Review,* July 29, 1956.

Donoghue, Denis. "The Brainwashing of Lemuel Gulliver." *Southern Review* 32, no. 1 (1996): 128–46.

Dorman, Thomas. "Brainwashing." Mind Control Forum. http://www.mindcontrol forums.com/brain_washing.htm. Accessed January 7, 2004.

Dos Passos, John. *The Major Nonfictional Prose.* Ed. by Donald Pizer. Detroit, Mich.: Wayne State Univ. Press, 1988.

Drought, James. *The Secret.* New York: Avon, 1963.

Dulles, Allen, W. "Brain Warfare—Russia's Secret Weapon." *U.S. News and World Report,* May 8, 1953.

————. *The Craft of Intelligence.* London: Weidenfeld and Nicolson, 1963.

Edwards, Paul M. *A Guide to Films on the Korean War.* Westport, Conn.: Green-wood, 1997.

Edwards, Thomas R. " People in Trouble." *New York Review of Books,* July 20, 1972.

Effinger, George Alec. *When Gravity Falls.* New York: Bantam, 1988.

Ehrhart, W. R., and P. K. Jason, eds. *Retrieving Bones: Stories and Poems of the Korean War.* New Brunswick, N.J.: Rutgers Univ. Press, 1999.

Ellison, Harlan. "The Terminal Man." *Vertex* 2, no. 2 (June 1974): 21–25, 76–77.

Ellison, Ralph. *Invisible Man.* Harmondsworth, U.K.: Penguin, 1976.

————. *Shadow and Act.* New York: Vintage, 1972.

Elliston, Jon. "Subliminal CIA." *Metareligion.* http://www.meta-religion.com/Secret_ societies/Mind_control/subliminal_cia.htm. Accessed January 13, 2004.

Elsaesser, Thomas. "Screen Violence: Emotional Structure and Ideological Function in *A Clockwork Orange.*" In *Approaches to Popular Culture,* ed. C. W. E. Bigsby, 171–200. London: Arnold, 1976.

Endicott, Stephen, and Edward Hagerman. *The United States and Biological Warfare: Secrets from the Early Cold War and Korea.* Bloomington: Indiana Univ. Press, 1998.

Engelhardt, Tom. *The End of Victory Culture: Cold War America and the Disillusioning of a Generation.* London: Harper Collins, 1995.

Estabrooks, George H. *Hypnotism.* London: Museum, 1959.

————. "Hypnotism Comes of Age." *Science Digest* (April 1977): 44–50.

Farber, I. E., Harry F. Harlow, and Louis Jolyan West. "Brainwashing, Conditioning, and *DDD* (Debility, Dependency, and Dread)." *Sociometry* 20 (1957): 271–85.

Faroohar, Kam. "William Burroughs: The Interview." *NSM* 4 (February 1988): 34–36.

Farrar-Hockley, Anthony H. *The Edge of the Sword.* London: Muller, 1954.

Finney, Jack. "The Body Snatchers." *Collier's,* part 1, November 26, 1954; part 2, December 10, 1954; part 3, December 24, 1954.

——. *Invasion of the Body Snatchers.* New York: Simon and Schuster, 1989.

Fleming, Ian. *The Man with the Golden Gun.* London: Hodder and Stoughton, 1990.

——. *On Her Majesty's Secret Service.* London: Hodder and Stoughton, 1989.

Flodstrom, John H. "Personal Identity in the Majipoor Trilogy, *To Live Again,* and *Downward to the Earth.*" In *Robert Silverberg's Many Trapdoors: Critical Essays on his Science Fiction,* ed. Charles L. Elkins and Martin H. Greenberg, 73–94. Westport, Conn.: Greenwood, 1992.

Flood, Charles B. *More Lives Than One.* Boston, Mass.: Houghton Mifflin, 1967.

Foucault, Michel. *Discipline and Punish: The Birth of the Prison.* Trans. Alan Sheridan. Harmondsworth, U.K.: Penguin, 1977.

Foundation of Human Understanding. *Brain-Washing: A Synthesis of the Russian Textbook of Psychopolitics.* Fort Worth, Texas: Foundation of Human Understanding, 1991.

Fox, Julian. Review of *Telefon. Films and Filming* 24, no. 9 (June 1978): 37–40.

Frame, Janet. *Faces in the Water.* London: Women's Press, 1989.

Francavilla, Joseph. "Disching It Out: An Interview with Thomas M. Disch." *Science-Fiction Studies* 12 (1985): 241–51.

Frank, Pat. *An Affair of State.* Philadelphia, Pa.: Lippincott, 1948.

——. *Forbidden Area.* Philadelphia, Pa.: Lippincott, 1956.

——. *Hold Back the Night.* London: Hamish Hamilton, 1952.

——. "In Enemy Hands." *Saturday Evening Post,* December 6, 1958.

Franklin, Bruce. "Foreword to J. G. Ballard's 'The Subliminal Man.'" In *SF: The Other Side of Realism: Essays on Modern Fantasy and Science Fiction,* ed. T. D. Clareson, 199–203. Bowling Green, Ohio: Bowling Green Popular Press, 1971.

French, Michael. *Circle of Revenge.* New York: Bantam, 1988.

Friedan, Betty. *The Feminine Mystique.* London: Gollancz, 1964.

Friedman, Sanford. *Totempole.* San Francisco, Calif.: North Point, 1984.

Friedman, Stanley. "Condon's *The Manchurian Candidate: Hamlet* Freely Adapted." *Journal of Popular Culture* 2, no. 3 (1968): 510–12.

Fromm, Eric. *The Sane Society.* London: Routledge and Kegan Paul, 1956.

Gallery, Daniel V. "We Can Baffle the Brainwashers!" *Saturday Evening Post,* January 22, 1955.

Gallico, Paul. *Trial by Terror.* New York: Knopf, 1952.

Gehrke, Pat J. "Deviant Subjects in Foucault and *A Clockwork Orange:* Congruent Critiques of Criminological Constructions of Subjectivity." *Critical Studies in Media Communication* 18, no. 3 (2001): 270–84.

Gernsback, Hugo. *Ralph 124C41+.* Lincoln: Univ. of Nebraska Press, 2000.

Gillmor, Don. *I Swear by Apollo: Dr Ewen Cameron and the* CIA *Brainwashing Experiments.* Montreal, Canada: Eden, 1987.

Ginsberg, Allen. *Deliberate Prose.* Harmondsworth, U.K.: Penguin, 2000.

Godshalk, William L. "Alfred Bester." In *Twentieth-Century Science-Fiction Writers, Part I,* ed. David Cowart and T. L. Wymer, 30–36. Detroit, Mich.: Gale Research, 1981.

Goffman, Erving. *Asylums.* Harmondsworth, U.K.: Penguin, 1991.

Goodman, Michael B., and Lemuel B. Coley. *William S. Burroughs: A Reference Guide.* New York: Garland, 1990.

Gorightly, Adam. "PKD, the Unicorn and Soviet Psychotronics." http://www.alphane. com/moon/PalmTree/unicorn.htm. Accessed April 8, 2004.

Grauerholz, James, ed. *Last Words: The Final Journals of William S. Burroughs.* New York: Grove, 2000.

Gregory, Chris. *Be Seeing You . . . Decoding the Prisoner.* Luton, U.K.: Univ. of Luton Press, 1997.

Hadas, Pamela White. "Green Thoughts on Being in Charge: Discovering Joseph McElroy's *Plus.*" *Review of Contemporary Fiction* 10, no. 1 (1990): 140–55.

Hammond, John, ed. *The Complete Short Stories of H. G. Wells.* London: Phoenix, 2000.

Harris, Harold, ed. *Astride Two Cultures: Arthur Koestler at 70.* London: Hutchinson, 1975.

Harris, Oliver, ed. *The Letters of William S. Burroughs, 1945–1959.* London: Picador, 1993.

Harris, Ralph, and Arthur Selden. *Advertising in a Free Society.* London: Institute for Economic Affairs, 1959.

Harrison, Emma. "Study Cites Basis of Brainwashing." *New York Times,* September 6, 1957.

Hartley, Leslie P. *Facial Justice.* London: Hamish Hamilton, 1960.

Hastings, Max. *The Korean War.* London: Michael Joseph, 1987.

Hayles, N. Katherine, "The Life Cycle of Cyborgs: Writing the Posthuman." In *Cybersexualities: A Reader on Feminist Theory, Cyborgs and Cyberspace,* ed. Jenny Wolmark, 157–73. Edinburgh, Scot.: Edinburgh Univ. Press, 1999.

Hebb, Donald O. "The Motivating Effects of Exteroceptive Stimulation." *American Psychologist* 13 (1958): 109–13.

Heinlein, Robert A. *Double Star.* Boston, Mass.: Gregg, 1978.

———. *The Puppet Masters.* Boston, Mass.: Gregg, 1979.

———. *6 X H: Six Stories.* New York: Pyramid, 1961.

Herman, Ellen. "The Career of Cold War Psychology." *Radical History Review* 63 (Fall 1995): 52–85.

Hibbard, Allen, ed. *Conversations with William S. Burroughs.* Jackson: Univ. Press of Mississippi, 1999.

Hill, Gladwin. "Brain-Washing: Time for a Policy." *Atlantic Monthly* 195, no. 4 (1955): 58–62.

Hinkle, Lawrence E., Jr., and Harold G. Wolff. "Communist Interrogation and Indoctrination of 'Enemies of the State'" A.M.A. *Archives of Neurology and Psychiatry* 76 (1956): 115–74.

Hinshelwood, Robert D. *Therapy or Coercion: Does Psychoanalysis Differ from Brainwashing?* London: Karnac, 1997.

Hinson, Hal. "The Manchurian Candidate." *Washington Post,* February 13, 1988.

Hjortsberg, William. *Gray Matters.* London: Gollancz, 1971.

Hoberman, J. "Paranoia and the Pods." *Sight and Sound* 4, no. 5 (May 1994): 28–31.

———. "When Dr. No Met Dr. Strangelove." *Sight and Sound* 13, no. 12 (Dec. 1993): 16–21.

Hooker, Richard. *MASH.* New York: William Morrow, 1968.

Hoover, Edgar J. "The H-Files: FBI Files on L. Ron Hubbard." Letter from J. Edgar Hoover to special agent in charge, Los Angeles, April 17 1956. *Operation Clambake*. www.xenu.net/archive/FBI/fbi-141.html. Accessed January 19, 2004.

Hubbard, L. Ron. "Dianetics: The Evolution of a Science." *Astounding Science Fiction* 45, no. 3 (May 1950): 43–87.

Hunter, Edward. *The Black Book on Red China*. New York: Bookmailer, 1961.

———. *Brainwashing from Pavlov to Powers*. Linden, N.J.: Bookmailer, 1965.

———. "Brain-Washing in 'New' China." *The New Leader*, October 7, 1950.

———. *Brain-Washing in Red China: The Calculated Destruction of Men's Minds*. 2d ed. New York: Pyramid, 1953.

———. *Brainwashing: The Story of the Men Who Defied It*. New York: Pyramid, 1957.

———. "'Brain-Washing' Tactics Force Chinese into Ranks of Communist Party." *Miami Sunday News*, September 24, 1950.

———. *Communist Psychological Warfare (Brainwashing): Consultation with Edward Hunter*. Washington, D.C.: Government Printing Office, 1958.

Hunter, Lynette. *George Orwell: The Search for a Voice*. Milton Keynes, U.K.: Open Univ. Press, 1984.

Huston, Penelope. "Tolchoked by Kubrick." *Times* (London), January 8, 1972.

Huxley, Aldous. *Brave New World*. London: Chatto and Windus, 1959.

———. *Complete Essays*. 6 vols. Ed. Robert S. Baker and James Sexton. Chicago: Ivan R. Dee, 2000–2002.

———. "A Footnote about *1984*." *World Review* 16 (June 1950): 66.

———. *The Human Situation*. London: Harper Collins, 1994.

———. *Letters*. Edited by Grover Smith. London: Chatto and Windus, 1969.

———. *Moksha: Writings on Psychedelics and the Visionary Experience, 1931–1963*. Ed. Michael Horowitz and Cynthia Palmer. Los Angeles, Calif.: J. P. Tarcher, 1982.

———. *Science, Liberty and Peace*. London: Chatto and Windus, 1947.

"Huxley Fears New Persuasion Could Subvert Democratic Procedures." *New York Times*, May 19, 1958.

Hyde, Margaret O. *Brainwashing and Other Forms of Mind Control*. New York: McGraw-Hill, 1977.

Icke, David. "Walter H. Bowart Radio Interview." *David Icke E-Magazine* 21 (Feb. 2001). www.davidicke.net/emagazine/vol21/research/bowart.html. Accessed January 7, 2004.

Ingersoll, Earl G., ed. *Putting the Questions Differently: Interviews with Doris Lessing, 1964–1994*. London: Harper Collins, 1996.

Ivie, Robert L. "Diffusing Cold War Demagoguery: Murrow versus McCarthy in 'See It Now'" In *Cold War Rhetoric. Strategy, Metaphor, and Ideology*, ed. M. J. Medhurst et al., 74–75. Westport: Greenwood, 1990.

Jackson, Tony. "*The Manchurian Candidate* and the Gender of the Cold War." *Literature/ Film Quarterly* 28, no. 1 (2000): 34–40.

Jameson, Storm. *Then We Shall Hear Singing: A Fantasy in C-Major*. London: Cassell, 1942.

Johnson, Eva. Review of *Night* by Francis Pollini. *San Francisco Chronicle*, September 10, 1961.

Johnson, Glen M. "'We'd Fight . . . We Had To': *The Body Snatchers* as Novel and Film." *Journal of Popular Culture* 13, no. 1 (1979): 5–14.

Jones, Anne Hudson. "Feminist Science Fiction and Medical Ethics: Marge Piercy's *Woman on the Edge of Time*." In *The Intersection of Science Fiction and Philosophy*, ed. R. E. Myers, 171–83.Westport, Conn.: Greenwood, 1983.

Karp, David. *The Last Believers.* London: Cape, 1965.

——. "A Look Back into the Tube." In *Pop Culture in America*, ed. David Manning White, 96–104. Chicago: Quadrangle, 1970.

——. *One.* London: Gollancz, 1967.

——. "Organization Men in Revolt." *Saturday Review*, June 15, 1957.

Kazin, Alfred, ed. *Writers at Work: The "Paris Review" Interviews.* Third Series. London: Secker and Warburg, 1968.

Kelley, Frank K. "Famine on Mars." *Astounding Stories* 14, no. 1 (Sept. 1934): 72–97.

Kennaway, James. *The Mind Benders.* New York: Signet, 1964.

Kenny, John, and Robert Neilson. "The Cyberpunk Techofeminist: Pat Cadigan Interviewed." *Albedo* 1, no. 5 (1994): 24–31.

Kent, S. A. "Brainwashing in Scientology's Rehabilitation Project Force (RDF)." http://www.skeptictank.org/hs/brainwas.htm. Accessed April 7, 2004.

Kesey, Ken. "The Art of Fiction CXXVI." *Paris Review* 130 (1994): 58–94.

——. *The Further Inquiry.* New York: Viking Penguin, 1990.

——. *Kesey's Garage Sale.* New York: Viking, 1973.

——. *One Flew Over the Cuckoo's Nest: Text and Criticism.* Ed. John C. Pratt. Harmondsworth, U.K.: Penguin, 1977.

Kessler, Carol F. "*Woman on the Edge of Time*: A Novel 'To Be of Use.'" *Extrapolation* 28, no. 4 (1987): 310–18.

Key, William Bryan. *Subliminal Seduction: Ad Media's Manipulation of Not So Innocent America.* New York: Signet, 1974.

Kies, Daniel. "Fourteen Types of Passivity: Suppressing Agency in *Nineteen Eighty-Four*." In *The Revised Orwell*, ed. Jonathan Rose, 47–60. East Lansing: Michigan State Univ. Press, 1992.

Kinkead, Eugene. *In Every War but One.* New York: Norton, 1959. U.K. title: *Why They Collaborated.*

Koestler, Arthur. *Darkness at Noon.* London: Cape, 1970.

——. *Drinkers of Infinity: Essays, 1955–1967.* London: Hutchinson, 1968.

——. *The Invisible Writing.* London: Hutchinson, 1969.

——. *The Yogi and the Commissar.* London: Cape, 1945.

Kostelanetz, Richard, ed. *American Writing Today.* Vol. 1. Washington, D.C.: International Communications Agency, 1982.

Kress, Kenneth A. "Parapsychology in Intelligence: A Personal Review and Conclusions." *Parascope.com.* http://parascope.com/ds/articles/parapsychologyDoc.htm. Accessed January 10, 2004. First published in *Studies in Intelligence* (Winter 1977). Released to the public in 1996.

Kubark. "KUBARK Counterintelligence Interrogation." *Parascope.com.* www.parascope. com/articles/0397/kubark06.htm. Accessed January 5, 2004.

Kubrick, Stanley. *Stanley Kubrick's Clockwork Orange.* New York: Ballantine, 1972.

Kumar, Krishan. *Utopia and Anti-Utopia in Modern Times*. Oxford, U.K.: Blackwell, 187.

Kunz, Don. "Mechanistic and Totemistic Symbolization in Kesey's *One Flew Over the Cuckoo's Nest*." In *A Casebook on Ken Kesey's "One Flew Over the Cuckoo's Nest*," ed. G. J. Searles, 81–101. Albuquerque: Univ. of New Mexico Press, 1992.

Laing, Ronald D. *The Divided Self: An Existential Study in Sanity and Madness*. Harmondsworth, U.K.: Penguin, 1978.

Lamott, Kenneth. "Memoirs of a Brainwasher." *Harper's Magazine* 212 (June 1956): 73–76.

Landesman, Jay, ed. *Neurotica 1948–1951*. London: Jay Landesman, 1981.

Lange, Oliver. *Vandenburg*. New York: Bantam, 1972.

Langford, David. "Dangerous Thoughts." *Foundation* 49 (Summer 1990): 56–57.

Lauter, Paul. Review of *Night*, by Francis Pollini. *New Republic*, September 11, 1961.

LaValley, Al, ed. *Invasion of the Body Snatchers*. New Brunswick, N.J.: Rutgers Univ. Press, 1989.

Lawrence, Lincoln, and Kenn Thomas. *Mind Control, Oswald and JFK: Were We Controlled?* Kempton, Ill.: Adventures Unlimited, 1995.

Leary, Timothy. *The Politics of Ecstasy*. London: Granada, 1970.

LeClair, Thomas. "Essential Opposition: The Novels of Anthony Burgess." *Critique: Studies in Modern Fiction* 12, no. 3 (1971): 77–94.

Lee, Martin A., and Bruce Shlain. *Acid Dreams: The Complete Social History of LSD. The CIA, the Sixties, and Beyond*. New York: Grove Weidenfeld, 1992.

Le Gacy, Arthur. "*Invasion of the Body Snatchers*: A Metaphor for the Fifties." *Literature/Film Quarterly* 6, no 3 (1978): 285–92.

Leiber, Fritz. "Snaring the Human Mind." *If: Worlds of SF* 1, no. 11 (Sept. 1954): 55–61.

Lessing, Doris. *Briefing for a Descent into Hell*. St. Albans, U.K.: Granada, 1980.

———. *The Four-Gated City*. London: McGibbon and Kee, 1969.

Leviero, Anthony H. "For the Brainwashed: Pity or Punishment?" *New York Times Magazine*, August 14, 1955.

Levin, Martin. "When the Enemy's Tired." Review of *When the Enemy Is Tired*, by Russell Braddon. *New York Times Book Review*, April 13, 1969.

Levine, Isaac Don. *The Mind of an Assassin*. New York: Farrar Straus and Cudahy, 1959.

Lifton, Robert Jay. *Thought Reform and the Psychology of Totalism: A Study of "Brainwashing" in China*. Harmondsworth, U.K.: Penguin, 1967.

Lilly, John C. *The Scientist: A Novel Autobiography*. Philadelphia, Pa.: Lippincott, 1976.

Linebarger, Paul M. A. [Cordwainer Smith, pseud.]. *Norstrilia*. Framingham, Mass.: NESFA, 1994.

———. *Psychological Warfare*, 2d ed. Washington, D.C.: Combat Forces, 1954.

———. [Cordwainer Smith, pseud.]. *The Rediscovery of Man*. Framingham, Mass.: NESFA, 1993.

Lockridge, Richard, and George H. Estabrooks. *Death in the Mind*. Cleveland, Ohio: World, 1947.

London, Perry. *Behavior Control*. New York: Harper and Row, 1969.

Loydell, Rupert, ed. *My Kind of Angel: i.m. William Burroughs*. Exeter, U.K.: Stride, 1998.

Lydenberg, Robin. *Word Cultures: Radical Theory and Practice in William S. Burroughs' Fiction.* Urbana: Univ. of Illinois Press, 1987.

Lynn, Jack. *The Turncoat.* London: Robson, 1976.

MacDonald, George P. "Control by Camera: Milos Forman as Subjective Narrator." In *A Casebook on Ken Kesey's "One Flew Over the Cuckoo's Nest,"* ed. George J. Searles, 163–72. Albuquerque: Univ. of New Mexico Press, 1992.

Macpherson, Pat. *Reflecting on* The Bell Jar. London: Routledge, 1991.

Manning, Nick. *The Therapeutic Community Movement: Charisma and Routinization.* London and New York: Routledge, 1989.

Marcus, Greil. "The Last American Dream." *The Threepenny Review* 38 (Summer 1989): 3–5.

———. *The Manchurian Candidate.* London: British Film Institute, 2002.

Mark, Vernon H., and Frank R. Irwin. *Violence and the Brain.* New York: Harper and Row, 1970.

Marks, J. H. *Conspiracy Theory.* New York: Signet, 1997.

Marks, John. *The Search for the "Manchurian Candidate": The CIA and Mind Control.* London: Allen Lane, 1979.

Marrs, Jim. *The Enigma Files: The True Story of America's Psychic Warfare Program.* Westminster, Md.: Harmony, 1995.

Mason, B. J. "New Threat to Blacks: Brain Surgery to Control Behavior." *Ebony*, February 1973.

Matheson, Richard. "The Waker Dreams." *Galaxy Science Fiction* 1, no. 3 (Dec. 1950): 93–105.

McCarthy, Kevin, and Ed Gorman, eds. *"They're Here . . ." Invasion of the Body Snatchers: A Tribute.* New York: Berkeley Boulevard, 1999.

McCracken, Samuel. "Novel into Film; Novelist into Critic: A Clockwork Orange . . . Again." *Antioch Review* 32, no. 3 (June 1973): 427–36.

McElroy, Joseph. "Neural Networks and Other Concrete Abstracts." *Tri-Quarterly* 34 (Fall 1975): 201–17.

———. *Plus.* New York: Knopf, 1977.

McGrath, Thomas. *The Gates of Ivory, the Gates of Horn.* Chicago: Another Chicago Press, 1987.

Medhurst, Martin J., et al., eds. *Cold War Rhetoric: Strategy, Metaphor and Ideology.* Westport, Conn.: Greenwood, 1990.

Meerloo, Joost A. M. "The Crime of Menticide." *American Journal of Psychiatry* 107 (1951): 594–98.

———. "Pavlovian Strategy as a Weapon of Menticide." *American Journal of Psychiatry* 110 (1954): 809–13.

———. "Pavlov's Dogs and Communist Brainwashers." *New York Times Magazine,* May 9, 1954.

———. *The Rape of the Mind: The Psychology of Thought Control, Menticide, and Brainwashing.* Cleveland, Ohio: World, 1956.

Melley, Timothy. *Empire of Conspiracy: The Culture of Paranoia in Postwar America.* Ithaca, N.Y.: Cornell Univ. Press, 2000.

Meyers, Jeffrey, ed. *George Orwell: The Critical Heritage*. London: Routledge and Kegan Paul, 1975.

Miles, Barry. *William Burroughs: El Hombre Invisible*. London: Virgin, 1993.

Miller, Alicia M. "Power and Perception in *Plus*." *Review of Contemporary Fiction* 10, no. 1 (1990): 173–80.

Miller, Arthur. *The Crucible*. Harmondsworth, U.K.: Penguin, 1970.

Miller, James G. "Brainwashing: Present and Future." *Journal of Social Issues* 13, no. 3 (1957): 48–55.

Miller, P. Schuyler "The Reference Library." *Analog* 89, no. 1 (Mar. 1972): 168–71.

Miller, Stephen P. *The Seventies Now: Culture as Surveillance*. Durham, N.C.: Duke Univ. Press, 1999.

Miller, Walter M., Jr. "Izzard and the Membrane." *Astounding Science-Fiction* 47, no. 3 (May 1951): 70–116.

Mills, James. *The Power*. New York: Warner, 1992.

Milosz, Czeslaw. *The Captive Mind*. Trans. Jane Zielonko. Harmondsworth, U.K.: Penguin, 1985.

Mind Control Glossary. "Eleanor White's 'Freedom Isn't Free!'" www.raven1.net/glossary.htm. Accessed January 19, 2004.

Moloney, James C. "Analyse 'Mind Washing.'" *Science News Letter* (May 16, 1953): 310–11.

Morgan, Ted. *Literary Outlaw: The Life and Times of William S. Burroughs*. New York: Henry Holt, 1988.

Morton, Frederic. "Review of *The Manchurian Candidate, by Richard Condon*." *New York Times*, April 26, 1959.

Mottram, Eric. *William Burroughs: The Algebra of Need*. London: Marion Boyars, 1977.

Moylan, Tom. *Demand the Impossible: Science Fiction and the Utopian Imagination*. New York: Methuen, 1986.

Murphy, Timothy S. *Wising Up the Marks: The Amodern William Burroughs*. Berkeley: Univ. of California Press, 1997.

Murray, Ian. "Orwell's List of Crypto-Communists and Fellow-Travellers." *Times* (London), July 11, 1996.

Mustazza, Leon, ed. *The Critical Reception of Kurt Vonnegut*. Westport, Conn.: Greenwood, 1994.

Nadel, Alan. *Containment Culture: American Narratives, Postmodernism, and the Atomic Age*. Durham, N.C.: Duke Univ. Press, 1995.

Nelson, Deborah. "Penetrating Privacy: Confessional Poetry and the Surveillance Society." In *Homemaking: Women Writers and the Politics and Poetics of Home*, ed. Catherine Wiley and F. R. Barnes, 87–114. New York: Garland, 1996.

Nickell, Joe. "Alien Implants: The New "Hard Evidence." *Skeptical Inquirer* (Sept.–Oct. 1998). http://www.findarticles.com/cf_dls/m2843/n5_v22/21076510/p1/article.html. Accessed April 8, 2004.

Niven, Larry. "Death by Ecstasy." In *World's Best Science Fiction 1970*, ed. D. A. Wollheim and Terry Carr, 46–105. New York: Ace, 1970.

Norris, Christopher. "Language, Truth and Ideology: Orwell and the Post-War Left."

In *Inside the Myth. Orwell: Views from the Left*, ed. Christopher Norris, 242–62. London: Lawrence and Wishart, 1984.

O'Brien, Cathy, with Mark Phillips. *Trance Formation of America*. Las Vegas, Nev.: Reality Marketing, 1995.

O'Donnell, Patrick. *Latent Destinies: Cultural Paranoia and Contemporary U.S. Narrative*. Durham, N.C.: Duke Univ. Press, 2000.

O'Neill, Dennis. "The Future in Books." *Amazing Stories* 43, no. 5 (Jan. 1970): 128–30.

O'Neill, Joseph. *Land Under England*. Harmondsworth, with an introduction by Anthony Storr. Harmondsworth, U.K.: Penguin, 1987.

O'Neill, William F., and George D. Demos. "The Yeshov Method." *ETC* 40, no. 4 (1983): 422–32.

Ore, Rebecca. *Gaia's Toys*. New York: Tor, 1995.

Orwell, George. *Complete Works*. Vol. 9, *Nineteen Eighty-Four*. Ed. Peter Davison. London: Secker and Warburg, 1997.

——. *Complete Works*. Vol. 12, *A Patriot after All, 1940–1941*. Ed. Peter Davison. London: Secker and Warburg, 1998.

——. *Complete Works*. Vol. 18, *Smothered under Journalism, 1946*. Ed. Peter Davison. London: Secker and Warburg, 1998.

——. *Complete Works*. Vol. 20, *Our Job Is to Make Life Worth Living, 1949–1950*. Ed. Peter Davison. London: Secker and Warburg, 1998.

——. *Nineteen Eighty-Four: The Facsimile of the Extant Manuscript*. Ed. Peter Davison. London: Secker and Warburg, 1998.

Ostrander, Sheila, and Lynn Schroeder. *PSI: Psychic Discoveries behind the Iron Curtain*. London: Sphere, 1976.

Packard, Vance. *The Hidden Persuaders*. London: Longmans Green, 1958.

——. *The People Shapers*. Boston, Mass.: Little, Brown, 1977.

Pavlov, Ivan Petrovich. *Conditioned Reflexes and Psychiatry*. Ed. and trans. W. H. Gantt. London: Lawrence and Wishart, 1941.

Pawel, Ernst. *From the Dark Tower*. New York: Macmillan, 1957.

Peary, Gerald, and Roger Shatzkin, eds. *The Modern American Novel and the Movies*. New York: Ungar, 1978.

Pease, Stephen E. *Psywar: Psychological Warfare in Korea, 1950–1953*. Harrisburg, Pa.: Stackpole, 1992.

Pêcheux, Michel. *Language, Semantics and Ideology*. Trans. Harbans Nagpal. New York: St. Martin's, 1982.

Perry, Paul, and Ken Babbs. *On the Bus*. New York: Thunder's Mouth, 1990.

Phillips, Gene D., ed. *Stanley Kubrick: Interviews*. Jackson: Univ. Press of Mississippi, 2001.

Piercy, Marge. *Woman on the Edge of Time*. London: Women's Press, 2000.

Pines, Maya. *The Brain-Changers: Scientists and the New Mind-Control*. London: Allen Lane, 1974.

Plath, Sylvia. *The Bell Jar*. New York: Bantam, 1979.

——. *Johnny Panic and the Bible of Dreams*. London: Faber, 1979.

——. *The Journals of Sylvia Plath*. Ed. Frances McCullough. New York: Ballantine, 1982.

——. *Letters Home.* Ed. Amelia Schober Plath. London: Faber, 1975.

Platt, Charles. *Dream Makers: The Uncommon People Who Write Science Fiction: Interviews.* New York: Berkeley, 1980.

Pohl, Frederik. *Alternating Currents.* New York: Ballantine, 1956.

——. *The Man Who Ate the World.* New York: Ballantine, 1960.

——. *Turn Left at Thursday.* New York: Ballantine, 1961.

——, and Cyril M. Kornbluth. *The Wonder Effect.* London: Gollancz, 1967.

Pollini, Francis. *Night.* Paris: Olympia, 1960; and London: John Calder, 1961.

——. *Three Plays.* London: Neville Spearman, 1967.

Porush, David. *The Soft Machine: Cybernetic Fiction.* London: Methuen, 1985.

Posner, Richard A. "Orwell Versus Huxley: Economics, Technology, Privacy, and Satire." *Literature and Philosophy* 24 (2000): 1–33.

Possony, Stefan T. "The Brain Wave Machine." In *There Will Be War IV: Day of the Tyrant,* ed. Jerry E. Pournelle and John F. Carr, 263–64. New York: Tor, 1985.

——. *A Century of Conflict: Communist Techniques of World Revolution.* Chicago: Henry Regnery, 1953.

——. "Psyops." In *There Will Be War IV: Day of the Tyrant,* ed. Jerry E. Pournelle and John F. Carr, 255–63. New York: Tor, 1985.

Pounds, Wayne. "The Postmodern Anus: Parody and Utopia in Two Recent Novels by William Burroughs." In *William S. Burroughs at the Front: Critical Reception, 1959–1989,* ed. Jennie Skerl and Robin Lydenberg, 217–32. Carbondale: Southern Illinois Univ. Press, 1991.

Priestley, J. B., and Jacquetta Hawkes. *Journey down a Rainbow.* London: Heinemann-Cresset, 1955.

Pynchon, Thomas. *Gravity's Rainbow.* New York: Penguin, 2000.

Radosh, Ronald, and Joyce Milton. *The Rosenberg File: A Search for the Truth.* London: Weidenfeld and Nicolson, 1983.

Rakoff, Ian. *Inside the Prisoner: Radical Television and Film in the 1960s.* London: Batsford, 1998.

Rand, Ayn. *Anthem.* New York: Signet, 1961.

Rayer, Francis G. *Tomorrow Sometimes Comes.* London: Home and Van Thal, 1951.

Reed, Ishmael. *The Free-Lance Pallbearers.* New York: Avon, 1977.

Regis, Ed. *Great Mambo Chicken and the Transhuman Condition.* New York: Penguin, 1992.

Rhine, Robert Stephen. *My Brain Escapes Me.* Northville, Mich.: Sun Dog, 1999.

Richter, Payton E., ed. *Utopia/Dystopia? Threats of Hell or Hopes of Paradise.* Cambridge, Mass.: Schenkman, 1975.

Riebling, Mark. "Tinker, Tailor, Stoner, Spy: Was Timothy Leary a CIA Agent? Was JFK the 'Manchurian Candidate'? Was the Sixties Revolution Really a Government Plot?" http://home.dti.net/lawserv/leary.html. Accessed January 14, 2004.

Robin, Ron. *The Making of the Cold War Enemy: Culture and Politics in the Military-Intellectual Complex.* Princeton, N.J.: Princeton Univ. Press, 2001.

Robinson, Spider. *Mindkiller.* New York: Berkley, 1983.

Roeburt, John. *The Long Nightmare.* New York: Crest, 1958.

Rogers, Dave. *The Prisoner and the Danger Man.* London: Boxtree, 1989.

Rogge, O. John. *Why Men Confess.* New York: Thomas Nelson, 1959.

Rogin, Michael. *"Ronald Reagan," the Movie and Other Episodes in Political Demonology.* Berkeley: Univ. of California Press, 1987.

Rogow, Arnold A. *The Psychiatrists.* London: Allen and Unwin, 1971.

Rohmer, Sax. *President Fu Manchu.* New York: Pyramid, 1963.

Rorvik, David M. *As Man Becomes Machine: The Evolution of the Cyborg.* London: Sphere, 1975.

———. "Someone To Watch Over You (Less Than 2¢ a Day)." *Esquire,* December 1969.

Rose, Barbara. "Cultural Paranoia, Conspiracy Plots, and the American Ideology: William Burroughs' *Cities of the Red Night.*" *Canadian Review of American Studies* 29, no. 2 (1999): 89–111.

Rose, Jacqueline. *The Haunting of Sylvia Plath.* London: Virago, 1991.

Rosenwein, Robert E. "A Place Apart: The Historical Context of Kesey's Asylum." In *A Casebook on Ken Kesey's "One Flew Over the Cuckoo's Nest,"* ed. George J. Searles, 41–47. Albuquerque: Univ. of New Mexico Press, 1992.

Ross, Andrew. *No Respect: Intellectuals and Popular Culture.* London: Routledge, 1989.

Ross, Colin. "The CIA and Military Mind Control Research: Building the Manchurian Candidate." CKLN-FM (Toronto, Canada). http://heart7.net/mcf/radio/ckln01.htm. Accessed January 6, 2004.

Rossmann, John F. *The Mind Masters.* New York: Signet, 1974.

Roszak, Theodore. *The Cult of Information: The Folklore of Computers and the True Art of Thinking.* Cambridge, U.K.: Lutterworth, 1986.

Rucker, Rudy. *Software.* Harmondsworth, U.K.: Penguin, 1985.

———. *Wetware.* London: New English Library, 1989.

Ruff, Lajos. *The Brain-Washing Machine.* London: Robert Hale, 1959.

Russell, Eric Frank. *Three To Conquer.* London: Methuen, 1987.

———. *With a Strange Device.* Harmondsworth, U.K.: Penguin, 1965.

Safer, Elaine B. "'It's the Truth Even If It Didn't Happen': Ken Kesey's *One Flew Over the Cuckoo's Nest.*" *Literature/Film Quarterly* 5, no. 2 (1977): 132–41. In *A Casebook on Ken Kesey's* One Flew Over the Cuckoo's Nest, ed. Searles, 151–61.

Sanders, Joe. "The Fantastic Non-Fantastic: Richard Condon's Waking Nightmares." *Extrapolation* 25, no. 2 (Summer 1987): 127–37.

Sargant, William. *Battle for the Mind: A Physiology of Conversion and Brain-Washing.* Rev. ed. London: Pan, 1959.

Saunders, Francis Stonor. *Who Paid the Piper? The CIA and the Cultural Cold War.* London: Granta, 1999.

Schaub, Thomas H. *American Fiction in the Cold War.* Madison: Univ. of Wisconsin Press, 1991.

———. *Pynchon: The Voice of Ambiguity.* Urbana: Univ. of Illinois Press, 1981.

Scheflin, Alan. "The History of Mind Control: What We Can Prove and What We Can't." CKLN-FM (Toronto, Canada). http://heart7.net/mcf/radio/ckln06.htm. Accessed December 30, 2003.

Scheflin, Alan W., and Edward M. Opton Jr. *The Mind Manipulators.* New York: Paddington, 1978.

Schein, Edgar H., Inge Schneier, and Curtis H. Barker, *Coercive Persuasion: A Socio-Political Analysis of the "Brainwashing" of American Civilian Prisoners by the Chinese Communists*. New York: Norton, 1961.

Scheinfeld, Michael. Review of *The Manchurian Candidate* by Richard Condon. *Films in Review* 39, no 11 (Nov. 1988): 538–46.

Schumacher, Skip. "USS Pueblo (Ager-2): Pueblo Incident." USS Pueblo Veteran's Association. www.usspueblo.org/v2f/incident/incidentframe.html. Accessed December 30, 2003.

Schuster, Melvin M. "Skinner and the Morality of Melioration" In *Utopia/Dystopia?* ed. Richter, 93–108.

Seabury, Martin B. "The Monsters We Create: *Woman on the Edge of Time*." *Critique: Studies in Contemporary Fiction* 42, no. 2 (2001): 131–43.

Searles, George J., ed. *A Casebook on Ken Kesey's "One Flew Over the Cuckoo's Nest."* Albuquerque: Univ. of New Mexico Press, 1992.

Sedgewick, Peter. *Psycho Politics*. New York: Harper and Row, 1982.

Seed, David. "Brainwashing and Cold War Demonology." *Prospects* 22 (1997): 535–73.

———. "Deconstructing the Body Politic in Bernard Wolfe's *Limbo*." *Science-Fiction Studies* 20, no. 2 (1997): 267–88.

Seldes, Gilbert. *The People Don't Know: The American Press and the Cold War*. New York: Gaer, 1949.

Shalizi, Cosma. Review of *Battle for the Mind* by William Sargant. *Bactra Review*. www.santafe.edu/~shalizi/reviews/battle-for-the-mind. Accessed December 30, 2003.

Shaviro, Steven. *Doom Patrols: A Theoretical Fiction about Postmodernism*. London: Serpent's Tail, 1997.

Shea, Robert, and Robert Anton Wilson. *Illuminatus!* Part 2. *The Golden Apple*. New York: Dell, 1975.

Shiner, Lewis. *Frontera*. New York: Baen, 1984.

Sigman, Joseph. "Science and Parody in Kurt Vonnegut's *The Sirens of Titan*." In *The Critical Response to Kurt Vonnegut*, ed. Leonard Mustazza, 25–41. Westport, Conn.: Greenwood, 1994.

Silverberg, Robert. *The Feast of St. Dionysus: Five Science Fiction Stories*. New York: Scribner, 1975.

———. *The Second Trip*. New York: Avon, 1981.

Siodmak, Curt. *Donovan's Brain*. New York: Berkley, 1969.

———. *Hauser's Memory*. London: Herbert Jenkins, 1969.

Skerl, Jennie, and Robin Lydenberg, eds. *William S. Burroughs at the Front: Critical Reception, 1959–1989*. Carbondale: Southern Illinois Univ. Press, 1991.

Skinner, B. F. *About Behaviorism*. London: Cape, 1974.

———. *Beyond Freedom and Dignity*. New York: Knopf, 1971.

———. *Science and Human Behavior*. New York: Free Press, 1965.

———. "Utopia as an Experimental Culture." In *America as Utopia*, ed. Kenneth M. Roemer, 28–42. New York: Burt Franklin, 1981.

———. *Walden Two*. New York: Macmillan, 1976.

Slaughter, Frank G. *Sword and Scalpel*. London: Jarrold's, 1957.

Small, Sidney Herschel. "The Brainwashed Pilot." *Saturday Evening Post*, March 19, 1955.

Smith, Harrison. "Rival to Orwell." *Saturday Review*, March 28, 1953.

Smith, J. Sydney, and L. G. Kiloh, eds. *Psychosurgery and Society*. Oxford, U.K.: Pergamom, 1977.

Smith, Robert A. *The Kramer Project*. London: Robert Hale, 1975.

Smith, Wilson. *Mechanisms of Virus Infection*. London: Academic, 1963.

Sobchack, Vivian. "Décor as Theme: *A Clockwork Orange*." *Literature/Film Quarterly* 9, no. 2 (1981): 92–102.

———. *The Limits of Infinity: The American Science Fiction Film, 1950–75*. Cranbury, N.J.: Barnes, 1980.

Society for the Investigation of Human Ecology. *Brainwashing: A Guide to the Literature*. Forest Hills, N.Y.: Society for the Investigation of Human Ecology, 1960.

Solomon, Carl. *Mishaps, Perhaps*. San Francisco, Calif.: City Lights, 1966.

Somit, Albert. "Brainwashing." In *International Encyclopedia of the Social Sciences*, vol. 2, ed. Daniel Sills, 138–42. New York: Macmillan and Free Press, 1968.

Sova, Mark. "Walter Bowart Interviewed." *Mind Control Forum*. www.mindcontrol forums.com/wbi.htm. Accessed January 15, 2004.

Stapledon, Olaf. *Darkness and the Light*. Westport, Conn.: Hyperion, 1974.

Stephenson, Neal. *Snow Crash*. Harmondsworth, U.K.: Penguin, 1993.

Strieber, Whitley. *Black Magic*. New York: William Morrow, 1982.

———. *Confirmation: The Hard Evidence of Aliens among Us*. New York: St. Martin's, 1998.

———. *Majestic*. New York: Putnam's, 1989.

———. *The Secret School: Preparation for Contact*. London: Harper Collins, 1996.

Sturgeon, Theodore. *Some of Your Blood*. New York: Ballantine, 1961.

———. "The Terminal Man." *New York Times Book Review*, April 30, 1972.

Sullivan, Harry Stack. *The Psychiatric Interview*. Ed. H. S. Perry and M. L. Gawel. New York: Norton, 1954.

Sutin, Lawrence, ed. *The Shifting Realities of Philip K. Dick: Selected Literary and Philosophical Writings*. New York: Pantheon, 1995.

Suykerbuyk, Benoit J., ed. *Essays from Oceania and Eurasia: Orwell in 1984*. Antwerp, Belgium: Antwerp Univ. Press, 1984.

Swirski, Peter. "Dystopia or Dischtopia? The Science-Fiction Paradigms of Thomas M. Disch." *Science-Fiction Studies* 18 (1991): 161–78.

Szasz, Thomas S. *Ideology and Insanity: Essays on the Psychiatric Dehumanization of Man*. London: Calder and Boyars, 1973.

———. "Some Call It Brainwashing." *The New Republic*, March 6, 1976.

Szasz, Thomas, ed. *The Age of Madness: The History of Involuntary Mental Hospitalization Presented in Selected Texts*. London: Routledge and Kegan Paul, 1975.

Tanner, Tony. *City of Words: American Fiction, 1950–1970*. London: Cape, 1971.

Tarsis, Valerij. *Ward 7: An Autobiographical Novel*. Trans. Katya Brown. London: Collins and Harvill, 1965.

Thomas, Gordon. *Journey Into Madness: The True Story of Secret CIA Mind Control and Medical Abuse*. New York: Bantam, 1990.

Thorin, Duane. *A Ride to Panmunjon.* Chicago: Henry Regnery, 1956.

Toole, John Kennedy. *A Confederacy of Dunces.* Harmondsworth, U.K.: Penguin, 1981.

Trembley, Elizabeth A. *Michael Crichton: A Critical Companion.* Westport, Conn.: Greenwood, 1996.

Trunnell, Eugene E. "George Orwell's *1984*: A Psychoanalytic Study." *International Review of Psycho-Analysis* 12 (1985): 263–71.

Turkle, Sherry. *Life on the Screen: Identity in the Age of the Internet.* London: Orion, 1997.

———. "Who Am We?" (1996). *Wired Magazine,* 4, no. 1 (January 1996). www.wired.com/wired/archive/4.01/turkle.html. Accessed January 19, 2004.

Turner, George. "The Double Standard: The Short Look, and the Long Hard Look." *SF Commentary* 76 (Oct. 2000): 16–20.

Twain, Mark. *A Connecticut Yankee in King Arthur's Court.* Ed. M. Thomas Inge. Oxford, U.K.: Oxford Univ. Press, 1998.

The U.S. Fighting Man's Code. Washington, D.C.: Office of Armed Forces Information, 1955.

Valenstein, Elliot S. *Brain Control: A Critical Examination of Brain Stimulation and Psychosurgery.* New York: John Wiley, 1973.

———. "Science-Fiction Fantasy and the Brain." *Psychology Today* 12, no. 2 (July 1978): 28–39.

Valenstein, Elliot S., ed. *The Psychosurgery Debate: Scientific, Legal and Ethical Perspectives.* San Francisco, Calif.: Freeman, 1980.

Van Coillie, Dries. *I Was Brainwashed in Peking.* Shertogenbosch: Nederlandse Boekdruk Industrie, 1969.

Van Vogt, Alfred E. *The Mind Cage.* New York: Belmont, 1970.

———. *Reflections of A. E. Van Vogt.* Lakemont, Ga.: Fictioneer, 1975.

———. "Van Vogt on Dianetics." *Spaceway* 2, no. 3 (Feb. 1955): 43–58.

———. *The Violent Man.* New York: Farrar, Strauss and Cudahy, 1962.

Varley, John. "PRESS ENTER." In *Best Science Fiction of the Year 14,* ed. Terry Carr, 11–72. London: Gollancz, 1985.

———. *Steel Beach.* London: Harper Collins, 1993.

Vernon, Jack. *Inside the Black Room: Studies of Sensory Deprivation.* Harmondsworth, U.K.: Penguin, 1966.

Victorian, Armen. *Mind Controllers.* London: Vision, 1999.

Vogeler, Robert A., with Leigh White. *I Was Stalin's Prisoner.* London: W. H. Allen, 1952.

Vonnegut, Kurt. *The Sirens of Titan.* London: Gollancz, 1986.

Wager, Walter. *Telefon.* London: Futura, 1976.

Wagner-Martin, Linda, ed. *Sylvia Plath: The Critical Heritage.* London: Routledge, 1988.

Walker, Richard L. *China Under Communism: The First Five Years.* New Haven, Conn.: Yale Univ. Press, 1955.

Walsh, Chad. *From Utopia to Nightmare.* London: Geoffrey Bles, 1962.

Warren, Bill. *Keep Watching the Skies! American Science Fiction Movies of the Fifties.* Vol. 1. Jefferson, N.C.: McFarland, 1982.

Warren, Robert Penn. *All the King's Men.* New York: Harcourt Brace, 1946.

Watson, John B. 1924. *Behaviorism*. 2d ed. London: Kegan Paul, Trench and Trubner, 1931.

Watson, Peter. *War on the Mind: The Military Uses and Abuses of Psychology*. New York: Basic, 1978.

Weissberg, Alex. *Conspiracy of Silence*. London: Hamish Hamilton, 1952.

Welch, Robert. *The Politician*. Blemont, Mass.: Welch, 1963.

Wells, H. G. *Men Like Gods*. London: Odhams, 1936.

Whyte, William H. *The Organization Man*. New York: Simon and Schuster, 1956.

Wiener, Norbert. *Cybernetics: or, Control and Communication in the Animal and the Machine*. 2d ed. Cambridge, Mass.: MIT Press, 1969.

Wiley, Catherine, and Fiona R. Barnes, eds. *Homemaking: Women Writers and the Politics and Poetics of Home*. New York: Garland, 1997.

Willeford, Charles. *The Machine in Ward Eleven*. London: World Distributors, 1964.

Williams, Tennessee. *Five Plays*. London: Secker and Warburg, 1962.

Williams, Tony. "College Course File: Television Studies / Television Theories — Series and Mini-Series." *Journal of Film and Video* 46, no. 1 (Spring 1994): 43–60.

Wilson, Robert Anton. *Prometheus Rising*. Tempe, Ariz.: New Falcon, 1997.

——, with Miriam John Hill. *Everything Is Under Control: Conspiracies, Cults, and Cover-Ups*. London: Macmillan, 1999.

Winance, Eleutherius. *The Communist Persuasion: A Personal Experience of Brainwashing*. Trans. E. A. Lawrence. New York: P. J. Kenedy, 1959.

Winn, Denise. *The Manipulated Mind: Brainwashing, Conditioning and Indoctrination*. London: Octagon, 1983.

Winokur, George. "'Brainwashing'—A Social Phenomenon of Our Time." *Human Organization* 13, no. 4 (1955): 16–18.

Wolfe, Bernard. *Limbo*. New York: Random House, 1952.

Wolfe, Tom. *The Electric Kool-Aid Acid Test*. London: Transworld, 1995.

Wood, Brent. "William S. Burroughs and the Language of Cyberpunk." *Science-Fiction Studies* 23, no. 1 (1996): 11–26.

Wright, Charles. *The Wig: A Mirror Image*. New York: Farrar, Straus, and Giroux, 1966.

Wubben, H. H. "America's Prisoners of War in Korea: A Second Look at the 'Something New in History' Theme." *American Quarterly* 12, no. 1 (Spring 1970): 3–19.

Wylie, Philip. *Generation of Vipers*. New York: Rinehart, 1942.

Wyndham, John. *Exiles on Asperus*. London: Hodder and Stoughton, 1979.

Young, Charles S. "Missing in Action: POW Films, Brainwashing and the Korean War, 1954–1968." *Historical Journal of Film, Radio and Television* 18, no. 1 (Mar. 1998): 49–74.

Yurick, Sol. "The Other Side." In *The 60s without Apology*, ed. Sohnya Sayres, et al., 304–8. Minneapolis: Univ. of Minnesota Press, 1985.

——. *Richard A: A Novel about Genius Rampant*. New York: Arbor, 1982.

Zamyatin, Yevgeny. *We*. Harmondsworth, U.K.: Penguin, 1993.

Zubizarreta, John. "The Disparity of Point of View in *One Flew Over the Cuckoo's Nest*." *Literature/Film Quarterly* 22, no. 1 (1994): 62–69.

Zweiback, Adam J. "The 21 'Turncoat GIs': Nonrepatriations and the Political Culture of the Korean War," *The Historian* (Winter 1998). http://www.findarticles.com/m2082/n2_v60/20427123/p1. Accessed January 4, 2003.

■ Films

Assignment Paris. Directed by Robert Parrish. Columbia Pictures, 1952.

The Brain Eaters. VHS. Directed by Bruno Vesota. AIP, 1958; Columbia TriStar Home Entertainment, 1993.

The Brain from Planet Arous. DVD. Directed by Nathan Hertz [also billed as Nathan Juran]. 1958; Image Entertainment, 2001.

A Breed Apart (Perfect Assassins). VHS. Directed by H. Gordon Boos. 1998; York Home Video, 1999.

A Clockwork Orange. DVD. Directed by Stanley Kubrick. 1971; Warner Studios, 2001.

Conspiracy Theory. DVD. Directed by Richard Donner. 1997; Warner Studios, 2002.

Donovan's Brain. DVD. Directed by Felix Feist. 1953; MGM, n.d.

I Married a Monster from Outer Space. VHS. Directed by Gene Fowler. 1958; Paramount, 2001.

Invaders from Mars. DVD. Directed by William Cameron. 1953; Image Entertainment, 2002.

Invasion of the Body Snatchers. DVD. Directed by Don Siegel. 1956; Republic Studios, 2002.

Invasion of the Body Snatchers. DVD. Directed by Philip Kaufman. 1978; MGM/UA Studios, 2001.

The Ipcress File. DVD. Directed by Sidney J. Furie. 1965; Anchor Bay Entertainment, 1999.

It Came from Outer Space. DVD. Directed by Jack Arnold. 1953; Umvd, 2003.

The Manchurian Candidate. DVD. Directed by John Frankenheimer. 1962; MGM/UA Studios, 2001.

The Manchurian Candidate. Directed by Jonathan Demme. Paramount, 2004.

MASH. DVD. Directed by Robert Altman. 1970; Twentieth Century Fox, 2002.

The Mind Benders. DVD. Directed by Basil Dearden. 1963; Anchor Bay Entertainment, 2001.

Naked Lunch. DVD. Directed by David Cronenberg. 1991; Criterion Collection, 2003.

Nineteen Eighty-Four. BBC TV dramatization. Directed by Rudolph Cartier, 1954.

Nineteen Eighty-Four. DVD. Directed by Michael Radford. 1984; MGM/UA Video, 2003.

Nineteen Eighty-Four. VHS. Directed by Michael Anderson, 1956; VHS, n.p., n.d.

On Her Majesty's Secret Service. DVD. Directed by Peter Hunt, 1969; MGM Home Entertainment (Europe), Ltd., 2003.

One Flew Over the Cuckoo's Nest. DVD. Directed by Milos Forman. 1975; Warner Studios, 1997.

The Prisoner. DVD. BBC TV series. 1967–68. Entire series available on DVD under the title *The Complete Prisoner Megaset.* A&E Entertainment, 2001.

The Prisoner. DVD. Directed by Peter Glenville. 1955; Columbia TriStar Home Entertainment, 2004.

The Puppet Masters. DVD. Directed by Stuart Orme. 1994; Buena Vista Home Video, 2002.

The Rack. Directed by Arnold Laven. MGM, 1956.

Red Nightmare. DVD. (Alternate title, *The Commies Are Coming, the Commies Are Coming.*) Directed by George Waggner. Made by Warner Brothers for U.S. Department of Defense, 1962; Video Yesteryear, 1969; Rhino Video, 1997.

The Running Man. DVD. Directed by Paul Michael Glaser. 1987; Republic Studios, 2002.

Suddenly. DVD. Directed by Lewis Allen. 1954; Parade, 1998.

Telefon. VHS. Directed by Don Siegel. 1977; Warner Studios, 1989.

The Terminal Man. VHS. Directed by Mike Hodges. 1974; Warner Studios, 1994.

Total Recall. DVD. Directed by Paul Verhoeven. 1990; Artisan (Fox Video), 2003.

Toward the Unknown. Directed by Mervyn Le Roy. Warner, 1956.

Index